D1550282

REVELATION, TRUTH, CANON AND INTERPRETATION

SUPPLEMENTS TO

VIGILIAE CHRISTIANAE

Formerly Philosophia Patrum

TEXTS AND STUDIES OF EARLY CHRISTIAN LIFE AND LANGUAGE

EDITORS

J. DEN BOEFT — R. VAN DEN BROEK — W.L. PETERSEN
D.T. RUNIA — J.C.M. VAN WINDEN

VOLUME LXIV

REVELATION, TRUTH, CANON AND INTERPRETATION:

STUDIES IN JUSTIN MARTYR'S DIALOGUE WITH TRYPHO

BY

CRAIG D. ALLERT

BRILL
LEIDEN · BOSTON · KÖLN
2002

This book is printed on acid-free paper.

Library of Congress Cataloging-in-Publication Data

Allert, Craig D.
 Revelation, truth, canon, and interpretation : studies in Justin Martyr's
Dialogue with Trypho / by Craig D. Allert.
  p. cm. — (Supplements to Vigiliae Christianae; v. 64)
 Includes bibliographical references and indexes.
 ISBN 9004126198 (alk. paper)
  1. Justin, Martyr, Saint. Dialogue with Trypho. 2. Revelation—History of
doctrines—Early church, ca. 30-600. 3. Truth (Christian theology)—History
of doctrines—Early church, ca. 30-600. 4. Bible—Canon. 5. Bible—Criticism,
interpretation, etc.—History—Early church, ca. 30-600. I. Title. II. Series.

BR65.J86 A44 2002
239'.2—dc21   2002027657

Die Deutsche Bibliothek – CIP-Einheitsaufnahme

Allert, Craig D.:
Revelation, truth, canon, and interpretation : studies in Justin Martyr's
dialogue with Trypho / by Craig D. Allert. – Leiden ; Boston ; Köln :
Brill, 2002
  (Supplements to Vigiliae Christianae ; Vol. 64)
  ISBN 90–04–12619–8

ISSN 0920-623X
ISBN 90 04 12619 8

CONTENTS

CHAPTER ONE

THE PURPOSE AND DESTINATION OF THE
DIALOGUE WITH TRYPHO

CHAPTER TWO

THE CONCEPT OF REVELATION
IN *DIALOGUE WITH TRYPHO*

CHAPTER THREE

THE CONCEPT OF TRUTH IN *DIALOGUE WITH TRYPHO*

CHAPTER FOUR

THE NEW TESTAMENT CANON AND THE
DIALOGUE WITH TRYPHO

CHAPTER FIVE

INTERPRETATIONAL FOUNDATIONS IN THE
DIALOGUE WITH TRYPHO

APPENDIX

GOSPEL QUOTATIONS AND ALLUSIONS FOUND
IN THE *DIALOGUE WITH TRYPHO*

ACKNOWLEDGEMENTS

This monograph is the culmination of research into the area of second century Christian theology and Justin Martyr's place therein. Its original form was that of a Ph.D. thesis at St. John's College, University of Nottingham under the direction of Dr. George Bebawi. I wish to acknowledge my gratitude to Brill for including this revised form in this series.

In many ways this work is not the result of one individual holed up in a study or library researching some obscure term or concept related to their topic. Much in the way of preparation needs to be accomplished in order to get the writer to that point. In my case that preparation began with my parents, Neil and Shirley Allert, to whom I owe much more than gratitude. They have given me the freedom to pursue my own interests and direction. This gift has meant more to me than they know. It has been manifested by their total support in all my endeavors. My wife, Corinne, has also been integral to that preparation. She knew the road that lay ahead for an aspiring graduate student with many years of schooling ahead. Yet she stood by her commitment to me with patience, perseverance, and love. Although Corinne has neither read nor necessarily understood what is between the covers of this monograph, it would not be a reality were it not for her. My in-laws, Aalt and Diny Bowman, have also played a major role in this preparation by giving Corinne and myself the freedom to make our own life when it would have been easy to criticize their son-in-law for not providing for their daughter. I sincerely wish to thank all of these for their vital part in my life and work.

I wish also to thank the following people who have played a significant role in this work. Dr. George Bebawi displayed a wonderful balance between task master and encourager through the composition of this thesis. He seemed to know when I needed encouragement, but balanced that with a healthy dose of criticism. I would like to thank him for encouraging me to "stop thinking like a Protestant." To Dr. John Goldingay, former Principal of St. John's College Nottingham, who paved the way for a smooth transition during a rather difficult time. Dr. Stephen Travis, research director at St.

John's, provided invaluable direction and practical advice as the thesis reached its final stages. Thanks is also extended to my Teaching Assistant at Trinity Western University for the 2001–2002 academic year, Thom Blair. Thom painstakingly entered and double checked the Greek text in the footnotes and Appendix, a daunting task which he accomplished with cheer and excellence.

I can think of no better people to dedicate this book to than my wife, Corinne, and our sons, Tyler and Zachary. They are truly a gift from God. It is because of their patience and understanding that I have the desire and ability to pursue my research.

Craig D. Allert
Abbotsford, B.C.
March 2002

ABBREVIATIONS

Acad. Pr.	Cicero, *Academica Priora*
ABD	Anchor Bible Dictionary
AnBib	Analecta biblica
1 Apol.	Justin Martyr, *First Apology*
2 Apol.	Justin Martyr, *Second Apology*
BHT	Beiträge zur historischen Theologie
BBR	*Bulletin for Biblical Research*
BETS	*Bulletin of the Evangelical Theological Society*
BJRL	*Bulletin of the John Rylands University Library of Manchester*
CH	*Church History*
CQ	*The Classical Quarterly*
CQR	*Church Quarterly Review*
CRINT	Compendia rerum iudaicarum ad novum testamentum
C. Cels.	Origen, *Against Celsus*
C. Eunom.	Basil, *Against Eunomius*
de E. ap Delph.	Plutarch, *On the E at Delphi*
De fin.	Cicero, *De finibus*
De Is. Et Osir.	Plutarch, *On Isis and Osiris*
De mut. nom.	Philo of Alexandria, *On the Change of Names* (*De Mutatione Nominum*)
De Platone	Apuleius of Madaura, *De Platone et eius Dogmate*
De post. Caini	Philo of Alexandria, *On the Posterity of Cain* (*De Posteritate Caini*)
De Sacrif.	Philo of Alexandria, *On the Sacrifices of Abel and Cain* (*De Sacrificiis Abelis et Caini*)
De Somn.	Philo of Alexandria, *On Dreams* (*De Somniis*)
De soph. el.	Aristotle, *De sophisticis elenchis*
Decr.	Athanasius of Alexandria, *On the Decrees of the Synod of Nicaea*
Dem.	Irenaeus of Lyons, *Proof of the Apostolic Preaching*
Dial.	Justin Martyr, *Dialogue with Trypho*
Didask.	Albinus, *Didaskalikos*
DJD	Discoveries in the Judean Desert
DR	*Downside Review*

ECQ	*The Eastern Churches Quarterly*
Encount	*Encounter*
Epitome	Albinus, *Epitome of the teachings of Plato*
Ep. ad Algasiam	Jerome, *Epistle to Algasiam*
Ep. ad Carpianum	Eusebius of Caesarea, *Epistle to Carpianum*
Ep. Afr.	Athanasius of Alexandria, *Epistle to the Bishops of Africa*
Ep. Fest.	Athanasius of Alexandria, *Festal Epistles*
ET	English Translation
EvQ	*Evangelical Quarterly*
FS	Festschrift
Frag. Origen	Theophilus of Alexandria, *Fragment from the Epistle Against Origen*
Gent.	Athanasius of Alexandria, *Against the Heathen (Contra gentes)*
Gorg.	Plato, *Gorgias*
Haer.	Irenaeus of Lyons, *Against Heresies*
Hom.	John Chrysostom, *Homilies*
HTR	*Harvard Theological Review*
HTS	Harvard Theological Studies
H.e.	Eusebius of Caesarea, *Ecclesiastical History*
Inc.	Athanasius of Alexandria, *On the Incarnation of the Word*
Int	*Interpretation*
Joh.	Origen of Alexandria, *Commentary on the Gospel of John*
JBL	*Journal of Biblical Literature*
J Early Chr St	*Journal of Early Christian Studies*
JR	*Journal of Religion*
JQR	*Jewish Quarterly Review*
JTS	*Journal of Theological Studies*
LCL	Loeb Classical Library
LXX	Septuagint
MT	Massoretic Text
Metaph.	Aristotle, *Metaphysics*
MGWJ	*Monatsschrift für Geschichte und Wissenschaft des Judentums*
Myst.	Pseudo-Dionysius, *The Mystical Theology*
ns	new series
NTS	*New Testament Studies*
NovT	*Novum Testamentum*
NovTSup	Novum Testamentum, Supplements

Or.	Tatian, *Orations to the Greeks*
Or.	Maximus of Tyre, *Oration*
Paed.	Clement of Alexandria, *Tutor* (*Paedagogus*)
Parm.	Plato, *Parmenides*
Phaed.	Plato, *Phaedo*
Phaedr.	Plato, *Phaedrus*
Phil.	Ignatius of Antioch, *Epistle to the Philadelphians*
P.e.	Eusebius of Caesarea, *Preparation for the Gospel* (*Praeparatio evangelica*)
Praescrip.	Tertullian of Carthage, *Prescription of Heretics*
Prax.	Tertullian of Carthage, *Against Praxeas*
Rep.	Plato, *Republic*
RestQ	*Restoration Quarterly*
RevExp	*Review and Expositor*
SJT	*Scottish Journal of Theology*
SecCent	*The Second Century*
SBLDS	Society of Biblical Literature Dissertation Series
SNTSMS	Society for New Testament Studies Monograph Series
SPCK	Society for the Promotion of Christian Knowledge
Soph.	Plato, *Sophist*
Str.	Clement of Alexandria, *Stromata*
StudEv	*Studia Evangelica*
St Miss	*Studia Missionalia*
StudPat	*Studia Patristica*
ST	*Studia Theologica*
Symp.	Methodius of Olympus, *Symposium*
Theaet.	Plato, *Theaetetus*
TS	*Theological Studies*
TU	Texte und Untersuchungen
Tim.	Plato, *Timaeus*
VC	*Vigiliae Christianae*
Virg.vel.	Tertullian, *On the Veiling of Virgins*
WTJ	*Westminster Theological Journal*
ZKG	*Zeitschrift für Kirchengeschichte*
ZNW	*Zeitschrift für die neutestamentliche Wissenschaft*
ZWT	*Zeitschrift für wissenschaftliche Theologie*

INTRODUCTION

It is not uncommon to hear Justin Martyr referred to as the most important of all the second century Apologists.[1] A main reason for this judgment may be the sheer volume of Justin's extant writings as compared to other second century writers. But volume of writings without substance would be little reason for such a judgment, and to judge Justin's writings as being without substance would be to misjudge them.

In Justin we have a man who sought to commend Christianity as the only true and pure philosophy to the contemporary Greek mind.[2] This is clearly exemplified in Justin's *Apologies*. In the *Apologies*, Justin attempts to answer those misconceptions about Christianity that were floating around the popular understanding of the movement.[3] Yet in the midst of this defense, Justin also presents the gospel in a way that, in his mind, would commend itself to this Greek mind.

But Greek philosophy, as influential as it was, was not the only mode of thought to which Justin sought to communicate the uniqueness and utter importance of Christ. The Jewish mind, out of which Christianity grew, also garnered the attention of Justin in his writings. This is exemplified in his *Dialogue with Trypho*.[4] Granted, the Jew to whom Trypho directed the *Dialogue* was a Hellenistic Jew, meaning he was influenced by the Greek thought of the second

---

[1] See e.g., F. L. Cross and E. A. Livingstone (eds.), *The Oxford Dictionary of the Christian Church* (rev. ed.; New York/Oxford: Oxford University Press, 1989) 770; R. M. Grant, *Greek Apologists of the Second Century* (Philadelphia: The Westminster Press, 1988) 50.

[2] The contemporary Greek mind of which I speak here is explained in more detail in Chapter 2.II–III.

[3] By their refusal to worship state deities Christians were accused of being atheists. Their gatherings for worship, instruction and participation in the Eucharist were being construed as gatherings for incest, child murder and cannibalism. See L. W. Barnard, *Justin Martyr. His Life and Thought* (Cambridge: Cambridge University Press, 1967) 2–4; H. Chadwick, "Justin Martyr's Defense of Christianity," *BJRL* 47 (1965) 279. Justin himself alludes to these popular misconceptions in *Dial.* 10.1. Trypho agrees that they are, indeed, misconceptions.

[4] I am fully aware of the discussion concerning the intended recipients of the *Dialogue*. My position is that the primary recipients are neither primarily Christians, nor pagans, but Jews. A summary discussion of the intended audience is presented in Chapter 1.

century. Justin's desire was to communicate to the Jew the centrality of Jesus in the economy of God.

Just as every individual, Justin is a child of his times. He was
influenced by his culture and made decisions, both consciously and
unconsciously, from within that culture. The *Dialogue with Trypho* was
written from within an era that was influenced, on the one hand,
by the prevailing Greek philosophic thought of the day. This mode
of thought is seen in the *Dialogue* as influencing not only Justin, the
author, but also Trypho and his Jewish companions. Yet, on the
other hand, as a Christian Justin was also influenced by Jewish scripture. This is fundamentally seen in his desire to remain faithful to
the Jewish scriptures interpreted through the event of Jesus Christ.
Thus, we see a situation in the *Dialogue* which is unique to it when
compared with Justin's *Apologies*.

I. *Revelation, Truth, Canon, and Interpretation*

The purpose of this introduction is five-fold. First, I will briefly
explain the foundation upon which this work rests and the rationale
for its title. Second, past works on Justin Martyr and their contributions
to the study at hand will be examined. Third, a biography of Justin
will be provided in order to place him in his proper context. Fourth,
Justin's extant writings will be reviewed. And finally, *The Dialogue
with Trypho* will be introduced as it fits into this corpus of writings.

Justin Martyr is a Christian. As a Christian, he was seeking to make
the message of Christ applicable to all of humanity—both Jew and
Greek. Justin's extant corpus of writings reveals this by their very
existence, written as they are to the Greek and to the Jew. I have
chosen herein to focus on Justin's communication of the gospel message to the Hellenistic Jew. And it is from within this context that
an introductory explanation of the title of this monograph is necessary.

Christianity is based on a person. "But to me the charters are
Jesus Christ, the inviolable charter is his cross, and death, and resurrection, and the faith which is through Him."[5] Ignatius of Antioch
states well the understanding that must accompany any study of
Christian theology in the patristic age. Difficulties with this foundational understanding begin to appear, however, when Christianity is

---

[5] Ignatius of Antioch, *Phil.* 8.2. ET from K. Lake (ed.), *The Apostolic Fathers* (2
Vols.; LCL; London: William Heinemann/New York: The Macmillan Co., 1914).

described as a "Religion of the Book."[6] This designation, while not altogether inaccurate, tends to "cook the books" in favor of a position with which Justin, and other Fathers, may not be entirely comfortable. That position centers on the relationship between Jesus Christ, revelation, and canon.

Here is where the impetus for this monograph stems. Justin resides in his thinking with the Greek Fathers who "did not lose sight of the fundamental point that Christianity is the religion not of a book but of a Person, that the Bible has its unique and irreplaceable authority in the Church because the prophets and apostles bear witness to him."[7]

What follows in this work stems from that foundational concept and grows to form what may be called the four pillars of the development of Christian theology in the patristic age.[8] Everything stems from the revelation of Jesus Christ as truth. "The supreme end to which Christian theology is directed is to the full intellectual expression of the truth which was manifested to men, once and for all, in the person and life of Jesus Christ."[9] Thus, the revelation of truth was manifest in Jesus Christ.[10] At first, traditions and teachings about Jesus Christ were spread orally—through the *kerygma*. But as time and distance separated that revelation a more reliable form of teaching became necessary—written documents.[11] But even this more reliable form of teaching is subject to differing interpretations.[12]

---

[6] C. A. Cory and D. T. Landry, *The Christian Theological Tradition* (Upper Saddle River, NJ: Prentice Hall, 2000) 101.

[7] H. Chadwick, "The Bible and the Greek Fathers," in D. E. Nineham (ed.), *The Church's Use of the Bible* (London: SPCK, 1963), 39. This, of course, must be understood in the context that Justin did not know of a closed New Testament canon. Thus, when we speak of a Justin in this regard we must understand his relationship with Christian writings that were later to be part of the NT canon. See Chapter 4.

[8] It is not the purpose of this introduction or monograph to expound a history of Christian doctrine. However, it is necessary here to provide a brief rationale for the title of this monograph.

[9] J. F. Bethune-Baker, *An Introduction to the Early History of Christian Doctrine to the Time of the Council of Chalcedon* (London: Methuen & Co., 1962) 2.

[10] See Cory & Landry (eds.), *The Christian Tradition*, 69–120; W. H. C. Frend, *The Rise of Christianity* (Philadelphia: Fortress, 1984) 11–270; J. Riches, "The Birth of Christianity," in I. Hazlett (ed.), *Early Christianity: Origins and Evolution to AD 600* (London: SPCK, 1991) 28–39.

[11] See H. Y. Gamble, *Books and Readers in the Early Church: A History of Early Christian Texts* (New Haven and London: Yale University Press, 1995); R. P. C. Hanson, *Tradition in the Early Church* (London: SCM Press, 1962); J. T. Lienhard, *The Bible, the Church, and Authority: The Canon of the Christian Bible in History and Theology* (Collegeville, MN: The Liturgical Press, 1995).

[12] See R. M. Grant, *The Letter and the Spirit* (London: SPCK, 1957); J. N. D.

Thus, we may at once see the relationship and the tension that is present within these four concepts of Revelation, Truth, Canon, and Interpretation. If Jesus is revelation and the embodiment of truth, how did the early church regard the writings about Jesus? Further, what norms were in place to ensure a unified understanding or interpretation of these writings? Justin Martyr provides a good case study of these issues.

These concepts represent and exemplify something that is fundamentally essential to the faith known as Christianity. It is certainly not my intention to force this schematic upon the conscious thought of any writer in patristic Christianity. It is, however, my intention to show what Justin Martyr's understanding of these concepts was. In so doing, it is my desire to show how Justin contributed to the development of Christian theology in the second century.

A. *Revelation*

By investigating a particular writer's concept of revelation one is really asking some pertinent foundational questions. In order to understand revelation, therefore, it is important to understand who is doing the revealing. The concept of revelation also requires an understanding of the very nature of revelation—what is it? When these questions are answered we are then in a position to examine where a writer presents this revelation as being available. Thus, revelation is a foundational concept because it is here that a basic understanding of a writer's concepts of God, epistemology and the message are found.

Surprisingly little has been said about Justin Martyr's concept of revelation in *Justinforschung*.[13] This is not to say that a concept of revelation has been ignored. In fact, the very opposite is true—most commentators on Justin Martyr simply assume a certain concept of revelation with no meaningful discussion concerning how Justin came

---

Kelly, *Early Christian Doctrines* (rev. ed.; San Francisco: Harper, 1978); T. G. Stylianopoulos, *The New Testament: An Orthodox Perspective. Volume One: Scripture, Tradition, Hermeneutics.* Brookline, MA: Holy Cross Orthodox Press, 1997). The classic example of this is found in the fact that the initial desire of the Nicenes at the Council of Nicaea was to combat Arianism using purely scriptural terms. But this was precisely where the problem lay—with the interpretation of scriptural terms. See Athanasius, *Ep. Afr.* and *Decr.*

[13] J. C. M. van Winden, *An Early Christian Philosopher. Justin Martyr's Dialogue with Trypho Chapters One to Nine* (Philosophia Patrum 1; Leiden: E. J. Brill, 1971) 1. "The works of Justin have already been the object of intensive study. The list of books and articles is so great that one rightly speaks of a *Justinforschung*."

to this concept of revelation or even what it is, i.e. its relationship to epistemology. For example, Goodenough makes the blanket statement in reference to Justin that "not by the efforts of man's own reason, but through revelation . . . is the truth to be had by men."[14] The type of assumption is also made by Shotwell who claims that Justin "had no need to state a concept of revelation, for both he and his opponents [in the *Dialogue*] used the Old Testament as the basis of their discussion."[15] Shotwell does maintain that revelation for Justin was two-fold in nature (the *Logos* and the Prophets),[16] but this assertion gets lost in the unexplained claim that Justin has a verbal theory of inspiration.[17] While Goodenough makes no such claim to verbal inspiration for Justin, both he and Shotwell assume a concept of revelation without really explaining what it is.

A detailed examination of Justin Martyr's concept of revelation has, in fact, been a neglected aspect of the study of his theology.[18] But herein it will be shown that Justin's concept of revelation is the

---

[14] E. R. Goodenough, *The Theology of Justin Martyr. An Investigation Into the Conceptions of Early Christian Literature and Its Hellenistic and Judaistic Influences* (Amsterdam: Philo Press, 1968) 72.

[15] W. A. Shotwell, *The Biblical Exegesis of Justin Martyr* (London: SPCK, 1965) 2.

[16] Shotwell, *The Biblical Exegesis of Justin Martyr*, 3.

[17] Shotwell, *The Biblical Exegesis of Justin Martyr*, 4.

[18] The term "theology" was first used by non-Christian authors, rarely in the later Christian sense of true doctrine concerning the true (Christian) God. In classical antiquity poets are called "theologians," meaning simply those who talk about divinity or the gods (Plato, *Rep.* 379; Cicero, *De nat. deor.* 3.53). Aristotle (*Metaph.* 1025) distinguishes between mathematics, and physics and theology. Here theology is the first philosophy, metaphysics. In *Metaph.* (Book XII) Aristotle gives a philosophical doctrine of God. During the Hellenistic period it became customary to speak of a *theologia tripartia*: poetic, political, and natural. This tripartite theology described three types of religious phenomena: those exemplified in the works of the poets, especially Homer; those which according to statesmen and historians guaranteed the prosperity of the civic community; and, finally, those in which philosophers focused their allegorical interpretation of the poets. Christian writers, the first being Origen of Alexandria (ca. 185–ca. 254), adopted this type of language. Greek Christian authors used it earlier than those in the West. Christian writers used the term θεολογία to mean "teaching about God" and θεολογέιν to mean "to speak about God" (Origen, *C. Cels.* 2.18; Eusebius, *H.e.* 1.1.7; 5.28.3ff.; Basil, *C. Eunom.* 1.2.5; 5.28.5; 10.4.7) See, A. Di Berardino & B. Struder (eds.), *History of Theology I: The Patristic Period* (ET M. J. O'Connell; Collegeville, MN: The Liturgical Press, 1997) 3. It would thus be anachronistic to say that Justin was a theologian in the Christian sense of the word since he predates the Christian use of the term in this way. But since the development of the term has evolved into this Christian use I will maintain the use of the word theology for Justin's enquiry concerning God. This in no way implies that Justin belonged to that age when Christianity took over these terms as their own.

result of his conversion from Middle Platonism to Christianity. The prologue to the *Dialogue with Trypho* (Chaps. 1–9) is important in this regard. Two monographs have appeared in the last 40 years that have examined this section of the *Dialogue* in great detail.[19] Van Winden claims that he and Hyldahl are in basic agreement in their examination of the text, but thinks that Hyldahl is overly influenced by theological presuppositions.[20] This being the case, van Winden offers a philological investigation of the prologue, in addition to an inquiry into Justin's philosophical ideas and their internal cohesion. Both commentators have contributed much to the understanding of the prologue to the *Dialogue*. However, the relationship between it and revelation has been overlooked. Both do recognize the fact that the aim of the prologue is to bring philosophy to the fore,[21] but the relationship of philosophy to the epistemological question and to Justin's concept of revelation is not addressed.

The fact that van Winden fails to address the epistemological significance of revelation is puzzling in light of some of his findings. He states, "The problem of God had, indeed, a central place in the Middle Platonic philosophy, the most important system in Justin's day. God, the ideas which are his thoughts, and the human soul in kinship with Him are precisely the main problems of this philosophy."[22] If this is so, it appears to me that the connection between Justin's concept of philosophy as a search for God and his concept of revelation needs to be examined. Both van Winden and Hyldahl overlook this important aspect of Justin's thought.

This is not to say that Justin's connection to the Middle Platonic philosophy of Justin's day has not been examined. There has been little doubt among Justin commentators that Justin was influenced

[19] N. Hyldahl, *Philosophie und Christentum. Eine Interpretation der Einleitung zum Dialog Justins* (Acta Theologica Danica 9; Copenhagen: Munksgaard, 1966); van Winden, *An Early Christian Philosopher*.

[20] van Winden, *An Early Christian Philosopher*, 2.

[21] Hyldahl is intent on minimizing the influence of Platonism on Justin before his conversion because of his underlying assumption that the prologue is literary fiction. This is based on the fact that the *Dialogue* was written some 15 to 20 years *after* the initial conversation with Trypho. Hyldahl sees the prologue as an idealized conversion story of Justin, not necessarily grounded in fact. Thus Hyldahl claims that Justin is refuting the philosophers of his time through this prologue. But van Winden claims that Justin is refuting nothing here, but rather, he is claiming that most philosophers are not concerned with the proper task of philosophy.

[22] van Winden, *An Early Christian Philosopher*, 23.

by the Platonism of his day. "There seems to be no mystery about
where Justin derived his ideal of philosophy that was so important
to him and prominent in his writings. He was a Platonist and these
were Platonic ideas."[23] The various opinions concerning Justin's
Platonism can be grouped under one of three categories:[24] total assimilation,[25] total rejection,[26] or assimilation with a critical reserve.[27]
Those who put forth the total assimilation view aim to show that
Justin's attempt to preach the message of Jesus Christ resulted in a
disintegration of the Christian message into existing Greek philosophical categories of thought. In reaction to this there arose the
total rejection theory. The proponents of this view claimed that
Christianity and Platonism were incapable of dialogue or assimilation because they were diametrically opposed to one another. Most
recently, however, a mediating position has largely won the day.
This being that the most likely description of Justin's post-conversion
Platonism is that of partial assimilation. In this position it is stated
that certain Platonic categories of thought were adopted as theological tools that did not override the pure Christian message. The
Platonism of which this position speaks, however, is that of Middle
Platonism. In fact, Goodenough has been credited with being the
first commentator on Justin who recognized that the Platonism of

---

[23] M. O. Young, "Justin, Socrates, and the Middle-Platonists," *StudPat* 18 (1989) 163.
[24] C. Nahm, "The Debate on the 'Platonism' of Justin Martyr," *SecCent* 9 (1992) 151.
[25] See e.g., Andresen, "Justin und der mittlere Platonismus" *ZNW* 44 (1952/53)
157–195; A. Harnack, *History of Dogma* (7 vols.; 2nd ed.; ET N. Buchanan; London:
Williams & Norgate, 1905) 2.179–188.; W. Jaeger, *Early Christianity and Greek Paideia*
(Cambridge, Mass./London: The Belknap Press, 1961); R. Joly, *Christianisme et philosophie. Études sur Justin et les Apologistes grecs du deuxième siècle* (Bruxelles: Editions de
l'Université de Bruxelles, 1973).
[26] See e.g., H. Dörrie, *Platonica minora* (München, 1976); Hyldahl, *Philosophie und
Christentum*; van Winden, *An Early Christian Philosopher*.
[27] See e.g., Barnard, *Justin Martyr*; H. Chadwick, *Early Christian Thought and the
Classical Tradition: Studies in Justin, Clement and Origen* (Oxford: Clarendon, 1984);
J. Daniélou, *Gospel Message and Hellenistic Culture* (The Development of Christian Doctrine
Before the Council of Nicaea Vol. 2; ET J. A. Baker; London: Darton, Longman
& Todd, 1973); R. Holte, "Logos Spermatikos: Christianity and Ancient Philosophy
According to St. Justin's Apologies," *StudTh* 12 (1958) 109–168; R. A. Norris, *God
and World in Early Christian Theology. A Study in Justin Martyr, Irenaeus, Tertullian and
Origen* (Studies in Patristic Thought; London: Adam & Charles Black, 1966); E. F.
Osborn, *Justin Martyr* (BHT Gerhard Ebeling; Tübingen: J. C. B. Mohr [Paul Siebeck],
1973); G. L. Prestige, *God in Patristic Thought* (London: SPCK, 1965); C. J. de Vogel,
"Platonism and Christianity: A Mere Antagonism or A Profound Common Ground?"
VC 39 (1985) 1–62; H. A. Wolfson, *The Philosophy of the Church Fathers* I: *Faith, Trinity,
Incarnation* (2d ed. rev.; Cambridge, Mass.: Harvard University Press, 1964).

the Middle Platonic period was an eclectic blend of Platonism, Aristotelianism, and Stoicism.[28]

The influence of Middle Platonism on Justin should not be over-looked. But Goodenough appears to do just this when he claims that Justin says very little about the world of Ideas, except to say that he had been thrilled by the contemplation of them (*Dial.* 2.6).[29] Goodenough claims that they appear to have played no essential part in his system and that he is puzzled about why Justin would be confused on where to find truth after his conversation with the old man.[30] Surely Goodenough misses the point here. I contend that Justin makes a great deal out of the Platonic word of Ideas. In fact, the entire prologue hinges on the differences between the Platonic theory of epistemology, which is represented by Justin the Platonist, and what may be considered as a Christian theory of epistemology, which is represented by the old man in the prologue.

For Justin epistemology centers on the question of how one may know God. And this is the very point of the prologue. While this is recognized by many commentators,[31] they fail to make a connection between it and revelation, which is the connection that Justin himself (through the old man) wishes to make. Osborn comes closest to rec-ognizing the significance of this connection.[32] He explains that in the prologue Justin is, in fact, relating a theory of knowledge. Thus, Chris-tianity is recognized by Justin to be the only sure philosophy because through it one may receive knowledge of God. But again, Osborn falls short in explicitly relating this to a concept of revelation in Justin.

Writings about Justin's theology are replete with the assertion that the *Logos* is God's revelation to humanity. But Justin also places a great deal of emphasis on the writings of the Prophets and the Memoirs of the Apostles. Are these revelation as well? Much dis-cussion has surrounded the Prophets and Memoirs, but there has been a lack of attention to this simple question.

Van Winden claims that writers on Justin Martyr generally fall into two groups: theologians and philologists, and their specialized

---

[28] This thesis was significantly carried forward by C. Andresen, "Justin und der mittlere Platonismus".

[29] Goodenough, *The Theology of Justin Martyr*, 65.

[30] *Dial.* 7.

[31] See e.g. Barnard, *Justin Martyr*, 36–37; C. I. K. Story, *The Nature of Truth in "The Gospel of Truth" and in the Writings of Justin Martyr* (NovTSup 25; Leiden: E. J. Brill, 1970) 66.

[32] Osborn, *Justin Martyr*, 66–73.

points of approach are a constant threat to a correct understanding of the text.[33] Thus, theologians usually start from an actual theological problem,[34] rather than from within his historical context. On the other hand, philologians tend to place Justin in the shadow of the classical era and see him simply as a second rate author and a plagiarist. Perhaps van Winden would object on these grounds that the approach I take herein distorts the true picture of Justin. But the attempt has been made to approach the *Dialogue with Trypho* from an historical perspective that is sensitive to both approaches while avoiding the pitfalls of each. This, in fact, is what van Winden himself attempts to accomplish.

In this light, I will argue that Justin's prologue must be taken seriously. It is an attempt, whether literary fiction or factual event,[35] to espouse a certain theory of knowledge. It has a logical sequence that posits philosophy as a search for God based on an understanding of a progression from a Middle Platonic epistemology to a Christian epistemology. Thus, Justin's epistemology informs us as to his concept of revelation.

In Chapter One of this monograph I ask how Justin's Middle Platonism affected his concept of epistemology, that is, how does one know God or how does God reveal himself? This is important background in understanding why he chose Christian revelation over Middle Platonic. It is concluded that Justin has two witnesses to revelation, or two places where the ultimate revelation of the Logos is predicted (the Prophets) experienced (the Apostles). It is, however, ultimately in the incarnate *Logos* that revelation resides. Piper claims that the Memoirs are valuable merely for historical data about the life of Christ.[36] But on the basis of my examination of the *Dialogue* I claim in Chapter One that the Memoirs must in fact be considered a witness to the *Logos*, and thus a witness to revelation. This aspect of Justin's theology seems to have been missed by most, if not all, commentators on Justin Martyr.

---

[33] van Winden, *An Early Christian Philosopher*, 1–2.

[34] van Winden specifically mentions the problem of the relationship between Christianity and philosophy. In this case he states that this approach causes theologians (usually Lutherans) to blame Justin for an alliance between philosophy and faith and distort a balanced historical approach to the text (pp. 1–2).

[35] On the question surrounding the historicity of Justin's conversion account see O. Skarsaune, "The Conversion of Justin Martyr," *ST* 30 (1976) 53–57.

[36] O. Piper, "The Nature of the Gospel According to Justin Martyr," *JR* 41 (1961) 159. Also Shotwell, *The Biblical Exegesis of Justin Martyr*, 25.

B. *Truth*

Investigation into the concept of truth is the logical step taken after
an understanding of revelation simply because truth is based upon
revelation. The message of truth is fundamentally related to revelation because the message of truth is that which is revealed. Understanding what that message of truth entails is the ultimate goal of
investigation into the concept of truth.

The above statement may seem obvious. But the situation with
Justin Martyr needs some clarification at the point of where his
Middle Platonism comes into contact with his Christianity. Justin
Martyr's connection to Middle Platonism has been seen as influential
upon his theology. His theology is the result of revelation, in other
words, he believes it to be truth. This being the case, it is surprising to see commentators neglecting the Justin's pre-conversion concept of truth. As it was with the study of Justin in relation to his
concept of revelation, so it is with Justin's concept of truth—it is
simply assumed by most.

Barnard's investigation into Justin's concept of truth can be summed
up in the undeveloped statement, "Only by revelation can we find
truth—and this revelation is enshrined in the teaching of the Prophets
and Jesus Christ."[37] When this statement is placed into the context
of second century Greek thought[38] it becomes a powerful argument
against those who would argue that Justin was unduly influenced by
Middle Platonic philosophy. But Barnard fails to do this and his
statement lacks the significance it should truly have.

Similarly, Osborn has failed to do justice to the concept of truth
in Justin. He recognizes the fact that Justin believed that truth can
only be directly known. And that it is not an abstract thing but a
loving person.[39] Osborn has two chapters devoted to the theme of
truth[40] which do a fine job of multiplying references in Justin to his
love of truth as argument and truth being the best argument, but
they never really explain the OT, NT, and Hellenistic concepts of
truth in relation to Justin Martyr.

---

[37] Barnard, *Justin Martyr*, 80. Also, "Christianity was, for him, truth itself and this
he served with unswerving devotion and courage" (p. 169).

[38] As I do below in Chapter 3.I–II.

[39] Osborn, *Justin Martyr*, 70; 80.

[40] Chapter 5, "The Knowledge of Truth" (pp. 66–76); Chapter 6, "The Love of
Truth" (pp. 77–86).

In Chapter Two I argue that it is entirely necessary to relate the differing concepts of truth that were prevalent in Justin's day. Certainly, this is not a new thing. It is, however, attended to in relation to Justin Martyr only sporadically. Thus, Piper recognizes the important distinction between Plato and Christianity.[41] In Plato no historical fact can be interpreted as the manifestation of truth. Plato is dominated by the ontic contrast between Idea and historical event. This is a very important statement because it illustrates the extreme difference between the manifestation of truth (Christian) and Being as truth (Plato).[42]

Richard Norris's valuable book entitled *God and World in Early Christianity* includes a section on Justin. But its limited scope (in connection with the topic at issue here) still leaves the important connection untouched. Norris's first chapter[43] does an excellent job of explaining the importance of Plato's doctrine of Forms and Middle Platonism. This informs his treatment of Justin in relation to his concept of God and world. But it is certainly asking more of this work to relate the issue to Justin's concept of truth.

Story, in the promising monograph, *The Nature of Truth in the "Gospel of Truth" and in the Writings of Justin Martyr,* offers a similar, if not longer, explanation.[44] Ostensibly the book is a comparison between two mid-second century authors concerning their concepts of truth. While we are not concerned here with the *Gospel of Truth*, the work does give us a good picture Justin's concept of truth in the *Dialogue*. He thus makes the important statement that truth is manifested in the realm of divinely ordered events.[45] But, unlike Barnard, Story recognizes some of the necessary background to properly understand this statement. Accordingly, in a very important part of his monograph, he discusses the idea of truth in the OT, the Intertestamental period, and in the NT.[46] Contained in the section on the NT

---

[41] Piper, "The Nature of the Gospel According to Justin Martyr," 158.

[42] J. Zizioulas recognizes the importance of this distinction in *Being as Communion: Studies in Personhood and the Church* (Crestwood, NY: St. Vladimir's Seminary Press, 1997 [1985]) 67–122. I summarize the importance of Zizioulas for this study in Chapter 3.I.C.

[43] "Greek and Hellenistic Cosmology," pp. 8–32.

[44] Story, *The Nature of Truth in "The Gospel of Truth" and in the Writings of Justin Martyr.*

[45] Story, *The Nature of Truth in "The Gospel of Truth" and in the Writings of Justin Martyr,* 68.

[46] Story, *The Nature of Truth in "The Gospel of Truth" and in the Writings of Justin Martyr,* 177–199.

concept of truth, Story contrasts it to the Greek concept to conclude that "Whereas Plato viewed truth as the dialectical process leading from real existence to the ideal, Paul understood truth to be the historical process leading from the provisional event (God the redeemer of his people Israel) to the final consummation (Christ the redeemer of the world)."[47] Later Story correctly transfers the Pauline understanding to Justin. He continues, however, to claim that as both a Christian and a philosopher, Justin attempts to do justice to both the NT (Pauline) conception and the Greek conception. He thus claims that by expressing truth in a static or propositional format, Justin is trying to do justice to the Greek concept of truth.[48] This is a puzzling statement. Simply because Justin expressed truth in propositions does not mean that he is trying to justice to the Greek concept of truth. Story himself has expressed the fact that Plato had no room for truth as a historical manifestation. This simple fact should indicate that, by claiming that truth is manifested in Jesus Christ, Justin has radically altered his previously held Middle Platonic conception. This is pivotal, and it is something which Story fails to recognize. Thus, this promising and very informative monograph somehow falls short in placing Justin's concept of truth in its proper second century context.

The present work thus makes the important distinctions between the OT, NT, and Hellenistic concepts of truth. This is nothing new. However, in relating these conceptions to Justin with the result that Justin's conception of truth as a manifestation radically altered his Middle Platonism is something that has been missing from other treatments of Justin. Justin simply could not have remained a Middle Platonist and accepted the manifestation of truth in the person of Jesus Christ.

Further, the dialogue genre that Justin chose to express the truth he found in revelation is important. Hirzel makes the claim that Justin wrote the *Dialogue with Trypho* in an unsuccessful attempt to imitate Plato's *Phaedrus*.[49] But he does not pursue the issue with any great fervor. The only commentator to pursue this aspect of the

---

[47] Story, *The Nature of Truth in "The Gospel of Truth" and in the Writings of Justin Martyr*, 177–196.

[48] Story, *The Nature of Truth in "The Gospel of Truth" and in the Writings of Justin Martyr*, 209–210.

[49] R. Hirzel, *Der Dialog. Ein literarhistorischer Versuch* (2 Vols.; Leipzig: S. Hirzel, 1895) 2.368.

Dialogue with Trypho in any depth is Sarah Denning-Bolle.[50] While Denning-Bolle's purpose was not to relate the genre of dialogue to Justin's concept of truth, it actually dovetails with that very issue.

Denning-Bolle briefly traces the history of the dialogue genre through the Ancient Near East and then moves right into the Platonic dialogues. She concludes that Justin's dialogue and Plato's dialogues display some astonishing similarities.[51] But they also reveal some important differences.[52] She concludes that in the hands of Justin the dialogue becomes a tool for apologetic. With this conclusion I cannot disagree. But, as I shall point out in the third chapter, Denning-Bolle does not explain the significance of pre-Socratic and Socratic dialogues in her brief history of the dialogue genre. If this is done one may see that the dialogue genre was instigated as a way to search for truth. But Justin goes beyond the normal purpose of the dialogue genre because he believes he has actually found truth. So, Justin actually uses the Platonic dialogue genre to eventually discredit Middle Platonic doctrine. This is something that has not been addressed in *Justinforschung* but which is seen as an important underlying *raison d'etre* in choosing the dialogue genre. In other words, by choosing the dialogue genre, Justin was claiming to say something about truth.

C. *Canon*

Understood as "rule" or "standard," this concept is perhaps more of a modern preoccupation which is deemed necessary in light of the development of the NT canon of writings.[53] The pivotal point

---

[50] S. Denning-Bolle, "Christian Dialogue as Apologetic: The Case of Justin Martyr in Historical Context," *BJRL* 69 (1987) 492–510.

[51] Denning-Bolle, "Christian Dialogue as Apologetic," 500–501.

[52] Denning-Bolle, "Christian Dialogue as Apologetic," 504–505.

[53] I mean here that in looking back at Justin with our written canon in hand, we tend to force questions about canon directly in the category of writings. This neglects the important aspect of Rule of Faith. The Greek term κανών originally meant "reed". Especially a reed as a tool for measurement or alignment, and therefore acquired the basic sense of "straight rod". From this literal sense there arose a metaphorical sense where it came to mean a "norm" or "ideal" or "standard" a firm criterion against which something could be evaluated or judged. In this broad sense, the word was used in a variety of contexts including art, music literature, ethics, Law, and philosophy. Early Christians first took up the word in the sense of a "norm" but not in connection with written materials, but rather with the Rule of faith. We find the substantive first applied to the Sacred Scriptures in the fourth century by Athanasius of Alexandria. See B. M. Metzger, *The Canon of the New Testament: Its Origin, Development, and Significance* (Oxford: Clarendon Press, 1987) 289–293.

here is discerning a particular author's views of documents of the era that are becoming more and more useful to Christian churches. The wider context of the development of the NT canon must be kept in view here, for if the canon of NT writings was not fully developed at the time of Justin Martyr's contribution to theology, it is anachronistic to think of him as conceiving of a written canon. This is important because, in the absence of a defined collection of Christian writings, there must be some standard to which that particular author turned for direction.

Justin's references to the ἀπομνημονεύματα (τῶν ἀποστόλων) and their relationship to the developing NT canon have long been a lively topic of research, as witnessed by the plethora of books and articles, whether in whole or in part, which are devoted to that topic.[54] In the present study I am not purporting to add new research

---

[54] See e.g. A. Baker, "Justin's Agraphon in the Dialogue With Trypho," *JBL* 87 (1968) 277–287; A. Baldus, *Das Verhältnis Justins des Märtyrers zu unsern synoptischen Evangelien* (Münster, 1895); A. J. Bellinzoni, "The Source of the Agraphon in Justin Martyr's Dialogue With Trypho 47:5," *VC* 17 (1963) 65–70; idem., *The Sayings of Jesus in the Writings of Justin Martyr* (NovTSup 17; Leiden: E. J. Brill); W. Bousset, *Die Evangeliencitate Justins des Märtyrers in ihrem Wert für die Evangelienkritik* (Göttingen: Vandenhoeck & Ruprecht, 1891); E. R. Buckley, "Justin Martyr's Quotations from the Synoptic Tradition," *JTS* 36 (1935) 173–176; C. H. Cosgrove, "Justin Martyr and the Emerging New Testament Canon. Observations on the Purpose and Destination of the Dialogue with Trypho," *VC* (1982) 209–232; C. A. Credner, *Beiträge zur Einleitung in die biblischen Schriften* (Halle, 1832); M. von Engelhardt, *Das Christentum Justins Märtyrers, Eine Untersuchung über die Anfänge der katholischen Glaubenslehre* (Erlangen: A. Deichert, 1878); D. A. Hagner, "The Sayings of Jesus in the Apostolic Fathers and Justin Martyr," in D. Wenham (ed.), *Gospel Perspectives Vol. 5: The Jesus Tradition Outside the Gospels* (Sheffield: JSOT Press, 1984) 233–268; A. Hilgenfeld, *Kristische Untersuchungen über die Evangelien Justin's, der Clementinischen Homilien und Marcion's* (Halle, 1850); C. E. Hill, "Justin and the New Testament Writings," *StudPat* 30 (1997) 42–48; L. L. Kline, "Harmonized Sayings of Jesus in the Pseudo-Clementine Homilies and Justin Martyr," *ZNW* 66 (1975) 223–241; H. Koester, *Ancient Christian Gospels. Their History and Development* (London: SCM/Philadelphia: Trinity Press International, 1990); E. Lippelt, *Quae fuerint Justini Martyris APOMNHMONEUMATA quaque ratione cum forma Evangeliorum syro-latina cohaeserint* (Halle, 1901); E. Massaux, *The Influence of the Gospel of Saint Matthew on Christian Literature Before Saint Irenaeus. Book 3: The Apologists and the Didache* (ET N. J. Belval & S. Hecht; New Gospel Studies 5/2; Leuven: Peeters, 1986); idem, "La Texte du Sermone sur la Montagne de Mattieu utilisé par Saint Justin," *EThL* 28 (1952) 411–448; E. F. Osborn, *Justin Martyr*, 120–138; W. L. Petersen, *Gospel Traditions in the Second Century. Origins, Rescensions, Text and Transmission* (Notre Dame: University of Notre Dame Press, 1989); idem., "From Justin to Pepys: The History of the Harmonized Gospel Tradition," *StudPat* 30 (1997) 71–96; idem., "Textual Evidence of Tatian's Dependence upon Justin's ἈΠΟΜΝΗΜΟΝΕΥΜΑΤΑ," *NTS* 36 (1990) 512–534; W. Sanday, *The Gospels in the Second Century* (London: Macmillan, 1876); K. Semisch, *Die apostolischen Denkwürdigkeiten des Märtyrers Justinus* (Hamburg, 1848) 389–392; G. N. Stanton, "The Fourfold

to this somewhat crowded field. Rather, I am dependent upon many of the works mentioned above to provide a foundation upon which I build an argument regarding Justin's relationship to the state of the developing NT canon.

Central to Justin's relationship to the developing NT Canon is his use of the term εὐαγγέλιον. The scholarly consensus concerning Justin's references to the εὐαγγέλιον[55] is that he is indeed referring to a written document. Further, the Memoirs of the Apostles are probably synonymous with this designation.[56] Recently, however, this assertion has been challenged by C. H. Cosgrove who believes that Justin is actually reluctant to call any writing εὐαγγέλιον.[57]

According to Cosgrove, this reluctance can be seen in the predominance of the term "Memoirs" over against the use of the term "gospels". He states that it is inconclusive to what gospel (if any) Justin refers in *Dial.* 100. Further, Cosgrove believes that this statement should be understood in light of the preceding statement of 10.2 where Trypho speaks of the precepts that are written in the

---

Gospel," *NTS* 43 (1997) 317–346; A. Thoma, "Justins literarisches Verhältnis zu Paulus und zum Johannesevangelium," *Zeitschrift für wissenschaftliche Theologie* 18 (1875) 383–412; G. Volkmar, *Über Justin den Märtyrer und sein Verhältnis zu unsern Evangelien* (Zurich, 1853); J. C. Zahn, "Ist Ammon oder Tatian Verfasser der ins Lateinische, Altfränkische und Arabische übersetzten Evangelien-Harmonie? Und was hat Tatian bei seinem bekannten Diatessaron oder Diapente vor sich gehabt und zum Grunde gelegt?" in C. A. G. Keil and H. G. Tzschirner, *Analekten für das Studium der exegetischen und systematischen theologie* 2/1 (Leipzig, 1814). As well as the numerous histories of the NT canon, J. Barton, *Holy Writings, Sacred Text. The Canon in Early Christianity* (Louisville, KY: Westminster John Knox Press, 1997); F. F. Bruce, *The Canon of Scripture* (Downers Grove: Inter-Varsity press, 1988); H. F. von Campenhausen, *The Formation of the Christian Bible* (ET J. A. Baker; London: Adam & Charles Black, 1969); H. Y. Gamble, *The New Testament Canon. Its Making and Meaning* (Guides to Biblical Scholarship; Philadelphia: Fortress, 1985); A. von Harnack, *The Origin of the New Testament and the Most Important Consequences of the New Creation* (ET J. R. Wilkinson; London: Williams & Norgate, 1925); L. M. McDonald, *The Formation of the Christian Biblical Canon* (rev. ed.; Peabody: Hendrickson, 1995); B. F. Westcott, *A General Survey of the Canon of the New Testament* (5th ed.; Cambridge and London: Macmillan, 1881); T. Zahn, *Geschichte des neutestamentlichen Kanons*, I.2 (Erlangen: Andreas Deichert, 1881).

[55] *Dial.* 10.2; 51.2; 100.1; 136.3; *1 Apol.* 66.3.

[56] See e.g., Barnard, *Justin Martyr*; Gamble, *The New Testament Canon*, 28–29; G. M. Hahneman, *The Muratorian Fragment and the Development of the Canon* (Oxford Theological Monographs; Oxford: Clarendon, 1992) 96–98; Hill, "Justin and the New Testament Writings," 42–48; Koester, *Ancient Christian Gospels*, 40–43; Sanday, *The Gospels in the Second Century*, 88–137; Stanton, "The Fourfold Gospel," 329–332; Westcott, *A General Survey of the History of the Canon of the New Testament*, 96–179.

[57] Cosgrove, "Justin Martyr and the Emerging Christian Canon," 209–232; esp. 221–22.

"so-called gospel". This suggests, to him, a certain reticence on the part of Justin to apply εὐαγγέλιον to any writing.[58]

The position advocated by Cosgrove is subtly arrived at through an investigation of some particularly salient points. At the outset, Cosgrove states the position that he will defend,

> This general consensus that Justin regards certain apostolic writings as Scripture or 'almost Scripture' must be given up in light of what will be shown to be the probable purpose and audience of the *Dialogue with Trypho*, the primary document upon which judgments concerning Justin's 'canon' are based. It will be argued that not only are the apostolic writings not esteemed as Scripture by Justin, but that he is in fact moving in an opposite direction from regarding them as such. Indeed, Justin represents a reversal of the trend of the church in the second-century toward regarding apostolic writings as canon.[59]

Evaluation of Cosgrove's position is best done under five main headings. I believe that the weakness of his position is seen in every point thus leading to a faulty foundation and conclusion to the issue of whether Justin actually calls the Memoirs "Gospels." In the form of questions, the five main headings are: 1) Who is the intended audience of the *Dialogue*?; 2) How much importance should be attributed to Marcion in NT canon formation?; 3) Did Justin employ a harmony?; 4) Is the use of the singular/plural of εὐαγγέλιον significant?; 5) Does Justin reverse the trend of placing apostolic writings on par with the Prophets?

1. *Who is the intended audience of the* Dialogue?

In pursuing the proof of his position Cosgrove opens the discussion with a section entitled, "The Legitimacy of Joining the Canon Question with Respect to Justin".[60] The issue of the intended audience of the *Dialogue* is examined in considerable detail. This is so because for Cosgrove the intended audience will reveal whether Justin intended to address the issue of canon in the document. In this respect, it is often assumed that because the *Dialogue with Trypho* was written to non-Christians, we should not expect Justin to address the internal issue of canon. On the other hand, if it can be shown that the

---

[58] This is a reasonable argument, but the fact remains that these are Trypho's words in 10.2, not Justin's.

[59] Cosgrove, "Justin Martyr and the Emerging Christian Canon," 209.

[60] Cosgrove, "Justin Martyr and the Emerging Christian Canon," 210–219.

Dialogue was, in fact, written to and for Christians, then we should expect the issue of canon to be present in the document.

Thus, according to Cosgrove, the implications of a non-Christian destination of the *Dialogue* are: 1) Statements about canon gain more weight by virtue of the fact that the global context militates against their introduction; 2) Absence of statements regarding canon are not an argument against the importance of the concept for the author. We simply do not know his views on the matter.[61] But, if the *Dialogue* is written to Christians, different implications result: 1) Statements regarding the author's conception of the canon tend to reflect more accurately his own opinions on the subject; 2) Absence of reference to the question of canon, where it would be expected in light of the audience, does suggest something about the author's thinking on the topic.[62]

At this point Cosgrove goes into the necessary examination of the destination of the *Dialogue*. He summarizes the history of the discussion well and argues for a strictly Christian audience.[63] Thus, because of his understanding that issues of canon will be addressed in a writing to Christians, Cosgrove believes he has good reason to proceed to the second part of the article entitled, "Justin's Canon".[64] He states, "The results of the foregoing suggest that Justin writes for Christians, and we may expect that he does so with the special problem of canon at least to some extent in mind."[65]

Cosgrove admits that his argument depends fundamentally upon the assertion that the intended audience of the *Dialogue* are in fact Christians.[66] While he does admit that this answer must be received somewhat guardedly,[67] he still places fundamental importance on the assertion. It is because he believes the *Dialogue* to be written to Christians that he can then pursue the issue of canon. For if Justin is writing to Christians it would be obvious to speak of a subject so important to the Christian cause. Even silence on the canon, according to Cosgrove, suggests Justin's view on the subject.

---

[61] Cosgrove, "Justin Martyr and the Emerging Christian Canon," 211.

[62] Cosgrove, "Justin Martyr and the Emerging Christian Canon," 211, 221.

[63] I summarize the history of the discussion and argue for a Jewish/Christian audience below in Chapter 1.

[64] Cosgrove, "Justin Martyr and the Emerging Christian Canon," 219–225.

[65] Cosgrove, "Justin Martyr and the Emerging Christian Canon," 219.

[66] I would add that it also fundamentally depends on the issue of whether or not Justin meant to pursue canon questions.

[67] Cosgrove, "Justin Martyr and the Emerging Christian Canon," 225.

But the question must be asked, "What if Cosgrove is wrong in his assertion of the intended audience?" I argue in Appendix II that the intended audience is primarily Jewish. If this is the case then, by Cosgrove's own admission, it would be illegitimate to ask questions about the canon with respect to Justin. For Cosgrove asserts that if the audience are non-Christian we should not expect Justin to argue for a concept that was unimportant to the audience.[68] But even aside from the issue of intended audience this line of argument is fundamentally flawed.

Attention must be drawn to the way Cosgrove simply assumes that the establishment of a written NT canon was an issue in Justin's day. This not only misrepresents a proper distinction between "scripture" and "canon,"[69] but it is also an anachronistic view of the history of the canon. In Chapter 3 of this monograph I argue that the issue of a closed canon of NT scripture was neither conceived of nor debated during Justin's day.[70] Arguments with heterodox movements were not settled by an appeal to a canon of written documents, but with an appeal to the doctrine of the church, the rule of faith. This was occurring even after Justin's era and on into the third century.[71] It was only with Athanasius in the mid-fourth century that canon was applied to a closed set of apostolic writings.[72]

This must cause revision in Cosgrove's assertion of the legitimacy of pursuing issues of canon in Justin. Cosgrove states that because the *Dialogue* was written to Christians, Justin's conception of the canon will be accurately reflected, and that silence on the issue of canon in itself is part of this reflection in that it speaks of a pattern in Justin to relegate the apostolic writings to a position of merely historic documents.[73] But if a written canon was not a conception in the thought of second and even third century writers how can Justin's silence on the matter be manipulated to form an opinion? Approaching Justin with questions of the NT canon may only be done in the

---

[68] Cosgrove, "Justin Martyr and the Emerging Christian Canon," 210–211.

[69] See below, Chapter 4.II.B-C.

[70] See below, Chapter 4.II.A.3.

[71] See e.g., Irenaeus, *Haer.* 1.8.1; 1.9.1–4; Tertullian, *Praescrip.* 8–9; Eusebius, *H.e.* 6.12.3–6.

[72] See Athanasius, *Ep. Fest.* 39. Irenaeus argued for a four Gospel collection in *Haer.* 3.1.1–2. While this shows a conscious attempt in the year 180 toward a fixed Gospel collection it is decidedly less developed than Athanasius's list in the year 367.

[73] Cosgrove, "Justin Martyr and the Emerging Christian Canon," 221–223.

proper historical context.[74] Failure to do so results in an anachronistic view of the history of the NT canon, and leads one understand second century writers to speak of a written NT canon when the concept was not even part of the contemporary thought.

2. How much importance should be attributed to Marcion in NT canon formation?

Cosgrove supports the presupposition that issues of canon will be addressed in the *Dialogue* by an appeal to the effect that Marcion had on the Roman church around the height of his anti-Jewish program. This assertion, of course, assumes a date for the writing of the *Dialogue with Trypho* sometime after 153.[75] The appeal to Marcion proceeds on the contention that he was the first to promulgate a fixed written canon. Because of this Justin would have found it necessary to deal with the question of canon as posed by Marcion. In stating this, Cosgrove has placed definitive importance on Marcion as the main motivation in the development of a new canon to counter Marcion's "canon".

The idea that Marcion was definitive in the decision of the church to form a NT canon is somewhat overstated by Cosgrove. Certainly no one can dispute the chronological priority of Marcion's "canon"— nothing like it precedes him. But this chronological precedence must be distinguished from the question of its influence on the church.[76] The fixation of a canon by Marcion did not lead to an immediate or concerted effort in the church to delimit its own literature. In fact, the number of writings valued by the church remained fluid for a long period after Marcion posited his collection.[77] The fact that the church catholic eventually decided upon a larger canon is adequately explained on the grounds that these documents were the ones which the church found most useful to their purposes.[78]

The influence of Marcion on the formation of the NT canon continues to be debated among scholars. By and large, the view

---

[74] This proper historical context is presented below, Chapter 4.II.B–III.B

[75] See below, section IV, for a discussion on the date of the *Dialogue with Trypho*.

[76] See Gamble, *The New Testament Canon*, 59–62.

[77] Two good examples of this fluidity are the Apocalypse of John in the East and Hebrews in the West. See Gamble, *The New Testament Canon*, 23–56; L. M. McDonald, *The Formation of the Christian Biblical Canon*, 191–226.

[78] This point is emphasized as the ultimate criterion of canonicity by McDonald, *The Formation of the Christian Biblical Canon*, 246–249.

promulgated by Harnack,[79] Goodspeed,[80] and Campenhausen,[81] that
Marcion's collection virtually forced the church to form its own
canon, has, to varying degrees, been revised.[82] The revision to see
Marcion more modestly, as perhaps not the crucial factor, but never-
theless hastening the canon's development causing the church to do
what it would have done already seems to be the general tone of
the revisions.[83] But Gamble believes even this judgment unjustified
"since it is not possible to know whether the process of canon formation would have moved at a different pace had there never been
a Marcion. In the absence of stronger evidence, it is gratuitous to
see in Marcion a decisive factor in the history of the NT canon."[84]
Thus, with his dependence on Campenhausen's overstated view of
the influence of Marcion on the NT canon Cosgrove has similarly
overstated his case.

3. Did Justin employ a harmony?

Cosgrove now moves into a discussion on Justin and the Gospels.
Two of Cosgrove's conclusions must be challenged here. First, he
states that the singular εὐαγγέλιον cannot refer to a Gospel harmony
since Tatian's *Diatessaron* had not yet been produced. But it is incorrect to posit Tatian's *Diatessaron* as the first Gospel harmony. While
the *Diatessaron* may be the first extant Gospel harmony, W. L. Petersen[85]
has clearly shown that the harmonized tradition antedates Tatian
and probably even Justin. Second, in light of the first point, it is

---

[79] A. von Harnack, *Marcion. The Gospel of the Alien God* (ET J. E. Steely & L. D.
Bierma; Durham, NC: Labyrinth, 1990); idem., *The Origin of the New Testament.*

[80] Goodspeed, *The Formation of the New Testament* (Chicago: University of Chicago
Press, 1962).

[81] H. F. von Campenhausen, *The Formation of the Christian Bible.*

[82] For discussion on this and other revisions of Harnack see D. L. Balás, "Marcion
Revisited: A 'Post-Harnack' Perspective," in W. E. March (ed.), *Texts and Testaments:
Critical Essays on the Bible and Early Church Fathers* (FS S. D. Currie; San Antonio:
Trinity University Press, 1980) 95–108.

[83] See e.g., E. C. Blackman, *Marcion and His Influence* (London: SPCK, 1948) 39;
F. V. Filson, *Which Books Belong in the Bible?* (Philadelphia: Westminster, 1957) 120.

[84] Gamble, *The New Testament Canon*, 62. G. M. Hahneman (*The Muratorian Fragment
and the Development of the Canon*, 90–93) even argues that it is a misnomer to call
Marcion's collection a "canon" and certainly misleading to credit him with creating a NT canon.

[85] W. L. Petersen, "From Justin to Pepys: The History of the Harmonized Gospel
Tradition," 73.

highly probable that Justin employed a harmony as a source for his quotations in the *Dialogue with Trypho*.[86]

4. *Is the singular/plural of εὐαγγέλιον significant?*

Still in the context of the previous point, Cosgrove believes that the singular εὐαγγέλιον in *Dial.* 10.2 is best explained as reflective of Justin's disinclination to equate the "gospel" with the apostolic writings themselves. "The singular connotes a certain element of abstraction as regards the idea of the gospel itself over against discrete Gospels."[87] In other words, Justin's avoidance of applying the term εὐαγγέλιον to the Gospels is because of the dynamic sense in which the gospel is conceived by him.[88]

Cosgrove seems to argue here for more than Justin himself states. Of the five instances where εὐαγγέλιον is used, only one is plural.[89] Cosgrove asserts that the plural is used there as an accommodation to a pagan audience.[90] This is possible, but it does not necessarily follow that Justin does not accept the appellation himself. The singular uses of the noun also do not support Cosgrove's assertion. The fact that the statement in 10.2 is uttered by Trypho should at least warn us of placing the statement in Justin's realm of understanding. But, aside from the fact that Trypho is a Jew and would not accept Christian writings, we cannot conclude from the statement alone that Trypho did not accept the appellation, for accepting the appellation does not necessarily imply acceptance of the teachings and narrative contained therein. The remaining use of the singular noun in *Dial.*

---

[86] The probability that Justin did employ a harmony is more fully discussed below, Chapter 4.I.C.

[87] Cosgrove, "Justin Martyr and the Emerging Christian Canon," 222.

[88] This point is also emphasized by O. A. Piper ("The Nature of the Gospel According to Justin Martyr"). "This whole activity of announcing the saving work of God is what Justin calls τὸ εὐαγγέλιον, and of it Jesus is both proclaiming agent and subject matter" (pp. 162–163).

[89] *1 Apol.* 66.3. It should be noted here that two of the five references are clearly not references to written documents—*Dial.* 51.2; 136.3. Cosgrove agrees.

[90] Cosgrove, "Justin Martyr and the Emerging Christian Canon," 230, footnote #47. Cosgrove may be alluding here to the fact that the Greek usage of the term εὐαγγέλιον carried with it the idea of a message of victory. But Cosgrove himself makes no explicit equation. See, U. Becker, "Gospel, Evangelize, Evangelist,' in C. Brown (ed.), *The New International Dictionary of New Testament Theology* (3 vols.; Grand Rapids: Zondervan, 1976) 2.107–115; G. Friedrich, "εὐαγγέλιον," in G. Kittel (ed.), *Theological Dictionary of the New Testament* (10 vols.; Grand Rapids: Eerdmans, 1964) 2.721–737.

100.1 contains a possible quotation of the Gospel of Matthew or
Luke, or a harmony of the two. The probability that Justin is quoting
from this type of source can thus explain the use of the singular here.[91]

The point here is that the uses of the singular and/or plural forms
of εὐαγγέλιον are little support for the conclusion that Justin did not
accept the appellation "Gospel" for a written source. Cosgrove appears
to making too much out of a rather insignificant point. The fact is
that each time Justin uses the term it is in reference to a written
source, and in *1 Apol.* 66.3 he equates the memoirs, Gospels, and
that which was handed down (παραδίδωμι).

5. *Does Justin reverse the trend of placing apostolic writings on a par with the
Prophets?*

After explaining that the gospel is conceived by Justin in a more
dynamic sense than simply apostolic writings, Cosgrove relates Justin's
view of the OT to his view of apostolic writings. In this respect he
employs Campenhausen's discussion of Justin's view of the OT.[92]
Cosgrove states, "Von Campenhausen demonstrates how in Justin's
response to Marcion's prediction fulfillment, inspiration by the
'prophetic Spirit,' non-contradiction, the appellation 'the Scriptures,'
the doctrine of the Logos, and a salvation-history solution to the
problem of the Mosaic law combine in what may be called a 'doctrine of holy scripture'."[93] To Cosgrove the remarkable thing is that
Justin employs no similar defense of the apostolic writings, even
though they were equally endangered by Marcion. This is accentu-
ated by the fact that Justin has adopted the general church practice
of reading the OT writings together with the apostolic writings at
worship services. According to Cosgrove this, in essence, represents
the church's general trend toward placing the OT writings on the
same level as the apostolic writings.[94]

In light of this Cosgrove asks why Justin then refrains from rein-
forcing this tendency by constructing for the Memoirs a doctrine of
scripture commensurate with or approaching that which he formu-
lates for the OT. "Why does he neglect to rescue Matthew, Mark,

---

[91] This point must, of course, be seen in the context of the previous one which
argues that Justin did, in fact, employ a harmony.
[92] Campenhausen, *The Formation of the Christian Bible*, 88–102.
[93] Cosgrove, "Justin Martyr and the Emerging Christian Canon," 222.
[94] Cosgrove, "Justin Martyr and the Emerging Christian Canon," 223.

Luke, and Paul from Marcionite rejection or unorthodox editing? Although the genre of 'dialogue with a Jew' may have put some restraints on Justin's presentation, he does not hesitate to introduce considerations which are relevant to his Christian audience but not to a debate with a Jew."[95] This is then understood to mean that there is no reason why Justin could not have developed some theory of "canon" for the Gospels. But, according to Cosgrove, Justin does less than fail to defend the Apostolic writings, he actually dethrones them from what actual status they may have attained by calling them "Memoirs". The widespread use of the term "Gospel(s)" in the church during Justin's time and his own appellation "Memoirs," suggest that he conceives of them as purely historical documents.

The idea that Justin actually "dethrones" the apostolic writings ignores a very important aspect of Justin's view of the Apostles and their writings. It is true that Justin employs the Memoirs in an historical manner.[96] But I will show in Chapter Two that the apostolic writings were not in any sense viewed by Justin as inferior to the Prophetic writings.[97] The Apostles themselves were held in very high esteem by Justin.[98] It is significant, in this respect, that following closely on the heels of the section which contains the concentrated references to the Memoirs written by the Apostles,[99] that Justin claims that the Gentiles repent of their sins as a result of hearing and learning the doctrine preached by the Apostles.[100] The esteem with which the Apostles are held by Justin is clearly transferred to the documents that were written by them and their associates. This is shown in the fact that both the Prophets and Apostles possessed the qualifications for communicating God's revelation because of the fact that they had both seen and heard God.[101] So rather than "dethroning" the apostolic writings, Justin views them as valuable. In fact, it can be stated that Justin actually views them as going hand in hand with the Prophetic writings in salvation-history.[102]

---

[95] Cosgrove, "Justin Martyr and the Emerging Christian Canon," 223.
[96] See below, Chapter 2.IV.B.
[97] See below, Chapter 2.IV.B.
[98] *Dial.* 42.1; 110.2; 119.6.
[99] *Dial.* 99–107.
[100] *Dial.* 109.1. See also *Dial.* 114 where Justin claims that the words uttered by the Apostles of Jesus circumcise Christians from idolatry and sin.
[101] See below, Chapter 2.IV.B-V.
[102] See below, Chapter 3.V.A-C.

Cosgrove's assertion that Justin himself did not employ the term εὐαγγέλιον as an appellation for Christian writings has many foundational and conceptual faults. As shown above, these include the following: a misunderstanding the chronology of canon formation which results in an anachronistic context in his discussion on Justin addressing the canon issue; an overstated understanding of the importance of Marcion in the formation of the NT canon; an apparent incognizance of Justin's use of a harmony; an inconsequential stress on the use of a singular noun and; a misunderstanding of the high esteem in which Justin held the Apostles and their writings. But even in light of the problems with Cosgrove's thesis it must be asked if the question of whether Justin *accepted* the appellation εὐαγγέλιον is almost irrelevant in the grand picture. For even Cosgrove admits that some in the Christian community are using the appellation of Christian writings.[103]

The issue of canon in Justin cannot be pursued without the proper historical and chronological context in full view. Cosgrove has failed to do this in many ways. By attempting to argue for a "dynamic" Gospel Cosgrove wants the reader to place the understanding of canon in his misunderstood context. Certainly the gospel of Jesus Christ is a concept that steps outside the boundary of mere writings, but in attempting to relate this dynamic Gospel to the question of canon Cosgrove has placed the question in a context to which it does not belong. This is his major fault and the one which renders his perceived problem moot for our discussion.

In many ways, Cosgrove is a good illustration of the misunderstandings that Chapter Three is attempting to correct. He represents a tendency of some scholars to equate the use of scripture with canonical status in the 2nd century.[104] But canon issues must be understood within a certain historical process that avoids an anachronistic view of the state of the canon in the second century. Foundational to this is proper historical context within which the relationship of the Rule of Faith and Canon functioned. Further, there must be a proper distinction between Canon and Scripture. This is all taken

---

[103] Cosgrove, "Justin Martyr and the Emerging Christian Canon," 223.

[104] See e.g., E. J. Goodspeed, *Formation of the New Testament* (Chicago: Chicago University Press, 1962) 37–38; R. L. Harris, *Inspiration and Canonicity of the Bible. An Historical and Exegetical Study* (Contemporary Evangelical Perspectives; Grand Rapids: Zondervan, 1968) 213.

into account in Chapter Three to conclude that Justin's contribution to the NT canon is best seen as a process toward a fixed collection rather than an example of a fixed collection.

D. *Interpretation*

Early Christianity claimed the Jewish scriptures as their own. In so doing, they were claiming that the message brought by Jesus fulfilled what the Prophets proclaimed. This certainly appeared presumptuous to the Jew. Thus, the Christians' task in claiming the Jewish scriptures as their own was to show how they spoke of Christ, and to convince the Jew that the Christian interpretation of the Hebrew scriptures was the true and proper interpretation. This necessitates explanation of the reasons why Christians thought they had the right to usurp the Hebrew scriptures as their own.

There have been many studies on Justin Martyr that attempt to locate background influences on his interpretation.[105] But the concern in Chapter Five is motivated by the question, "How is it possible

---

[105] See e.g., D. E. Aune, "Justin Martyr's use of the Old Testament," *BETS* 9 (1966) 179–197; Barnard, *Justin Martyr*; idem, "The Old Testament and Judaism in the Writings of Justin Martyr," *VT* 14 1964) 395–406; B. Z. Bokser, "Justin Martyr and the Jews," *JQR* 64 (1973–74) 97–122; 204–211; Daniélou, *Gospel Message and Hellenistic Culture*; P. J. Donahue, *Jewish-Christian Controversy in the Second Century: A Study in the Dialogue of Justin Martyr* (Yale University Ph.D. Dissertation, 1973); Goodenough, *The Theology of Justin Martyr*; A. J. B. Higgins, "Jewish Messianic Beliefs in Justin Martyr's *Dialogue with Trypho*," *NovT* 9 (1967) 298–305; M. Hirschman, "Polemic Literary Units in the Classical Midrashim and Justin Martyr's *Dialogue with Trypho*," *JQR* 83 (1993) 369–384; W. Horbury, "Old Testament Interpretation in the Writings of the Church Fathers," in J. M. Mulder (ed.), *Mikra: Text, Translation and Interpretation in the Hebrew Bible in Ancient Judaism and Early Christianity* (Assen, The Netherlands: Van Gorcum/Philadelphia: Fortress, 1988); T. W. Manson, "The Argument From Prophecy," *JTS* 46 (1945) 129–136; B. de Margerie, *An Introduction to the History of Exegesis Vol. 1: The Greek Fathers* (ET L. Maluf; Petersham, MA: Saint Bede's Publications, 1993); Osborn, *Justin Martyr*; H. Remus, "Justin Martyr's Argument with Judaism," in S. G. Wilson (ed.), *Anti-Judaism in Early Christianity Vol. 2: Separation and Polemic* (Studies in Christianity and Judaism 2; Waterloo: Wilfred Laurier University Press, 1986); D. T. Runia, *Philo in Early Christian Literature: A Survey* (CRINT 3/3; Assen: Van Gorcum/Philadelphia: Fortress, 1993); H. P. Schneider, "Some Reflections on the Dialogue of Justin Martyr with Trypho," *SJT* 15 (1962) 164–175; Shotwell, *The Biblical Exegesis of Justin Martyr*; M. Simon, *Verus Israel. A Study of the Relations Between Christians and Jews in the Roman Empire (135–425)* (ET H. McKeating; The Littmen Library of Jewish Civilization; Oxford: Oxford University Press, 1986); P. R. Weiss, "Some Samaritanisms of Justin Martyr," *JTS* 45 (1944) 199–205; P. Widdicombe, "Justin Martyr, Allegorical Interpretation, and the Greek Myths," *StudPat* 31 (1997) 234–239; R. L. Wilken, "The Old Testament in Controversy with the Jews," *SJT* 8 (1955) 111–126; S. G. Wilson, *Related Strangers. Jews and Christians 70–170 CE* (Minneapolis: Fortress, 1995).

26 INTRODUCTION

that two different interpretations (Trypho's interpretation vs. Justin's interpretation) can arise from the same scriptural passage?" This question must be answered, of course, based on the assumptions and presuppositions that each brings to scripture. This necessitates a contextual examination of the text that is sensitive to the reasons Justin himself gives for his Christian interpretation of the Hebrew scriptures.

In 1975 Theodore Stylianopoulos stated that one of the most distinctive aspects of Justin's contribution to the ongoing Christian interpretation of the Law was his historical conception of the purpose of the Law.[106] But Stylianopoulos bemoans the fact that the Law in Justin has received little attention in secondary literature.[107] This is not to say that there has been a complete disregard for the Law in Justin Martyr.[108] But still, even Goodenough, who produced arguably the most important monograph on Justin this century, says virtually nothing about the problem of the Law.[109]

Since the publication of Stylianopoulos's monograph the scene has changed little. Barnard's standard on Justin Martyr does contain a chapter on the Apologist's relationship to Judaism but offers nothing on his interpretation of the Law.[110] Pierre Prigent offers a brief analysis of the problem of the Law in Justin,[111] but his main purpose was not a study of Justin's interpretation of the Law, but rather the discovery of a foundational document behind the *Dialogue* and the *Apologies*.[112] Stylianopoulos's work filled a much needed gap in Justin studies by answering three foundational questions:[113] 1) Why is the Law a problem for Justin?; 2) What is Justin's conceptions of the Mosaic law?; 3) What arguments does Justin marshall to demonstrate the invalidity of the Law, on the one hand, and its purpose on the other?

The fourth chapter of this monograph recognizes the debt owed to Stylianopoulos in formulating the above questions and providing

---

[106] T. Stylianopoulos, *Justin Martyr and the Mosaic Law* (SBLDS 20; Missoula, MON: Scholars Press, 1975) 1.

[107] Stylianopoulos, *Justin Martyr and the Mosaic Law*, 2.

[108] As witnessed in the older monographs of K. Semisch, *Justin des Märtyrer* (2 Vols.; Breslau, 1840–1842) 2.58–70; von Englehardt, *Das Christentum Justins des Märtyrers*, 241–270.

[109] Goodenough, *The Theology of Justin Martyr*. Also, A. von Harnack, *Judentum und Judenchristentum in Justins Dialog mit Trypho* (TU 39; Leipzig, 1913) 47–92.

[110] Barnard, *Justin Martyr*, 39–52.

[111] P. Prigent *Justin l'Ancien Testament* (Paris: Gabalda, 1964) 234–285.

[112] Stylianopoulos, *Justin Martyr and the Mosaic Law*, 3.

[113] Stylianopoulos, *Justin Martyr and the Mosaic Law*, 4.

answers. I would be cautious, however, and state with Stylianopoulos[114] that Chapter 5 is not a study of the scriptural exegesis of Justin, nor of his use of the OT as such. Rather, it is an analysis of his theological foundations for christological interpretation of the OT.

Central to the discussion is the "pattern of twos"[115] which I suggest are the hermeneutical key to Justin's OT interpretation. The two Laws and the two advents are the two most important concepts with which Justin deals.

Following the examination of these pattern of twos Chapter Five then moves into a key, and much discussed, concept in Justin's interpretation of scripture—illumination. My discussion here seeks to relate Justin's doctrine of illumination to the centrality of Christ. It is Christ who is the illuminator and any Christian possesses this illumination.

The above four concepts are seen as foundational because they get to the heart of the issues in early Christianity. Who is God? How do we know him? What is his message? Who is Jesus? What writings are authentic expositions of the faith? To what standard do we look for direction in belief? How are the Jewish scriptures Christian if their message is different than the Jewish writings? Is the Law still valid? These and many other questions are paramount as Christianity attempted to establish itself as the one true religion. They are represented and answered within this schematic of the four pillars.

This is the reason why I have approached Justin Martyr's *Dialogue with Trypho* with a view to discerning his concepts of revelation, truth, canon, and interpretation. They are windows into a larger world—a world which explains Justin's theology as it is presented in the *Dialogue*.

II. *The Life of Justin*

The details of Justin Martyr's birth, life, and death are relatively obscure and sketchy. Any understanding of the life of Justin must be examined from two types of sources. First, we can piece together a rather skeletal amount of autobiography from Justin's extant works, *1 Apology*, *2 Apology*, and *Dialogue with Trypho*. Second, events of Justin's life can also be gleaned from a few ancient writers who mention

---

[114] Stylianopoulos, *Justin Martyr and the Mosaic Law*, 4.
[115] See below, Chapter 5.II.

Justin in their own writings. These include mainly Eusebius, but Justin is also mentioned by Irenaeus and Tatian. In this vein, we will first examine Justin's autobiographical sections and then move on to these other writers. In this fashion a summary "life" of Justin can be constructed.

A. *Justin's Autobiography*

1. *Birth*

Justin offers no hint to the date of his birth. Most have been satisfied with the simple and broad conclusion that he was born near the end of the first century or the beginning of the second.[116] He does state that he is the son of Priscus and the grandson of Bacchius.[117] His grandfather's name is thus Greek, while his father's, as is his own, is Latin. In the same passage in *1 Apology* Justin states that he was born in Flavia Neapolis in Palestine. Flavia Neapolis, which was not far from Shechem and was established by the Emperor Vespasian as a colony in 72 AD,[118] was in Samaritan territory.[119] Today the town is known as Nablus, Israel.

2. *Life*

Justin claims that he is a Gentile convert to Christianity,[120] and is thus uncircumcised.[121] *Dial.* 2 indicates that he received a Greek education while the entire prologue to the *Dialogue* (chaps. 1–9) shows that he lived the life of an educated pagan. Also, in the prologue we see that he showed intellectual vigor in his investigation and successive rejection of most of the established schools of philosophy.[122] Justin certainly considered himself a philosopher. The prologue clearly

---

[116] H. Chadwick ("Justin Martyr's Defense of Christianity," 276) simply asserts a second century birthdate. E. F. Osborn (*Justin Martyr*, 6) claims that Justin was born in the early second century. L. W. Barnard (*Justin Martyr*, 5) states that because we only know that Justin taught at Rome during the reign of Antoninus Pius and that he was martyred under Marcus Aurelius, we can infer that his birth occurred either in the late first century or the early second.

[117] *1 Apol.* 1.1.

[118] Barnard, *Justin Martyr*, 5; Osborn, *Justin Martyr*, 6.

[119] Chadwick, "Justin Martyr's Defense of Christianity," 276. This is probably the reason why Justin refers to himself as a Samaritan in *Dial.* 120.6.

[120] *1 Apol.* 53; *Dial.* 41.3.

[121] *Dial.* 28.2; 29.

[122] Osborn, *Justin Martyr*, 6.

indicates that he was a follower of the philosophy of Plato,[123] and that after his conversion he still considered himself a philosopher. In fact, Justin, even after his conversion, wore the philosopher's cloak.[124]

Justin actually gives two reasons for his conversion to Christianity. The first, as seen in the prologue to the *Dialogue*, is because of the arguments of the respectable old Christian man whom he met by the sea. The man recognized Justin's Middle Platonic leanings and proceeded to refute Justin's Platonism and convince him of the necessity of the Prophets and Apostles in the true philosophy. The second reason for his conversion to Christianity is that even though he had seen the Christians slandered and persecuted, he saw that they had fear neither of death nor of terrible harm. In this fearlessness Justin saw that it was impossible that they could be living in the wickedness that was so often portrayed of them.[125]

B. *Justin's Biography*

1. *Birth*

No ancient writer even mentions an approximate date of Justin's birth.

2. *Life*

As for Justin's life, however, more is stated in the ancient writers. But the information about Justin's life, which is found mainly in Eusebius' *Ecclesiastical History*[126] is largely what we have already learned from Justin himself. From the passages in Eusebius it is confirmed that Justin was converted from philosophy to Christianity. He thus became a lover of the true philosophy. After his conversion he continued to wear the philosopher's cloak and was still involved in the study of Greek literature.

In addition to these details that are mentioned by Justin himself, Eusebius also tells us that Justin was especially prominent during the days of Antoninus Pius (reigned 137–161). Further, we learn that Justin lived at Rome. This is confirmed in *The Martyrdom of the Holy*

[123] Cf. Also *2 Apol.* 12.1.
[124] Chadwick ("Justin Martyr's Defense of Christianity," 277) states that during this time the philosopher's cloak possessed something of the significance of the modern clerical collar and provoked the same kind of mixed reaction in the public mind.
[125] *2 Apol.* 12.1.
[126] *H.e.* 4.8.3–5; 4.11.8–11; 4.16.1–4.18.10.

Martyrs[127] which states that, at the time of Justin's trial, he was in
Rome for the second time. From this, Barnard posits that Justin
appears to have stayed in Rome for some time. The fact that Justin
resided in Rome twice is consistent with what is known of the various schools of thought which were established by Christians in Rome.
Thus, while Valentinus used Rome as a base, he also had connections
with Alexandria and Cyprus. Marcion's nickname, "sea-captain," suggests that he made a number of voyages away from Rome. And
Greek philosophers such as Lucian of Samosata taught in province
after province. It is therefore more probable that Justin did not establish a permanent school in Rome, but that he was more of an itin-
erant teacher who traveled while using Rome as more of a base.[128]

3. *Death*

Justin's martyrdom, as stated above, is recorded in *The Martyrdom of
the Holy Martyrs*. It is a rather short account of the beheading of
Justin and six others after being questioned by the prefect Junias
Rusticus. The account relates how decrees were passed against
Christians in Rome to force them to offer libations to idols. The
men are questioned and subsequently asked to offer sacrifice to the
gods. Each refuses and each is therefore decapitated.

The account of Justin's death is consistent with various statements
of Eusebius,[129] Tatian,[130] and with the mind of Justin himself.[131]
Because the account clearly states that Justin was martyred during
the reign of Junias Rusticus as prefect (162–168), this gives us a fairly
narrow window for the actual date of his death.[132]

Justin was martyred while Antoninus Pius was Emperor (161–169).
Eusebius claims that he was martyred as a consequence of a plot
by the Cynic Crescens, whom Justin is said to have publicly refuted
on a number of occasions.[133] This piece of information is also related

---

[127] ET found in A. Roberts & J. Donaldson, *Ante-Nicene Fathers* (10 Vols.; Peabody,
MA: Hendrickson, 1994 [Originally: Buffalo, NY: Christian Literature Publishing
Company, 1885]) 1.303–306.
[128] Barnard, *Justin Martyr*, 12.
[129] *H.e.* 4.16.
[130] *Or.* 19.
[131] Osborn, *Justin Martyr*, 8.
[132] Chadwick ("Justin Martyr's Defense of Christianity," 278) states that this is
why most encyclopedias record the date of Justin's death as 167.
[133] *H.e.* 4.16.1.

by Tatian.[134] But Eric Osborn believes that Eusebius has "exceeded the evidence for the cause of his death."[135]

Osborn accepts the fact that Justin himself claimed that he expected to be plotted against by someone like Crescens.[136] And Justin's pupil, Tatian, even claims that Crescens' plots were directed at him as well.[137] But Osborn does not trust Tatian's account because of the "wild hyperbole" employed by Tatian in describing Crescens' character.[138] But in light of this even Tatian does not claim that Crescens is responsible for Justin's death. Eusebius, argues Osborn, can only have made this claim based on his misinterpretation of Tatian. Besides, even if Tatian were correct in claiming that Crescens plotted against both he and Justin, the fact that he failed in getting Tatian suggests that he also failed in getting Justin.[139]

As proof of his misgivings about Crescens being responsible for Justin's death, Osborn suggests a closer look at the account of Justin's martyrdom. In this respect, Osborn offers two reasons to reject Crescens' responsibility for Justin's death.[140] First, the martyrdom account clearly shows that Justin was condemned with six others in a normal legal process. At the outset of the account a decree is pointed to as the "culprit" of the martyrdom. Second, there is no hint of a suggestion that one particular person had especially accused Justin.

Osborn proceeds to support this argument by calling into question Eusebius' claim that Justin frequently debated with Crescens.[141] On this Osborn suggests that "Justin claims to have interrogated him [Crescens] more than once and to have found him ignorant; but Justin is not sure whether this ignorance is due to a failure of Crescens to read the teachings of Christ or a failure to understand them. If there had been protracted disputations, Justin could not have been uncertain concerning these alternatives."[142]

---

[134] *Or.* 19.
[135] Osborn, *Justin Martyr*, 9.
[136] *2 Apol.* 3.1.
[137] *Or.* 19.
[138] Osborn, *Justin Martyr*, 9. Tatian refers to Crescens as a "sodomite" and a "money grabber."
[139] Osborn, *Justin Martyr*, 9.
[140] Osborn, *Justin Martyr*, 9.
[141] *H.e.* 4.16.1.
[142] Osborn, *Justin Martyr*, 9–10.

III. *The Writings of Justin*

Of Justin Martyr's writings only three are extant, his two *Apologies*[143] and his *Dialogue with Trypho the Jew*. This, however was not the extent of Justin's literary activity.[144] Justin himself claims to have written a treatise against all heresies.[145] Eusebius indicates that he wrote at least seven more which have subsequently been lost to us.[146] They include a third *Apology*, a work against the Greeks, a work entitled *Refutation*, one under the title *On the Sovereignty of God*, a work entitled *Psaltes*, a "disputation on the soul," and a writing against Marcion.[147]

The texts of all our extant writings of Justin are available in the single medieval manuscript, Paris 450.[148] Also contained in that manuscript are the texts of nine other documents reputed to be Justinian. Justin became a fairly well-known author and because of this his fame grew in the later church. It is not surprising, therefore, that many writings were either deliberately or mistakenly attributed to him. This is the case with the nine other writings included in Paris 450.[149] The arguments against accepting any of these works as genuine have been conclusively stated by Harnack.[150]

IV. *The* Dialogue with Trypho

A. *Date*

The date of the composition of the *Dialogue* cannot be nailed down with any precision. There is a significant piece of evidence within

---

[143] What are commonly referred to today as Justin's two *Apologies* are, in fact, one *Apology* which has been divided into two—the text and the Appendix. This monograph will retain the accepted titles *1 Apology* and *2 Apology* for these respective works.

[144] In addition to these extant works there are four fragments of Justin preserved in later writers which are almost certainly genuine. See R. M. Grant, "The Fragments of the Greek Apologists and Irenaeus," in J. N. Birdsall and R. W. Thompson (eds.), *Biblical and Patristic Studies in Memory of Robert Pierce Casey* (Freiberg: Herder, 1963) 182–188.

[145] *1 Apol.* 26.

[146] *H.e.* 4.11.7–11; 4.16.1–9.

[147] Irenaeus (*Haer.* 4.6.2) also mentions Justin's work against Marcion.

[148] The date on the manuscript itself is 11 September 1363. It is beyond dispute that of all the extant works attributed to Justin only the *Apologies* and the *Dialogue* are genuine. See Barnard, *Justin Martyr*, 14; J. Nilson, "To Whom is Justin's *Dialogue with Trypho* Addressed?" *TS* 38 (1977) 539.

[149] These spurious writings are: *Address to the Greeks; Hortatory Address to the Greeks; On the Unity of God; A Fragment on the Resurrection; Exposition of the True Faith; Letter to Zenas and Serenus; Refutation of Certain Aristotelian Doctrines; Questions and Answers to the Orthodox; Christian Questions Asked to the Greeks.*

[150] See Barnard, *Justin Martyr*, 172.

the work itself where Justin refers to his *1 Apology*.[151] Because Justin refers to his previous writing in the *Dialogue* it is therefore certain that he composed the *Dialogue with Trypho* after he penned *1 Apology*. This being the case, it is helpful to ascertain the date of the writing of Justin's *1 Apology*.

The address of *1 Apology* is to Antoninus Pius and to his two sons, Verissimus and Lucius. Antoninus' son Lucius was born in 130, and Antoninus reigned from 137–161. In the address of the *Apology* Justin claims that Lucius was a "philosopher" and a "lover of learning." Barnard thus reasons that allowing time for Lucius to attain this description, the writing of the *Apology* cannot be placed earlier than 145.[152]

Along with this is the reference of Justin in *1 Apology* to Marcion and his following as "spread over every race of men."[153] Marcion came to Rome and taught in the reign of Hyginus (139–142). This fits well with a composition date *after* 145 because sufficient time needs to be allowed for Marcion's teachings to receive such a wide audience.[154] Further, Justin states[155] that he is writing 150 years after Christ's birth.

Finally, Justin makes reference to a petition recently presented to Felix, the governor of Alexandria.[156] Cullen Story explains that a number of papyri establish the date of the prefecture of this Felix with considerable certainty.[157]

1) In 1896, Frederick Kenyon[158] identified the Felix of *1 Apol.* 29.2 with a Munatius Felix who succeeded Honoratus.

2) The Berlin Papyrus 265 shows Honoratus to have been prefect in 148 AD.[159] But according to another papyrus, Felix's date of ascension was 151.[160]

3) Another papyrus with the date 186 AD mentions a trial held in 151 before the prefect of Egypt, Munatius.

---

[151] *Dial.* 120.5.
[152] Barnard, *Justin Martyr*, 19.
[153] *1 Apol.* 26.
[154] Barnard, *Justin Martyr*, 19.
[155] *1 Apol.* 46.
[156] *1 Apol.* 29.
[157] C. I. K. Story, *The Nature of Truth in "The Gospel of Truth" and in the Writings of Justin Martyr*.
[158] F. Kenyon, "The Date of the Apology of Justin Martyr," *The Academy* 49 (1896) 98.
[159] Story, *The Nature of Truth in "The Gospel of Truth" and in the Writings of Justin Martyr*, XIV.
[160] Barnard, *Justin Martyr*, 19.

4) Another Berlin papyrus (no. 448) gives the first name of the prefect Munatius Felix as Lucius.

5) Kenyon[161] cites another papyrus which mentions a prefect Lucius of the reign of Antoninus Pius, probably the same as Felix.

In light of the above, it is probable that Felix held office between 151–154. Thus, the date of the Apology lies somewhere between these two dates.

If *1 Apology* lies between 151–154, and because the *Dialogue* mentions the *Apology* it is certain that the *Dialogue* was composed after that date. Any conjecture regarding a more exact date than 155–167 is only that. We must, therefore, be satisfied with an imprecise date for the *Dialogue with Trypho*.

B. *Text*

As mentioned above, the text of the *Dialogue* comes to us in Paris 450, a medieval manuscript dated 11 September 1363. Unfortunately, the state of the text of *Dialogue* leaves something to be desired. Some have suggested that because there is no introductory dedication preceding the *Dialogue* that this has been lost from the original.[162] But there is more definite evidence of mutilation of the text. There appears to be a lacuna in *Dial.* 74.3 which Chadwick believes extended for several pages.[163] There is a further lacuna in *Dial.* 73 where the exposition of Ps 96 is suddenly interrupted, never to be resumed again. There is also internal evidence that suggests the discussion between Justin and Trypho lasted two separate days.[164] But the *Dialogue*, as we have it, shows no trace of either the end of the first day or the beginning of the second. In light of this, perhaps the words of Schneider are appropriate, "Solutions in this field are difficult and must be left to the technical experts. While it would be of immeasurable gain if the mutilations of the text could be resolved, they are fortunately not of such an extent as to make any attempt at evaluation and interpretation useless or grossly inaccurate."[165]

---

[161] F. Kenyon, *Greek Papyri in the British Museum*, II (Oxford: Oxford University Press, 1898) 171.

[162] On this point Schneider ("Some Reflections on the Dialogue of Justin with Trypho," 166) expresses his agreement with Goodenough (*The Theology of Justin Martyr*, 97). Agreement on this point is far from uniform.

[163] Chadwick, "Justin Martyr's Defense of Christianity," 278.

[164] *Dial.* 56.16; 85.4; 95.2. See also the same assertion by Eusebius, *H.e.* 4.18.6–8.

[165] Schneider, "Some Reflections on the Dialogue of Justin Martyr with Trypho," 166.

Throughout this monograph the Greek text used for Justin's extant works is Goodspeed's.[166] All English translations of the *Dialogue* are my own while English translations of the *Apologies* are from Roberts and Donaldson,[167] unless otherwise noted.

---

[166] E. J. Goodspeed (ed.), *Die ältesten Apologeten. Texte mit kurzen Einleitungen* (Gottingen: Vandenhoeck & Ruprecht, 1915).

[167] A. Roberts & J. Donaldson (eds.), *Ante-Nicene Fathers* (10 Vols.; Peabody, MA: Hendrickson, 1994) 1.159–193.

CHAPTER ONE

THE PURPOSE AND DESTINATION OF THE
DIALOGUE WITH TRYPHO

At a perfunctory level of understanding, the interpretation of scripture in Justin's *Dialogue with Trypho* presents us with interpretive issues directed toward a Jewish audience. Thus it appears clear that Justin's choice and use of certain OT texts are made because of the presuppositions of his audience, who are Jews. The *Dialogue* has often been described as a foundational document for an understanding of the theological discussions and contacts between Christians and Jews of the second century.[1] This is based on the foundational understanding that the intended audience of the *Dialogue* was Jews, as a defense of the Christian faith to them.

This traditional view concerning the intended audience of the *Dialogue* was held by the majority of scholars until the twentieth century. But since then it has been faulted for being uncritical.[2] But it is not difficult to assert that the *Dialogue* was written to and for the Jews of the second century. Any casual reading of the document reveals its focus on the Law, the Jewish messianic hope, and the concept of Israel as the chosen people of God. Further, the two main participants, Justin, a Christian, and Trypho,[3] a Jew, tends to

---

[1] L. W. Barnard, *Justin Martyr. His Life and Thought* (Cambridge: Cambridge University Press, 1967) 39–52; E. Flesseman Van Leer, *Tradition and Scripture in the Early Church* (Van Gorcum's Theologische Bibliotheek; Assen: Van Gorcum, 1954) 71–72; W. A. Shotwell, *The Biblical Exegesis of Justin Martyr* (London: SPCK, 1965) 2; G. N. Stanton, "Aspects of Early Christian-Jewish Polemic and Apologetic," *NTS* 31 (1985) 378; D. Trakatellis, "Justin Martyr's Trypho," *HTR* (1986) 287.

[2] See e.g., C. H. Cosgrove, "Justin Martyr and the Emerging Christian Canon," *VC* (1982) 211.

[3] The information Justin gives us about Trypho can be collected from *Dial.* 1.1–3; 9.3; 16.2; 18.3; 38.1; 94.4. From this data L. W. Barnard ("The Old Testament in the Writings of Justin Martyr," *VT* 14 [1964] 395–396) describes Trypho as a Jew who fled from the war in Palestine, spending much time in Greece and Corinth. His culture was Gentile because he states that he was instructed by Corinthus the Socratic in Argos. Trypho distinguishes himself from 'our teachers' and includes himself among those who have been warned against entering into discussions with Christians. Barnard believes this to be a good indication that Trypho was a layman and not a Rabbi—a fact corroborated by his lack of knowledge of the Hebrew language. Trypho's "conception of Judaism will represent a position different from

support the idea that the target audience is Jewish. These appear to
be distinctly Jewish concerns in order to convince them that the messianic expectation of Israel is found in Jesus.

In spite of this, however, the present century has offered several
reasons for arguing against the traditionally held understanding of
Jewish addressees. In this vein, some have argued for a pagan audience,[4] some for a gentile Christian audience,[5] and some for a combined Jewish and Christian audience.[6] The major arguments for
denying Jewish addressees will be summarized and examined below.[7]

I. Pagan Destination

A. The Address to Marcus Pompeius

The possibility that the *Dialogue* is addressed to a man named Marcus
Pompeius has been used to deny Jewish addressees and posit pagan
addressees. Marcus is explicitly referred to in *Dial.* 141.5 as ὦ φίλτατε
Μᾶρκε Πομπήϊε. Earlier in the *Dialogue*[8] there is simply a reference
to φίλτατε. In spite of the fact that only 141.5 makes explicit reference to Marcus, Nilson takes the term φίλτατε to be a reference to
him as well.[9] Nilson believes he has good reason for so doing because
of the mutilated state of the Greek text of the *Dialogue*.[10] Thus, if

---

the strict Palestinian Pharisaic orthodoxy which was being enforced following on
the reconstruction of Jamnia after 70 AD." (p. 396)

[4] E. R. Goodenough, *The Theology of Justin Martyr. An Investigation Into the Conceptions
of Early Christian Literature and Its Hellenic and Judaistic Influences* (Amsterdam: Philo
Press, 1968); A. Harnack, "Judentum und Judenchristentum in Justins Dialog mit
Tryphon," TU 39 (1913) 47–98; N. Hyldahl, *Philosophie und Christentum. Eine Interpretation
der Einleitung zum Dialog Justins* (Acta Theologica Danica 9; Copenhagen: Munksgaard,
1966); J. Nilson, "To Whom is Justin's *Dialogue with Trypho* Addressed?" TS 38 (1977)
538–546.

[5] Cosgrove, "Justin Martyr and the Emerging Christian Canon."

[6] T. Stylianopoulos, *Justin Martyr and the Mosaic Law* (SBL Dissertations 20;
Missoula: Scholars Press, 1972) 10–20; 169–195.

[7] I must acknowledge, at the outset, a relative dependence upon Stylianopoulos's
oustanding Appendix in *Justin Martyr and the Mosaic Law*, 169–195.

[8] *Dial.* 8.3.

[9] Nilson, "To Whom is Justin's *Dialogue with Trypho* Addressed?" 540.

[10] Concerning the mutilation of the text of the *Dialogue*, the details are well-
known. They centre mainly in the lost part of the Introduction and lacuna in 74.3
and a more serious lacuna in 73 where the exposition of Ps. 96 is suddenly interrupted and not resumed. From a quotation by Eusebius (*H.e.* 4.18.6–8) and internal evidence (*Dial.* 56.16; 85.4; 92.5) it is apparent that the discussion was presented
as lasting two days or more. But there is no trace in the *Dialogue* either of the end-
ing of the first day or the beginning of the second. See, H. P. Schneider, "Some
Reflections on the Dialogue of Justin Martyr With Trypho," *SJT* 15 (1962) 166.

one considers the mutilated state of this text it would not be hard to conceive of the *Dialogue* as originally featuring an introductory dedication which included the name of the addressee.[11] Nilson accepts this possibility and posits Marcus Pompeius in the position of addressee. Because the name Marcus Pompeius is strongly Roman, it suggests, therefore, that Marcus is a Roman, and, as such, a Gentile. Thus, if he is a Roman and the *Dialogue* is addressed to him, the hypothesis that the *Dialogue* is addressed to a pagan audience gains considerable weight and argues against a Jewish audience.[12]

Four criticisms of this point have been offered. First, it is entirely possible that the name Marcus Pompeius could belong to a Gentile Christian or even a Jew.[13] For ". . . the adoption of Greek and Roman names by Jews in hellenistic times was not unusual as in the case of Flavius Josephus. The name Marcus is a good Jewish name."[14] Second, the name only explicitly appears once in the entire *Dialogue*, and there is evidence that the work went through more than one edition.[15] Third, the references in 8.3 and 141.5 really say nothing about the addressees of the *Dialogue*. They are simply isolated references which add nothing to a work that focuses on the encounter between a Jew and a Christian.[16] Goodenough's suggestion that the *Dialogue* originally contained a dedication which included the name of the addressee and a key to the purpose of the book has neither textual nor internal support. But, in light of the probability that the *Dialogue* is an imitation of Platonic style,[17] the work may begin as it does for maximum dramatic effect. This would mean, then, that the question of the identity of Marcus Pompeius, much like the identity of Luke's Theophilus,[18] recedes into the background with minimal significance on the question of the addressee(s) of the work. Thus,

---

[11] This possibility is also asserted by E. R. Goodenough, *The Theology of Justin Martyr*, 97.

[12] Nilson, "To Whom is Justin's *Dialogue with Trypho* Addressed?" 540.

[13] Cosgrove, "Justin Martyr and the Emerging Christian Canon," 212; Stylianopoulos, *Justin Martyr and the Mosaic Law*, 170.

[14] Stylianopoulos, *Justin Martyr and the Mosaic Law*, 170, footnote #10. See also, H. C. Kee; E. Albu, C. Lindberg, W. J. Frost & D. L. Robert, *Christianity: A Social and Cultural History* (2nd ed.; Upper Saddle River, NJ: Prentice-Hall, 1998) 11.

[15] Cosgrove, "Justin Martyr and the Emerging Christian Canon," 212. Cosgrove does not offer any support for his assertion of multiple editions and it is difficult to see where he is headed with the point. Perhaps he intends to imply that the name could actually be a scribal addition.

[16] Stylianopoulos, *Justin Martyr and the Mosaic Law*, 170–171.

[17] I argue this below, Chapter 3.II.

[18] Luke 1:3; Acts 1:1.

both the dedication (if it did exist) and the two references to the
stated addressee may merely be a literary gesture.[19] Fourth, *Dial.*
80.3 presents strong evidence for moving away from a single addressee,
as well as confirming the formality of Justin's address to Marcus.

In *Dial.* 80.3 Justin says to Trypho, "But so that you know that I
do not say this to you alone, I promise to create a whole book, as
far as I am able, of all the arrangements we will make, in which I
also will write all that I confess to you."[20] This is the only place in
the entire *Dialogue* where Justin takes note of his own intention in
writing it. The wider context of chapter 80 is on Christian eschatological
hope. Trypho questions Justin as to whether he actually believes in
the rebuilding of Jerusalem, the millennium, and the resurrection,
or whether he has simply asserted these in order to win the argument. Justin states that he says exactly what he means and that, in
order to prove it, he will commit their discussion to writing. This
passage in itself does not prove who the addressees of the *Dialogue*
are, it is merely an incidental point in the work. But the passage
does show that the work appears to be directed at a wider audience
than simply Trypho and his friends.[21] This wider audience argues
against a single addressee such as Marcus Pompeius which certainly
does not rule out the possibility of the audience being Jewish.

B. *The Philosophical Prologue*

The philosophical prologue of *Dial.* 1–9 is also used to argue against
a Jewish audience. Justin's introductory presentation here of Christianity
as the true philosophy, in comparison with the "many-headed" versions of philosophy which neglect God,[22] is said to create a setting in
the *Dialogue* which is much more appealing to a Gentile than a Jewish
audience.[23] Nilson states that in the prologue "Philosophy is given a
position of highest esteem; indeed, it is the category under which
revelation itself is treated. Discussing revelation in terms of philosophy
would give a Gentile audience a way to relate revelation to their own

---

[19] This was suggested by R. Hirzel, *Der Dialog: ein literarhistorischer Versuch* (Leipzig,
1895) II.368ff. See Stylianopoulos, *Justin Martyr and the Mosaic Law,* 171.

[20] *Dial.* 80.3. ὅτι δ᾽ οὐκ ἐφ᾽ ὑμῶν μόνων τοῦτο λέγειν με ἐπίστασθε, τῶν γεγενημένων
ἡμῖν λόγων ἁπάντων, ὡς δύναμίς μου, σύνταξιν ποιήσομαι, ἐν οἷς καὶ τοῦτο ὁμολογοῦντά
με, ὃ καὶ πρὸς ὑμᾶς ὁμολογῶ, ἐγγράψω.

[21] Stylianopoulos, *Justin Martyr and the Mosaic Law,* 172–173.

[22] See below, Chapter 3.IV.A.2.

[23] Nilson, "To Whom is Justin's *Dialogue with Trypho* Addressed?" 540.

cultural background and appeal to those who had been disillusioned by its inability to fulfill its promise."[24] The argument continues that for a Jew philosophy is not a category for discussing revelation.

Goodenough takes issue with the discontinuity between the prologue, which discusses philosophical questions, and the main body, which discusses issues arising out of the Jewish-Christian debate.[25] He concludes that the *Dialogue* must therefore be recognized as addressed to a man interested in philosophy and not as a record of controversy. Thus, the *Dialogue* is a vindication of revelation over philosophy. The main body of the *Dialogue* shows the unity of this revelation, which disagreements between Christians and Jews may set into question. This concept of the purpose of the *Dialogue*, thus prefers a pagan reader.[26]

Nilson's position above that philosophy is not a category for a Jew to discuss revelation is somewhat misleading. The question which must be asked of Nilson's assertion is this; Does Justin present philosophy as the category to discuss revelation? The answer must be no. Justin defines philosophy as knowledge of all that exists.[27] In Justin's concept of God, existence was dependent upon God as the First Cause, the Unmoved Mover, or as the Unbegotten and Incorruptible.[28] Thus, everything which exists does so because of him and according to his will, and is dependent upon his sovereignty. In defining philosophy, therefore, as knowledge of that which exists Justin was postulating a definition which had knowledge of God at the very center. He was actually defining philosophy as knowledge of God.

In defining philosophy as knowledge of God (or a search for the knowledge of God) Justin also indicates that revelation is where this knowledge is attained. The whole point of the inclusion of the discussion with the old man in the *Dialogue* is to show Trypho where one may attain knowledge of God. This knowledge cannot be attained through philosophy because philosophers have not fulfilled the requirements of seeing and hearing. The sources of this knowledge are the Prophets and the Memoirs of the Apostles.

According to Justin this is how knowledge of God is attained. This is the revelation. In this light, Nilson's assertion that revelation is

---

[24] Nilson, "To Whom is Justin's *Dialogue with Trypho* Addressed?" 540.
[25] Goodenough, *The Theology of Justin Martyr*, 96–100.
[26] Goodenough, *The Theology of Justin Martyr*, 100.
[27] *Dial.* 3.4. For a discussion of Justin's understanding of philosophy see Chapter 3.IV.
[28] See below, Chapter 2.III

discussed within philosophical categories must be radically revised
and placed within its contextual understanding. Nilson misunder-
stands the fact that Justin desires to show that contemporary philosophy is inadequate for discussing revelation, and posits a corrective
definition of philosophy in its place. In so doing revelation is discussed in terms of witness, not philosophical categories. Thus Nilson's
argument is inconsistent with the context of the prologue.

Goodenough recognizes the fact that Justin places revelation over
contemporary philosophy, yet he still posits a pagan audience. He
does so by maintaining that the prologue shows that the whole is
to be seen not as a record of controversy but as addressed to a man
interested in philosophy, thus it must be addressed to a pagan. The
obvious question here is; Why can't a Jew be interested in philosophy? Of Trypho we know that he had philosophic training, for upon
his meeting with Justin he started the conversation because he was
taught in Argos by Corinthius the Socratic to converse with anyone
wearing a philosopher's cloak.[29] From the first chapter of the *Dialogue*
it is easy to deduce that Trypho was most likely a Hellenistic Jew.[30]
And this would certainly not rule out the possibility that Trypho could
be interested in philosophy. Further, as Stylianopoulos queries, "must
the *Dialogue*'s philosophical aspects exclude this document from being
a record of a controversy, or a text book for controversy, against
Judaism?"[31] There is no reason to discount the understanding that the
Dialogue may well arise out of the Jewish-Christian debate and still
contain philosophical interests sustained by the larger cultural climate.

C. *The Use of the Hebrew Scriptures*

Another argument used to cast doubt upon an intended audience
that is Jewish is the manner in which Justin employs OT scripture.
This assertion generally has two parts. First, it is argued that because
the quotations of OT scripture are so long and numerous and never
alluded to as common knowledge of the participants, this rules out

---

[29] *Dial.* 1.2.

[30] Goodenough himself recognizes that Trypho was indeed a Jew interested in
philosophy. See E. R. Goodenough, *Jewish Symbols in the Graeco-Roman Period Vol. 1:
The Archeological Evidence From Palestine* (New York: Pantheon, 1953) 42–53. The relationship between hellenistic Judaism and philosophy is also discussed in J. Daniélou,
Gospel Message and Hellenistic Culture (A History of Early Christian Doctrine Before
the Council of Nicaea, Vol. 2; ET J. A. Baker; London: Darton, Longman &
Todd/Philadelphia: Westminster, 1973) 323–333.

[31] Stylianopoulos, *Justin Martyr and the Mosaic Law*, 188.

Jewish addressees. Certainly Justin could approach the OT with a common knowledge as to its contents if the audience was Jewish. But this characteristic is only understandable if the audience had little or no familiarity with the texts.[32]

The second part of this argument centers on Justin's exclusive use of the Septuagint in his quotations. Justin's use of the Septuagint was during a time of increasing Jewish resentment over the Christian appropriation of their sacred texts. If Justin was addressing his *Dialogue* to Jews it is thus argued that he would be ill-advised to use the Septuagint because of Jewish discontent. But if Justin was addressing his *Dialogue* to a Gentile audience his use of the Septuagint would not be surprising.

These arguments, however, fail to convince. The length of the citations of scriptural passages is not necessarily indicative of a pagan audience. As Stylianopoulos points out, a comparison between the OT citations in the *Apology* and in the *Dialogue* shows that the citations in the *Apology*, a work unquestionably addressed to pagans, are actually much less extensive.[33] In fact, the *Dialogue* appears to presuppose a familiarity with and even intimate knowledge with Judaism which cannot be presupposed of a wider Graeco-Roman audience.[34] Both knowledge of the OT and the Mosaic Law are presupposed in the *Dialogue*, as is knowledge of the Gospels. Each of these topics is introduced into the discussion with no explanation.[35] Further, some passages in the *Dialogue* even presuppose knowledge of OT contexts.[36]

The extensive use of scripture by Justin certainly does not argue against the address of the *Dialogue* to a pagan audience.[37] But, by

---

[32] Nilson, "To Whom is Justin's *Dialogue with Trypho* Addressed?" 541. See also Cosgrove, "Justin Martyr and the Emerging Christian Canon," 215–216.

[33] Stylianopoulos, *Justin Martyr and the Mosaic Law*, 193.

[34] Stylianopoulos, *Justin Martyr and the Mosaic Law*, 192.

[35] See *Dial.* 8.4; 9.1; 10.2; cf. 1.3.

[36] See e.g., *Dial.* 10.3–4 where Gen 17:14 is quoted. The references to the purchased slaves and to circumcision as a "covenant" presuppose the wider context of Gen 17.

[37] A. Harnack ("Die Altercatio Simonis Judaei et Theophili Christiani nebst Untersuchungen über die antijüdische Polemik in der alten Kirche," TU 1 [1883]) argued that any *adversus Judaeos* literature in the second century can not be used as evidence of any real Jewish-Christian polemic. In fact, Harnack argues that there was no real relations between Jews and Christians at this time. Because of this he sees *adversus Judaeos* literature as necessarily directed toward a pagan audience. See M. Simon, *Verus Israel. A Study in the Relations Between Christians and Jews in the Roman Empire (135– 425)* (ET H. McKeating; The Littman Library of Jewish Civilization; Oxford: Oxford University Press, 1986) 136–141.

the same token, the primary stated purpose of the *Dialogue* was to commend the Christian faith to a group of Jews, and this was done by an appeal to a mutual respect for the OT scriptures. This appeal gave the arguments force because they proceeded from a common ground. On the other hand, however, arguments from scripture tended to lose some of their force when Christian addressed them to pagans.[38] Because the acceptance of scripture is assumed by both Jew and Christian in the *Dialogue*, the main issue is proper interpretation of said scripture. Thus, the extensive use of OT scripture tends to argue against a pagan audience.

The issue of Justin's use of the Septuagint must be considered on internal grounds. Nilson does recognize[39] that official Jewish rejection of the Septuagint was not until long after the *Dialogue* was written.[40] And I agree that Justin does reflect the Jewish discontent with the Septuagint during the middle of the second century.[41] But the way in which Justin deals with these issues surrounding the Septuagint show that they are not of great consequence to him.

The *Dialogue* reveals only one OT passage which Trypho objects to Justin quoting from the Septuagint, Isa 7:10–17.[42] All other differences in translation between the Hebrew and Greek text are pointed out by Justin himself.[43] The Isaiah passage hinges on the insertion of "virgin" in the Septuagint in place of the Hebrew "young woman." While it is true that Justin argues for the accuracy of the Septuagint translation,[44] he also indicates that his point is proven even without it. This is done in two ways. First, Justin is aware that he will get nowhere in trying to admit passages into the discussion which Trypho will not admit as genuine. This being the case, he states that he will only use scriptures which the Jews admit as genuine.[45] In other words, he will only use scriptures with which Trypho will have no objection. Even after Trypho asks Justin to list the pas-

[38] Simon, *Verus Israel*, 139.
[39] Nilson, "To Whom is Justin's *Dialogue with Trypho* Addressed?" 542.
[40] Simon, *Verus Israel*, 299. "From the third century onwards the Jews as a community seem to have abandoned it and substituted for it new translations, in particular, that of Aquila."
[41] See *Dial.* 43; 68; 71.
[42] *Dial.* 43; 66; 67; 68; 71; 84.
[43] Gen 49:10 (*Dial.* 120); Ps 81:1–8 (*Dial.* 124); Deut 32:7–9 (*Dial.* 131). In *Dial.* 72–73, at Trypho's request, Justin also lists passages which he claims the elders omitted from their translation. Trypho is presented as being ignorant of these.
[44] *Dial.* 43; 66; 67; 68; 71.
[45] *Dial.* 71.

sages which Justin claims were deleted by the Jews,[46] Justin claims that these will not be admitted because they make no difference to what has already been proven in the *Dialogue* by scriptures accepted by Trypho.[47]

The second way in which Justin argues that his point about Christ is proven is through the occurrence of an event. *Dial.* 84 is illustrative of this. There the discussion is on the difference in translation of Isa 7:14. Justin makes the point that the irrefutable proof of what he is asserting is that it actually took place. This, in effect, places the stress of the issue on the proof from prophecy. It is after the event occurs that it is properly understood. And this is no less true for the virgin birth of Christ.

So, the argument that Justin's use of the Septuagint militates against a Jewish audience is weakened. In the grand scheme of things Justin is perfectly willing to prove his points, and he believes that he has, with appeals to passages which the Jews accept as genuine. He is perfectly aware of the Jewish disdain for certain translations. But the fact that he believes he can prove his argument without appeal to these passages shows that the Septuagint is not problematic in his argument. Further, his emphasis on the event proving the proper interpretation is key in understanding that the differences in translation fade into the background of the larger picture.

D. *Appeals to Gentiles*

Also used to argue against a Jewish audience is the hypothesis that certain passages of the *Dialogue* seem to ring out as appeals to Gentiles, not Jews. T. Zahn was the first to suggest that *Dial.* 23.3; 24.3; and 32.5 are addressed to Gentile readers.[48] Later Harnack suggested the same for *Dial.* 29.1; 64.2; 80.3; and 119.4.[49] Both Cosgrove and Stylianopoulos have shown the inadequacy of the hypothesis held by these scholars.[50] Each requires examination.

---

[46] *Dial.* 71–73.
[47] *Dial.* 73.6.
[48] T. Zahn, "Studien zu Justin III," *ZKG* 8 (1885–1886) 56–61.
[49] Harnack, "Judentum und Judenchristentum in Justins Dialog mit Tryphon," 51–52, footnote #2.
[50] Cosgrove, "Justin Martyr and the Emerging Christian Canon," 212–215; Stylianopoulos, *Justin Martyr and the Mosaic Law*, 173–187. The above summary and criticism depends on these sources.

1. Dialogue *23.3*

> And when no one was answering [I continued], "Wherefore, O Trypho,
> I proclaim to you, and to the ones who may want to become prose-
> lytes, the divine message which I heard from that [old] man. Do you
> not see that the elements are idle and keep no sabbaths? Stay as you
> were at birth! For if there was no need of circumcision before
> Abraham . . . [they are] not [needed] now . . ."[51]

The key to this passage being understood as an address to pagans
is the use of the term προσήλυτοις ("proselytes"). Zahn views this term
in a purely technical sense designating only Gentile converts to
Judaism, and not Jewish or Gentile converts to Christianity. So, Zahn
identifies the προσήλυτοις here as Gentile converts to Judaism, who
are not yet full proselytes but only "fearers of God".[52] These proselytes, according to Zahn, have not yet been circumcised because
Justin supposedly alludes to this when he states, "Stay as you were
at birth", that is, uncircumcised.[53]

Zahn's argument is unconvincing for three reasons. First, Justin does
not use the term προσήλυτοι or the phrase φοβούμενοι τὸν θεόν in the
technical sense which Zahn intimates.[54] Second, the same is true of
the phrase φοβούμενοι τὸν θεόν, which is used in a general, rather
than a technical, sense.[55] Third, the distinction that Zahn wishes to
maintain between Justin's address to Trypho and his address to
Trypho's friends is difficult to maintain. Throughout the *Dialogue* the
distinction is rather between Trypho and his teachers,[56] not between
Trypho and his companions. Thus, the appeal to "Stay as you were
at birth" (uncircumcised) includes Trypho and his companions.[57]

---

[51] Καὶ μηδὲν μηδενὸς ἀποκρινομένου· Διὰ ταῦτά σοι, ὦ Τρύφων, καὶ τοῖς βουλομένοις
προσηλύτοις γενέσθαι κηρύξω ἐγὼ θεῖον λόγον, ὃν παρ' ἐκείνου ἤκουσα τοῦ ἀνδρός.
ὁρᾶτε ὅτι τὰ στοιχεῖα οὐκ ἀργεῖ οὐδὲ σαββατίζει. μείνατε ὡς γεγένησθε. εἰ γὰρ πρὸ τοῦ
Ἀβραὰμ οὐκ ἦν χρεία περιτομῆς . . . οὐδὲ νῦν . . .

[52] *Dial.* 10.4. φοβούμενοι τὸν θεόν.

[53] *Dial.* 23.3. μείνατε ὡς γεγένησθε.

[54] This is seen in *Dial.* 28.2 and 122.5 where προσήλυτος and προσήλυσις are
clearly used for converts to the Christian faith.

[55] The general usage of the phrase is indicated in *Dial.* 24.3; 98.5; and especially
106.1–2.

[56] *Dial.* 9.1; 36.2; 38.1–2; 62.2; 68.7; 71.1; 110.1; 112.4–5; 117.4; 120.5; 134.1;
137.2; 140.2; 142.2.

[57] Stylianopoulos (*Justin Martyr and the Mosaic Law*, 176) notes that *Dial.* 28.1–2
totally shatters Zahn's view because it contains all these above elements together.
"Justin here not only uses the noun προσήλυσις in connection with his inviting
Trypho and his companions to become *Christian* proselytes, but also groups Trypho
and his companions together without distinction, as the plural in both Trypho's

2. Dialogue *24.3 and 29.1*

These are parallel passages and may be examined together.

> Come with me, then, all the ones fearing God, the ones wanting to see the good of Jerusalem. Come, let us proceed to the light of the Lord. For he has liberated his people, the house of Jacob. Let us gather together in Jerusalem.[58]

> Let us glorify God together with all the nations, for he is concerned about us. Let us glorify him through the King of glory, through the Lord of power. For he was gracious towards the nations, and he receives our sacrifices more gratefully than yours.[59]

Here we have to do unambiguously with gentiles (τὰ ἔθνη). The hortatory subjunctive is used in both these passages as indicating the direct audience of the passage—Gentiles. The question is, however, whether these references signify pagan Gentiles, and not rather Christian Gentiles.

Basing their argument on an article by D. Gill,[60] Cosgrove and Stylianopoulos point out that although the hortatory δοξάσωμεν of 29.1 appears to include Trypho and his companions, the passage closes with a contrasting our/your motif which makes this unlikely. Further, the probability that these are Christian Gentiles here is further demonstrated by the wider use of the term ἔθνη in the *Dialogue*.[61] If this is the case, then the call of *Dial.* 29.1 is not to conversion, but to worship.[62]

---

and Justin's lips indicates. Most telling of all is the implicit contrast which Justin draws on the one hand between himself, an uncircumcised gentile (ἀπερίτμητος) and, on the other hand, those whom he is here addressing, Trypho and his companions who are circumcised Jews."

[58] *Dial.* 24.3. δεῦτε σὺν ἐμοὶ πάντες οἱ φοβούμενοι τὸν θεόν, οἱ θέλοντες τὰ ἀγαθὰ Ἰερουσαλὴμ ἰδεῖν. δεῦτε, πορευθῶμεν τῷ φωτὶ κυρίου· ἀνῆκε γὰρ τὸν λαὸν αὐτοῦ, τὸν οἶκον Ἰακώβ. δεῦτε πάντα τὰ ἔθνη, συναχθῶμεν εἰς Ἰερουσαλὴμ ...

[59] *Dial.* 29.1. Δοξάσωμεν τὸν θεόν, ἅμα τὰ ἔθνη συνελθόντα, ὅτι καὶ ἡμᾶς ἐπεσκέψατο· δοξάσωμεν αὐτὸν διὰ τοῦ βασιλέως τῆς δόξης, διὰ τοῦ κυρίου τῶν δυνάμεων. εὐδόκησε γὰρ καὶ εἰς τὰ ἔθνη, καὶ τὰς θυσίας ἥδιον παρ' ἡμῶν λαμβάνει.

[60] D. Gill, "A Liturgical Fragment in Justin, Dialogue 29.1," *HTR* 59 (1966) 98–100.

[61] Justin uses the term ἔθνη in the *Dialogue* primarily as a designation for Christians. The term is Septuagintal language derived from prophetic texts which Justin quotes as predictions of the true Israel, the church, now fulfilled (*Dial.* 11.3–5; 24.4; 26.2–4; 28.5; 30.2–3; 118–141). Justin can use the same term to designate unbelieving pagans in general (*Dial.* 10.3; 17.1; 21.1) but in each case the fact that they are unbelievers is made clear. See Stylianopoulos, *Justin Martyr and the Mosaic Law*, 179–180.

[62] The idea that this is a call to worship is furthered by Gill ("A Liturgical Fragment in Justin, Dialogue 29.1") who believes 29.1 to be a liturgical fragment inserted into the *Dialogue* at this point by Justin. Stylianopoulos (*Justin Martyr and the Mosaic Law*, 177–178), based on Gill's assertion, sees no reason why the same cannot be said for 24.3.

Dial. 24.3 also contains the hortatory subjunctive, in this case δεῦτε. Stylianopoulos explains that this passage presupposes the contrast between the true and false Israel which is prevalent throughout the *Dialogue*.[63] 24.1 shows this contrast in its references to those who believe in the "blood of circumcision"[64] and those who have believed in "the blood of salvation."[65] The "righteous nation" and the "faith-keeping people"[66] of 24.2 are the Gentiles who, unlike Israel, have already responded to God's call. The theme of true and false Israel is actually the subject of the larger context of both of these passage.[67] This corroborates the probability that references to ἔθνη in 24.3 and 29.1 are to Christian Gentiles, not pagans.

3. Dialogue *32.5*

> But all this I said to you in digression, in order that you may now be convinced of that which has been prescribed against you by God, that you are foolish sons . . . Stop leading yourselves astray, and those hearing you, and learning from us, the ones having been made wise (enlightened) by the grace of Christ.[68]

The important reference here is Justin's appeal for Trypho and his companions to stop leading themselves astray, as well as the ones hearing them. So, the question is, who are the ones hearing the Jews and consequently being lead astray by them. Zahn's conclusion that they are, like Trypho's friends, students of Jewish teachers has been adequately dismissed above.[69] But this does not dismiss the possibility that they are pagans. This possibility is in fact confirmed upon a closer examination of the passage. There appears to be three distinct groups here. Justin includes himself in "the ones having been enlightened by the grace of Christ," which must be a reference to Christians. The Jews are set off from the Christians as "yourselves"

---

[63] Stylianopoulos, *Justin Martyr and the Mosaic Law*, 178–179. True Israel is treated in concentration in *Dial.* 119–125 and 130–141. The theme is also present throughout the *Dialogue* breaking in at many points of the discussion (*Dial.* 11.4–5; 32.5; 39.1–5; 43.2).

[64] τὸ αἷμα τῆς περιτομῆς.

[65] αἷματι σωτηρίῳ.

[66] ἔθνος δίκαιον and λαὸς φυλάσσων πίστιν.

[67] *Dial.* 24–26 and 28–30.

[68] *Dial.* 32.5. καὶ ταῦτα δὲ πάντα ἃ ἔλεγον ἐν παρεκβάσεσι λέγω πρὸς ὑμᾶς, ἵνα ἤδη ποτὲ πεισθέντες τῷ εἰρημένῳ καθ' ὑμῶν ὑπὸ τοῦ θεοῦ, ὅτι Υἱοὶ ἀσύνετοί ἐστε . . . παύσησθε καὶ ἑαυτοὺς καὶ τοὺς ὑμῶν ἀκούοντας πλανῶντες, καὶ παρ' ὑμῶν μανθάνοντες τῶν σοφισθέντων ἀπὸ τῆς τοῦ Χριστοῦ χάριτος.

[69] See above, I.D.1.

(καὶ ἑαυτοὺς), while the other group is set off from these as the ones being lead astray by the Jews (καὶ τοὺς ὑμῶν ἀκούοντας πλανῶντες). The only option, therefore, is that they are, in fact, pagans.

Given the fact that pagans are in view here, does this argue for a pagan destination? The probability for this is low. This is most likely a remark made in passing by Justin. The isolated remark is quite lost in the entire *Dialogue*, and arguing that this rather insignificant remark is indicative of the audience as a whole violates Justin's straightforwardness and boldness in the work.[70] In other words, a writer with Justin's passion and candor is not likely to leave matters of important concern merely in the background. Thus, *Dial.* 32.5 simply contains an indirect and allusive reference to pagans who are receptive to Judaism but cannot be considered the addressees of the *Dialogue*.

4. Dialogue *64.2*

> and in fact, I do the same to all men of every nation, who wish to examine along with me, or make inquiry at me, regarding this subject.[71]

Harnack's claim that this passage implies a pagan readership is easily overcome. It is quite obvious that Justin is simply indicating that, despite Trypho's belligerence, he will continue his explanation—just as he would for any other person. He is not *addressing* Gentiles here, he is simply indicating his willingness to engage any person in conversation about the Christian faith, the passage does not disclose the addressees of the *Dialogue*.

5. Dialogue *119.4*

> Wherefore, we are not a contemptible people, nor a tribe of barbarians, nor just any nation as the Carians or the Phrygians, but the chosen people of God who appeared to those who did not seek him. "Behold," He said, "I am God to a nation that has not called upon my name." For, this is really the nation promised to Abraham by God, when he told him that he would make him a father of many nations.[72]

---

[70] See Stylianopoulos, *Justin Martyr and the Mosaic Law*, 183, footnote #45.

[71] *Dial.* 64.2. καὶ τὸ αὐτὸ καὶ πρὸς πάντας ἁπλῶς τοὺς ἐκ παντὸς γένους ἀνθρώπων, συζητεῖν ἢ πυνθάνεσθαί μου περὶ τούτων βουλομένους πράττω.

[72] *Dial.* 119.4. οὐκοῦν οὐκ εὐκαταφρόντος δῆμός ἐσμεν οὐδὲ βάρβαρον φῦλον οὐδὲ ὁποῖα Καρῶν ἢ Φρυγῶν ἔθνη, ἀλλὰ καὶ ἡμᾶς ἐξελέξατο ὁ θεὸς καὶ ἐμφανὴς ἐγενήθη τοῖς μὴ ἐπερωτῶσιν αὐτόν. Ἰδοὺ θεός εἰμι, φησί, τῷ ἔθνει, οἳ οὐκ ἐπεκαλέσαντο τὸ ὄνομά μου. τοῦτο γάρ ἐστιν ἐκεῖνο τὸ ἔθνος, ὃ πάλαι τῷ Ἀβραὰμ ὁ θεὸς ὑπέσχετο, καὶ πατέρα πολλῶν ἐθνῶν θήσειν ἐπηγγείλατο.

Harnack's contention that Justin has pagans in view here is contradicted
by two things. First, it is clear that Justin identifies himself with the
group here in view. Thus leading us to believe that he has Christians
in mind. Second, this is confirmed by the preceeding context of the
passage. Justin, in *Dial.* 119.3 has already identified ἡμεῖς as those
who are already God's people ("But we are not only a people, but
a holy people"). Therefore, the references in 119.4 to personal pro-
nouns in the first person plural are further explanation of the initial ἡμεῖς of 119.3.

From the foregoing it must be concluded that arguments for pagan
addressees of the *Dialogue with Trypho* based on the above passages
are unconvincing.

E. *The Literary Form of the Dialogue*

This point argues that the literary form of the *Dialogue*, which is neither Jewish nor Christian, but pagan and Greek, implies that this
document has been written for cultured pagan readers. But several
things argue strongly against such a conclusion. This point is fundamentally flawed in that it identifies the question of cultural setting
with that of the addressees.[73] The mistake here is that a literary feature indicating cultural milieu of the *Dialogue* also indicates the actual
addressees of the *Dialogue*. But, as Styianopoulos explains, ". . . just
as a Christian or a Jew living in the Graeco-Roman world, as well
as a pagan, can be expected to share the philosophical concerns of
the age, so also a Christian or a Jew, as well as a pagan, can equally
be expected to find the literary form of the dialogue attractive."[74]
We must not forget that Justin himself wrote the *Dialogue* as a
Christian. Further, the Jews had already adopted Greek literary forms
prior to Justin's *Dialogue*, and Christians employed such forms as is
evidenced in the Greek epistolary style of NT letters.[75]

The above five arguments may be considered the classical arguments for a pagan readership of the *Dialogue with Trypho*. But these
arguments appear to be decisively controverted by the evidence presented above. In addition to the above five points J. Nilson has pro-

---

[73] Stylianopoulos, *Justin Martyr and the Mosaic Law*, 191.
[74] Stylianopoulos, *Justin Martyr and the Mosaic Law*, 191.
[75] Cosgrove, "Justin Martyr and the Emerging New Testament Canon," 212.
Cosgrove uses, as a reference for the Christian use of the Greek epistolary style,
H. D. Betz, "The Literary Composition and Function of Paul's Letter to the
Galatians," *NTS* 21 (1975) 353–379.

vided three others that demand consideration if we are to properly dismiss the pagan readership hypothesis.[76]

F. *Other Arguments for a Pagan Readership*

1. *Misconceptions About Christianity*

Nilson notes five times in the *Dialogue* where Justin complains about the Jews spreading misconceptions about Christianity.[77] Justin accuses the Jews of disseminating their slanders "into all the earth",[78] and not only among the Jews. In other words, the Gentiles are hearing these misconceptions and are being deceived by them. Nilson believes that this points to a widespread proselytization effort of the part of the Jews. He suggests that it would be very unlikely that Christians would allow this type of thing to continue without some sort of challenge. Thus, he posits the *Dialogue* as Justin's attempt, in the form of a dialogue with a Jew, to correct these Gentile misunderstandings.

While it may be true that Christians in general desired to correct these Gentile misconceptions about Christianity, it does not necessarily follow that the *Dialogue* is an attempt to do so. It is perfectly understandable that Justin makes these accusations against the Jews in a document that is addressed to Jews. In fact, this would be a more likely explanation. Here Justin is simply voicing his objections that the Jews are spreading these misconceptions about Christianity. He is confronting the Jews on a point of order.

2. *The Theme of Forgiveness*

Nilson also believes that the theme of forgiveness in the *Dialgue* is something that should not be taken lightly when considering its audience. The admission of one of Trypho's companions in *Dial.* 94 concerning the correct interpretation of the brazen serpent is key here. The significance of this admission is relative to the meaning of the serpent as it is given by Justin. The serpent was a foreshadowing of forgiveness of sins through Jesus who died on the cross. Nilson appeals to J. Parkes[79] who claims that it was exactly this lack of a doctrine of forgiveness of sins that put Judaism at a disadvantage vis-à-vis

---

[76] Nilson, "To Whom is Justin's *Dialogue with Trypho* Addressed?" 542–546.
[77] *Dial.* 17; 32; 93; 108; 117.
[78] *Dial.* 17.1. εἰς πᾶσαν τὴν γὴν.
[79] J. Parkes, *The Conflict of the Church and the Synagogue* (New York: 1964) 115–116.

Christianity in appealing to Gentile converts. Therefore, in the context of a proselytization effort by both Christianity and Judaism, Justin was showing to pagans that even the Jews admit their lack of a doctrine of forgiveness.

The problem here is that Christians would employ the same argument in appeals to Jews. The foundational theme in presenting Christianity's supremacy over Judaism is the fact that the old covenant has been surpassed by the new covenant because the old covenant could not supply forgiveness of sins. To assume that pagans were in view because of this theme and not Jews relegates the universality of the new covenant. Certainly this argument alone does not necessarily rule out pagan addressees,[80] but neither does it argue against a Jewish audience. In fact, one would be more inclined to see this as more indicative of a Jewish audience in view of the fact that the Jews were conscious of their sinful standing before God and their need for forgiveness.

3. *The Historical Context of the Dialogue*

Nilson also claims that while the *Dialogue* is showing the superiority of Christianity over Judaism, it also formulating a response to a common pagan objection to Christianity, that is, that it was a religion without roots in antiquity that would commend it to Gentiles. Justin is thus doing in the *Dialogue* what he had done already in the *First Apology*. He is showing the antiquity of Christianity by appropriating for it the antiquity of Judaism.

The problems with this line of argument are similar to the problems with the theme of forgiveness argument—it does not necessarily argue for a pagan readership. It would make perfect sense, in a dialogue with a Jew, for Justin to argue the connection of Christianity with Judaism. Throughout the *Dialogue* Justin maintains his respect and historical connection with Judaism through his dependence on the Prophets. He desires to maintain this link with Judaism as the common ground upon which he may pursue the discussion. If Justin was aiming this line of argument at the pagans then why would he make a point, at the outset of his discussion with Trypho, of maintaining that the Jews and Christians worship the same God?[81] The whole point here is that this is the foundation upon which Justin's

---

[80] The combined force of the arguments presented above and below, however, do.
[81] *Dial.* 11.

argument for the superiority of Christianity over Judaism progresses. Therefore, the Jews are not expected to forsake the God of their fathers, but only to recognize the difference between the old and new covenants.

4. *Tertullian's* Adversus Judaeos

A final argument presented by Nilson is based on what he calls the scholarly concensus that the *Dialogue with Trypho* was a source for Tertullian's *Adversus Judaeos*.[82] Tertullian's work is a reconstruction of a dispute between a Christian and a Jewish proselyte, whom Tertullian describes as "a man from the Gentiles and not from the race of the Jews of Israel."[83] The intended audience of Tertullian's treatise was not the Jewish community at Carthage but sympathetic pagans who might be confronted and confused by missionaries from both religions. Nilson thus reasons, in light of Tertullian's audience, a document which had been composed earlier for a similar audience for a similar purpose would naturally commend itself to him as a source.

Cosgrove points out the problem here of the disputability of Nilson's first two "ifs".[84] But even if these two "ifs" may be granted, it only allows for the possibility that this may have been addressed to pagans, not a probability. Could Tertullian not have made use of any sources which he found helpful, regardless of their original purposes? Just because one document uses another as a source, does not mean that they both had the same target audience in mind.

Based on the examination and criticisms above of the arguments for a pagan address of the *Dialogue* the hypothesis must be rejected. This leaves us to the task of offering a better hypothesis. The two obvious choices, therefore, are a Christian audience,[85] or a Jewish audience.[86]

---

[82] As scholarly consensus Nilson offers only J. Quasten, *Patrology* (3 Vols.; Utrecht, 1953) 2.269. He does mention that T. D. Barnes (*Tertullian: A Historical and Literary Study* [Oxford: Oxford University Press, 1971] 175–176) disputes Tertullian's dependence on Justin's *Dialogue* as a source for his *Adversus Judaeos*.

[83] Tertullian, *Adversus Judaeos* 1.2. *homo ex gentibus nec de prosapia Israelitum Iudaeus.*

[84] The first "if" is if Tertullian did rely on Justin's work. The second "if" is if Justin's *Dialogue* is aimed at pagans who are confused between missionaries from both religions. See Cosgrove, "Justin Martyr and the Emerging Christian Canon," 215.

[85] Cosgrove, "Justin Martyr and the Emerging Christian Canon".

[86] Stylianopoulos, *Justin Martyr and the Mosaic Law*. It should be noted that Cosgrove correctly points out that Stylianopoulos's position is that the *Dialogue* is addressed to Christians and Jews. But this is maintained by Stylianopoulos because he believes that any document written within the Christian community, no matter who the addressees were, would naturally commend itself to other Christians (p. 32).

II. *Christian Destination*

Cosgrove also concludes that a pagan destination for the *Dialogue* is uncompelling. In its place he offers 3 main reasons why he would offer an exclusively Christian destination.[87] Because these arguments are best understood and criticized as a whole I will delineate all three and then offer criticisms.

A. *The Address to Gentiles in* Dialogue *24.3 and 29.1*

It was understood above[88] that these two passages are undoubtedly references to Gentiles. Cosgrove believes that because these verses suggest the necessity of positing at least a partly Christian audience, the Jewish hypothesis is obviated by the fact that the *Dialogue*'s preoccupation with issues of the Jewish/Christian debate is adequately explained by an exclusive Christian audience.[89]

B. *The Liturgical Styling of* Dialogue *24.3 and 29.1*

Again, using the same passages as above, Cosgrove argues that because *Dialogue* 24.3 and 29.1 are liturgical fragments inserted by Justin[90] that this would make it very awkward for Jewish readers.[91]

C. *Justin's Portrayal of Jews*

Here Cosgrove argues that Justin portrays Trypho and Jews in general in such a derogatory way that it is difficult to conceive of his *Dialogue* as an evangelistic appeal to Jews. At points Trypho and his companions are cast in an extremely unfavorable light.[92]

D. *Criticism's of Cosgrove's Position*

There is no difficulty with positing an address to Christians in *Dialogue* 24.3 and 29.1. However, Cosgrove makes quite a leap from these two references to Christians to his claim that they virtually rule out

---

[87] Cosgrove, "Justin Martyr and the Emerging Christian Canon," 217–218.
[88] See above, I.D.2–5.
[89] Cosgrove, "Justin Martyr and the Emerging Christian Canon," 217.
[90] See Gill, "A Liturgical Fragment in Justin Martyr," 98–100; Stylianopoulos, *Justin Martyr and the Mosaic Law*, 184.
[91] Cosgrove, "Justin Martyr and the Emerging Christian Canon," 217.
[92] *Dial.* 14.2; 134.2; 30.2.

a Jewish audience. The inconsistency in this argument is immediately seen when one examines the references to a Jewish audience.[93] Cosgrove bases his argument here on a number of points that makes an exclusively Christian audience the "least problematic."[94] But Stylianopoulos has, in a similar vein, argued that a combined Jewish/Christian audience can also be described as "least problematic."[95] Stylianopoulos delineates items of specifically Jewish concern in the *Dialogue*. In this light, Cosgrove's contention that the Jewish hypothesis is obviated by its preoccupation with issues of the Jewish/Christian debate being adequately explained by an exclusive Christian audience is called into question.

Cosgrove's contention that the insertion of the liturgical fragments at *Dial.* 24.3 and 29.1 would make it awkward for Jewish readers is not a very strong evidence for an exclusively Christian audience. The simple insertion here of a liturgical fragment does not necessarily rule out a Jewish audience for the entire work. In fact, the insertion of these calls to Christian worship do fit in with the actual context of an appeal to Jews.

Dial. 24 follows directly after a lengthy presentation by Justin concerning the inadequacy of the Mosaic Law.[96] Therein Justin speaks of the true meaning of the precepts that the Jews were to follow. Thus, the rite of circumcision was necessary only for the Jews, to mark them off.[97] But since circumcision was not necessary for salvation, the Jews are in need of the true Christian circumcision.[98] In the same manner, sacrifices to God were instituted so that this weak people (the Jews) would not fall into idolatry, and the sabbaths so that they would remember God.[99]

A similar line of argument is followed by Justin in *Dial.* 20–23 with regard to dietary laws, the Sabbath, sacrifices and oblations. Justin's reason for the lengthy discussion on these Jewish rites is summed up in *Dial.* 23 where he states, "Therefore, we must conclude that God, who is immutable, ordered these and similar things to be done only

---

[93] See e.g., *Dial.* 9.1; 11.1; 16.4; 17.1; 19.2; 21; 22; etc.
[94] Cosgrove, "Justin Martyr and the Emerging Christian Canon," 218–219.
[95] Stylianopoulos, *Justin Martyr and the Mosaic Law*, 32–44. Stylianopoulos's arguments will be presented below.
[96] *Dial.* 11–23.
[97] *Dial.* 19.2.
[98] *Dial.* 19.3.
[99] *Dial.* 19.6.

because of sinful men . . .".[100] This emphasizes Justin's point that they have no salvific value but are only instituted temporarily.[101]

Dial. 24 follows directly after this lengthy argument, and is indeed dependent on it. As confirmation of this, Justin clearly states what he means, "this blood of circumcision has been rendered useless, and we have now come to trust in the blood of salvation, [there is] now another covenant, and another law has come out of Zion."[102] Here circumcision is presented as representing the entire discussion on the Jewish rites which preceded. The thrust is upon the old covenant being made obsolete by a new covenant. Thus, the circumcision of Christ is to preferred over the circumcision of Moses, and those who receive this circumcision will become a righteous nation.[103] Here is where the liturgical fragment is inserted. It is most certainly a call for those who have received the circumcision of Christ to worship. And in the context it fits perfectly with Justin's line of argument.

Rather than appearing here as an awkward insertion, I would argue that Justin is simply showing here that true worship of God is only possible by those who have made the realization that the old Law is abolished. The call to worship is made to those who can truly worship God. In light of the preceeding context Justin is assuming that they would understand this. There is no awkwardness here for a Jewish readership. Justin cannot call Jews to true worship. So, in calling Christians to true worship he is building on the previous discussion that only they, and not the Jews, can worship. It is an appeal that must be understood in its context. The call to worship in *Dial.* 29.1 is made on the same grounds.

Cosgrove also argues for an exclusively Christian audience on the basis of his belief that the Jews are presented in an extremely unfavorable light. But this argument cannot explain passages where Justin is especially conciliatory. Certainly there are passages where Justin is especially harsh with Trypho and his friends.[104] But the *Dialogue* is not totally defined by polemics against the Jews. As Stylianopoulos

---

[100] *Dial.* 23.2. δι' αἰτίαν δὲ τὴν τῶν ἁμαρτωλῶν ἀνθρώπων τὸν αὐτὸν ὄντα ἀεὶ ταῦτα καὶ τὰ τοιαῦτα ἐντετάλθαι ὁμολογεῖν.

[101] Cf. *Dial.* 10–12 where Justin stresses the new and eternal covenant which is instituted with the coming of Jesus.

[102] *Dial.* 24.1. τὸ αἷμα τῆς περιτομῆς ἐκείνης κατήργηται, καὶ αἵματι σωτηρίῳ πεπιστεύκαμεν· ἄλλη διαθήκη τὰ νῦν, καὶ ἄλλος ἐξῆλθεν ἐκ Σιὼν νόμος.

[103] *Dial.* 24.2. The allusion here to Christians being the true Israel cannot be missed.

[104] *Dial.* 14.2; 134.2; 30.2.

points out,[105] when compared with the ancient literature of *Adversus Judaeos* from Barnabas to Chrysostom's homilies against the Jews, the amazing thing about Justin's *Dialogue* is its distinct effort to be conciliatory, not its uncompromising spirit.[106] In this regard, it is quite significant that the *Dialogue* does not conclude with the conversion of Trypho and his companions. This state of affairs does not result in denouncement by a "cascade of polemics"[107] against Trypho. The door is left open. When this is considered in light of Tertullian's *Adversus Judaeos*, which was written for Christians as a sort of handbook to refute the Jews, the conciliatory tone of the *Dialogue* suggests that the author is writing not only for the benefit of those who are on his side, the Christians, but also for those to whom he ostensibly appeals to, the Jews.[108]

III. *Other Arguments for a Jewish Audience*

With the pagan destination well refuted and Cosgrove's confident assertion of an exclusively Christian audience cast in doubt we now examine the final reasons for asserting a Jewish/Christian audience.

A. *Jewish-Christian Polemics*

The shared respect by both Trypho and Justin of the OT scriptures has an important corollary. The very existence of *Adversus Judaeos* literature, combined with the fact that the adversary in such works was sketched as a Jew implies that Christians were bothered by Jewish questions and that the Jewish community was not totally indifferent to the Jewish-Christian debate.

With respect to Justin's *Dialogue*, two reasons make this argument stronger.[109] First, Justin shows a remarkable acquaintance with postbiblical Judaism. It has been shown by W. Shotwell that Justin uses

---

[105] Stylianopoulos, *Justin Martyr and the Mosaic Law*, 35.
[106] See e.g., the many occasions where Justin refers to Trypho and his companions as "friends" (*Dial.* 8.4; 10.1; 68.2; 72.1; 85.7; 142.1). Justin even addresses them as "brothers" (58.3; 137.1). Justin also wishes to sustain the dialogue even when Trypho, at times, seems to tax Justin's patience by reclaiming points already conceded (67.7, 11; cf. 38.2; 44.1; 64.2). Further, in 79.2, when Trypho is ready to break off the discussion, Justin accommodates to his anger.
[107] Stylianopoulos, *Justin Martyr and the Mosaic Law*, 35.
[108] Stylianopoulos, *Justin Martyr and the Mosaic Law*, 36.
[109] Stylianopoulos, *Justin Martyr and the Mosaic Law*, 37–38.

post-biblical haggadic material not simply in order to refute it but
also incorporated it into his own argument much like a rabbinic
teacher would.[110] Of itself, this fact does not necessarily imply that
Justin wrote the *Dialogue* for the Jews. But it does show Justin's
unusual proximity to the faith which he as an apologist attempts to
refute, as well as indicating a genuine interest at a real discussion
with his opponents. Again, it may be reiterated that the amazing
thing here is not the polemics against the Jews, but the effort to
walk on as much of the opponents ground as Justin seems to do.

Second, Justin is a strong testimony to a variegated Jewish Christian
community in his time,[111] and he hints that successful missionary
activity was occurring between Christians and Jews, and between
Jewish Christians and Gentile Christians. The setting of the *Dialogue*
is a proselytic encounter between a Christian and a Jew.[112] Not only
does Justin call for Trypho's conversion throughout the *Dialogue*, but
Trypho also shows interest in Justin converting to Judaism.[113] Justin
is aware of Jewish and Jewish Christian attempts to convince Gentile
Christians to observe the Mosaic Law.[114] In this respect he seems to
assume that some of these attempts were successful.[115] So, in Justin's
time, there are traces of actual proselytizing activity not only between
Jews and Christians, but also between Jewish Christians and Gentile
Christians. The setting of the *Dialogue* as a literary genre seems to
presuppose a concrete situation, where this proselytizing was occurring. If this was the case, it may be possible that the *Dialogue with
Trypho* was Justin's contribution to this mission field, i.e., as a writing addressed to Jews, as well as to Christians.

Stylianopoulos has pointed out that *Dial.* 47 would find interest
among a variety of Jews and Christians:[116] (1) Jews who were receptive to the Christian faith; (2) Christians who wanted to defend their
rejection of the Mosaic Law; (3) Gentile Christians who doubted the
legitimacy of rejecting the Mosaic Law; (4) Jewish Christians who
lived within the Gentile church but still practiced the Law; (5) Jewish
Christians who lived apart from the gentile church and tried to
induce Gentile Christians to observe the Mosaic Law.

---

[110] W. A. Shotwell, *The Biblical Exegesis of Justin Martyr* (London: SPCK, 1965) 88–89.
[111] *Dial.* 47.2ff.
[112] *Dial.* 8.2, 4.
[113] *Dial.* 8.4; 47.1.
[114] *Dial.* 47.1–3.
[115] *Dial.* 47.4.
[116] Stylianopoulos, *Justin Martyr and the Mosaic Law*, 38, footnote #73.

B. *Eschatological Remnant of Jews*

Perhaps the strongest evidence for a Jewish audience is Justin's conviction that a remnant of the Jews, according to God's plan, remains yet to be saved.[117] According to Stylianopoulos, even though this receives explicit formulation several times in the *Dialogue*, it has gone largely unnoticed but explains both Justin's persistence in trying to convert Trypho as well as his hope of success in such efforts. The significant passages in this respect are *Dial.* 32.2; 55.3; 64.2–3.

1. Dialogue *32.2*

> But now I am bringing all my proofs by all the words that I adduce from the passages of scripture, which are held by you to be holy and to belong to the prophets, because I hope that some of you can be found to belong to [the seed] which, according to the grace given by the Lord of Sabaoth is left over unto eternal salvation.[118]

Here there are two very important indications regarding the purpose and intent of the *Dialogue*. Justin indicates here that the purpose of the *Dialogue* is to demonstrate the truth of Christian claims using the same scripture which the Jews accept. The intent is likewise to convince some of the Jews of the truth of these claims. Justin's repeated calls for Trypho's conversion is explicitly based on the idea of the remnant as is Justin's application of this theme to the Jews of his time. According to Justin, not all Jews will accept the Christian interpretation of scripture, but only those Jews who according to God's plan included in the eschatological remnant.

2. Dialogue *55.3*

> God, because of your iniquity, hid from you the ability to perceive the wisdom that there is in his words, with the exception of them who, after the grace of his abundant kindness, "He left," as Isaiah said, "a seed" for salvation, in order that your race should not perish completely, like the men of Sodom and Gomorrah.[119]

---

[117] Stylianopoulos, *Justin Martyr and the Mosaic Law*, 39–44.

[118] *Dial.* 32.2. νῦν δὲ διὰ πάντων τῶν λόγων ἀπὸ τῶν παρ' ὑμῖν ἁγίων καὶ προφητικῶν γραφῶν τὰς πάσας ἀποδείξεις ποιοῦμαι ἐλπίζων τινὰ ἐξ ὑμῶν δύνασθαι εὑρεθῆναι ἐκ τοῦ κατὰ χάριν τὴν ἀπὸ τοῦ κύριου Σαβαὼθ περιλειφθέντος εἰς τὴν αἰώνιον σωτηρίαν.

[119] *Dial.* 55.3. διὰ τὴν ὑμετέραν κακίαν ἀπέκρυψεν ὁ θεὸς ἀφ' ὑμῶν τὸ δύνασθαι νοεῖν τὴν σοφίαν τὴν ἐν τοῖς λόγοις αὐτοῦ, πλήν τινων, οἷς κατὰ χάριν τῆς πολυσπλαγχνίας αὐτοῦ, ὡς ἔφη Ἡσαΐας, ἐγκατέλιπε σπέρμα εἰς σωτηρίαν, ἵνα μὴ ὡς Σοδομιτῶν καὶ Γομορραίων τέλεον καὶ τὸ ὑμέτερον γένος ἀπόληται.

Here, after explaining that God has hidden the true meaning of scripture from the Jews because of their iniquity, Justin explains that a small number of Jews will be given understanding through God's grace. This is based on the Prophet Isaiah's promise that of an eschatological remnant from Judaism will remain so that Israel may not be totally lost.

3. Dialogue *64.2–3*

> Trypho, if I were fond of strife and superficial like you, I should not continue to join in this discussion with you . . . But now, since I fear the judgment of God, I am in no hurry to express my opinion about any one of your race, whether he is not of those who can be saved in accordance with the grace of the Lord of Sabaoth. Therefore even though you act maliciously, I will continue answering . . . That therefore they from your race who are saved by this man, and are in his portion, you would, if you had paid attention to the passages from the scriptures which I have cited, have already understood.[120]

This passage virtually summarizes Justin's intentions in the *Dialogue*. First, Justin is convinced that the scriptures proclaim salvation through Jesus alone, even for Jews. Second, Justin believes he is in no position to judge who is and who is not to be included in the eschatological remnant. Thus, Trypho and his companions, or any other Jew for that matter, may still be converted according to God's plan for the eschatological remnant. Third, the zeal and patience of Justin is according to the same conviction concerning the remnant.

Justin's seriousness concerning the matter of the eschatological remnant cannot be doubted. He makes several references to his responsibility to communicate the truth and to the fact that he will be accountable for it in the day of judgment.[121] Indeed, as Stylianopoulos claims,[122] the *Dialogue* may have been written by Justin as an expression of his conviction about the eschatological remnant and his desire to do his part for the rescue of the remnant according to God's will.

---

[120] *Dial.* 64.2–3. ᾮ Τρύφων, εἰ ὁμοίως ὑμῖν φιλέριστος καὶ κενὸς ὑπῆρχον, οὐκ ἂν ἔτι προσέμενον κοινωνῶν ὑμῖν τῶν λόγων . . . νῦν δέ, ἐπεὶ κρίσιν θεοῦ δέδοικα, οὐ φθάνω ἀποφαίνεσθαι περὶ οὐδενὸς τῶν ἀπὸ τοῦ γένους ὑμῶν, εἰ μήτι ἐστὶν ἀπὸ τῶν κατὰ χάριν τὴν ἀπὸ κυρίου Σαβαὼθ σωθῆναι δυναμένων. διὸ κἂν ὑμεῖς πονηρεύησθε, προσμενῶ . . . ἀποκρινόμενος . . . ὅτι οὖν καὶ οἱ σωζόμενοι ἀπὸ τοῦ γένους τοῦ ὑμετέρου διὰ τούτου σώζονται καὶ ἐν τῇ τούτου μερίδι εἰσί, τοῖς προλελεγμένοις ὑπ᾽ ἐμοῦ ἀπὸ τῶν γραφῶν εἰ προσεσχήκειτε, ἐνενοήκειτε ἂν ἤδη.

[121] *Dial.* 38.2; 44.1; 68.1.

[122] Stylianopoulos, *Justin Martyr and the Mosaic Law*, 44.

IV. *Conclusion*

The conclusion concerning the intended audience of the *Dialogue with Trypho* should be clear from the preceding discussion. The arguments for a pagan audience have been well-criticized and refuted. Cosgrove's assertion of an exclusively Christian audience is plausible on the face of it, but his contention that it is least problematic fails to convince— especially in light of Stylianopoulos's important contributions concerning the non-polemic tone of the *Dialogue* and the eschatological remnant.

In this light, I agree with Stylianopoulos's hypothesis that the *Dialogue* was written for a Jewish audience in the context of missionary activity between Jews and Christians. But because the *Dialogue* was written within the Christian community it would naturally commend itself to a Christian audience. Justin, realizing this, may have had Jewish Christians as well as Gentile Christians in mind. It has been shown that the *Dialogue* answers issues that would be a concern to each of these groups. Therefore, even though the *Dialogue* has primarily a Jewish audience in mind, a combined Jewish/Christian audience can reasonably be posited.

CHAPTER TWO

THE CONCEPT OF REVELATION IN
DIALOGUE WITH TRYPHO

I. *Introduction*

"In most versions of Christianity, revelation has served as the epistemological basis for theology; that is, an appeal has often been made to revelation in order to account for knowledge of God."[1] It is my contention that this line of thinking coincides with Justin Martyr's in the *Dialogue with Trypho*. It must be remembered, however, that because the *Dialogue* is not a systematic presentation of Justin's theological beliefs, it was not necessarily Justin's intent to espouse his understanding of revelation in the pages of that work. Rather, in the *Dialogue*, Justin covers topics and issues pertinent to the existing context. The task in this chapter is to examine the context of the *Dialogue* with the view to understanding how Justin understood revelation.

At its root, the idea of revelation carries with it the disclosure of something which was previously only partly known.[2] For whatever reason something is disclosed that was previously hidden from knowledge or understanding. Knowledge, therefore, appears to be the goal in revelation. Knowledge of something or someone which was previously incomplete or partly known. In what follows, this link between revelation and epistemology take center stage as we discuss Justin Martyr's concept of revelation.

In Christian theology the focus of revelation has been the self-revealing God. As sovereign creator, God is viewed as eternal and without equal, wholly other than humankind's existence.[3] Because of

---

[1] G. Stroup, "Revelation," in P. C. Hodgson & R. H. King (eds.), *Christian Theology. An Introduction to Its Traditions and Tasks* (London: SPCK, 1983) 88.

[2] W. Pannenberg, *Systematic Theology* (3 vols.; Edinburgh: T. & T. Clark, 1991) 1.189.

[3] Biblical passages often presented as exemplary of this belief include: 1 Chr 29:11; Isa 40:22–23; Ps 22:28; 47:7–8, Dan 5:21; Ps 75:7; Jer 30:24. For the relationship of these and other verses to this concept, see e.g., D. G. Bloesch, *Essentials of Evangelical Theology Volume I: God, Authority, & Salvation* (San Francisco: Harper & Row, 1978) 24–50; L. Gilkey, "God," in Hodgson & King (eds.), *Christian Theology*, 62–87; S. J. Grenz, *Theology for the Community of God* (Nasville: Broadman & Holman, 1994)

this we are utterly unable to understand God on our own. The need to know who God is, what God does, and our relationship to him therefore rests in God's self-disclosure. In other words, only God can reveal himself.[4]

The OT scriptures are illustrative of this focus. God's self-disclosure can be seen in his activity—his mighty acts. This is emphasized in many ways throughout the OT. The call of Abraham, through whom God would build his nation, showed the Israelites that God revealed his purposes to them. The miraculous provision of Isaac as an heir to the promise further showed his nation that God carried out his promises to them. The deliverance of Israel from Egypt and the conquest of the promised land further strengthened the Israelite dependence on God's self-revealing acts. These, and many other, mighty acts by God on behalf of the nation of Israel revealed God's care and plan for it, they are not only revelations of his power, but are also revelations of his character. God's self-disclosure can also be seen in his speech. The Prophets were very conscious that the message they were delivering was not their own, it was from God. The Prophets could therefore state, "The word of the Lord came to me, saying . . .".[5] God, therefore, was not only revealing himself but also his plan and purposes.

Justin Martyr reflects this focus that views God as wholly other, yet as one who chooses to make self-disclosure through his mighty acts. Concerning Justin's concept of revelation in the *Dialogue with Trypho*, W. A. Shotwell has stated, "In the *Dialogue with Trypho* there was no need for Justin to state a concept of revelation, for both he and his opponent used the Old Testament as the basis for their discussion."[6] Shotwell proceeds to explain Justin's concept of revelation based upon the *Apologies* with little reference to the *Dialogue*. As this chapter will show, Shotwell is correct in his statement that Justin considers the OT scriptures as a witness to God's character. However, he has neglected to mention and give account for two other very important issues that must be discussed in connection with Justin's concept of revelation in the *Dialogue with Trypho*. First, the concept

---

35–161; J. N. Hart, "Creation and Providence," in Hodgson & King (eds.), *Christian Theology*, 115–140; T. C. Oden, *The Living God. Systematic Theology: Volume One* (San Francisco: Harper, 1992) 15–82, 270–316; Pannenberg, *Systematic Theology*, 1.337–421.

[4] Pannenberg, *Systematic Theology*, 1.1–2.

[5] See e.g., Jer 18:1; Ezek 12:1, 8, 17, 21, 26; Hos 1:1; Joel 1:1; Amos 3:1.

[6] W. A. Shotwell, *The Biblical Exegesis of Justin Martyr* (London: SPCK, 1965) 2.

of revelation must be placed within Justin's understanding of philosophy as a search for God. Justin's background and the influence
of Middle Platonic philosophy upon him cannot be disregarded in
the *Dialogue*. Failure to do so oversimplifies the issue to the extreme
of misunderstanding it. Second, the importance of the *Logos* in Justin's
concept of revelation must also be examined, for, it will be shown,
the *Logos* is the glue which holds Justin's concept of revelation together.

The purpose in this chapter is not to discuss modern views of revelation, or even the general theme of revelation. The task before us
here is to discuss Justin's foundational understanding of God's revelation as presented in the *Dialogue with Trypho*. We will see that
Justin understands this revelation in terms of salvation history in
which the incarnation of the *Logos* is central. Under-girding Justin's
understanding here is the belief that God actually breaks into the
human situation from beyond—God acts in the human situation.
Justin claims that God has acted, and is acting, historically to rescue humanity from its plight.[7]

This chapter has three main foci. First, by way of background,
the foundational issue of epistemology must be discussed with a view
toward how Justin believed knowledge of God is attained. In this
section, Justin's connection with the Middle Platonic theory of knowledge will be explained and its significance stated. Second, also by
way of background, Justin's concept of God will be discussed with
a view toward seeing the link between it and the Platonic concept

---

[7] G. D. Kaufman, *Systematic Theology: A Historicist Perspective* (New York: Charles
Scribner's Sons, 1968) 13–40, 378–388. Kaufman claims that because man and
woman are historical beings, salvation from humanity's plight must also be historical—it must come through events which further transform history, thus finally heal-
ing humanity itself. He identifies several of the most important stages in this salvation
history. "The *first*, symbolized in Genesis by the 'call of Abraham,' was the preparation of a certain receptiveness in man to the fact that God's requirements are
distinct from man's (autonomous) desires" (p. 379). "The *second* stage or event of
salvation-history . . . is the exodus-covenant complex through which the people of
Israel bound themselves in a historical compact to the God Yahweh. Here the totali-
tarian character of the loyalty claimed by God began to become apparent, together with
the genuinely personal character of the relation between God and man" (p. 380).
"With this development we are into the *third* stage or event of salvation-history.
Yahweh, it now became evident, is the absolute Lord of all history; the whole course
of history, therefore, must be understood as working out his personal purposes"
(p. 381). "The *fourth* stage of this historical movement toward man's salvation bears
the name Jesus Christ . . . This event includes the actual 'bridging of the gap'
between God and man, and the broadening out once again of what had seemed
to be the particular history of an obscure nation into universal history, with the
emergence of a community destined to include all nations" (p. 383).

of God. Both of these first two main sections will show that even though Justin retained some Platonic categories of thought after his conversion to Christianity, he could no longer call himself a true Platonist.[8] This has significant implications for his view of epistemology and its relationship to revelation. The third major section will discuss the implications of Justin's epistemology and Theology Proper on his concept of revelation. In other words, the *Dialogue with Trypho* will be examined with a view towards seeing how Justin practically works out his concept of revelation.

II. *Background—Epistemology*

In the prologue to the *Dialogue with Trypho* (chaps. 1–9) the reader is immediately ushered into the philosophic tone of the treatise. A detailed examination of the prologue will arrive in due course as this chapter progresses. However, the somewhat latent philosophical presuppositions upon which the entire prologue is based must be understood in its relationship to Justin's conversion. In other words, we must ask how Justin's philosophical presuppositions affected his conversion and, ultimately, his conception of revelation. This is the foundational issue upon which and from which all thought and argument progress in the prologue.

I have suggested above that the root idea of revelation carries with it disclosure of something that was previously hidden or partly known. We have thus entered into the epistemological question—"How do we know what we know?" In a very real sense, this is Justin's concern in the *Dialogue with Trypho*. It is my contention that Justin retained certain Platonic presuppositions even after his conversion to Christianity.[9] However, in order to show this, certain aspects of Platonic thought must be explained within the context of its contact with Justin. At the top of the list is Platonic epistemology. Justin's conversion from Platonism to Christianity cannot be properly understood without understanding the Platonic theory of knowledge. His conversion indicates a fundamental shift concerning how one attains knowledge of God. This shift, in turn, is foundational to the concept of revelation in the *Dialogue*.

---

[8] It will be shown that Justin is indebted to the more eclectic form of Platonism of the second century that has been described as Middle Platonism.

[9] As will be shown below, Justin's Platonic epistemology is radically altered while his Platonic concept of God is, by and large, retained.

A. *Platonic Epistemology*

It is clear that Justin considered himself a philosopher—both before and after his conversion to Christianity.[10] As a philosopher, he believed it was his task (along with philosophers in general) to inquire about God. In fact, according to Justin, this inquiry is necessary for happiness.[11] Trypho becomes intrigued by this assertion and asks him to define God and philosophy. Justin does so by recounting his trek through the philosophies of his day and through his meeting with a certain respectable old man who would eventually convince him to accept Christianity as the true philosophy. It is by way of Justin's recounting his meeting with the old man that Justin answers Trypho's questions of definition. Justin states that philosophy "is the knowledge of that which is (ἐστὶ), and knowledge of the truth."[12] In his reply to Justin's definition the old man seizes upon a very important issue for revelation—epistemology. And it is in this reply that we see the foundational importance of epistemology in Justin's concept of revelation.

By replying that philosophy is "knowledge of that which is" Justin is recalling his debt to Middle Platonism. He had already offered an indication of this debt to Middle Platonic thought in *Dial.* 2.6,

> I thereupon spent as much of my time as was possible with one who had lately settled in our city—a sagacious man, holding a high position among the Platonists,—and I progressed, and made the greatest improvements daily. And the perception of immaterial things quite overpowered me, and the contemplation of Ideas furnished my mind with wings, so that in a little while I supposed that I had become wise; and such was my stupidity, I expected forthwith to look upon God, for this is the end of Plato's Philosophy.[13]

Justin's Platonism was distinctly the eclectic Middle Platonism of the second century. He employs the same terms in describing the act of knowing the Christian God[14] as he uses of knowing philosophical

---

[10] *Dial.* 1.
[11] *Dial.* 1.3.
[12] *Dial.* 3.4 ἐπιστήμη ἐστὶ τοῦ ὄντος καὶ τοῦ ἀληθοῦς ἐπίγνωσις.
[13] καὶ δὴ νεωστὶ ἐπιδημήσαντι τῇ ἡμετέρᾳ πόλει συνετῷ ἀνδρὶ καὶ προΰχοντι ἐν τοῖς Πλατωνικοῖς συνδιέτριβον ὡς τὰ μάλιστα, καὶ προέκοπτον καὶ πλεῖστον ὅσον ἑκάστης ἡμέρας ἐπεδίδουν. καί με ᾕρει σφόδρα ἡ τῶν ἀσωμάτων νόησις, καὶ ἡ θεωρία τῶν ἰδεῶν ἀνεπτέρου μοι τὴν φρόνησιν, ὀλίγου τε ἐντὸς χρόνου ᾤμην σοφὸς γεγονέναι, καὶ ὑπὸ βλακείας ἤλπιζον αὐτίκα κατόψεσθαι τὸν θεόν· τοῦτο γὰρ τέλος τῆς Πλάτωνος φιλοσοφίας. Cf. Albinus, *Didask.* 2.
[14] *Dial.* 8.

truth. Both passages are based on a passage in Plato.[15] This text was
a favorite among Middle Platonists.[16] For the Middle Platonic school
the experience of the highest good in the intelligible world was central. Thus, Justin's interpretation of Plato here is in line with the
Middle Platonic thought of his day when he describes the experience of the Idea as the end of Platonic philosophy. When Justin
understands Plato's ontological sentences as theological it is an interpretation that is well-known in Middle Platonism. For example, when
Albinus speaks about God being discernable to the mind alone, he
is using as his base *Phaedr.* 247C. But he (like Justin) applies the passage which deals with knowledge of the intelligible world of the True
and the Good to the knowledge of God.[17] Celsus uses the passage
from Plato in a similar way.[18] Thus, while it is true that the *telos* of
Platonism was not to look upon God, it must be remembered that
Justin was not a Platonist in the pure sense of that school of thought.
He was a Middle Platonist and his understanding of Plato was an
interpretation. The central metaphysical theme for Justin is no longer,
as it was for the historical Plato, the doctrine of Ideas, but God.
For Plutarch the ὄντως ὄν is God.[19] But for Plato it was the Ideas.[20]
This fact should not cause surprise since Justin is here recording his
own words prior to his conversion to Christianity. By answering in
such a way, Justin has exposed himself as espousing, to a certain
degree, the Platonic theory of knowledge.[21] This, in turn, is important when we look at Justin's Christian epistemology.

Plato presents the world in which we live as a product of the
interaction between two distinct principles—"Becoming" and "Being."

---

[15] Plato, *Ep.* 7.341D.
[16] Albinus, *Didask.* 10; Maximus of Tyre, *Or.* 29.5; Plut. *De Is. Et Osir.* 77.
[17] Albinus, *Didask.* 10.
[18] Celsus, *Fr.* 6.64.
[19] Plutarch, *de E. ap Delph.* 19, 20.
[20] Plato, *Phaedr.* 247E; *Tim.* 27D; 28A.
[21] For more on Justin's Middle Platonism see above, section III.A.1.b. For the
relationship between Justin's Platonism and Middle Platonisn see also, C. Andresen,
"Justin und der mittlere Platonismus," *ZNW* 44 (1952/53) 157–195; Barnard, *Justin
Martyr*, 34–37; J. Daniélou, *Gospel Message and Hellenistic Culture*. (The Development
of Christian Doctrine Before the Council of Nicaea Vol 2; ET J. A. Baker; London:
Darton, Longman & Todd, 1973) 107–113; Droge, "Justin Martyr and the Restoration
of Philosophy," 304–307; G. May, *Creatio Ex Nihilo: The Doctrine of 'Creation out of
Nothing' in Early Christian Thought* (ET A. S. Worall; Edinburgh: T. & T. Clark, 1994)
1–5; Story, *The Nature of Truth in "The Gospel of Truth" and in the Writings of Justin
Martyr*, 58–59.

Becoming is defined as the visible, tangible reality which is perceived by the senses. Of the two, this kind of reality is lower and inferior to Being. Being, on the other hand, is a higher reality that is found in the intelligible realm, the realm of Forms or Ideas.[22]

1. *"Becoming"*

Becoming has two essential characteristics:[23] (a) it is physical or material in nature and thus occupies both space and time and, (b) because it occupies both space and time it is always in a state of flux or change. Because nothing is permanent or stable, nothing quite succeeds in *being* what it is. This is because it is always in the state of *becoming* something else. The result of this state of *becoming* is that because of this state of flux or change there is no basis for reliable knowledge of any kind.[24]

The crux of the issue here is that of sensible perception, or knowledge of objects of which we are made aware of by our senses. Plato sets out to show that knowledge gained by perception does not fulfill the requirements of true knowledge at all, since, according to him, knowledge must be infallible and of what *is* (Being). As far as knowledge of sensible things go, Plato is quite fond of pointing out how fallible this knowledge is. One such example is found in *Theaetetus*.[25] Here, Theaetetus has just asserted to Socrates that "knowledge is nothing else than perception."[26] In reply, Socrates points out that sometimes when two men are feeling the same wind blow, one may feel cold while the other does not, or, one may feel only slightly

---

[22] Plato states, "Now first of all we must, in my judgment, make the following distinction. What is that which is Existent always and has no Becoming? And what is that which is Becoming always and never is Existent? Now the one of these is apprehensible by thought with the aid of reasoning, since it is ever uniformly existent; whereas the other is an object of opinion with the aid of unreasoning sensation, since it becomes and perishes and is never really existent. Again, everything which becomes must of necessity become owing to some Cause; for without a cause it is impossible for anything to attain becoming" (Plato, *Tim.* 27D–28A).

[23] R. A. Norris, *God and World in Early Christian Theology: A Study in Justin Martyr, Irenaeus, Tertullian, and Origen* (Studies in Patristic Thought; London: Adam & Charles Black, 1966) 13.

[24] Plato, *Theaet.* 181–183.

[25] Plato, *Theaet.* 152. Other examples of Plato pointing out the fallibility of sensible knowledge include *Tim.* 48–51; *Theaet.* 182–188; *Phaed.* 73–75; *Rep.* 413, 475–480. See also, F. Copleston, *A History of Philosophy* (9 vols.; new rev. ed; Garden City, NY: Image Books, 1962) 1/1.167.

[26] Plato, *Theaet.* 151E.

cold while the other is exceedingly cold.[27] "Then in that case, shall we say that the wind is in itself cold or not cold; or should we accept Protagoras's saying that it is cold for him who feels cold and not for him who does not?"[28]

The point here is that for Plato sense-perception is not infallible. This is because one object can be described as being two opposite things. This is expanded upon by Plato (through Socrates) when he states that

> ... you could not rightly ascribe any quality whatsoever to anything, but if you call it large it will also appear to be small, and light if you call it heavy, and everything else in the same way, since nothing whatever is one, either a particular thing or of a particular quality; but it is out of movement and motion and mixture with one another that all those things become which we wrongly say "are"—wrongly, because nothing ever is, but is always becoming.[29]

Further, if knowledge must be knowledge of that which *is*, then sense-perception fails again, because the fact that two people can perceive the same object in contradictory ways proves that the objects of sense-perception are always in a state of change or flux. Since sense-perception is built on opinion rather than knowledge[30] it is not reliable. Opinions are not "real". They may, therefore contradict one another. Thus, perception is not knowledge because it is fallible and is not knowledge of Being but only of Becoming.

2. *"Being"*

This state of affairs leaves one thinking that any search for a stable knowledge is a vain search. But Plato offers a remedy to this. True knowledge, to Plato, is knowledge that can be comprehended by reason, by the powers of the mind. This higher reality is that of Being,[31] and is described as the realm of Forms or Ideas.

For Plato, Forms (εἴδη) or Ideas (ἰδέαι) are neither physical nor mental—they are outside of space and time. It is the Forms that are real while the physical and material world is but a poor reflection.[32]

---

[27] Plato, *Theaet.* 152B.
[28] Plato, *Theaet.* 152B.
[29] Plato, *Theaet.* 152D–E.
[30] Plato, *Rep.* 357C; 402C–D; 475–480; 585C; *Tim.* 53; 121–123.
[31] Plato, *Rep.* 575–580.
[32] Plato, *Parm.*, passim.

Plato was here influenced by the methods and achievements of mathematics in his day. The truth of mathematics were of a special sort—they are grasped intellectually, by a process of intuition and deductive reasoning. They are reflected or illustrated in the physical world, but only imperfectly. They can only be truly understood by the mind which abstracts from the unreliable evidence of sense and relies on the capacities of reason alone.[33] And Plato thinks that as it is with the truths of mathematics, so also with other matters as well.[34] Thus, objects of true knowledge must be stable and abiding, fixed, capable of being grasped in clear scientific definition. This knowledge which is attained of the stable is knowledge of universals, of Forms or Ideas.[35]

3. *Plato's Allegory of the Cave*[36]

Plato himself offers an allegorical explanation of how his theory of knowledge should be understood. His allegory of the Cave[37] may thus be seen as a summary of his theory of Forms or Ideas and his mission as a philosopher. If one were to diagram this allegory, it would look like this:[38]

Cave Entry

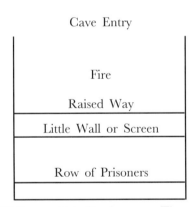

Fire

Raised Way

Little Wall or Screen

Row of Prisoners

Wall on which Shadows are Thrown

---

[33] Plato, *Rep.* 434D–435E; *Theaet.* 165.
[34] Norris, *God and World in Early Christian Theology*, 14.
[35] Copleston, *History of Philosophy*, 1/1.174.
[36] Plato actually related 3 different comparisons to help express various aspects of his epistemology. In addition to the Allegory of the Cave (*Rep.* 514–519) Plato also used the Divided Line (*Rep.* 510–511) and the Simile of the Sun (*Rep.* 505–509). The Divided Line and the Simile of the Sun will be discussed in Chapter 3 as they apply to Justin's concept of truth.
[37] Plato, *Rep.* 514A–519A.
[38] Copleston, *A History of Philosophy*, 1/1.185.

Plato asks the reader to imagine a cave which has an opening towards
a light. In the cave are living human beings where, from birth, their
legs and necks have been chained in such a way that they can look
neither left, nor right, but only forward to the back wall of the cave.
The prisoners have thus never actually seen the light of the sun.
Between the prisoners and the mouth of the cave is a fire, and
between the fire and the prisoners is a raised way and a low wall
like a screen. Along this raised way people pass carrying statues and
figures of animals and other objects. They are carried in such a way
that they appear over the top of the screen. Because the prisoners
are facing the inside wall of the cave, they neither see one another
nor the objects being carried, but only shadows of themselves and
of the objects which are thrown on the wall they are facing.

The prisoners represent the majority of humankind who are in a
state in which they see only shadows of reality and hear only echoes
of truth. It is a distorted view of the world. If these prisoners were
to suddenly break free and told to look at the realities of which they
had only formerly seen shadows, they would be blinded by the glare
of the light, and would imagine that the shadows are far more real
than the realities. But if one of the escaped prisoners grows accus-
tomed to the light, he would be able to look at the concrete sensible objects, of which he had formerly only known shadows. This
escaped prisoner can now see his fellow prisoners in the light of the
fire (which represents the visible sun). He has thus been "converted"
from the shadow world to the real world. He now sees the prisoners
for what they really are. If this converted prisoner now comes out
of the cave into the sunlight, he will see a world of sun-illumined
and clear objects (which represent intelligible realities), and will eventually be able to see the sun itself, which represents the Idea of the
Good, the highest Form. If someone, after ascending to the sun-
shine, were to go back into the cave, he would be unable to see
properly because of the darkness. If he tried to free another and
lead him to the light, the prisoners, who love the darkness and consider the shadows to be true reality, would put the offender to death.

So, from the allegory of the cave, one sees that the philosopher
who has seen the world of Ideas is in the best position to explain
the realities better than those who have only seen the shadowy world
of sense.[39] The allegory also makes it clear that there is a concept

---

[39] Ferguson, *Backgrounds of Early Christianity*, 314.

of progress which requires great effort and mental discipline. This is why Plato insists on the importance of education. For it is through education that the young may be brought, through progression, to behold eternal and absolute truths and values, and so saved from passing their lives in the shadowy existence of sense.[40]

B. *Justin's Platonic Epistemology*

Justin uses his meeting with the old man by the sea[41] to introduce a Christian epistemology, as opposed to the Platonic epistemology described above.[42] The old man is given some initial indication of Justin's Platonic leanings in two ways upon their meeting. First, when the old man asks Justin why he is walking alone, Justin replies that he likes to walk alone by the sea because his attention is not distracted and dialogue with himself is uninterrupted.[43] Second, Justin declares reason (λόγος) to be the source which governs all. Once a person has laid hold of reason he or she is able to look down on the errors of others. But without reason prudence would not be present in any man.[44] These two indications show that Justin is concerned with using the faculty of his mind to inquire and progress in philosophy—a matter that sounds very much like Plato's philosophy outlined above.

At this point in the *Dialogue* it appears as though Justin is presenting the old man as slowly trying to press Justin concerning his Platonism, and the next two indications confirm this. The first indication, which has already been discussed, is Justin's definition that philosophy "is the knowledge of that which is (ἐστὶ)."[45] The second indication is Justin's definition that God is "That which always has the same manner and existence and is the cause of all other things."[46] From these two further indications, the old man's suspicions are confirmed that Justin is, in fact, a Platonist. Justin has just stated a belief in the

[40] Copleston, *A History of Philosophy*, 186.

[41] *Dial.* 3.1.

[42] It should be noted that at this point in the *Dialogue* Justin is using the old man as a "foil" for Platonic epistemology. Therefore, Justin is reflecting back on his conversion from Platonism to Christianity. It is thus Justin the Platonist here.

[43] *Dial.* 3.2.

[44] *Dial.* 3.3.

[45] *Dial.* 3.4. The dependence of this statement upon Platonic philosophy is discussed above, section II.A.

[46] *Dial.* 3.5. Τὸ κατὰ τὰ αὐτὰ καὶ ὡσαύτως ἀεὶ ἔχον καὶ τοῦ εἶναι πᾶσι τοῖς ἄλλοις αἴτιον.

higher order of knowledge—Being. Thus, for Justin the Platonist, God is that which is and that which remains the same—Being.

The old man recognizes that Justin has placed himself within Plato's theory of knowledge.[47] Therefore, he presses the epistemological question—How do we know God? According to the old man knowledge is not always apprehended in the same ways. Justin is therefore asked if knowledge is not a word applied commonly to different matters. Some knowledge, such as military strategy, navigation, and medicine comes from study and practice. But some knowledge, specifically knowledge in Divine and human affairs, cannot be gained in this way, it must be gained by sight or hearing from someone who has seen. The example given by the old man for this type of knowledge is the idea that, hypothetically, there exists an animal in India which is different than any other. If one had not seen this animal he would have no definite knowledge of it. The only other way one could describe it therefore is if one had heard of it from someone who had seen the animal.[48] Justin agrees with the old man's reasoning, and upon this agreement the old man gets to the heart of the issue: "Then how . . . can philosophers set forth truthfully or speak that which is true concerning God when they have no knowledge of him, having never seen or heard him?"[49]

Justin's reply, once again, is Middle Platonic, ". . . the Divine is not visible to the eyes, as other living things, but is discernible to the mind alone, as Plato says—and I believe him."[50] If the old man had any doubt as to Justin's philosophical bias, it has now been answered. The phrase "discernible to the mind alone" embodies the core of Platonic philosophy.[51] Now that the old man can place Justin as a follower of Plato, he knows what Justin believes regarding the attainment of knowledge. And it is these beliefs that the old man sets out to discredit in favor of a Christian epistemology.

---

[47] As it has been understood in second century Middle Platonism. See sections II.A & III.A.1.b.

[48] *Dial.* 3.6.

[49] *Dial.* 3.7 Πῶς οὖν ἄν, ἔφη, περὶ θεοῦ ὀρθῶς φρονοῖεν οἱ φιλόσοφοι ἢ λέγοιέν τι ἀληθές, ἐπιστήμην αυτοῦ μὴ ἔχοντες, μηδὲ ἰδόντες ποτὲ ἢ ἀκούσαντες;

[50] *Dial.* 3.7. Ἀλλ' οὐκ ἔστιν ὀφθαλμοῖς, ἦν δ' ἐγώ, αὐτοῖς, πάτερ, ὁρατὸν τὸ θεῖον ὡς τὰ ἄλλα ζῶα, ἀλλὰ μόνῳ νῷ καταληπτόν, ὥς φησι Πλάτων, καὶ ἐγὼ πείθομαι αὐτῷ.

[51] van Winden, *An Early Christian Philosopher*, 69.

C. *Toward a Christian Epistemology*

The old man starts discrediting Justin's Middle Platonic epistemology by questioning Justin's belief that the mind actually has the power to do such a thing. He counters Justin's belief with his own that the mind of man cannot see God without the aid of the Holy Spirit. Justin then replies that the mind is of such a nature that it has been given for this end—to see that very Being when the mind is pure. This Being actually comes into the souls on account of their affinity to and desire for seeing God.[52] For Plato, and thus for Justin here, the soul is immortal (having neither beginning nor end). But not only is the soul immortal, it is also immaterial or spiritual and therefore belongs to the same reality as Forms or Ideas. This is important, for "Only like can know like; only a subject which is itself eternal and incorporeal can grasp the truth of an eternal and incorporeal reality."[53]

The old man then seizes upon Justin's statement about the soul. He recognizes that Justin is claiming that the soul is immaterial, immortal, and eternal, i.e. that it is uncreated. This is why, in *Dial.* 4–6 Justin uses the old man to discredit the Platonic idea that the soul is part of the order of Forms or Ideas. For if the soul is not immortal then it cannot be a part of the Platonic version of reality. Thus, neither the soul nor the mind has affinity to God. And if the soul and the mind has no affinity to God, if it is of a different order of reality, then there is no chance that the mind may see God because "only like can know like."[54] The old man is making an argument that could conceivably cause Justin's entire epistemological framework to collapse.

The climax to the old man's argument is found in chapter 7, where he offers his alternative Christian epistemology. But the summary of his argument against Middle Platonic epistemology is found in chapter 6. It is well worth quoting.

> The soul certainly is, or has, life. If, therefore, it is life, it would cause other life, not itself—just as motion moves something other than itself. No one denies that the soul lives. But if it lives, it does not live as

---

[52] *Dial.* 4.1.
[53] Norris, *God and World in Early Christian Theology*, 16. See also, van Winden, *An Early Christian Philosopher*, 74–75.
[54] Norris, *God and World in Early Christian Theology*, 16.

being life, but rather as a partaker of life. And the one partaking of
something is different from that of which it partakes. So the soul partakes of life because God wills it to live. Thus, it cannot partake of
life if God does not will it to live. For to live is not its own [attribute]
as it is God's.[55]

The old man is placing the soul within the realm of the will of God,
in other words, the soul lives only because God wills it to live. It is
not an uncreated reality, but rather, it is subject to the will of God
as the giver of life. The soul and God are different, thus, the soul
has no affinity to God.

Immediately after the old man's summary of Platonic epistemology the climax of his argument is reached. Justin is introduced to
the Prophets and Apostles of Christ who can actually relate knowledge of God. Justin rejects his previously held Platonic epistemology
and accepts the old man's argument—a Christian epistemology.[56]

By eventually accepting this Christian way of attaining knowledge
about God Justin has severed an important link to his Middle
Platonism. Plato did not believe in a God who reveals himself in
time and history, much less in theophanies, as did Jewish and Christian
writers. Basically "god," for Plato, was anything which participates
in Being as opposed to Becoming. "God" is thus anything which
belongs by nature to the realm of immortal and intelligible existence.[57] As we have seen,[58] it is the Forms or Ideas which belong to
this realm of immortal and intelligible existence. All of these Forms
or Ideas are summed up in the ultimate ideal, which Plato calls the
Good. Even though this idea of the Good has been thought of as
the nearest approximation in Plato to the biblical idea of God, it
must be remembered that the Good is a Form, and not a living
God. Strictly speaking, Plato does not have a personal God, rather,
only an impersonal principle.[59] It is out of these concepts that Justin
emerged to maintain a belief in the personal God of the Prophets

---

[55] *Dial.* 6.1–2. ἡ ψυχὴ ἤτοι ζωή ἐστιν ἢ ζωὴν ἔχει. εἰ μὲν οὖν ζώη ἐστιν, ἄλλο τι ἂν
ποιήσειε ζῆν, οὐχ ἑαυτήν, ὡς καὶ κίνησις ἄλλο τι κινήσειε μᾶλλον ἢ ἑαυτήν. ὅτι δὲ ζῇ
ψυχή, οὐδεὶς ἀντείποι. εἰ δὲ ζῇ, οὐ ζωὴ οὖσα ζῇ, ἀλλὰ μεταλαμβάνουσα τῆς ζωῆς·
ἕτερον δέ τι τὸ μετέχον τινὸς ἐκείνου οὗ μετέχει. ζωῆς δὲ ψυχὴ μετέχει, ἐπεὶ ζῆν αὐτὴν
ὁ θεὸς βούλεται. οὕτως ἄρα καὶ οὐ μεθέξει ποτέ, ὅταν αὐτὴν μὴ θέλοι ζῆν. οὐ γὰρ ἴδιον
αὐτῆς ἐστι τὸ ζῆν ὡς τοῦ θεοῦ·

[56] *Dial.* 7–8. This is discussed in more detail below, sections IV–V.

[57] Norris, *God and World in Early Christian Theology*, 20.

[58] See above, section II.A.

[59] Ferguson, *Backgrounds of Early Christianity*, 313.

and Apostles. His task, therefore, was to transform Platonic notions of this impersonal "god" into a more acceptable personal God of the scriptures of Christianity.

D. *Concluding Remarks on Epistemology*

The differences here between Middle Platonic epistemology and the old man's Christian epistemology, which Justin accepts, are foundational to understanding why Justin uses both the Prophets and Memoirs of the Apostles as sources of the knowledge of God, and, most importantly, the incarnation of the *Logos* as revelation of God.[60] The old man builds upon a common ground between Middle Platonic epistemology and his Christian epistemology. That common ground is found in the definition of philosophy as "knowledge of that which is (ἐστί)"[61] and the belief that God is that which remains the same (Being).[62]

But from this common ground arises the question, "How do we know God?" This is the real crux of the issue between Middle Platonic and Christian epistemology. The old man discredits the Platonic idea that the soul and the mind have an affinity for God because they are of a different order of reality. Thus, the only way gain knowledge about God is from those who had seen or heard him.[63] This is a major difference in how to attain knowledge about God. No longer is the intelligible world seen as deceptive. Rather, it is this very intelligible world that gives us knowledge about God. Simply stated, one cannot accept the Christian epistemology described by the old man and still remain a Platonist.

III. *Background—Theology Proper*

This issue of epistemology must never be far from a contextual reading of the *Dialogue with Trypho* regarding revelation. The old man's Christian epistemology literally revolutionized the way Justin acquired knowledge about God. It is quite clear, therefore, that Justin has not retained his previously held Platonic epistemology. Can the same be said, however, for his concept of God?

---

[60] These 3 subjects form the headings for the section below on the Witnesses to Revelation and the *Logos* as Revelation. See sections IV–V.

[61] *Dial.* 3.4.

[62] *Dial.* 3.5.

[63] *Dial.* 7–8. This is discussed in greater detail in sections IV–V.

A. *Common Staring Point?*

Having placed Justin's conversion to Christianity in its proper context of epistemology and his discussion with the old man, we may now turn to Justin's discussions with Trypho and his companions. It is clear, once again, that this discussion also centers on the concept of epistemology.

In *Dial.* 10 Justin asks Trypho for an explanation of the accusations he and other Jews make against the Christians. Trypho's answer is that the Christians live a life that is no different than the Gentiles, neither keeping the feasts and Sabbaths, nor practicing the rite of circumcision. Therefore, what Trypho requires of Justin is an explanation of why he, as a Christian, can scorn the covenant of circumcision, spurn the commands that come after it, and still think that he knows God. To Trypho it is impossible for a person to know (εἰδότες) God without practicing those things which God requires. In Trypho's eyes, Justin is no different than the Gentiles. He and other Christians do not segregate themselves from other Gentiles, and really live a life that is no different from them. This is evidenced for Trypho in Justin's disregard for the feasts and sabbaths, as well as his disregard for the rite of circumcision. For Trypho, knowledge of God is attained through adherence to the Law. Therefore, failure to practice the Law results in a failure to know God. Following this explanation of his accusations Trypho then sets the stage for the ensuing dialogue, "If, therefore, you have satisfactory verbal defense of these [accusations], and can show in what way you hope for anything whatsoever, even though you do not observe the Law, we would most willingly listen to you, and we will also make similar investigations."[64]

Justin begins his reply by focusing in on the common ground between Trypho the Jew and Justin the Christian. That common ground relates to God.

> There will never be, Trypho, nor has there ever been from eternity (I thus addressed him), any other except the one who created and arranged all. Nor do we think that our God is different from yours, for this is the God who, with a strong hand and outstretched arm, led your fathers out of the land of Egypt. Nor have we placed our

---

[64] *Dial.* 10.4 εἰ οὖν ἔχεις πρὸς ταῦτα ἀπολογήσασθαι, καὶ ἐπιδεῖξαι ᾧτινι τρόπῳ ἐλπίζετε ὁτιοῦν, κἂν μὴ φυλάσσοντες τὸν νόμον, τοῦτό σου ἡδέως ἀκούσαιμεν μάλιστα, καὶ τὰ ἄλλα δὲ ὁμοίως συνεξετάσωμεν.

hope in any other (for there is no other), but in this same one in whom you also have placed your hope, the God of Abraham and of Isaac and of Jacob.[65]

Here Justin is attempting to begin on the same footing with Trypho by stating that his doctrine of God is the same as Trypho's. As a philosopher,[66] God was one of Justin's main concerns.[67] But can Justin's statement be taken at face value? Is Justin's conception of God the same as Trypho's conception? This question is best answered under three main headings: Justin's Concept of God, Trypho's Judaism, and Apophatic Theology.

1. *Justin's Concept of God*

a. *Pre-Conversion*

In *Dial.* 5.4–6 Justin appeals to Plato's *Timaeus* for support in his belief that only God is unbegotten (ἀγέννητος) and incorruptible (ἄφθαρτος). "Because of this God is God, and all other things after him are created and corruptible."[68] This idea is the Platonic premise that what has a beginning must have an end.[69] The world or anything else is not God and continues to exist only by God's will—only God is without beginning and end.[70] The dependence on Plato then continues in the same vein,

> Hence there are not many things which are unbegotten. For if there was difference between them, you could search and not find the difference, but after sending the intellect always to the infinite, you would become weary and take your stand on the one unbegotten, and say that this one is the cause of all things. Did such things escape the notice of Plato and Pythagoras, the wise men who became just like a wall and a bulwark to our philosophy?[71]

---

[65] *Dial.* 11.1 Οὔτε ἔσται ποτὲ ἄλλος θεός, ὦ Τρύφων, οὔτε ἦν ἀπ᾽ αἰῶνος, ἐγὼ οὕτως πρὸς αὐτόν, πλὴν τοῦ ποιήσαντος καὶ διατάξαντος τόδε τὸ πᾶν. οὐδὲ ἄλλον μὲν ὑμῶν, ἄλλον δὲ ὑμων ἡγούμεθα θεόν, ἀλλ᾽ αὐτὸν ἐκεῖνον τὸν ἐξαγαγόντα τοὺς πατέρας ὑμῶν ἐκ γῆς Αἰγύπτου ἐν χειρὶ κραταιᾷ καὶ βραχίονι ὑψηλῷ· οὐδ᾽ εἰς ἄλλον τινὰ ἠλπίκαμεν, οὐ γὰρ ἔστιν, ἀλλ᾽ εἰς τοῦτον εἰς ὅν καὶ ὑμεῖς, τὸν θεὸν τοῦ Ἀβραὰμ καὶ Ἰσαὰκ καὶ Ἰακώβ.

[66] *Dial.* 8.

[67] *Dial.* 3.

[68] *Dial.* 5.4 ὁ θεὸς καὶ διὰ τοῦτο θεός ἐστι, τὰ δὲ λοιπὰ πάντα μετὰ τοῦτον γεννητὰ καὶ φθαρτά.

[69] Plato, *Tim.* 52.

[70] E. F. Osborn, *Justin Martyr* (BHT Gerhard Ebeling; Tübingen: J. C. B. Mohr [Paul Siebeck], 1973) 21.

[71] *Dial.* 5.6 ὅθεν οὐδὲ πολλά ἐστι τὰ ἀγέννητα· εἰ γὰρ διαφορά τις ἦν ἐν αὐτοῖς, οὐκ

Here, Justin describes God as the First Cause[72] upon whom all else is dependent. The argument that God is the First Cause of all things had been stated in its simplest form by both Plato and Aristotle.[73] Justin takes this concept and appropriates it to his understanding of the Christian God.[74]

b. *Post-Conversion*

In piecing together Justin's post-conversion understanding of God it is necessary to proceed from his Middle Platonism. It is not difficult to maintain that a complete intellectual break from a previous world-view is practically impossible—regardless of whether the retention of certain ideas is intentional or unintentional. When Justin accepted Christianity as the true philosophy he did so from the position of one influenced by the Platonism of his day. It would therefore be understandable if certain Middle Platonic categories of thought manifested themselves in certain areas of Justin's thought. Most scholars have come to the conclusion that there was some retention of Platonic categories of thought following Justin's conversion.[75]

ἂν εὕροις ἀναζητῶν τὸ αἴτιον τῆς διαφορᾶς, ἀλλ᾿, ἐπ᾿ ἄπειρον ἀεὶ τὴν διάνοιαν πέμπων, ἐπὶ ἑνός ποτε στήσῃ ἀγεννήτου καμὼν καὶ τοῦτο φήσεις ἁπάντων αἴτιον. ἢ ταῦτα ἔλαθε, φημὶ ἐγώ, Πλάτωνα καὶ Πυθαγόραν, σοφοὺς ἄνδρας, οἳ ὥσπερ τεῖχος ἡμῖν καὶ ἔρεισμα φιλοσοφίας ἐξεγένοντο;

[72] While Justin does not necessarily employ the term "First Cause," the concept is definitely present. Note the text quoted in the passage above (*Dial.* 5.6) where Justin states that the "unbegotten" is the "cause (αἴτιος) of all things." See also *Dial.* 3.5, "That which always has the same manner and existence and is the cause (αἴτιος) of all other things—this indeed is God."

[73] Aristotle *Metaphysics* 1071–1075; Plato, *Laws* 893–896. Barnard (*Justin Martyr. His Life and Thought* [Cambridge: Cambridge University Press, 1967] 35) states, "Both Justin and Albinus combine Platonic and Aristotelian elements in their systems, which strongly suggests the eclecticism of Middle Platonism."

[74] For a more detailed discussion on the similarities and differences between Plato and Aristotle on this point see, G. Ryle, "Aristotle," in P. Edwards (ed.), *The Encyclopedia of Philosophy* (8 vols.; New York: The Macmillan Company and the Free Press, 1967) 1.151–162; R, Taylor, "Causation," in *The Encyclopedia of Philosophy*, 2.56–57; A. D. Woozley, "Universals," in *The Encyclopedia of Philosophy*, 8.194–198.

[75] Some of the more notable contributions include, C. Andresen, "Justin und der mittlere Platonismus," *ZNW* 44 (1952/53) 157–195; Barnard, *Justin Martyr*; A. J. Droge, "Justin Martyr and the Restoration of Philosophy," *CH* 56 (1987) 303–309; M. J. Edwards, "On the Platonic Schooling of Justin Martyr," *JTS* ns 42 (1991) 17–34; C. Nahm, "The Debate on the 'Platonism' of Justin Martyr," *SecCent* 9 (1992) 131; Osborn, *Justin Martyr*; C. I. K. Story, *The Nature of Truth in "The Gospel of Truth" and in the Writings of Justin Martyr* (NovTSup 25; Leiden: Brill, 1970); van Winden, *An Early Christian Philosopher*; D. F. Wright, "Christian Faith in the Greek World: Justin Martyr's Testimony," *EvQ* 54 (1982) 77–78; M. O. Young, "Justin, Socrates, and the Middle Platonists," *StudPat* 18 (1989) 161–189. For a discussion on the opinions concerning Justin's Platonism see above, Introduction I.A.

The Platonism of which this speaks, however, is not the Platonism of an earlier age, but that of Middle Platonism. The period of Middle Platonic philosophy was an eclectic blend found in those philosophers who wrote before the Neo-Platonic philosopher Plotinus, and exhibit an important debt to Plato.[76] F. Copleston calls the period to which Middle Platonism belongs the second major phase of Hellenistic-Roman Philosophy. During this time,

> Eclecticism on the one hand and skepticism on the other hand continue into the second period (from about the middle of the first century BC to the middle of the third century AD), but this period is characterized by a return to philosophical "orthodoxy." Great interest is taken in the founders of the Schools, their lives, works and doctrines, and this tendency to philosophical "orthodoxy" is a counterpart to the continuing eclecticism. But the interest in the past was also fruitful in scientific investigation, e.g. in editing the works of the old philosophers, commenting on them and interpreting them.[77]

The era of Middle Platonism was a time marked by a weakening in the original creative thought of Plato. The change can be seen in three distinct ways:[78] (1) it was an era of skepticism in the Academy; (2) it was an era of commentaries and introductions to both Plato and Aristotle which corroded the dogmatism and anti-conformity so essential to the Platonic and Aristotelian schools and gave way to the teaching of transmitted doctrine; and (3) it was an era of syncretism. These three changes combined in Justin's era to form what has come to be known as Middle Platonism.

The main beliefs of Middle Platonism included an insistence on Divine transcendence, a theory of intermediary beings, and a belief in mysticism.[79] The Middle Platonists devoted much time to studying the dialogues of Plato which resulted in a reverence for his person and actual words. Consequently, there arose a tendency to stress the differences between Platonism and other philosophies. Thus, the syncretism and the movement toward philosophical "orthodoxy" was in obvious conflict. The result of the conflict was that the movement did not represent the character of a unitary whole. In fact, different thinkers amalgamated various elements in different ways. Thus,

---

[76] M. J. Edwards, "Justin's Logos and the Word of God," *J Early Chr St* 3 (1995) 264.

[77] Copleston, *A History of Philosophy*, I/2.126.

[78] Story, *The Nature of Truth in "The Gospel of Truth" and in the Writings of Justin Martyr*, 61–62.

[79] Copleston, *A History of Philosophy*, 1/2.195.

Middle Platonism is accordingly *Middle* Platonism; that is to say, it bears the mark of a transition stage: it is only in Neo-Platonism that anything like a real synthesis and fusion of the various currents and tendencies can be found. Neo-Platonism is thus like the sea, to which the various contributing rivers are flowing in and their waters are at length mingled.[80]

Many scholars agree that the best example of Middle Platonism in Justin's day can be found in the second century philosopher Albinus.[81] Albinus distinguished the πρῶτος θεός, νοῦς, and ψυχή.[82] The πρῶτος θεός is unmoved (Aristotle) but is not mover. Since the πρῶτος θεός is unmoved but not mover, it operates through the Νοῦς or World-Intellect.[83] Between God and the Platonic Ideas are the star-gods and others, οἱ γεννητοὶ θεοί. In his fusion of Platonic and Aristotelian elements Albinus helped to prepare the way for Neo-Platonism.

Middle Platonism had a strong tendency towards theology which gave it a strong affinity with Christianity in the second century.[84] Whereas Plato's central metaphysical theme was the doctrine of Ideas,[85] for Middle Platonists, like Plutarch, it was God.[86] Albinus shows that Middle Platonists identified the Demiurge of *Timaeus* with

---

[80] Copleston, *A History of Philosophy*, 1/2.196. See also, Norris, *God and World in Early Christian Theology*, 8.

[81] Andresen, "Justin und der mittlere Platonismus"; Barnard, *Justin Martyr*, 29–30; E. R. Goodenough, *The Theology of Justin Martyr. An Investigation Into the Conceptions of Early Christian Literature and Its Hellenistic and Judaistic Influences* (Amsterdam: Philo Press, 1968) 21–32; Norris, *God and World in Early Christian Theology*, 27–28; R. E. Witt, *Albinus and the History of Middle Platonism* (Cambridge: Cambridge University Press, 1937) 144.

[82] The following description of Albinus' Middle Platonism is dependent on Copleston, *A History of Philosophy*, 1/2.199–200.

[83] G. B. Kerford ("Logos," in *The Encyclopedia of Philosophy*, 5.83–84) explains that νοῦς and λόγος both have a similar background understanding in philosophy as the rational governing principle of the universe. The *logos* doctrine of Heraclitus combines three ideas: our human thought about the universe, the rational structure of the universe itself, and the source of that rational structure. To Heraclitus, the *logos* as source of rationality in the universe was an immanent principle, neither conscious nor intelligent. Anexagoras took this same type of principle and called it *nous* and not *logos*. The identification of *logos* and *nous* was perhaps first made in the pseudo-Platonic *Epinomis* 986c4, although Plato had treated the two terms as meaning very nearly the same thing in his account of the human soul in the *Republic*. See also, Origen of Alexandria, "Dialogue with Heraclides," in H. Chadwick and J. E. L. Oulten (eds.), *Alexandrian Christianity* (2 vols.; Library of Christian Classics; London: SCM, 1954) 2.430–455.

[84] G. May, *Creatio Ex Nihilo: The Doctrine of 'Creation out of Nothing' in Early Christian Thought* (ET J. S. Worall; Edinburgh: T. & T. Clark, 1994) 3.

[85] Plato, *Phaedr.* 247E; *Tim.* 27D; 28A.

[86] Plutarch, *de E. ap Delph.* 19, 20.

the Supreme God, who is thought of as *Nous* and the sum of Ideas.[87]

When the Platonism of Justin is discussed, therefore, it must rest on the understanding that it is not the earlier "orthodox" Platonism, but rather the Middle Platonism of the second century CE. It is quite clear that, even in the *Dialogue*, Justin still displays some affinity to this philosophy, but not to the extent that it dilutes the Christian message. This can be seen in Justin's description and understanding of God.

Justin appropriates to Christianity the Middle Platonic concept of God as the First Cause or Unmoved Mover in two ways in the *Dialogue*. First, in his descriptions of God it can be seen that Justin has retained, and even expanded on these concepts. Because God is unbegotten there has never been, nor will there ever be any other God except the one who created and formed the universe.[88] He asserts that God is immutable, benevolent, prescient, needful of nothing, just, and good.[89] These are all concepts which inherently speak not only of God's supremacy as First Cause, but they also speak of God's character as good and just.

The second way in which Justin uses the concept of an unbegotten God as First Cause or Unmoved Mover is in stating that because of this everything exists or occurs according to his will or purposes. In this respect, God is said to have foreknowledge of future events and that he prepares beforehand what individuals deserve.[90] For example, in explaining the incarnation of the *Logos* and the creation of Adam and Eve, Justin states that God foretold these events would occur and that they happened according to his purpose. Thus, if God wills it, nothing is impossible for him.[91] More specifically, the place of Jesus in God's plan and will is of importance to Justin. In explaining the meaning of Ps 22 to Trypho Justin asserts that "the Father decreed that the one whom he had begotten should be put to death, but only after he had grown into manhood and proclaimed the word which went out from him."[92] In fact, throughout chaps. 97–107 Justin demonstrates from Ps 22 that the life, death and resurrection of Jesus was according to the will and plan of God. And

---

[87] Albinus, *Didask.* 10.
[88] *Dial.* 11.1; 34.8; 116.3.
[89] *Dial.* 23.2.
[90] *Dial.* 16.3.
[91] *Dial.* 84.
[92] *Dial.* 102.2. μετὰ γὰρ τὸ κηρύξαι αὐτὸν τὸν παρ᾽ αὐτοῦ λόγον ἀνδρωθέντα ὁ πατὴρ θανατωθήσεσθαι αὐτὸν ἐκεκρίκει ὃν ἐγεγεννήκει.

this, in turn, is ultimately in accordance with the divine plan of redemption for humankind.[93]

Justin's understanding of God is that he, as the Supreme Being, is in control and that all things work according to his will and purpose. In Justin's mind, therefore, revelation of his character and plan flow from this God. It is in this understanding of God that the epistemological question becomes relevant to Justin's understanding of revelation. In philosophy, epistemology is concerned with the nature and source of knowledge. It asks, "How do we know what we know?" In a very real sense this is Justin's concern in the *Dialogue with Trypho*.

It was also from Plato that Justin retained the idea that God is the Maker and Father of all,[94] a concept manifestly biblical as well (Gen 1). In fact, Justin's most frequent description of God is as Father and Maker of all things—terms which link fatherhood with creation.[95] Even though Justin usually couples these terms with a biblical quotation, they are most likely ultimately derived from Plato. In the *Republic* (506E) he speaks of the Form of the Good as "Father," and in the *Timaeus* (28C) he describes the creator as "the Maker and Father of this Universe."[96] The creator of the world is its Maker and its Father. After Plato the concept of divine fatherhood can be traced through Middle Platonism. Thus, Justin makes use of it because it is common in his day.

Another example of the appropriation of Middle Platonic concepts in Justin's theology can be seen in his understanding of God being unbegotten—that God has neither beginning nor end.[97] In Justin's appropriation of this philosophical concept, however, it is clear that he has used it to strengthen the Christian understanding of God.[98]

2. *Trypho's Judaism*

The type of Judaism represented by Trypho has been debated for many years. Basically, two opposing schools of thought have been offered.[99] One school of thought presents Trypho's interpretations of

---

[93] *Dial.* 103; 120.1.
[94] See Osborn, *Justin Martyr*, 17–20; Plato, *Tim.* 33D.
[95] *Dial.* 7.3; 56.1; 60.2, 3; 117.5.
[96] ποιητὴν καὶ πατέρα τοῦδε τοῦ παντός. See also Plato, *Tim.* 50–51.
[97] Osborn, *Justin Martyr*, 20–27.
[98] *Dial.* 5.4; 5.6; 6.2; 114.3.
[99] This debate is succinctly summarized by E. R. Goodenough, *Jewish Symbols in the Graeco-Roman Period Vol. 1: The Archeological Evidence From Palestine* (New York:

the Bible and the Law as closely resembling those of the rabbinic tradition and being completely dependent on his teachers.[100] The second school of thought views Trypho as a fully Hellenized Jew and minimizes the rabbinic elements stressed by the former school. M. Freimann is representative of this view. Freimann believed that Trypho was a part of Hellenized Judaism of the diaspora which long had little contact with rabbinism.[101] It was the Judaism of the diaspora which was the foundation of the spread of Christianity because the rabbis gradually withdrew from relations with the world. But by no means did all of these Jews become Christians. Concerning Freimann's understanding of this Judaism Goodenough comments,

> Many of them had a deep commitment to the Jewish group, and even though they had a philosophic training like Philo, they wanted as far as possible to observe the ceremonial law dear to their ancestors, and could have no use whatever for a gospel which preached the end of the Law and a crucified Messiah. It was these Jews who became the chief opponents of Christianity in the Roman world, and they attacked Christianity on broad hellenistic grounds rather than on a narrow Pharisaic level.[102]

Goodenough states that he has much sympathy with this view but that it suffers from putting too wide of a cleft between "hellenistic" and "rabbinic" Judaism. Therefore, these are not two sharply defined categories into which all Jews should fit. Justin simply tried to reproduce the attitude and arguments of the Jews he knew and this is why the evidence must be taken from the *Dialogue* itself to ascertain the type of Judaism to which Trypho adhered.

If this direction is pursued one can deduce from the *Dialogue* that Trypho was a Jew who fled from the war in Palestine,[103] and now resided in Corinth.[104] He obviously had philosophic training, for upon his chance meeting with Justin he started the conversation because

---

Pantheon, 1953) 42–44. See also Goodenough, *The Theology of Justin Martyr*, 33–56 where these two opposing schools of thought are identified as Judaism proper and Hellenistic Judaism, or Palestinian Judaism and Alexandrian Judaism.

[100] See e.g., A. H. Goldfahn, "Justinus Martyr und die Agada," *MGWJ* 22 (1873) 49–60, 104–115, 145–153, 193–202, 257–269; A. Harnack, "Judentum und Judenchristentum in Justins Dialog mit Trypho," *TU* 39, I.47–92.

[101] M. Freimann, "Die Wortführer des Judentums in den ältesten Kontroversen zwischen Juden und Christen," *MGWJ* 55 (1893) 555–585.

[102] Goodenough, *Jewish Symbols in the Graeco-Roman Period*, 44.

[103] *Dial.* 1.3; 9.3; 16.2; 18.3. In all probability, the war referred to is Bar Kochba, 132–135 CE.

[104] *Dial.* 1.3.

he was taught in Argos by Corinthus the Socratic to converse with
anyone wearing the philosopher's cloak, like Justin.[105] Thus, from the
first chapter of the *Dialogue* we know not only that Trypho was a Jew,
but one with philosophic training, in other words, he was a Hellenistic
Jew. But even in light of the probability that Trypho is a Hellenistic
Jew, Justin's arguments are constantly made with reference to the
Jewish scriptures, a fact which Trypho recognizes and appreciates.[106]

Trypho is often presented as one who is not an independent
thinker, dependent entirely upon his teachers for his understanding
of Judaism. To a certain degree this is correct, for in many instances
Trypho expresses what he believes to be the collective Jewish doctrine on a matter.[107] But to state, as some do,[108] that Trypho was
entirely dependent upon his teachers may be overstating the case.
In fact, there is evidence to the contrary. At one point in the *Dialogue*
Trypho and his companions express a dissatisfaction with the Jewish
interpretation of a scriptural passage.[109] He also states that he has
read the Gospels[110] and in the very act of conversing with Justin has
disobeyed his teachers.[111] Further, even though Trypho often clearly
disagrees with Justin, he is not afraid to show his agreement on some
matters.[112] This assent on Trypho's part is most likely due to his
concern for being informed,[113] a concern that appears to fly in the
face of his teachers.[114]

Trypho's Judaism has been expressed by some scholars as un-
classifiable and difficult to define.[115] But these sharply defined cat-

---

[105] *Dial.* 1.2.

[106] *Dial.* 56.16; 80.1.

[107] See e.g., passages where Trypho makes reference to his beliefs as those of a
group ("we"; "we Jews"; "our belief"; "we doubt"), *Dial.* 46; 49; 56; 64; 79; 89;
90; 94; 142.

[108] See e.g., J. Nilson, "To Whom is Justin's *Dialogue with Trypho* Addressed?" *TS*
38 (1977) 541.

[109] *Dial.* 94.4.

[110] *Dial.* 10.2.

[111] *Dial.* 38.1.

[112] See e.g., *Dial.* 36; 39; 49; 57; 60; 63; 65; 67; 77; 89; 123; 130.

[113] *Dial.* 87.1. "Do not now suppose that I am endeavoring, by asking what I do
ask, to overturn the statements you have made; but I wish to receive information
respecting those very points about which I now inquire." Μή με λοιπὸν ὑπολάμβανε,
ἀνατρέπειν πειρώμενον τὰ ὑπὸ σοῦ λεγόμενα, πυνθάνεσθαι ὅσα ἂν πυνθάνωμαι, ἀλλὰ
βούλεσθαι μανθάνειν περὶ τούτων αὐτῶν ὧν ἂν ἐρωτῶ.

[114] See also *Dial.* 9.2 where Trypho is unwilling to participate in the rude behavior
of his companions. Rather, than laughing and shouting rudely at Justin Trypho
appeals to Justin to remain and continue the conversation on the controversial issues.

[115] See e.g. L. W. Barnard, *Justin Martyr*, 398; D. Trakatellis, "Justin Martyr's
Trypho," *HTR* 79 (1986) 289–297.

egories of Hellenistic and Rabbinic Judaism are perhaps too sharply delineated. The mixture of philosophy, metaphysical and mystical allegory along with bits of halakoth that were accepted or created by the rabbis is perhaps exactly what we should expect Hellenized Judaism to have been. It is quite probable that Trypho is valuable in that he shows that no single "norm" or "orthodoxy" dominated Judaism in the diaspora. The goal of historians to set up one single point of view for all Hellenized Judaism serves only to violate the complexities of the data. Perhaps the chief value of Justin's Trypho is that we get a complex picture of the Judaism that he represented. Trypho is thus quite typical of diaspora Judaism not because of the specific points of Hellenism or legalism that he represents, but rather, because his Judaism is a mixture of Hellenistic and halachic traditions.[116]

3. *Apophatic Theology*

As we now return to our original question of a common starting point between Trypho's Jewish conception of God and Justin's Christian conception of God we find that there are, in fact, commonalities between the two. In fact, "the contacts between Judaeo-Christian thought and Hellenistic philosophy were much closer than had been supposed."[117] These commonalities converge in what has been called apophatic theology. When dealing with the concept of God in the second century the central issue is God's transcendence and the language used to express it.

In his περὶ μυστικῆς θεολογίας (*The Mystical Theology*),[118] Pseudo-Dionysius indicates two methods of speaking about God.[119] He made

---

[116] Goodenough, *Jewish Symbols in the Graeco-Roman Period*, 42–53. See also R. M. Price, " 'Hellenization' and Logos Doctrine in Justin Martyr," *VC* 42 (1988) 18–19.

[117] J. Daniélou, *Gospel Message and Hellenistic Culture*, 323.

[118] *The Mystical Theology* in C. Luibheid (ed.), *Pseudo-Dionysius: The Complete Works* (Classics of Western Spirituality; New York: Paulist Press, 1987) 133–141.

[119] The history of Pseudo-Dionysius, or Dionysius the Pseudo-Areopagite, (c. 500) is a fascinating one. This is the name given to the author of a corpus of theological writings (*Corpus Areopagiticum*) to which the Monophysites appealed at an assembly in the year 532. It seems as though the Monophysites believed the writings to be from Dionysius the Areopagite who was converted by Paul as recorded in Acts 17:34. Through the efforts of many scholars, the works of the *Corpus* have conclusively been found not to be of the first century. On this see, H. Koch, "Der pseudoepigraphische Character der dionysischen Schriften," *Theologische Quartalschrift* 77 (1895) 353–421; J. Stiglmayr, "Der Neuplatoniker Proclus als Vorlage des sog. Dionysius Areopagita in der Lehre vom Übel," *Historisches Jahrbuch* 16 (1895) 253–273. For more on Pseudo-Dionysius see, R. F. Hathaway, *Hierarchy and Definition of Order in the Letters of Pseudo-Dionysius* (The Hague, 1969); A Louth, *Denys the Areopagite* (Outstanding Christian Thinkers Series; London: Geoffrey Chapman, 1981).

a distinction between what he called κατάφασις and ἀπόφασις.[120] At its most basic level, the *kataphatic* (or affirmative) approach believes that we can attain some knowledge of God, even though it may be limited, by attributing the created order to him as source. *Apophatic* (or negative) affirms God's absolute transcendence and unknowability to such an extent that no affirmative concepts may be applied to him. Both ways take creation as their starting point, yet end up at either end of a pole. *Kataphatic* asserts that since God is creator, he can be known through his creation. *Apophatic*, on the other end of the pole, asserts that God is beyond creation, that he cannot be known in any way through it.

Daniélou has shown that Hellenistic Judaism and Middle Platonism of the second century both exhibit a sudden and simultaneous emergence of negative phrases (*apophatic*) for describing God.[121] Thus, theology is defined by terms applied to the divine that emphasize his "otherness" such as God being timeless, invisible, impassible etc. The importance of Daniélou's study for our purposes lies in his detailed comparison of God's transcendence in Hellenistic Judaism and Middle Platonism, thus corresponding to both Trypho's understanding and Justin's understanding of God. In the following, it will be clearly seen that there is tremendous overlap in both concepts of God. For it is in "the development of the theology of God's transcendence, that the influence of Hellenistic Judaism is . . . at its most pronounced."[122]

There were three contexts in which the vocabulary of negative theology was elaborated which all have links to Hellenistic Judaism.[123] The first of these three contexts was the polemic against idolatry.[124]

---

[120] "What has actually to be said about the Cause of everything is this. Since it is the Cause of all beings, we should posit and ascribe to it all the affirmations we make in regards to human beings, and, more appropriately, we should negate all these affirmations, since it surpasses all being. Now we should not conclude that the negations are simply the opposites of the affirmations, but rather that the cause of all is considerably prior to this, beyond privations, beyond every denial, beyond every assertion" (*Myst.* 1000B). See also, D. Carabine, *The Unkown God. Negative Theology in the Platonic Tradition: Plato to Eriugena* (Louvain Theological & Pastoral Monographs 19; Louvain: Peeters Press/Grand Rapids: Eerdmans) 2–7.

[121] Daniélou, *Gospel Message and Hellenistic Culture*, 323–333. See also, D. W. Palmer, "Atheism, Apologetic, and Negative Theology in the Greek Apologists of the Second Century," *VC* 37 (1983) 234–259.

[122] Daniélou, *Gospel Message and Hellenistic Culture*, 324.

[123] Daniélou, *Gospel Message and Hellenistic Culture*, 324.

[124] Daniélou, *Gospel Message and Hellenistic Culture*, 324–326.

Within Hellenistic Judaism there was a large amount of this type of literature. This also constitutes the setting of the work of the second century Apologists, who, in this respect are dependent upon Hellenistic Judaism. In this polemic both the Jewish and the Christian writers were seeking to establish opposition to things like idolatry, mythology, astrology, and demonology by asserting the spiritual, unique, and uncreated nature of God.[125]

The second context of this negative theology was Philo.[126] Daniélou calls Philo "the first theologian to treat fully the divine transcendence."[127] As time progressed, the need to demonstrate that God was spirit, in opposition to paganism, was not enough. It soon became necessary to prove God's transcendence in order to combat philosophic rationalism. Philo made a monumental contribution to the creation of a vocabulary for use in negative statements about God. He did this either by adapting to the subject of God terms originally used for other purposes, or by inventing new ones. Philo used three categories to describe God apophatically. First, for Philo, God is "the one who cannot be circumscribed" (ἀπερίγραφος).[128] Second, Philo uses terms which assert that God transcends any name given to him (ἀνωνόμαστος, ἀκατονόμαστος).[129] Third is the term which Philo did the most to enhance, ἀκατάληπτος.[130]

The final context in which the vocabulary of apophatic was elaborated relates to certain epithets which stress the unapproachableness of God.[131] These terms originate from Palestinian apocalyptic. Also in this category may be included certain Paulinisms.[132]

We can see, therefore, that negative theology in the second century arose from the influence of Hellenistic Judaism. This means that both Justin and Trypho would have used and understood this type of vocabulary. Similarly, there are other terms that derive from

---

[125] Daniélou goes on to cite some examples of the kind of language used by these writers in this context, pp. 324–326.

[126] Daniélou, *Gospel Message and Hellenistic Culture*, 326–327.

[127] Daniélou, *Gospel Message and Hellenistic Culture*, 326.

[128] *De Sacrif.* 59; 124.

[129] *De somn.* I, 67.

[130] *De somn.* I, 67; *De mut. nom.* 10; *De post. Caini* 169.

[131] Daniélou, *Gospel Message and Hellenistic Culture*, 327–328.

[132] E.g., ἀνεξιχνίαστος, "untraceable" (Rom 11:33; Eph 3:8); ἀνεξερεύνητος, "inscrutable" (Rom 11:33); ἀπρόσιτος, "unapproachable" (1 Tim 6:18). Daniélou continues on to cite examples of the terms used in second century writers.

Middle Platonism. Certainly the development of apophatic in Middle
Platonism owed a great deal to the Jewish sense of God's transcendence.
But nonetheless, this Middle Platonism influences the Apologists also,
and has left discernible traces in their vocabulary as well.[133]

Justin sees no conflict in this description of God in comparison
with what he believed Trypho's understanding of God to be, influenced
as it was by Hellenistic Judaism. The essential point in both understandings is that God is sovereign in carrying out his will and his
purposes. Daniélou has shown that many of the terms used in the
apophatic theology of the second century were understood in the
same manner by both Hellenistic Jews and by Christian Middle
Platonists such as Justin.[134] It is quite reasonable, therefore, for Justin
to compare his understanding of God with the Trypho's understanding of God.

In light of Daniélou's informative study the question posed earlier
becomes somewhat clearer. The question concerned the accuracy of
Justin's statement of whether the doctrine of God in Christianity and
Judaism is the same. When taken in the context of Trypho's Hellenistic
Judaism and Justin's Middle Platonism, it appears that Justin is making an accurate statement. Both Trypho's and Justin's understanding of the nature of God is comparable.[135]

B. *Knowledge of God and Revelation*

If we now relate Justin's concept of God with the conversation
between the old man and Justin, we can see that because of it the

---

[133] Daniélou, *Gospel Message and Hellenistic Culture*, 329–333.
[134] Daniélou, *Gospel Message and Hellenistic Culture*, 322–333.
[135] Carabine (*The Unknown God*, 6–7) stresses the fact that both *kataphatic* and
apophatic theology belong together since they are two aspects of the one divine truth
of revealed religion: God is both hidden and present, known and unknown, tran-
scendent and immanent. "Any failure to take both aspects of this simultaneous truth
into account in a discussion of the divine nature could result in a distorted view"
(p. 6). G. L. Prestige (*God in Patristic Thought* [London: SPCK, 1956] 4) emphasizes
the fact that negative forms are enriched with a wealth of positive association. Thus,
"when it is asserted that God is free from various limitations and controls, the effect
is to assert his entire freedom to be Himself and act according to His own nature
and will." This fits well with Justin's negative theology. His *apophatic* is balanced
well by his *kataphatic*. As will be seen below, his negative theology proceeds into
positive theology because of the incarnation of the Logos, which, in turn, has tremendous importance in his understanding of revelation. This will be evident as the
chapter progresses.

old man can enter into the epistemological question with relative ease. Justin's definition of philosophy is that it was knowledge of that which is.[136] But in Justin's concept of God existence was dependent on a personal God as the First Cause, the Unmoved Mover, or as the Unbegotten and Incorruptible. Everything which exists does so because of him and through his will. Existence was dependent on the sovereign God. Therefore, in defining philosophy as knowledge of that which exists, Justin was postulating a definition which had the knowledge of God at the very center. Granted, his concept of God had changed from Middle Platonic to Christian, but this does not negate the fact that, as a philosopher, he felt it was his task to seek knowledge of God. This is what he was concerned with before he was a Christian in his philosophical travels, and this is also what he was concerned with in his acceptance of Christianity as the true philosophy. In actuality, Justin was defining philosophy as knowledge of God.

In defining philosophy as knowledge of God (or a search for knowledge of God) Justin has given a strong indicator concerning his view of revelation.[137] When Justin recounts his discussion with the old man to Trypho he does so in order to show Trypho where he attains knowledge about God, which is the goal of his philosophy. The remainder of the *Dialogue* consists of Justin's explaining this knowledge of God, his concept of truth. How this knowledge of God is attained, therefore, is revelation. This will be made clear in the following sections concerning the witnesses to revelation which Justin presents. The following sections will therefore answer the question: How and where does God reveal knowledge about himself and his plans or will?

---

[136] *Dial.* 3. For a fuller treatment of Justin's understanding of philosophy see Chapter 3.IV.A–C.

[137] As will be explained below in this chapter, Justin's concept of revelation is connected with epistemology—the nature and source of knowledge about God. This knowledge cannot be attained through philosophy. The sources of this knowledge are the Prophets and the memoirs of the Apostles. The Prophets are witnesses to revelation because they saw and heard God, thus qualifying them to communicate knowledge about God and the incarnation of the Logos. The memoirs of the Apostles are witnesses to revelation for two reasons: First, they bear witness to that which the Prophets foretold and; Second, they saw and heard the ultimate revelation of God—the incarnate Logos. The Apostles witnessed that which the Prophets foretold.

IV. *Witnesses to Revelation*

A. *The Prophets*

In light of the relationship between revelation and epistemology the
old man expands on his initial request for Justin to define philosophy. He asks, "How do you define God?"[138] This question is entirely
legitimate for he understood that, as a Middle Platonist, Justin was
concerned with knowledge of God. God was the First Cause of creation, therefore he was also the First Cause of knowledge about himself. The old man's position is that only those who have seen God
or heard from someone who has seen God can know him.[139] Because
the philosophers have done neither they do not qualify. Justin's
response is to defer to agreement with Plato who states that God
cannot be perceived in the same way as other things. He is to be
perceived with the mind alone.[140]

Justin proceeds to give a Middle Platonic understanding of how
God is known.[141] The mind is thus given a special power to see the
very being who is the cause of everything (God). This power is given
to souls who are well disposed because of their affinity to and desire
of seeing him. This is clearly in the tradition of the above mentioned representative of Middle Platonic philosophy, Albinus. In his
Didaskalikos, Albinus states that God,

> . . . is ineffable and apprehensible by the mind alone, as has been said,
> because He is neither genus nor species nor specific difference. We
> cannot predicate of Him evil (for it is unholy to utter such a thing)
> or good (for in this case He would have to participate in something
> else, namely goodness). Nor does He experience anything indifferent
> (for this is not in harmony of our notion of Him). We cannot predi-
> cate of God qualities since His perfection is not the result of having
> received qualities, nor can we say He lacks qualities since He has not
> been deprived of any quality the befits Him. God is neither a part of
> something else nor a whole having parts; He is not the same as any-
> thing nor different from anything, for nothing can be predicated of
> Him which would separate Him from other things. He does not move
> nor is He moved.[142]

---

[138] *Dial.* 3.5 Θεὸν δὲ σὺ τί καλεῖς;

[139] *Dial.* 3.5–7.

[140] *Dial.* 3.7.

[141] *Dial.* 4.1. See above, Chapter 2.II.B. See also Norris, *God and World in Early
Christian Theology*, 13–32; Van Winden, *An Early Christian Philosopher*, 69–118.

[142] Albinus, *Didask.* 10.3. ET in J. P. Hershbell (ed.) *The Platonic Doctrines of Albinus*

The old man refutes this idea and concludes that the philosophers who propound such a doctrine know nothing.[143]

In refuting the ideas of these philosophers the old man refuted Justin's way of acquiring knowledge about God. Justin realizes this and asks, "What teacher should one avail oneself to, or where can one be aided if these ones [the philosophers] do not know what the truth is?"[144] The truth which Justin inquires about is the knowledge of God. The old man's reply is worth reproducing at length.

> There were some men who existed long before the time of all those reputed philosophers, men who are ancient, blessed, just, and loved by God, speaking by the spirit of God and prophesying things which were about to take place which, indeed, are now taking place. We call these men Prophets. They alone both saw and announced the truth to men, neither fearing nor reverencing anyone, and not overcome with a desire for glory. But they alone, being filled with the holy spirit, communicated that which they heard and saw. Their writings are still now unchanged, and the one reading them is greatly aided concerning the beginning and end of all things, and that which the philosopher needs to know, believing these things. For they did not give proof at that time of their words, for they were above all proof, being higher witnesses to the truth. And these things which have happened and are now happening force you to agree with what they are saying. Indeed, because of the powers which they displayed they are worthy of belief, since they glorified God, the creator and father of all, and also announced the Christ, his son.[145]

(ET J. Reedy; Grand Rapids: Phanes Press, 1991). The Greek text of this work can be found in *Enseignement des doctrines de Platon/Alcinoos; introduction, texte établi et commenté par John Whittaker ettraduit par Pierre Louis* (Paris: Belles lettres, 1990).

[143] *Dial.* 4–6.

[144] *Dial.* 7.1 Τίνι οὖν. φημί, ἔτι τις χρήσαιτο διδασκάλῳ ἤ πόθεν ὠφεληθείη τις εἰ μηδὲ ἐν τούτοις τὸ ἀληθές ἐστιν;

[145] *Dial.* 7.1–3 Ἐγένοντό τινες πρὸ πολλοῦ χρόνου πάντων τούτων τῶν νομιζομένων φιλοσόφων παλαιότεροι, μακάριοι καὶ δίκαιοι καὶ θεοφιλεῖς, θείῳ πνεύματι λαλήσαντες καὶ τὰ μέλλοντα θεσπίσαντες, ἃ δὴ νῦν γίνεται· προφήτας δὲ αὐτοὺς καλοῦσιν. οὗτοι μόνοι τὸ ἀληθὲς καὶ εἶδον καὶ ἐξεῖπον ἀνθρώποις, μήτ᾽ εὐλαβηθέντες μήτε δυσωπηθέντες τινά, μὴ ἡττημένοι δόξης, ἀλλὰ μόνα ταῦτα εἰπόντες ἃ ἤκουσαν καὶ ἃ εἶδον ἁγίῳ πληρωθέντες πνεύματι. συγγράμματα δὲ αὐτῶν ἔτι καὶ νῦν διαμένει, καὶ ἔστιν ἐντυχόντα τούτοις πλεῖστον ὠφεληθῆναι καὶ περὶ ἀρχῶν καὶ περὶ τέλους καὶ ὧν χρὴ εἰδέναι τὸν φιλόσοφον, πιστεύσαντα ἐκείνοις. οὐ γὰρ μετὰ ἀποδείξεως πεποίηνται τότε τοὺς λόγους, ἅτε ἀνωτέρω πάσης ἀποδείξεως ὄντες ἀξιόπιστοι μάρτυρες τῆς ἀληθείας· τὰ δὲ ἀποβάντα καὶ ἀποβαίνοντα ἐξαναγκάζει συντίθεσθαι τοῖς λελαλημένοις δι᾽ αὐτῶν. καίτοι γε καὶ διὰ τὰς δυνάμεις, ἃς ἐπετέλουν, πιστεύεσθαι δίκαιοι ἦσαν, ἐπειδὴ καὶ τὸν ποιητὴν τῶν ὅλων θεὸν καὶ πατέρα ἐδόξαζον καὶ τὸν παρ᾽ αὐτοῦ Χριστὸν υἱὸν αὐτοῦ κατήγγελλον

Within the context of epistemology several things merit attention in
this quotation. First, the Prophets existed "long before" all the philosophers. Second, they predicted things that would take place in the
future, these things were consequently taking place in Justin's era
through the Son. Third, the filling (πληρόω) of the Holy Spirit was
key in what they saw and heard. It was through this filling that the
Prophets were able to see and hear the truth about God.[146] Fourth,
the truth about God that the Prophets saw and heard through the
filling of the Holy Spirit was communicated to men. And fifth, the
communication of the Prophets is still extant. These are the reasons
that the Prophets know God. They are in the position to communicate this to others because they fulfil the old man's requirements.

    In the above quotation the issue of epistemology has come full
circle. Knowledge about God and his truth cannot be known through
the mind alone. If we recall Justin's concept of deity this becomes
much clearer. God, being outside of our existence and wholly other
cannot be known through the usual means (the mind alone). He
must be known through someone who has had access to him. The
philosophers do not know God but the Prophets do because they
had this special access through the filling of the Holy Spirit. The
Prophets look forward to the *Logos* incarnate. It was this philosophy
that gripped Justin. *Dialogue* 8 shows that Justin accepted the old
man's arguments concerning the truth and knowledge of God being
apprehendable through the Prophets. The knowledge contained therein
was a knowledge that regarded the salvation of souls and a knowledge of the Christ of God.[147] It is this knowledge that leads one to
enjoy a happy life.[148]

---

[146] It appears here that Justin is speaking of prophetic inspiration, i.e., a state of
ecstasy. Justin does explicitly state that the prophets Daniel and Zechariah were in
a state of ecstasy when they received their prophecies (*Dial.* 31.7; 115.3). In this
light it is probable that he viewed other Prophets as receiving their prophecies in the
same manner. See R. M. Grant, *The Letter and the Spirit* (London: S.P.C.K., 1957) 75–78.

[147] Justin's concept of Salvation is discussed below, Chapter 2.VI.

[148] *Dial.* 8.2. Philosophical discussion of the concept of "happiness" is associated
primarily with the names Jeremy Bentham and John Stuart Mill. Mill attempted
to combine two traditions of thought about happiness—the identification of happiness and pleasure, what we may call "hedonism." This can be contrasted with what
has been called the "eudaimonistic" conception of happiness. The word comes from
the Greek *eudaimonia*, literally "having a good guardian spirit," i.e., the state of having an objectively desirable life which was universally agreed by ancient philosophical theory and popular culture to be the supreme human good. Thus, the
term *eudaimonia* refers not so much to a psychological state as to the objective char-

Justin's acceptance of the old man's argument changed the way he acquired knowledge. Because the philosophers had no knowledge of God, Justin turned to those who witnessed and predicted his coming in the *Logos*, the Prophets. The knowledge that the Prophets communicated was true and reliable because "they alone, being filled with the Holy Spirit, communicated that which they heard and saw."[149] The knowledge which the Prophets communicated is said to be written down and still available for study.[150] And it is this communication from the Prophets upon which Justin places a great deal of weight for the acquisition of knowledge about God and his plan of salvation.

There is little doubt that Justin believed the writings of the Prophets to be a primary place from which to obtain knowledge about God. The culmination of the old man's argument above was not simply that the Prophets were qualified to provide knowledge about God, but also that we have access to this knowledge in written form. The old man tells Justin that their writings (συγγράμματα) are still extant and can be read (ἐντυχόντα).[151] It is these writings to which Justin continuously refers. After his encounter with the old man Justin accepted the argument concerning the writings of the Prophets because Justin believed these to be a place to attain knowledge of God.

The entire focus of the *Dialogue* confirms that Justin has indeed understood the writings of the Prophets to contain knowledge about God because they witness to the coming of the *Logos*. In *Dial.* 8 Trypho explains to Justin that he does not think that Jesus is the long awaited Jewish messiah. He believes that Christians have simply believed a foolish rumor and have invented a messiah whom they blindly worship. Justin's answer in *Dial.* 9 is that the Jews have been instructed by teachers who are ignorant of the meaning of scriptures. This is significant in setting the playing ground on which

---

acter of a person's life. The classic account of *eudaimonia* is found in Aristotle who emphasizes that it has to do with the quality of one's life as a whole. Happiness is to be identified above all with the fulfillment of one's human potentialities which are located in the exercise of reason. See Aristotle, *The Nicomachean Ethics*, Book I and X; R. J. Norman, "Happiness,' in T. Honderich (ed.), *The Oxford Companion to Philosophy* (Oxford/New York: Oxford University Press, 1995) 332–333; C. C. W. Taylor, "*eudaimonia*," in *The Oxford Companion to Philosophy*, 252.

[149] *Dial.* 7.1 ἀλλὰ μόνα ταῦτα εἰπόντες ἃ ἤκουσαν καὶ ἃ εἶδον ἁγίῳ πληρωθέντες πνεύματι.

[150] *Dial.* 7.2.

[151] *Dial.* 7.2.

the following discussion will ensue, the interpretation of the scriptures and the importance of the Law.

Justin included the account of his conversion with the old man to
show that the Prophets are integral in a proper understanding of
God and his plan for salvation. This belief is made manifest through
his constant use of and reference to OT scripture as the basis of his
claims. So, following his claim that the Jewish teachers are ignorant
of the true meaning of scripture he proceeds to support his arguments by using scripture.[152] Thus, immediately in *Dial.* 11 Justin
introduces the discussion concerning the obsolescence of the old Law
and the superiority of the new Law with words from the Prophets
Isaiah and Jeremiah. This method of argument is typical throughout the *Dialogue*.[153] In so doing Justin makes clear the importance of
the Prophets for the knowledge of God. "Their [the Prophets] writings are still now unchanged, and the one reading them is greatly
aided concerning the beginning and end of all things, and that which
the philosopher needs to know, believing these things."[154] The things
which the philosopher needs to know center around God. Thus,
Justin is stating that things about God can be known through studying the Prophets and their witness to the *Logos*. In his presentation
of truth to Trypho Justin thus attempts to convince him that he
must disregard the teachings of the rabbis and apply himself to the
study of the Prophets, for they possess a special knowledge.[155]

The knowledge that the Prophets possessed was, in Justin's view,
knowledge that is accessible to all because it was written down, communicated to humanity. But the knowledge that is now accessible
was not always so. Because of this Justin often couches statements
in terms of making something that was previously hidden or misunderstood more clear. For example, he explains that the mysterious meaning of the rites of the external Law were "revealed" or
"displayed" (ἐπιδείκνυμι) through the Prophets.[156] Ostensibly, the rite

---

[152] While it is Justin's particular interpretation that is important for his understanding of the OT scriptures as Christian, the point still stands that he attempts
to use the OT as the basis for his presentation. The specific issues of interpretation will be discussed below in Chapter 5.

[153] Instances of this method of argument are so numerous that only a few will
be listed as exemplary. See e.g., *Dial.* 14; 16; 22; 28; 34; 43; 58; 80.

[154] *Dial.* 7.2 συγγράμματα δὲ αὐτῶν ἔτι καὶ νῦν διαμένει, καὶ ἔστιν ἐντυχόντα τούτοις
πλεῖστον ὠφεληθῆναι καὶ περὶ ἀρχῶν καὶ περὶ τέλους καὶ ὧν χρὴ εἰδέναι τὸν φιλόσοφον,
πιστεύσαντα ἐκείνοις.

[155] *Dial.* 112.

[156] *Dial.* 24.

of the external Law existed only for the Jews and prefigured a greater purpose.[157] But through a study of the Prophets it can be shown what the true meaning of these rites were.[158] A knowledge of the previously hidden plan of God can therefore be attained.

Many times Justin refers to various prophecies which "show" or "display" (ἀποδείκνυμι) that something has occurred or will occur.[159] In other words, Justin uses scripture to prove the attainment of some kind of knowledge. Further, Justin often describes scripture as "making something clear" (δηλόω) through a Prophet.[160] In each case the item that was made clear was knowledge that was previously hidden or misunderstood. The same can be said in passages where scripture is claimed by Justin to "make manifest" or "make clear" (φανερός, φαίνω, φανέντος, ἐκφαίνω) events which were misunderstood or hidden.[161]

The point here need not be pressed. As any cursory reading of the *Dialogue with Trypho* will attest, Justin believed knowledge about the plan of God could be ascertained from the Prophets. This plan centered on the incarnate *Logos*. The Prophets possessed a special knowledge because they had seen and heard the truth about God. This knowledge is to be seen as a witness to revelation for three reasons. 1) In personal revelation one must choose to reveal oneself.[162] Thus it is through the *Logos* that God has chosen to reveal himself.[163] In Justin's estimation philosophy is properly concerned with the knowledge of God. Therefore, because the Prophets attained their knowledge of God from him,[164] it is God who chose to reveal himself. In other words, the knowledge about God came from God—it was revealed by him.

2) The knowledge that was revealed to the Prophets was not self-evident. It was not knowledge that could be attained by the Prophets

---

[157] *Dial.* 11.

[158] It should be noted here that this is only half of the argument. The study of the Prophets was accomplished through decidedly Christian tradition. Therefore, it was not necessarily the Prophets alone, but rather the Prophets through the lens of Christian tradition. See Chapter 3.V.A.1 & V.A.3.

[159] See e.g., *Dial.* 39.5; 39.8; 43.1; 54.2; 59.1; 72.3; 85.4; 92.6; 99.1.

[160] See e.g., *Dial.* 62.1; 75.1; 75.3; 85.6; 99.3.

[161] See e.g., *Dial.* 56.12; 70.4; 89.1; 90.3.

[162] For an outstanding discussion concerning the philosophical/theological presuppositions of the concept of revelation see, C. E. Gunton, *A Brief Theology of Revelation* (Edinburgh: T&T Clark, 1995) *passim.*, esp. 20–39.

[163] As I explain below, the Logos is God and this is the ground and climax of revelation. See Chapter 3.V.C.

[164] *Dial.* 7.

on their own. Because of the "otherness" of God only he can reveal himself. Thus, what God reveals about himself is knowledge that only he knows and is able to reveal. This is what necessitates the revelation. Just as God revealed the Law at Horeb, he also revealed the fact that the old Law would be surpassed and made obsolete. But still contained in the old Law were the hidden precepts of the new Law.[165] Thus, revelation was a knowledge of the plan (οἰκονομία) of God.

3) The Prophets saw and heard what they communicated to humankind. This gave the Prophets a qualification that the philosophers did not possess. No one could claim to communicate knowledge of God that was audibly and observationally received except the Prophets. This, in turn, allowed those who heard and read the Prophets to communicate this same knowledge based on their qualifications.

B. *The Memoirs of the Apostles*[166]

References and allusions to OT scripture are plentiful in the *Dialogue*. But it also contains numerous references and allusions to written documents that are not found in OT scripture. Even though references to these other documents are not as frequent as those to the Prophets it is clear that Justin placed a great deal of importance on these documents as well.

Following his conversion to Christianity Justin makes the above mentioned appeal to the Prophets as a place to gain knowledge about God.[167] The appeal, however, does not end at the Prophets. He also states that his "heart was set on fire" and that an affection for the "friends of Christ" took hold of him. This addition cannot be a description of the Prophets because Justin is clearly differentiating between Prophets and friends of Christ. Later in the same chapter, Trypho accuses Justin of following "worthless men" who propagate false teachings. In Trypho's expression the same holds true because it is difficult to accept that a Jew would call the Prophets worthless men expounding false teachings.

---

[165] The old Law is witness to revelation because it contained "hidden precepts." These hidden precepts are discussed in detail below, Chapter 5.II.

[166] A more detailed examination of the Memoirs of the Apostles as they relate to issues of the NT canon can be found below in Chapter 4.

[167] *Dial.* 8.

G. Stanton believes this is a reference to the Apostles.[168] One would be hard pressed not to agree with him. The Apostles do figure quite prominently in certain places throughout the *Dialogue* as followers of Jesus who preach the same message as the Prophets.[169] In one instance Justin even states that the Prophets preached the gospel of Jesus and proclaimed him to all men.[170] This is a significant description in light of the use of the terms "Gospel" and "Memoirs of the Apostles".

Justin uses the term εὐαγγέλιον (gospel) and its derivatives a total of four times in the *Dialogue*. One of the four has already been mentioned as a description of what the Prophets proclaimed.[171] *Dial.* 51.2 states that part of John the Baptist's prophetic ministry was preaching the gospel. The description of the gospel which follows is that the Kingdom of Heaven is imminent, that Jesus had to suffer, be crucified, and rise the third day, and that he would appear again to his disciples at the second advent. It is, therefore, not a great stretch to say that the Prophets preached the gospel, for this is Justin's whole point in the argument from prophecy.[172]

The two remaining uses of εὐαγγέλιον differ from the ones above.

> Trypho said . . . But I believe your precepts in the so-called Gospel are so wonderful and so great that no one is able to keep them for I have carefully read them.[173]

> but also in the Gospel it is written that he [Jesus] said, "Everything has been handed over to me by the Father . . ."[174]

Here it is apparent that the references are to some sort of written document(s). Justin makes many appeals to the words of Jesus and proceeds to quote them.[175] While these quotations aren't explicitly

---

[168] G. Stanton, "The Fourfold Gospel," *NTS* 43 (1997) 332. O. Skarsaune ("The Conversion of Justin Martyr," *ST* 30 [1976] 58) along with van Winden (*An Early Christian Philosopher*, 118) believe that the phrase "friends of Christ" refers to Christians in Justin's own time, and especially their capacity as martyrs. My reasons for disagreement with Skarsaune and van Winden follow.

[169] See e.g. *Dial.* 42.1–2; 76.6; 88.3; 106.1; 109.1; 110.2; 119.6.

[170] *Dial.* 136.3.

[171] *Dial.* 136.3.

[172] For a discussion on Justin's "Argument from Prophecy," see below, Chapter 3.V.A.

[173] *Dial.* 10.2 ὑμῶν δὲ καὶ τὰ ἐν τῷ λεγομένῳ εὐαγγελίῳ παραγγέλματα θαυμαστὰ οὕτως καὶ μεγάλα ἐπίσταμαι εἶαι, ὡς ὑπολαμβάνειν μηδένα δύνασθαι φυλάξαι αὐτά· ἐμοὶ γὰρ ἐμέλησεν ἐντυχεῖν αὐτοῖς

[174] *Dial.* 100.1 καὶ ἐν τῷ εὐαγγελίῳ δὲ γέγραπται εἰπών· Πάντα μοι παραδέδοται ὑπὸ τοῦ πατρός . . .

[175] See e.g., *Dial.* 17.3–4; 35.2–3; 51.3; 76.3–6, 7; 81.4; 93.2; 96.3; 99.1–2; 100.1, 3; 103. 5; 105.5–6; 107.1; 115.6; 122.1; 125.1, 4.

stated to come from a written document, it is hard to conceive of Justin not obtaining these words of Jesus from a written document—especially in light of some of the detail included in them. In reading the *Dialogue* Justin makes many appeals to these words of Jesus and to events that occurred throughout his lifetime.[176] It is natural to inquire about the source of these words and events.

The ἀπομνημονεύματα τῶν ἀποστόλων (Memoirs of the Apostles) appear to be the best explanation of the source of these words and events. Justin makes reference to the Memoirs in one concentrated section of the *Dialogue* a total of 13 times.[177] These Memoirs were written documents which were composed by the Apostles and those who followed them. We know they are written because Justin quotes from them as written.[178]

The cluster of references to the Memoirs of the Apostles found in *Dial.* 100–107 informs us that these written documents record the life of Jesus. From them we learn, among other things, that he is the Son of God, that he was silent before Pilate, that he sweat drops of blood, and that at his nativity a star arose. Much discussion has surrounded the question of locating exactly what these Memoirs are. While this is not the place for that type of discussion[179] it must be stated that in all probability the Memoirs are the Synoptic Gospels (and possibly the Gospel of John).[180]

---

[176] See e.g., *Dial.* 35; 39; 78; 82.

[177] *Dial.* 100.4; 101.3; 102.5; 103.6; 104.1; 105.1, 5, 6; 106.1, 3, 4; 107.1.

[178] Justin uses various formulas to introduce a quotation from the memoirs. *Dial.*100.1 γέγραπται εἰπών, 103.6 ἐν τοῖς ἀπομνημονεύμασι τῶν ἀποστόλων γέγραπται. 104.1 ὅπερ καὶ τοῖς ἀπομνημονεύμσι τῶν ἀποστόλων αὐτοῦ γέγραπται γενόμενον. 105.6 ταῦτα εἰρηκέναι ἐν τοῖς ἀπομνημονεύμασι γέγραπται. 106.4 ὡς γέγραπται ἐν τοῖς ἀπομνημονεύμασι τῶν ἀποστόλων αὐτοῦ. 107.1 γέγραπται ἐν τοῖς ἀπομνημονεύμασιν τῶν ἀποστόλων αὐτοῦ. Justin claims that the Memoirs were συντετάχθαι (lit. "put together") by the Apostles and their followers—in other words, they were written by them (*Dial.* 103.8).

[179] A detailed examination of what exactly the Memoirs may be is discussed below in Chapter 4.

[180] See Barnard, *Justin Martyr*; H. Y. Gamble, *The New Testament Canon. Its Making and Meaning* (Guides to Biblical Scholarship; Philadelphia: Fortress, 1985) 28–29; G. M. Hahneman, *The Muratorian Fragment and the Development of the Canon* (Oxford Theological Monographs; Oxford: Clarendon, 1992) 96–98; H. Koester, *Ancient Christian Gospels. Their History and Development.* London: SCM/Philadelphia: Trinity Press International, 1990) 40–43; W. Sanday, *The Gospels in the Second Century* (London: Macmillan and Co., 1876) 88–137; B. F. Westcott, *A General Survey of the History of the Canon of the New Testament* (5th ed.; Cambridge and London: Macmillan and Co., 1881) 96–179.

More important for the purpose in this chapter is the connection that these Memoirs have with the prophecy of Ps 22. In each of these references to the Memoirs of the Apostles the phrase serves to quote, or refer to Christian writings which demonstrate that the prophecy of Ps 22 has been fulfilled in Jesus. Thus they are used as reliable records, as written documents which are accessible to all. The authors of these documents were men who lived with Jesus or, as their followers, received their information from them as reliable witnesses.[181] In this sense the Memoirs serve as good examples of Justin's argument from prophecy.[182]

The Memoirs of the Apostles are put to significant use by Justin in his argument from prophecy. As reliable records the Memoirs prove that the events predicted by the Prophets have actually occurred—they witness to these events. The question may justifiably be asked, therefore, whether the significance of the Memoirs lies solely in their historical verifiability. There is strong indication that this is not the case. Certainly there is great significance in the fact that the Memoirs verified the Prophets. But Justin did not view the Apostles as simply recorders of history or inferior to the Prophets in what they communicated.

Rather, the Apostles are also held in very high esteem. In explaining the bells of Exod 28:33–34 that are attached to the robe of the high priest, Justin states that this, "was a symbol of the twelve Apostles—the ones depending on the eternal priest and through whom all the earth has been filled with the glory and grace of God and of his Christ."[183] This type of language describing the work of the Apostles is reminiscent of how Justin describes the Prophets. Justin also describes the Apostles as supplying knowledge of true worship of God,[184] a task presumably accomplished (in part at least) through their written Memoirs.

Another very strong indication of the high esteem in which the Apostles were held by Justin is found in *Dial.* 119. There Justin begins developing the theme of Christians being the True Israel. The patriarch Abraham is recalled to mind as receiving God's promise

---

[181] *Dial.* 103.
[182] See below, Chapter 3.V.A.
[183] *Dial.* 42.1 τῶν ἐξαφθέντων ἀπὸ τῆς δυνάμεως τοῦ αἰωνίου ἱερέως Χριστοῦ, δι᾽ ὧν τῆς φωνῆς ἡ πᾶσα γῆ τῆς δόξης καὶ χάριτος τοῦ θεοῦ καὶ τοῦ Χριστοῦ αὐτοῦ ἐπληρώθη, σύμβολον ἦν.
[184] *Dial.* 110.2.

that he would be the father of many nations. It is stated that Christ
called Abraham with his voice, and it is with this same voice that
Christ calls the True Israel. "For that manner in which he [Abraham]
believed the voice of God, it was reckoned to him as righteousness;
in this same manner also we have believed the voice of God, which
was spoken through the Apostles of Christ and through which it was
further proclaimed to us by the Prophets."[185] Here the Apostles are
said to have performed the same function as the Prophets, that is,
they communicated knowledge of God. So, in Justin's thinking, there
was no hierarchy of status between the Prophets and the Apostles,
both communicated the voice of God.

Thus, the Memoirs of the Apostles are witnesses to revelation.
The Memoirs can be so described for two main reasons. First, they
supply knowledge of God in a manner similar to the Prophets.[186]
Second, as will be explained in more detail in the following section,
the writers of the Memoirs pass the epistemological test of witness-
ing the *Logos*.

V. *The* Logos *as Revelation*

The crux of the relationship between the Prophets and the Apostles
is located in the epistemological significance of seeing and hearing.
In other words, the qualification of the Prophets for communicating
revelation rested in the fact that they had seen and heard God. This
is the key issue. The qualification of the Apostles rested in their witness to the *Logos* incarnate. This is shown in two ways. First, one of
the old man's requirements for gaining true and accurate knowledge
of anything, in this case God, was that the knowledge had to be
communicated by someone who had heard from someone who had
seen.[187] For this requirement the Apostles rested on the communication of the Prophets. They had seen and heard that which they
communicated, therefore the Apostles were able to use their writings for gaining true and accurate knowledge of God.

---

[185] *Dial.* 119.6 ὃν γὰρ τρόπον ἐκεῖνος τῇ φωνῇ τοῦ θεοῦ ἐπίστευσε καὶ ἐλογίσθη αὐτῷ
εἰς δικαιοσύνην, τὸν αὐτὸν τρόπον καὶ ἡμεῖς τῇ φωνῇ τοῦ θεοῦ, τῇ διά τε τῶν ἀποστόλων
τοῦ Χριστοῦ λαληθείσῃ πάλιν καὶ τῇ διὰ τῶν προφητῶν κηρυχθείσῃ ἡμῖν . . .

[186] *Dial.* 110.2.

[187] See *Dial.* 3, 7 & 8.

The second way in which the qualification of the Apostles rested in seeing and hearing is somewhat more significant *JR* and requires more explanation. This second demonstration is anchored in the event of Jesus Christ. Justin's *Logos* theology has a great deal of significance in Justin's understanding of truth.[188] The ultimate importance of the *Logos*, who is identified as Jesus, is seen in his incarnation in space and time. The *Logos* became human and fulfilled the will of the Father.

In becoming human the *Logos* fulfilled the predictions of the Prophets. One of the functions of the *Logos* prior to the incarnation was to point to the coming of the full manifestation of the *Logos* through the Prophets. With the coming of the man, Jesus, that function of the *Logos* was no longer needed. With the incarnate Logos came the full manifestation of the *Logos* in Jesus Christ.[189] Justin expresses this full manifestation of the *Logos* through his concept of the "resting" of the spirit.[190]

In *Dial.* 87 Trypho requests of Justin an explanation of Isa 11:1–3.[191] The context of chap 86 indicates that Trypho's question stems from Justin's interpretation of the phrase which indicates that Jesus would come as a rod from the root of Jesse. Through this statement Justin finds Jesus prefigured in a number of different scriptural references,[192] and ultimately fulfilled in his crucifixion on a cross made of wood. Thus, it is because Justin initially brought this passage in Isaiah into the discussion that Trypho desires to pursue it in *Dial.* 87.

In *Dial.* 87 Trypho clarifies what he believes Justin to be saying— that Jesus already existed as God, that he was incarnate according to the will of God, and that he became human by the virgin. Trypho then asks his question: "How can it be demonstrated that he is able to be pre-existing, he who is filled with the Holy Spirit (as the word by Isaiah enumerates) as if he were in need of possessing this [Holy

---

[188] For a detailed presentation Justin's Logos theology see below, Chapter 2 V.C

[189] As opposed to a germ of the *Logos* which was the possession of every person. See Chapter 3.IV.A.2.d; 2.V.C.6; 5.III.B–C.

[190] O. A. Piper, "The Gospel According to Justin Martyr," *JR* 61 (1961) 158.

[191] *Dial.* 87.2. "Explain to me the following words of Isaiah, 'There shall come forth a rod out of Jesse, and a flower shall rise up out of his root. And the spirit of God shall rest upon him, the spirit of wisdom and understanding, the spirit of counsel and fortitude, the spirit of knowledge and piety; and he shall be filled with the spirit of the fear of the Lord.'"

[192] Ps 1:3; 92:12; Gen 18:1; Ex 15:27; Num 33:9; Ps 23:4; 2 King 6:1–7; Gen 38:25.

Spirit]?"[193] Trypho sees a difficulty here with Justin's claim of pre-
existence and Justin's interpretation of Isa 11. For if Jesus pre-existed
as God then he lacked nothing. But, Isaiah states that the Holy
Spirit would rest upon him, as though Jesus lacked the Spirit.

Justin recognizes Trypho's difficulty and replies that these powers
of the Spirit came upon Jesus, not because he stood in need of them,
but because they would find their rest in him.[194] With the coming
of Jesus all prophecy had ceased because he was the fulfillment or
accomplishment of the spirit of prophecy, he was the new covenant
(καινὴ διαθήκη) which was previously announced by the Prophets.[195]
This is why there are no more Prophets after the baptism of Jesus.[196]
With the coming of the man Jesus, a goal or a fulfillment had been
reached. In the will of God the incarnation of the *Logos* signified the
accomplishment of humankind's redemption.

The significance of this goal or fulfillment cannot be overstated,
for it centers on the relationship of the Father and the incarnate
Logos. This relationship is expressed by Justin in two ways. First,
Justin is sure to retain the numerical distinction between the Father
and the *Logos*.[197] The *Logos* is "different from God, the creator of all
things; different, I mean, numerically but not in will. For I affirm
that he has at no time ever done anything which he who created
the world (above whom there is no other God) wished him to per-
form or associate with."[198] Second, even though he is sure to retain
this numerical distinction, he is also sure to state that the Logos is
to be worshipped as God.[199] The importance of the *Logos* is that
through him humankind attains salvation, we come to God through
the *Logos*.[200] But this salvation is not received by the *Logos* simply
directing or pointing to the Father. The relationship between the
Father and the *Logos* is much more intimate than that. There is no

---

[193] *Dial.* 87.2 πῶς δύναται ἀποδειχθῆναι προϋπάρχων, ὅστις διὰ τῶν δυνάμεων τοῦ
πνεύματος τοῦ ἁγίου, ἃς καταριθμεῖ ὁ λόγος διὰ Ἡσαΐου, πληροῦται ὡς ἐνδεὴς τούτων
ὑπάρχων;
[194] *Dial.* 87.3.
[195] *Dial.* 51.3.
[196] *Dial.* 51; 52.4; 87.3.
[197] *Dial.* 56; 61; 128; 129.
[198] *Dial.* 56.11 ἕτερός ἐστι τοῦ τὰ πάντα ποιήσαντος θεοῦ, ἀριθμῷ λέγω ἀλλὰ οὐ
γνώμῃ· οὐδὲν γάρ φημι αὐτὸν πεπραχέναι ποτὲ ἢ ἅπερ αὐτὸς ὁ τὸν κόσμον ποιήσας,
ὑπὲρ ὃν ἄλλος οὐκ ἔστι θεός, βεβούληται καὶ πρᾶξαι καὶ ὁμιλῆσαι.
[199] See e.g., *Dial.* 63.5; 74.3.
[200] *Dial.* 43.2; 64.3; 133.6.

question that Jesus taught that which the Father willed to be taught.[201] But in certain places in the *Dialogue* the incarnate *Logos* himself is sometimes described by Justin as being the revelation of the Father to humankind.

One description of the *Logos* employed by Justin is that of the Father begetting himself a certain rational Power, with this Power being indicated with various titles. Justin states,

> My friends, I will give to you another testimony from the scriptures. God begat a beginning before all creatures a rational power from himself, who is called by the Holy Spirit the Glory of the Lord, now also Son, now also Wisdom, now also Angel, now also God, now also Lord and Word—he even called himself Captain, when he appeared in human form to Joshua, son of Nun. For he possesses all these names because he serves the will of the Father and was also begotten by the will of the Father.[202]

The titles ascribed to the *Logos* are said to be appropriate because the *Logos* performs the Father's will and also because he was begotten by an act of the Father's will. These titles, therefore, all express Justin's understanding of the close relationship of the *Logos* with the Father.[203] The *Logos* witnesses to the Father, reveals the Father, and is paramount in the Father's plan of salvation.

Near the end of the *Dialogue* Justin explains the function of this rational Power which is important for understanding revelation. In *Dial.* 128 Justin desires to teach that the Power was begotten of the Father and is distinct from the Father but that the relationship with the Father is still intimately maintained. As an illustration he points to fires being kindled from another. The enkindled fires are distinct from the original fire which, though it ignites many other fires, still remains the same undiminished fire. It is this close relationship, allegorized in the fire, which Justin retains as important in his concept of revelation. For the Power begotten by the Father (the *Logos*)

---

[201] *Dial.* 76.3.
[202] *Dial.* 61.1 Μαρτύριον δὲ καὶ ἄλλο ὑμῖν, ὦ φίλοι, ἔφην, ἀπὸ τῶν γραφῶν δώσω, ὅτι ἀρχὴν πρὸ πάντων τῶν κτισμάτων ὁ θεὸς γεγέννηκε δύναμίν τινα ἐξ ἑαυτοῦ λογικήν, ἥτις καὶ δόξα κυρίου ὑπὸ τοῦ πνεύματος τοῦ ἁγίου καλεῖται, πότε δὲ υἱός, ποτὲ δὲ σοφία, ποτὲ δὲ ἄγγελος, ποτὲ δὲ θεός, ποτὲ δὲ κύριος καὶ λόγος, ποτὲ δὲ ἀρχιστράτηγον ἑαυτὸν λέγει, ἐν ἀνθρώπου μορφῇ φανέντα τῷ τοῦ Ναυῆ Ἰησοῦ· ἔχει γὰρ πάντα προσοινομάζεσθαι ἔκ τε τοῦ ὑπηρετεῖν τῷ πατρικῷ βουλήματι καὶ ἐκ τοῦ ἀπὸ τοῦ πατρὸς θελήσει γεγεννῆσαι.
[203] See, C. Stead, *Divine Substance* (Oxford: Clarendon Press, 1977) 168–170.

announces the Father to humanity.[204] This Power has many titles, each corresponding to a particular function. For example, he is called Glory because he sometimes appears in visions that cannot be contained; is called man and human being because he appears in such forms as please the Father. But the Power functions as the Logos because "he carries communication from the Father to men."[205] It is important here that the "communication" (ὁμιλία) referred to in this context is that the Power, hence the *Logos*, does the will of the Father. Therefore, the communication is that which the Father wanted it to be.

Exactly what the above communication consisted of in the form of the *Logos* has already been made clear to Trypho earlier in *Dial.* 69. There Justin uses Isa 35:1–7 to show that the ones who were destitute of a knowledge of God, the Gentiles, would abandon their idols and put their hope in Jesus. After quoting the passage from Isaiah Justin explains,

> The fountain of living water which gushed forth from God on a land devoid of a knowledge of God, namely the land of the Gentiles, was this Christ, who also appeared to your offspring, and he healed those who from birth were disabled, deaf and lame in the body, causing them to leap, to hear and to see by his word. And by raising the dead and causing them to live he convinced men of the ascertainment of knowledge about him [God].[206]

By becoming incarnate, the *Logos* provided knowledge of God to a people that were destitute of a knowledge of God. This knowledge of God was provided by the events and words surrounding the incarnate *Logos* and in his very person as the *Logos* of God. The Logos is the way to God.[207]

---

[204] *Dial.* 128.2 δι' αὐτῆς τὰ παρὰ τοῦ πατρὸς τοῖς ἀνθρώποις ἀγγέλλεται

[205] *Dial.* 128.2 καὶ τὰς παρὰ τοῦ πατρὸς ὁμιλίας φέρει τοῖς ἀνθρώποις.

[206] *Dial.* 69.6 πηγὴ ὕδατος ζῶντος παρὰ θεοῦ ἐν τῇ ἐρήμῳ γνώσεως θεοῦ τῇ τῶν ἐθνῶν γῇ ἀνέβλυσεν οὗτος ὁ Χριστός, ὃς καὶ ἐν τῷ γένει ὑμῶν πέφανται, καὶ τοὺς ἐκ γενετῆς καὶ κατὰ τὴν σάρκα πηροὺς καὶ κωφοὺς καὶ χωλοὺς ἰάσατο, τὸν μὲν ἄλλεσθαι, τὸν δὲ καὶ ἀκούειν, τὸν δὲ καὶ ὁρᾶν τῷ λόγῳ αὐτοῦ ποιήσας· καὶ νεκροὺς δὲ ἀναστήσας καὶ ζῆν ποιήσας, καὶ διὰ τῶν ἔργων ἐδυσώπει τοὺς τότε ὄντας ἀνθρώπους ἐπιγνῶναι αὐτόν.

[207] See e.g., *Dial.* 30.3; 43.2; 49.8; 64.3. In *Dial.* 93 Justin makes reference to a knowledge in every type of man which knows adultery, fornication, murder, and so on being evil. Those who commit such acts are sinning. This reference to a conscience is the only place in the entire *Dialogue with Trypho* where Justin possibly discusses the subject of natural revelation. His silence on the matter is most likely due to his overriding christocentric purpose.

Much of the *Dialogue* records Trypho's objection to Justin's assertion that Jesus is the Christ. As the Christ Justin believes that he is intimately involved in the salvation of humankind. Indeed, the Son fulfilled the Father's plan of our redemption.[208] It is apparent that the watershed issue in the discussion between Justin and Trypho is over the messiahship of Jesus. Trypho simply cannot accept that the Christ is a suffering Christ.[209] Justin employs an explanation of the events of the life of the incarnate *Logos* together with the prophecies made of him to convince Trypho that the one who did suffer is the one of whom the Prophets speak. This is succinctly exemplified in *Dial* 89.

> 'If, then, Christ was not meant to suffer,' I said to him, 'and the Prophets not foretold that on account of the sins of the people he would be lead to death and be dishonored and scourged, and counted among the sinners, and be lead like a sheep to slaughter, whose birth, the Prophets makes known, no one can declare, then you might have cause to wonder. But, if these things are characteristic of him and disclose him to all, how can we not, with confidence, believe in him? Whoever understands the Prophets, upon simply hearing that he was crucified, will say that this is the one and none other.'[210]

The above paragraph and quotation must be put within the context that the actions of the *Logos* were all in accordance with the will of the Father. When this is done it can be seen that in these actions predicted by the Prophets, knowledge of God's plan was being revealed through the actions of the incarnate *Logos*. Because all that he did was in accordance with the will and plan of the Father, it logically follows that his life, death and crucifixion were within that plan as well. Thus in the event of his life, death and resurrection, the *Logos* fulfilled the Father's plan of humankind's redemption.[211] In so fulfilling the Father's plan the *Logos* was also revealing it through his actions.

---

[208] *Dial.* 103.3.

[209] *Dial.* 89.1.

[210] *Dial.* 89.3 Εἰ μὲν μὴ ἔμελλε πάσχειν ὁ Χριστός, φημὶ αὐτῷ ἐγώ, μηδὲ προεῖπον οἱ προφῆται ὅτι ἀπὸ τῶν ἀνομιῶν τοῦ λαοῦ ἀχθήσεται εἰς θάνατον καὶ ἀτιμωθήσεται καὶ μαστιχθήσεται καὶ ἐν τοῖς ἀνόμοις λογισθήσεται καὶ ὡς πρόβατον ἐπὶ σφαγὴν ἀχθήσεται, οὗ τὸ γένος ἐξηγήσασθαι ἔχειν οὐδένα φησὶν ὁ προφήτης, καλῶς εἶχε θαυμάζειν. εἰ δὲ τοῦτό ἐστι τὸ χαρακτηρίζον αὐτὸν καὶ πᾶσι μηνύον, πῶς οὐχὶ καὶ ἡμεῖς θαρροῦντες πεπιστεύκαμεν εἰς αὐτόν; καὶ ὅσοι νενοήκασι τὰ τῶν προφητῶν, τυῦτον φήσουσιν, οὐκ ἄλλον, εἰ μόνον ἀκούσειαν ὅτι οὗτος ἐσταυρωμένος.

[211] See e.g., *Dial.* 30.3; 31.1; 34; 43; 45.3–4; 53; 60; 63; 67.6; 74; 76; 87.5; 92.6; 103.3; 110; 120.1; 128; 136.

This intimate connection between the Father's will and its revelation through the incarnate *Logos* is expressed through the οἰκονομία
of the Father. Justin uses the term (and its derivatives) a total of
thirteen times in the *Dialogue*.[212] Of these, seven are of special significance because Justin relates it to Christ's incarnation, birth, human
life, and passion.[213] In its verbal form, οἰκονομέω means primarily
administering or overseeing an office, like a bishopric or a civil community.[214] The noun thus carries the sense of administration or
management.[215] But there is also an important theological use of
term as a noun, and this is where Justin's use of the term becomes
important in its relationship to revelation.

Justin views God's οἰκονομία as his will and purposes—his plan for
humanity. The οἰκονομία is concerned with things as mundane as
God's provision of the gourd to shelter Jonah from the heat.[216] But
ultimately the theological implications of the word are seen in its
relationship to the incarnation, death, and resurrection of the *Logos*.
". . . He [the *Logos*] endured all these things not as if he were justified
by them, but completing the dispensation [οἰκονομίαν] which his
Father, the Maker of all things, and Lord and God, wished him [to
complete]."[217] God's οἰκονομία is the explanation for Christ's suffering,[218]
victory over demons,[219] the first and second advents,[220] the crucifixion,[221]
and the entire incarnation.[222] All these are viewed as part of the plan
(οἰκονομία) of God. The οἰκονομία and the will of the Father are thus
synonymous with his plans and purposes.

The implications of this for Justin are important. Although the
Father and the *Logos* are numerically distinct,[223] the *Logos* always performs the will of the Father.[224] This is why the *Logos* becomes so

---

[212] 30.3; 31.1; 45.4; 67.6; 87.5; 103.3; 107.3 (2x); 120.1; 125.2 134.2 (2x); 141.4.
[213] 30.3; 31.1; 45.4; 67.6; 87.5; 103.3; 120.1.
[214] For an explanation on the uses of the verb in the early Church see Prestige,
God in Patristic Thought, 57–62.
[215] For an explanation of the uses of the noun in the early Church see Prestige,
God in Patristic Thought, 62–64.
[216] *Dial.* 107.3.
[217] *Dial.* 67.6. ἀλλ᾽ οὐχ ὡς δικαιούμενον αὐτὸν διὰ τούτων ὡμολόγησα ὑπομεμενηκέναι
πάντα, ἀλλὰ τὴν οἰκονομίαν ἀπαρτίζοντα, ἣν ἤθελεν ὁ πατὴρ αὐτοῦ καὶ τῶν ὅλων
ποιητὴς καὶ κύριος καὶ θεός.
[218] *Dial.* 30.3; 31.1; 67.6; 103.3.
[219] *Dial.* 30.3; 45.4.
[220] *Dial.* 31.1; 45.4.
[221] *Dial.* 103.3.
[222] *Dial.* 67.6; 87.5.
[223] *Dial.* 56; 61; 128; 129.
[224] *Dial.* 56; 61.1; 76.3.

essential in Justin's thinking. The *Logos* is with God at creation, throughout the lives of the patriarchs, and in the theophanies.[225] But, this same *Logos* became incarnate through the will of the Father,[226] and ministers according to the will of the Father.[227] This same *Logos* was also proclaimed as the new covenant by the Prophets.[228] The incarnate *Logos* "announces"[229] God to humanity and "carries communication"[230] from the Father to humanity. In fact, now that the *Logos* has become incarnate, humanity comes to God through him because he fulfilled the Father's plan of redemption.[231] It is through the incarnate *Logos* that those destitute of a knowledge of God would attain knowledge of the Father because he is related to the Father in will and purpose.[232]

Thus, the οἰκονομία, redemption, and revelation are closely connected. The plan of the Father was redemption accomplished through the *Logos*. This is why there are no more Prophets after the baptism of Jesus—after his baptism the Prophets had nothing to announce since the incarnate *Logos* is that to which they pointed.[233] The *Logos* is the revelation of the Father. The plan of the Father was redemption through the *Logos*. Since this *Logos* is the previously announced new covenant, he renders the old covenant obsolete and necessitates a new interpretation of the OT scriptures.[234] The *Logos* reveals God's οἰκονομία to humanity.

The knowledge that was communicated by the *Logos* about the Father and his plan is revelation. Because the will of the *Logos* is exactly the same as the will of the Father who sent him, that which the *Logos* reveals about the Father is that which the Father wanted revealed. The knowledge is therefore ultimately revealed by the Father. Justin emphasizes this intimate relationship. The relationship is dependent upon the will of the Father for it is he who accomplishes his purposes. But his will and purposes are accomplished ultimately through his Power which is revealed in the incarnate *Logos*. "For he who is ignorant of Him is likewise ignorant of God's

---

[225] *Dial.* 56–58; 61–64; 86; 87; 113; 128.
[226] *Dial.* 56.11; 61.1–2; 101.1; 102.5; 127.4.
[227] *Dial.* 56; 61.1; 76.3.
[228] *Dial.* 51.3.
[229] ἀγγέλλεται *Dial.* 128.2.
[230] ὁμιλίας φέρει *Dial.* 128.2.
[231] *Dial.* 30.3; 43.2; 49.8; 64.3; 102; 103.3; 133.6.
[232] *Dial.* 69.9.
[233] *Dial.* 51; 52.4; 87.3.
[234] See Chapter 5.

purpose, and he who insults and hates him clearly also hates and insults Him who sent Him. And he who does not believe in Him does not believe the words of the Prophets, who spoke the good news and proclaimed him to all men."[235]

God's purpose is revealed through the coming of the incarnate *Logos*. While it is true that the Prophets gave us a certain amount of knowledge about God, they also predicted a further and more significant knowledge. The Apostles saw, heard, and experienced that which the Prophets predicted. With Christ the salvation of God through his *Logos* was made plain for all humankind. With the *Logos*, God's total purpose was revealed. It is this to which the Apostles bear witness and communicate in writing. Their writings, therefore, are linked with revelation—they communicate knowledge about God and his purposes, which rest in the person of the incarnate *Logos*. But more importantly, the *Logos* himself is revelation, for in his very person he carries the will of the Father and it is through him that humankind understands God's plan of salvation and attains life.

The *Logos* appeared for the purpose of revealing the will and message of God.[236] But Justin does not present the *Logos* as revealing this message and will only at the incarnation. The revealing *Logos* is pervasive throughout salvation history. He is thus an agent in creation,[237] and is active throughout the time of the patriarchs as the theophanies of God, thus revealing knowledge about God even then.[238] But the goal of the revelation of God through the *Logos* is found in his incarnation where God's plan is made manifest in the person of Jesus. Justin's concept of the Logos as God's revelation can thus be seen as a process which is gradually unfolded in history.[239]

VI. *Salvation*

In the preceding sections on the Witnesses to Revelation and The *Logos* as Revelation several references have been made to the signi-

---

[235] *Dial.* 136.3 ὁ γὰρ τοῦτον ἀγνοῶν ἀγνοεῖ καὶ τὴν βουλὴν τοῦ θεοῦ, καὶ ὁ τοῦτον ὑβρίζων καὶ μισῶν καὶ μισῶν καὶ τὸν πέμψαντα δῆλον ὅτι καὶ μισεῖ καὶ ὑβρίζει· καὶ εἰ οὐ πιστεύει τις εἰς αὐτόν, οὐ πιστεύει τοῖς τῶν προφητῶν κηρύγμασι τοῖς αὐτὸν εὐαγγελισαμένοις καὶ κηρύξασιν εἰς πάντας.

[236] Osborn, *Justin Martyr*, 41.

[237] *Dial.* 61–64.

[238] *Dial.* 56–58; 86; 87; 113; 128.

[239] Story, *The Nature of Truth in "The Gospel of Truth" and in the Writings of Justin Martyr*, 100.

ficance of salvation in Justin Martyr's thinking. In this vein, the
knowledge contained in the Prophets was a witness that regarded
salvation and a witness to Christ.[240] The Apostles performed the same
function as the Prophets, they witnessed saving knowledge of God.
With the coming of the man Jesus, a goal had been reached. In the
οἰκονομία of God the incarnation of the *Logos* signified the accomplishment of humankind's redemption. In light of this larger section
on the Witnesses to Revelation and the *Logos* as Revelation[241] it could
be stated that central to them is salvation. In other words, it appears
that Justin is positing the reception of salvation as the central purpose of the *Logos* incarnate, while the central purpose of the Prophets
and the Apostles was the communication of this event.

If this is the case, the question quite naturally arises regarding the
meaning of salvation for Justin. It is certainly more than just a curi-
ous incongruity that of the two reasons which Justin himself gives
for his conversion to Christianity, neither are the result of conviction of sin as a state of corruption.[242] Rather, Justin has little concern for inherited guilt or original sin. In fact, in the pre-Nicene
church, there is remarkably little elaboration of the doctrine of salvation.[243] Indeed, the great creedal statements of the early Church
show no elaboration on any specific theory of the atonement.[244] "The
development of the Church's ideas about the saving effects of
the incarnation was a slow, long drawn-out process. Indeed, while the
conviction of redemption through Christ has always been the motive
force of Christian faith, no final and universally accepted definition
of the manner of its achievement has been formulated to this day."[245]

Some have explained that the reason for this lack of elaboration
is because the early church was so certain that the life and death

---

[240] *Dial.* 8.

[241] Chapter 2.IV–V.

[242] The first reason Justin gives for his conversion, as recorded in the prologue
of the *Dialogue with Trypho*, is that the respectable old man by the sea had convinced him of the necessity of the Prophets and Apostles in his search for the true
philosophy. The second reason Justin gives for his conversion, as recorded in *1
Apol.* 12.1, was the courage that Christian converts were displaying in the midst of
terrible persecution.

[243] For example, Origen dwells at length with many Christian doctrines but
nowhere does he deal specifically with the death of Christ and its significance for
salvation. The same is true of Greek theology in general.

[244] See J. McIntyre, *The Shape of Soteriology: Studies in the Doctrine of the Death of Christ*
(Edinburgh: T&T Clark, 1992) 1–3. McIntyre calls this lack of a specific theory of
the death of Christ a "stumbling-block" to definitive understanding.

[245] J. N. D. Kelly, *Early Christian Doctrines* (rev. ed.; San Francisco: Harper Collins,
1978) 163.

of Christ had effected an atonement between God and humanity. This was the very heart and strength of Christians from the earliest days so "they did not need to theorize about it; they were content to know and feel it."[246] This explanation has lead some to pursue the issue further.[247] If this is done, two reasons may be posited as to why there is an absence of a developed theory of the atonement in the early Church.[248]

The first reason lies in the eucharistic liturgies of the early Church. The strong connection of the death of Christ and the forgiveness of sins is central in these liturgies that derive from the institution narrative of 1 Cor 11:23–34. In the eucharist the sacrificial death of Christ was grasped because of the meaning attached to it in the institution of the eucharist by Christ. The significance of this for our purpose here is that once it is understood that the eucharist was central to Christian worship[249] we see that thinking about the atonement was more integral to the worship life of the Church than the thought life of the theologians. Thus, thinking about a systematic theory of the atonement was not necessary as it was an assumed pillar in the worship of the Church. At issue here is the difference between something said and something done.[250] If the atonement was seen as articulated in the worship of the church, the people felt no need to investigate it further.

The second reason for the absence of a developed theory of the atonement in the early Church is the absence of any protracted heretical attacks on established soteriological positions. In the early Church, the doctrine of the atonement did not see the same level of controversy and doctrinal focus as controversy about the Son's relationship to the Father, as at Nicaea (325) and Constantinople (381), or the controversy concerning the nature of the Son, as at Chalcedon (451). This lack of controversy, or attack on doctrine, concerning the atonement simply did not force the Church to sys-

---

[246] J. F. Bethune-Baker, *An Introduction to the Early History of Christian Doctrine to the Time of the Council of Chalcedon* (London: Methuen & Co. Ltd., 1963) 327. See also, L. W Grensted, *A Short History of the Doctrine of the Atonement* (Manchester: Manchester University Press, 1962) 11. "It was not in theory but in life that the Living Fact approved itself to men, and so it is natural that the early days of the Church should be marked by emphasis on the Atonement as fact."
[247] McIntyre, *The Shape of Soteriology*, 7–8.
[248] McIntyre, *The Shape of Soteriology*, 8–16.
[249] "the eucharist *was* Christian worship . . .", McIntyre, *The Shape of Soteriology*, 10.
[250] G. Dix, *The Shape of the Liturgy* (Westminster: Dacre Press, 1947) 12.

tematically articulate that which was being pictured in her worship. In fact, the history of theology shows us that it was controversy that forced the Church to formulate the doctrine of the atonement in a more systematic manner.[251]

Justin belongs to this age of an undeveloped doctrine of the atonement. His description of the eucharist is testimony to the importance of it in early Christian worship.[252] But Justin does not present the reader with a systematic and organized presentation of the purpose of the incarnation. His concerns are not the concerns of later theology and the implications of his beliefs have not been scrutinized by the passage of time and the development of doctrine.

There is really only a cluster of passages in all of Justin's extant writings that give us indication of his doctrine of the atonement— of creation, the Fall and sin, and redemption. Of this cluster, two stand out as particularly relevant. The first, which appears in *1 Apology*, is helpful as the focal point for understanding his doctrine of creation, while the other, in the *Dialogue with Trypho*, is helpful as the focal point for understanding his doctrines of the Fall and sin, and redemption. I shall quote both here.

> And we have been taught that He [God] in the beginning did of his goodness, for man's sake create all things out of unformed matter; and if men by their works show themselves worthy of His design, they are deemed worthy, and so we have received—of reigning in company with Him, being delivered from corruption and suffering. For as in the beginning He created us when we were not, so do we consider that, in like manner, those who choose what is pleasing to him are, on account of their choice, deemed worthy of incorruption and of fellowship with Him. For the coming into being at first was not in our own power; and in order that we may follow those things which please Him, choosing them by means of the rational faculties He has Himself endowed us with, He both persuades and leads us to faith. And we think it for the advantage of all men that they are not restrained from learning these things, but are even urged thereto. For the restraint which human laws could not effect, the Word, inasmuch as He is divine, would have effected, had not the wicked demons, taking as their ally the lust of wickedness which is in every man, and which

---

[251] McIntyre, (*The Shape of Soteriology*, 15–25) discusses the three main issues that eventually forced the Church to formulate a position: (1) Anselm's *Cur Deus-homo?*; (2) The Reformation, and; (3) The traditional metaphysical transcendental expressions of the attributes of God.

[252] *1 Apol.* 66.

draws variously to all manner of vice, scattered many false and pro-
fane accusations, none of which attach to us.[253]

Now we know that he [Jesus] did not go to the river because he
stood in need of baptism, or of the descent of the Spirit like a dove;
even as he submitted to be born and to be crucified, not because he
needed such things, but because of the human race, which from Adam
had fallen under the power of death and the guile of the serpent, and
each one of which had committed personal transgression. For God,
wishing both angels and men, who were endowed with free will, and
at their own disposal, to do whatever he had strengthened each to do,
made them so, that if they chose the things acceptable to himself, he
would keep them free from death and from punishment; but that if
they did evil, he would punish each as he sees fit.[254]

A. *Creation*

Justin really says three things about the creation of the world:[255] God
made it, he made it for humanity, and he made it out of formless
matter. These three are quite explicitly stated above in the quotation from *1 Apology*. The first two points, that God made the world,
and that he made it for humanity find little conflict with later eastern theology.[256]

The third of the three points above is where the difference lies
between later eastern theology and Justin. Whereas Athanasius puts
great stress on creation *ex nihilo*,[257] with Justin *ex nihilo* creation is
absent. So, once again, from the passage in *1 Apology* Justin states
that God created things "out of unformed matter."[258]

---

[253] *1 Apol.* 10.2–6. English translation of Justin's *Apologies* are from A. Roberts
and J. Donaldson (eds.), *Ante-Nicene Fathers* (10 Vols.; Peabody, MA: Hendrickson,
1994) 1. 159–193.

[254] *Dial.* 88.4.

[255] Osborn, *Justin Martyr*, 45.

[256] These two points are also stated in other passages of Justin. *Dial.* 11.1, "There
will never be, Trypho, nor has there ever been from eternity (I thus addressed
him), any other except the one who created and arranged all." *2 Apol.* 4.2, "We
have been taught that God did not make the world aimlessly, but for the sake of
the human race."

[257] Athanasius, *Inc.* 1–9.

[258] The assertion of creation from unformed matter is also stated in *1 Apol.* 67.7
where Justin, in explaining the weekly worship of Christians, states, "But Sunday
is the day on which we all hold our common assembly, because it is the first day
on which God, having wrought a change in the darkness and matter, made the
world;" This creation from unformed matter is also extended to humanity in *Dial.*
62.2 where after quoting Gen 1:26–27 to support his belief that the Logos was present with God at creation, Justin says to Trypho, "And that you may not change
[the force of the] words just quoted, and repeat what your teachers assert,—either

Also helpful in this regard is Justin's most extended account of creation.

> And that you may learn that it was from our teachers—we mean the account given through the prophets—that Plato borrowed his statement that God, having altered matter which was shapeless, made the world, hear the very words spoken through Moses, who, as above shown, was the first prophet, and of greater antiquity of than the Greek writers; and through whom the Spirit of prophecy, signifying how and from what materials God at first formed the world spake thus: "In the beginning God created the heaven and the earth. And the earth was invisible and unfurnished, and darkness was upon the face of the deep; and the Spirit of God moved over the waters. And God said, Let there be light; and it was so." So that both Plato and they who agree with him, and we ourselves, have learned, and you also can be convinced that by the word of God the whole world was made out of the substance spoken of before by Moses. And that which the poets call Erebus, we know was spoken of formerly by Moses.[259]

While this may be Justin's most extended account of creation, it still does not give an extended explanation on creation. According to Justin, Plato followed Moses in his account of creation. Plato clearly taught that the cosmos was created out of formless matter.[260] Justin identifies the formless state of the world as ὕλην ἄμορφον (shapeless matter). Order came through the word of God. Unfortunately, Justin does not specifically address the question of whether matter existed eternally in antithesis to God or whether God created the formless matter himself and then made it into the phenomenal world.[261] For Justin creation is defined with reference to God's work of salvation. God creates and sustains the world so that humanity may turn to him and grasp the salvation offered through Christ.[262]

---

that God said to himself, 'Let us make,' just as we, when about to do something, often say to ourselves, 'Let us make;' or that God spoke to the elements, to wit, the earth and other similar substances of which we believe man was formed, 'Let us make,' ..."

[259] *1 Apol.* 59.
[260] Plato, *Tim.* 29–30; 32; 51.
[261] For the relationship between Hellenic understanding of creation and Justin's understanding see, May, *Creatio Ex Nihilo*, 120–133.
[262] *1 Apol.* 10.2–6; *2 Apol.* 4.2; 5.2; *Dial.* 41.1.

B. *Fall and Sin*

In the passage from *Dial.* 88 quoted above Justin indicates his doctrine of the Fall, inadequate as it is.[263] A number of things need to be highlighted in this regard. First, Justin asserts that humanity since Adam had fallen under the power of death. Second, humanity is given moral freedom or free will to choose whatever he or she desires. Third, the serpent is the responsible agent for leading humanity astray.

The first point, that humanity had fallen under the penalty of death, is linked to the latter two. Justin asserts that humanity has moral freedom to choose. This we can see in the two particularly relevant passages quoted above. So, in *1 Apol.* 10.2–6 Justin states that men choose things on account of their own choice. And *Dial.* 88.4 shows that even though humanity had fallen under the power of death since Adam because of the serpent, it is still an act of personal transgression through humanity's moral freedom.[264] It is important to point out here that in *Dial.* 88 Adam's sin is mentioned not as the cause of human sin, but as marking the origin of human sin and death.[265] This is significant because it indicates Justin's view of original sin. In Justin, because humanity is endowed with moral freedom, there is no inherited sinfulness apart from our chosen acts of sin. "The sin of Adam is typical of our sin; the sins of our ancestors result in an evil atmosphere into which we must be born, a constant evil influence in which we must grow up, there is no inherited guilt, and no racial depravity aside from the totality of individual offences."[266]

1 Apol. 10.4 indicates that by virtue of the rational powers God has given humanity we have the choice of living a life which is acceptable to God or not. As a result, we are without excuse in God's eyes when we do wrong.[267] Sin, therefore is not choosing to

---

[263] One cannot speak of a systematic doctrine of the Fall in Justin. He makes no exact reference to the causal link between humanity's first sin and the sin of Adam's posterity. As will be shown in the present section, Justin does, in some sense regard the sin of Adam as having some effect on the human race, but the specifics of this influence is not exegeted. Indeed, Justin makes more reference to the influence of evil demons in the sin of humanity than to Adam's sin. See also, N. P. Williams, *The Ideas of the Fall and of Original Sin: A Historical and Critical Study* (London: Longmans, Green and Co. Ltd., 1927) 171–175.

[264] Other passages which Justin asserts humanity's moral freedom include *1 Apol.* 28.3; *Dial.* 124.3; 140.4 141.

[265] Barnard, *Justin Martyr*, 115.

[266] Goodenough, *The Theology of Justin Martyr*, 227.

[267] *1 Apol* 28.3.

live for God according to the reason implanted in humanity—an erroneous belief and ignorance of what is good.[268] But if humanity is originally created with this knowledge of right and wrong, and the complete freedom to choose, why do we choose the wrong? The answer given by Justin is hinted at in the above quoted *Dial.* 88.4, where he states humanity had fallen under the power of death and the guile of the serpent. Justin asserts that demons are to blame for the fact that humanity chooses evil over good.[269] So, the underlying suggestion in *Dial.* 88 is that the sin of Adam and Eve, which consisted of a yielding to the devil's coaxing words, is the proto-type for humanity's sin.[270] "The human race has fallen under the power of death and guile of the serpent from the time of Adam (not from the offense of Adam), and each member of the race has committed personal transgression. Men and angels alike are free to make their own decision on the important question. That is, the activity of the serpent began with Adam and has continued ever since that time."[271] Thus, man is a sinner because he allows the demons to lead him into rebellion against the Law of God which every man has within him as a part of the divine equipment in life.[272] Salvation is needed because his rebellion has made him like the demons and worthy to share in their condemnation.[273]

Here, then we have the belief that the Fall is not an inherited guilt from Adam, but rather a choice every human makes to sin. Sin is rebellion against God, not a state of corruption. This sin results in punishment—eternal damnation. So, Justin looks for a salvation that will remove this penalty of sin and ensure escape from hell.

C. *Redemption*

The salvation of humanity is certainly wrapped up in the incarnation for Justin. But it appears as though the primary purpose of the incarnation was didactic. In other words, the primary purpose of Christ's coming to save men from evil deeds and powers is to teach assured truth.[274] So, Christ came to impart saving knowledge[275] which

---

[268] See *Dial.* 28.4; 141.1; *2 Apol.* 14.1.
[269] *1 Apol.* 5.2; *2 Apol.* 5.3f.; 17.2f.
[270] Kelly, *Early Christian Doctrines*, 167.
[271] Goodenough, *The Theology of Justin Martyr*, 228.
[272] *Dial.* 141.1.
[273] Goodenough, *The Theology of Justin Martyr*, 228.
[274] *1 Apol.* 23.2; *2 Apol.* 9. Barnard, *Justin Martyr*, 122.
[275] *Dial.* 18.2; 11.2; cf. 43.1; 51.3.

consisted of the realization of the oneness of God and the belief in a moral law.[276] In Justin men are saved primarily in two ways.[277] First Christ saves as teacher. Since the demons had lead astray humanity we have only a dim understanding until the incarnation of the Logos. With the coming of the Logos humanity has the whole truth.[278] Second, Christ saves by his cross and resurrection. Justin makes this claim more than any other Apologist of the second century.[279] He makes it clear that Christ's death and resurrection is a triumph over the demons[280] and this makes the demons subject to Christ.[281] Thus, the reason why humanity needs this revelation of the redeeming work of Christ as teacher is that the defeat of Jesus over the demons and the didactic content of his truth actually brings about a real moral change in the heart of the believer.[282]

Justin's many references to the cross and the resurrection are a frustrating thing to the interpreter of Justin. He often refers to them as central to our salvation but fails to fit them specifically into his theology of the atonement.[283] In this regard, Barnard and Chadwick each state it quite succinctly,

> The significance of Justin's statements about the Cross should not be underestimated. In strict logic his philosophical presupposition, which controlled his intellectual apprehension of Christianity, had no place for any objective theory of the Atonement. The fact that he has so much to say about the cross and what it had effected is a strong proof that the Church of his day held this belief. Its faith rested not only on the Word of truth which Christ had spoken but also on the redemption which he had wrought by his death and resurrection. Christ's power lay not only in his character and example; not only in his power to inflame and illuminate the hearts of men; but in what he was believed to have done for men on the cross. Justin accepted this faith

---

[276] *1 Apol.* 12–19. Kelly, *Early Christian Doctrines*, 196.

[277] Barnard, *Justin Martyr*, 122–125.

[278] See below, Chapter 3.V.C.

[279] Barnard, *Justin Martyr*, 124. For example see *1 Apol.* 32; 56; 63; *2 Apol.* 13; *Dial.* 13; 40; 49; 54; 86; 94–96; 98; 103; 111; 115; 116; 143; 137; 138.

[280] *1 Apol.* 46; *2 Apol.* 6; *Dial.* 91; 131.

[281] *Dial.* 30.

[282] *1 Apol.* 23.2; *Dial.* 30.3; 83.4.

[283] Goodenough (*The Theology of Justin Martyr*, 258) states "Justin may have connected the cross with the breaking of the power of the demons because of the conspicuous part which the Cross played in exorcisms. The formula of exorcism which JM has preserved lays great stress upon the crucifixion (*Dial.* 85.2 cf. 30.3) . . . But just how Justin conceived that the Cross achieved this victory is not explained."

as fundamental although it did not easily fit into the philosophy which he had imbibed. Justin is thus revealed as one who accepted, in this connection without question, the traditional faith of the Church.[284]

Justin's theology deserves the epithet "popular" in the sense that he wants to stress the points prominent in the mind of ordinary Christian folk with a practical concern for moral responsibility and a devotion quickened to life by the dramatic story of the divine acts of redemption through Christ and the work of the spirit. His faith is juxtaposed with an open optimism towards Greek philosophy, and he seems hardly to be aware of a deep tension between the two.[285]

VII. *Summary and Conclusion*

Justin's study of philosophy directed him to seek a revelation of God. Philosophy's task is to inquire about God. Only God himself is without beginning and end. Thus, in apophatic theology Justin found one of the main ideas that shaped his idea of revelation. God is the cause of all, and everything that exists does so as a result of his will and purposes. God himself must necessarily take the step of revealing his character to whomever he wills.

Justin's concept of revelation as it is presented in *Dialogue with Trypho* has been examined through three main concepts. First, it was stated that revelation is closely related to epistemology—the issue of the nature and source of knowledge. Justin's interest in philosophy gave him an interest about where he could discover knowledge about God, for this was the goal of his philosophy. Before his meeting with the old man Justin believed he could attain knowledge about God through Middle Platonic philosophy. But the old man showed him the epistemological significance of the Prophets. In contrast to the Plato, the Prophets had actually seen and heard God. Thus, the Prophets were qualified to communicate knowledge about God because they had witness to him.

Second, in the section on the Witnesses to Revelation, the places where one can find witness to God was examined. As mentioned above, the Prophets were an obvious place to look. But there was also a brief discussion surrounding the Memoirs of the Apostles as places in which this witness could be attained. The connection between

---

[284] Barnard, *Justin Martyr*, 125. See also Kelly, *Early Christian Doctrines*, 170.
[285] H. Chadwick, "Justin Martyr's Defence of Christianity," *BJRL* 47 (1965) 293.

the Prophets and the Memoirs of the Apostles was made clear with
the conclusion that the Apostles are held in high esteem because
they bear witness to the events that the Prophets foretold. As reliable records of the events of Jesus' life they recount that which the
Prophets predicted would occur.

But the significance of the Memoirs of the Apostles does not lie
solely in their function as historical records. More importantly, it
rests in the fact that they saw and heard the ultimate revelation of
God—the incarnation of the *Logos*. The Apostles witnessed that to
which the Prophets pointed. The Apostles thus fulfill the criteria by
which knowledge of God may be attained and communicated. They
heard from the Prophets who had seen God, but more importantly,
they actually saw God's will and plan for salvation played out before
their very eyes. In other words, through the incarnate *Logos* the
Apostles saw the fulfillment of God's will in his very being, and in
his actions. He is the ultimate revelation of God because by becoming incarnate the *Logos* performed the Father's will thus providing
knowledge to the Apostles. As witnesses to this action the Apostles
were thus qualified to communicate the revelation of God to humankind. The *Logos* was also seen as a progressive revelation throughout God's salvation history. He was an active agent throughout God's
οἰκονομία which culminated in his becoming the manifestation of
God's power.

Because the Prophets and the Memoirs of the Apostles witness to
God they pass the "epistemological test", they are therefore qualified
to communicate this witness to humankind. The Prophets saw and
predicted, the Apostles heard the Prophets and witnessed the events
which they predicted. The process is revealed in their writings. But
the goal of revelation is the *Logos*, culminating in his becoming incarnate. The agency of the *Logos* in the οἰκονομία of God thus reveals
God's plan for humankind's salvation.

The incarnation of the Logos incarnate allowed humankind to see
God's plan of salvation acted out as event in space and time. All
that was pointed in the old Law and the Prophets was fulfilled in
the event of the incarnation of the *Logos*. The tiny nation of Israel,
in effect, provided the stage for the event of Jesus.[286]

---

[286] A similar expression of this concept can be found in M. Muggeridge, "The
Universe Provides a Stage: Jesus is the Play," in G. Barlow (ed.), *Vintage Muggeridge.
Religion and Society* (Grand Rapids: Eerdmans, 1985) 35–43.

In Justin's concept of revelation both the event of Jesus and the communication of his coming (Prophets and Memoirs) have a place. The incarnation was an event limited in space and time but not limited in its significance for salvation. This significance for salvation necessitates its communication which, in turn, allows those who predicted and those who witnessed this event to speak concerning the revelation of God.

CHAPTER THREE

THE CONCEPT OF TRUTH IN *DIALOGUE WITH TRYPHO*

I. *Truth in Its Second Century Context*

The concept of truth is a rather slippery one to grab hold of. It is not necessary here to delve into the modern discussion on this issue. But we would certainly be remiss to ignore the concept of truth in the era of Justin Martyr. It is highly probable that Justin retained a love for truth that was also the possession of Plato. Plato stressed the love of truth as the essential aim of the philosopher. It is truth that should be honored above all else.[1] A love for truth and hatred of falsehood should thus dominate the life of the philosopher.[2]

It is certainly proper for the Christian to agree with the biblical assertion that Jesus is truth.[3] But the question of the truth of the Christian faith and the reason why Jesus is that truth cannot be answered by this simple assertion.[4] An accurate understanding of truth from the Christian perspective in the second century entails a brief look at the context in which the issue arose. This context is encompassed by the influence of three strands of thought—Hebrew thought, Platonic thought, and NT thought.

A. *Truth in Hebrew Thought*

The Hebrew concept of truth is usually described as characteristically concerned with history.[5] The Hebrew term אֱמֶת (truth) is both a legal and a religious term.[6] In law, it suggests veracity in speech,

---

[1] Justin, *1 Apol.* 3.6; Plato, *Rep.* 595.

[2] Plato, *Rep.* 585.

[3] John 14:6.

[4] W. Pannenberg, "What is Truth?" in idem., *Basic Questions in Theology: Collected Essays* (2 Vols.; ET G. H. Kehm; Philadelphia: Fortress, 1971) 2.2.

[5] C. I. K. Story, *The Nature of Truth in "The Gospel of Truth" and in the Writings of Justin Martyr* (NovTSup 25; Leiden: E. J. Brill, 1970) 181; J. D. Zizioulas, *Being as Communion: Studies in Personhood and the Church* (Contemporary Greek Theologians 4; Crestwood, NY: St. Vladimir's Seminary Press, 1997) 68.

[6] G. Quell, "ἀλήθεια, ἀληθής, ἀληθινός, ἀληθεύω" in G. Kittel (ed.), *Theological Dictionary of the New Testament* (10 Vols.; Grand Rapids: Eerdmans, 1964, 1.232–237.

as well as correspondence to facts. In religion, the term is used in connection with God being rich in faithfulness and truth in relation to his promises. Thus, two things are implied:[7] (1) In the OT, truth points to what has occurred or what will occur in history[8] and, (2) the God who deals in truth calls for men to respond in like manner.[9] In other words, ". . . it is God's promises which may be considered as ultimate truth, and these promises coincide with the goal or fulfillment in history. It is in short an eschatological truth which orients the human spirit towards the future."[10]

In the Hebrew understanding, the truth about God and who he is is revealed to humankind in historical events through his promises. This truth evokes relationships with humanity calling forth a response. The response is seen as an attitude of faith based on truth, i.e. the fact that God will carry out his promises.[11] Truth, therefore, is a Divine power that anticipates a future fulfillment. The Hebrew conception of truth is thus not only eschatological, but ontological as well.[12] It is ontological in that it reveals the nature of God and the way God communicates his truth to man. It is eschatological in that it anticipates the unfolding of God's purposes for the world.

B. *Truth in Platonic Thought*

In Platonic thought, truth is intimately connected with the theory of Forms and the Good. This connection is best seen through the three comparisons that Plato uses to highlight the various aspects of his epistemology. In addition to the analogy discussed in Chapter 1 of the Cave,[13] Plato also used two others—the Divided Line[14] and the Simile of the Sun.[15] Since the Analogy of the Cave was already discussed the focus here will be on the latter two. In so doing the point will be made that truth for Plato may only be found in the realm of Forms which is ultimately found in the Good.

---

[7] Story, *The Nature of Truth in "The Gospel of Truth" and in the Writings of Justin Martyr*, 181.
[8] H. F. von Soden, "Was ist Wahrheit? Vom geschichtlichen Begriff der Wahrheit" (Marburg: N. G. Elwert'sche Verlagsbuchhandlung, 1927) 14.
[9] von Soden, "Was ist Wahrheit?", 14.
[10] Zizioulas, *Being as Communion*, 68.
[11] O. Procksch, *Theologie des Alten Testaments* (Gütersloh: C. Bertalsman, 1950) 606.
[12] Story, *The Nature of Truth in "The Gospel of Truth" and in the Writings of Justin Martyr*, 184–188.
[13] See above, Chapter 2.II.A.3.
[14] Plato, *Rep.* 509–511.
[15] Plato, *Rep.* 506–509.

1. *The Divided Line*

The Divided Line is used by Plato to illustrate the relationship of knowledge to opinion, reality to appearance, metaphysics to epistemology, and the worlds of Being and Becoming.[16] Basically, the Divided line distinguishes between degrees or levels of knowledge with the four metaphysical levels of reality corresponding to four epistemological ways of apprehending them. In a schematic, the comparison would look something like this:[17]

HIGHEST

	METAPHYSICS	EPISTEMOLOGY	
BEING νοητά	Higher Forms—The Good ἀρχαί	A. Understanding νόησις	**KNOWLEDGE** ἐπιστήμη
	Lower Forms— Human Forms μαθηματικά	B. Reasoning διάνοια	
BECOMING δοξαστά	Sensible Objects ζῷα	C. Perception πίστις	**OPINION** δόξα
	Images & Shadows εἰκόνες	D. Illusion εἰκασία	

LOWEST

The concept herein explained is the development of the human mind on its way from ignorance to knowledge which lies over the two fields of Opinion (δόξα) and Knowledge (ἐπιστήμη). It is only the latter that can properly be termed Knowledge. Opinion is said to be concerned with images (εἰκόνες), while Knowledge, at least in the higher forms, is concerned with originals or archetypes (ἀρχαί).[18]

---

[16] Plato, *Rep.* 508E–509A.
[17] Adapted from F. Copleston, *A History of Philosophy* (9 vols.; new rev. ed.; Garden City, NY: Image Books, 1962) 1.1.176; D. J. Soccio, *Archetypes of Wisdom: An Introduction to Philosophy* (2nd ed.; Belmot, CA: Wadsworth, 1995) 155.
[18] Copleston, *A History of Philosophy*, 1.1.176.

This development of the human mind from ignorance to knowledge is movement through "levels of awareness."[19] The lowest level of awareness is the level of Illusion (εἰκασία, D in the schematic). This realm is not always inhabited but we occasionally slip into it purposely when we watch magic shows or go to the movies. But Plato says that we can also slip into illusion without being aware of it when our opinions are based solely on appearances, unanalyzed impressions, uncritically inherited beliefs, and unevaluated emotions.

The second level of awareness is that of Perception (πίστις, C in the schematic). The objects of the Perception level are the real objects corresponding to the Images and Shadows of the line. Perception involves a wider range of opinions about what most of us think of as reality. These Opinions are based on observations of physical objects as distinguished from the level of Illusion which is based on beliefs, impressions, or emotions. Of this line Plato includes "the animals which we see, and everything that grows or is made."[20] The implication here is that, for example, the man whose only idea of a horse is that of particular real horses, and who does not see that particular horses are imperfect imitations of the ideal horse, that is, the universal, is at the level of Perception. He has no real knowledge of the horse, only perception. Thus, the person who does not see that the Sensible Objects (ζῷα) are imperfect realizations of the specific type has only Perception (πίστις).[21] This person, is one step up on the inhabitant of the level of Illusion, but still has not attained Knowledge. Of these levels Plato asks rhetorically, "Would you not admit that both the sections of this division have different degrees of truth, and that the copy is to the original as the sphere of opinion is to the sphere of knowledge?"[22]

The next two levels of awareness pass from the realms of Becoming and Opinion and into the realms of Being (νοητά) and Knowledge (ἐπιστήμη), hence the bold line of demarcation in the schematic. In this section, that of Knowledge (ἐπιστήμη), the first level of true knowledge is acquired through reasoning (διάνοια, C in the schematic). In order for this level to be true knowledge, it is not knowledge of those at the level of Perception or Illusion, since these levels belong to the realm of Becoming and thus are subject to flux. Reasoning

---

[19] Cf., Soccio, *Archetypes of Wisdom*, 136–137.
[20] Plato, *Rep.* 510.
[21] Copleston, *A History of Philosophy*, 1.1.178.
[22] Plato, *Rep.* 510.

knowledge must be of a Form, for the Form does not grow or change.

The highest level of awareness is that of understanding (νόησις, A in the schematic). Here the soul has no need of perception or interpretation for it directly apprehends the absolute Form of the Good.

Of this comparison of the Divided Line Plato has indicated that there is a scale of the faculties of our minds. These four faculties "have clearness in the same degree that their objects have truth."[23] In other words, each successive level of awareness is another step toward the ultimate truth which resides in the realm of Being in the Form of the Good.

2. *The Simile of the Sun*

For Plato, the Good is the absolute Form. In the Simile of the Sun he compares the Good to the sun. He relates the concept that just as the sun is necessary for vision and life, it is the Good which makes reality, truth and existence of everything else possible.

The simile begins with Glaucon imploring Socrates (representing Plato himself) to give an explanation of the Good.[24] Socrates begins by reviewing some pertinent points that have already been presented.[25] In doing this he sums up the idea of universals and particulars—the concept of Forms.

> ... but I must first come to an understanding with you, and remind you of what I have mentioned in the course of this discussion, and at many other times.
>
> What?
>
> The old story, that there is a many beautiful and a many good, and so of other things which we describe and define; to all of them 'many' is applied.
>
> True, he [Glaucon] said.
>
> And there is an absolute beauty and an absolute good, and of other things to which the term 'many' is applied there is an absolute; for they may be brought under a single idea, which is called the essence of each.
>
> Very true.
>
> The many, as we say, are seen but not known, and the ideas are known but not seen.[26]

Following this contextual explanation, Socrates goes on to focus in on the sense of sight as a way to link the importance of that which

---

[23] Plato, *Rep.* 511.
[24] Plato, *Rep.* 506.
[25] Plato, *Rep.* 507.
[26] Plato, *Rep.* 507.

makes things visible. It is the sun which makes the eye to see and
the visible to appear, therefore, this great light is implied to be of
a higher order.[27] In fact, Socrates states that "the power which the
eye possesses is a sort of effluence from the sun."[28] Thus, the sun is
not sight, but is the author of sight.

At this point the Simile of the Sun is brought to a sort of climax
where Socrates gets to the point he is trying to make. It is worth
quoting at length.

> And this is he whom I call the child of the good, whom the good
> begat in his own likeness, to be in the visible world, in relation to
> sight and the things of sight, what the good is in the intellectual world
> in relation to mind and the things of the mind.
>   Will you be a little more explicit? He [Glaucon] said.
>   Why, you know, I said, that the eyes, when a person directs them
> towards objects on which the light of day is no longer shining, but
> the moon and stars only, see dimly, and are nearly blind; they seem
> to have no clearness of vision in them?
>   Very True.
>   But when they are directed towards objects on which the sun shines,
> they see clearly and there is sight in them?
>   Certainly.
>   And the soul is like the eye: when resting upon that on which truth
> and being shine, the soul receives and understands and is radiant with
> intelligence; but when turned towards the twilight of becoming and per-
> ishing, then she has opinion only, and goes, blinking about, and is first
> of one opinion and then of another, and seems to have no intelligence?
>   Just so.
>   Now, that which imparts truth to the known and the power of know-
> ing to the knower is what I would have you term the idea of good,
> and this you will deem to be the cause of science, and of truth in so
> far as the latter becomes the subject of knowledge; beautiful too, as
> are both truth and knowledge, you will be right in esteeming this other
> nature as more beautiful than either: and as is the previous instance,
> light and sight may be truly said to be like the sun, and yet not to
> be the sun, so in this other sphere, science and truth may be deemed
> to be like the good, but not the good; the good has a place of hon-
> our yet higher.[29]

> You would say, would you not, that the sun is not only the author of
> visibility in all things, but of generation and nourishment and growth,
> though he himself is not generation?

[27] Plato, *Rep.* 508.
[28] Plato, *Rep.* 508.
[29] Plato, *Rep.* 508.

Certainly.

In like manner the good may be said to be not only the author of knowledge to all things known, but their being and essence, and yet the good is not essence, but far exceeds essence in dignity and power.[30]

It is difficult to miss the ultimate regard Plato held for the Good. The Good transcends all and attains to the highest honor.

3. *Platonic Truth*

With these two comparisons we see the relationship that exists with truth, Forms, and the Good. The relationship of truth to Forms is seen in the fact that truth resides in the Forms. Truth is thus seen as changeless and eternal. With the Divided Line Plato shows that there are degrees of truth and that he clearly taught that the highest level of truth resides in the Good. With the Simile of the Sun we saw the utmost regard Plato held for the Good as the ultimate Form. It is the Good which gives the objects of knowledge their truth and the mind the power of knowing.

So, for Plato, truth was to be understood from the side of that which was true itself.[31] This places us squarely within the realm of Forms.[32] Thus, in contrast to the Hebrew conception, truth actually transcends history. Platonic thought held an essential unity between the intelligible world (νοητά), the thinking mind (νοῦς), and Being (εἶναι). And it is in this unity that truth is to be found.[33] Truth for the Platonist never really entered the world in a concrete form. The best the Platonist can say in this respect is that the world contains pointers to the truth which is ultimately found in the world of Forms.[34] Thus, the Platonic concept of truth is that it is not historical, that it is not worked out in historical events.

C. *Truth in New Testament Thought*

The NT era represents a convergence of the disparate views of the Hebrew and the Platonic forms of thought. This disparity, then, presented the NT writers with a conflict which they had to somehow

---

[30] Plato, *Rep.* 509.
[31] Pannenberg, "What is Truth?" 11.
[32] See above, Chapter 2.II.A.1–3.
[33] Zizioulas, *Being as Communion*, 69.
[34] Story, *The Nature of Truth in "The Gospel of Truth" and in the Writings of Justin Martyr*, 196.

resolve. Greek ontology has a problem with the status given to history by the Hebrew concept. The conflict between the Hebrew and the Greek concepts of truth for the Christian are succinctly summarized in the question, "How can a Christian hold to the idea that truth operates in history and creation when the ultimate character of truth, and its uniqueness, seem irreconcilable to change and decay to which history and creation are subject?"[35] In other words, the Platonic world of Forms is the realm of Being, not Becoming. The realm of history and creation are in the realm of Becoming and are therefore not "real." Pannenberg calls this the "hidden impasse in the Greek idea of truth."[36] What he means is that the essence of truth for the Platonist must be its Being—its unchangeableness. The event character of truth must be disregarded because it stood in firm contradiction to the unchangeable character of truth.

What we are left with when dealing with the Hebrew and Greek concepts of truth is an apparent impasse, as Pannenberg accurately identifies. It was the task of the NT writers to break the deadlock that existed between these two influential ways of conceiving truth. Many have viewed the NT writers as simply restating and expanding the OT concept of truth. With this assertion Zizioulas would disagree. "It would be wrong to deduce too easily," states Zizioulas, "that biblical thinking, particularly in its New Testament form, is to be identified with what one would call Hebrew or Jewish thought-forms. When St Paul presents the cross of Christ as the content of his preaching, he stands against the Greek and Jewish mentalities simultaneously. The Christian message may be confused neither with the 'wisdom' of the Greeks nor with the Jewish preoccupation with 'signs' (1 Cor 1:22)."[37]

For Zizioulas, the NT way of understanding truth, with its distinct christological character, differs from both Hebrew and Greek ideas as presented above.[38] Thus, by referring to Christ as the Alpha

---

[35] Zizioulas, *Being as Communion*, 70.

[36] Pannenberg, "What is Truth?" 19.

[37] Zizioulas, *Being as Communion*, 68. Zizioulas explains that in 1 Cor 1:22 Paul says that the "signs" which the Jews seek are manifestations of God's presence and his activity in history. By and in these signs, truth makes itself known historically as God's faithfulness towards his people (p. 68). The Greek, on the other hand, is concerned with the wisdom of the mind in perceiving truth.

[38] Zizioulas, *Being as Communion*, 70.

and Omega of history,[39] the NT radically transforms the linear historicism or eschatological aspect of Hebrew thought. This is because the NT asserts a *realized* eschatology in that the end of history in Christ becomes present here and now. Likewise, in affirming that the historical person of Jesus Christ is the truth,[40] the NT transforms and challenges Greek thought. This is because it is in the flow of history and through it, with all its changes and ambiguities, that humanity is called to discover the meaning of existence.

In typical erudite fashion, Zizioulas sums up the issue,

> If, therefore, we want to be faithful to the christological character of truth, we must affirm the historical character of truth and not despise it for the sake of its "meaning." . . . it must be affirmed if by this "historicity" of the truth we understand a linear, Jewish historicism, for which the future constitutes a reality still to come, as though it had not at all arrived in history, then we are departing radically from the conception of the truth found in the New Testament. Thus, the problem which the christological character of truth has presented the Church from its earliest days may be summarized in the following question: How can we hold at one and the same time to the historical nature of truth and the presence of ultimate truth here and now. *How, in other words, can truth be considered simultaneously from the point of view of the "nature" of being (Greek preoccupation) from the view of the goal or end of history (preoccupation of the Jews), and from the viewpoint of Christ, who is both a historical person and the permanent ground (the λόγος) of being (the Christian claim)—and all the while preserving God's "otherness" in relation to creation?*[41]

With this transformation of the idea of truth in the Christian era comes the responsibility of communicating that idea of truth. In this vein, when we come to Justin Martyr we must pose two questions. First, we must understand how Justin understood truth—Hebrew, Greek, or New Testament? Did Justin hold on to his Platonic way of understanding truth after his conversion or did he retain a strictly linear view from his reading of the Prophets? Or, is Justin in line with a christologically transformed view of truth in keeping with Christian writings? Second, What exactly is Justin's message of truth? As this chapter progresses the latter question will be discussed and evaluated in light of the former.

---

[39] Rev 21:6.
[40] John 14:6.
[41] Zizioulas, *Being as Communion*, 71–72. Italics in original.

II. *Dialogue as a Search for Truth*

Justin did not casually set forth his case in the genre of dialogue. This genre was chosen for a reason—one that builds an important foundation in this investigation of Justin's concept of truth.

A. *Ancient Near Eastern Dialogues*

Relatively little research has been done in investigating the genre of dialogue in relation to Justin's *Dialogue with Trypho*. Recently, however, S. Denning-Bolle has offered a constructive article on this very subject.[42] Denning-Bolle begins her essay by briefly tracing the use of dialogues before Plato.[43] Mesopotamia and Egypt are shown as producing a number of purely dialogic texts.[44] The purpose for introducing and summarizing this genre in the Ancient Near East is to show that these dialogues were used for the purpose of arriving at truth. As Denning-Bolle explains, "In the Ancient Near East, man wrote dialogues to probe the gravest matters he encountered and it was *through* the dialogue form that he discovered solutions he could live with."[45]

B. *Pre-Socratic and Socratic Dialogues*

The Ancient Near Eastern dialogue is presented as a prologue to the Platonic dialogue. But Denning-Bolle unfortunately neglects placing the Platonic dialogue within the context of Socrates and his predecessors. If this is done one discovers that the genre of dialogue contains the philosophical art of dialectic, which originates from the Greek expression for the art of conversation (διαλεκτικὴ τέχνη).[46] Simply stated, dialectic is the art of conversation through which is developed knowledge by question and answer.[47]

---

[42] S. Denning-Bolle, "Christian Dialogue as Apologetic: The Case of Justin Martyr Seen in Historical Perspective," *BJRL* 69 (1987) 492–510. B. Z. Bokser ("Justin Martyr and the Jews," *JQR* 64 [1973–74] 97–122, 204–211) also touches on the connection of the dialogue genre with Justin's *Dialogue with Trypho*, but not near to the extent as Denning-Bolle.

[43] Denning-Bolle, "Christian Dialogue as Apologetic," 493–495.

[44] Egyptian dialogues include, "The Dispute Between a Man and His Soul," and "Eloquent Peasant". Mesopotamian dialogues include, "Babylonian Theodicy," and "Dialogue of Pessimism".

[45] Denning-Bolle, "Christian Dialogue as Apologetic," 495.

[46] R. Hall, "Dialectic," in P. Edwards (ed.), *The Encyclopedia of Philosophy Vols. 1–2* (New York: Macmillan & The Free Press/London: Collier Macmillan, 1972) 385.

[47] Hall, "Dialectic", 385; E. Zeller, *Outlines of the History of Greek Philosophy* (ET L.

Dialectic is believed to have originated in the fifth century BCE with the author of the famous paradoxes, Zeno of Elea. This was recognized by Aristotle who saw these paradoxes as outstanding examples of dialectic in the sense of refutation of hypotheses by opponents drawing unacceptable conclusions from these hypotheses.[48] Thus, for Zeno, dialectic came to be used as logical arguments to defeat an opponent for purely philosophical reasons. However, later in the hands of the Sophists, it came to be used simply as an instrument to win arguments. Plato labeled this type of dialectic "eristic"[49] from the word ἔρις (strife). Eventually, eristic began to make use of invalid argumentation and sophistical tricks.[50]

Socrates stands in contrast to the Sophist use of eristic dialectic. Socrates was only interested in bringing the truth to light, not in winning an argument.[51] This is not to say that Socrates was above winning an argument, as can be seen in what is called *elenchus*, a major element in his dialectic. Concerning the *elenchus*, Hall states that it was a "refined form of the Zenonian paradoxes, a prolonged cross-examination which refutes the opponent's original thesis by getting him to draw from it, by means of a series of questions and answers, a consequence that contradicts it."[52]

C. *Platonic Dialogues*

The choice of dialogue form was not an arbitrary one for Plato. Plato chose the dialogue form as nearest to the teaching method of Socrates.[53] Some even credit Plato as raising the form of the Socratic dialogue to an art form.[54] In general, Platonic *Dialogues* proceed in the following manner:[55] Someone, generally a representative of an

---

R. Palmer; 13th ed. rev.; London: Kegan Paul, Trench, Trubner & Co./New York: Harcourt, Brace & Co., 1931) 129.

[48] Hall, "Dialectic," 385.

[49] Plato, *Soph.* 231E.

[50] Hall, "Dialectic," 386.

[51] Plato, *Gorg.* 475E. P. Friedländer, *Plato Vol. 1: An Introduction* (ET H. Meyerhoff; Bollingen Series 59; New York, Pantheon, 1958) 155.

[52] Hall, "Dialectic," 386.

[53] H. Cairns, "Introduction," in E. Hamilton & H. Cairns (eds.), *The Collected Dialogues of Plato* (Bollingen Series 71; New Jersey: Princeton University Press, 1982) xiv; E. Ferguson, *Backgrounds of Early Christianity* (2nd ed.; Grand Rapids: Eerdmans, 1993) 312.

[54] Friedländer, *Plato*, 157.

[55] C. E. M. Joad, *Great Philosophies of the World* (Benn's Sixpenny Library 24; London: Ernest Benn Limited, 1928) 7–8.

average "man-in-the-street," brings up a subject in the realm of religion or politics in which some word like "just" or "true" or "beautiful" appears. Socrates, the chief figure in Plato's *Dialogues*, asks the
man what he means by the word. The man attempts an explanation, but encounters many difficulties along the way. Other speakers come to the aid of the man and offer suggestions as to what he
meant but Socrates refutes them one by one. Finally, Socrates is
challenged to give his own meaning to the disputed term. The rest
of the *Dialogue* is then a long explanation by Socrates, interspersed
with objections or requests for restatement in the interests of clarity
by the other speakers.

The essence of Platonic dialogue is definition. In Plato's dialogues
Socrates is presented as the midwife, aiding in the process of knowing. By his continual questioning of a person two things are thus
brought to light: (1) a necessary recognition by the other person that
he does not know what he thought he did (admitting his ignorance);
and, (2) arriving at the essence of something by a careful definition.[56]

Because dialectic literally means "conversational method," Denning-
Bolle continues her description of Platonic dialogues by pointing out
two main observations.[57] First, the notion of a conversation implies
a certain informality, people simply conversing with one another.
From a chance meeting a conversation arises which proceeds to a
specific issue. This was not the kind of conversation concealed in
special terminology to which only a few individuals were able to participate. Rather, the discussion was open to whomever was able to
exercise reason and enter into the search. Second, because dialectic
is a conversational method many illustrations are used. Analogies,
metaphors, and similes from everyday life are used when an idea is
being explained. This infuses the conversation with life because it is
adapted to the experiences of the listener.

In his *Republic* Plato places dialectic as the supreme philosophical
method, the coping-stone of the sciences which is set over them and
over which nothing can be placed.[58] Denning-Bolle claims that for
Plato it is through the dialogue that one arrives at truth; through a
carefully constructed conversation one finds solutions. However, this

---

[56] Cairns, "Introduction," xiv; Denning-Bolle, "Christian Dialogue as Apologetic,"
496; Friedländer, *Plato*, 156.
[57] Denning-Bolle, "Christian Dialogue as Apologetic," 496–498.
[58] Plato, *Rep.* 534E.

attainment of truth may be allowing more to the Platonic dialogue than Plato's philosophy itself will allow.

In this light, certain differences between the Socratic and the Platonic way of philosophizing must be maintained in a discussion of dialectic or dialogue.[59] Aristotle described the Socratic method by stating that "Socrates asked questions, but he did not answer; for he professed not to know".[60] Thus Socrates, in contrast to Plato, concludes with an assertion of not knowing. But Plato was compelled to carry the Socratic dialectic beyond itself, not to a skeptically negative conclusion, but to an answer to the questions posed by it.

> For Plato the dialectical path leads to that which is "beyond being." The "beyond" (*epekeina*) is not knowable; hence, not communicable. Only the way to it can be prepared. The dialogue, therefore, is such a way, leading, step by step, to a goal that, beyond the Socratic admission of ignorance and beyond the inexpressible [*sic*] of the highest Platonic vision, is ultimately vouched for as real by the living person of the master. And just as it is characteristic of the Socratic conversation to conclude with an admission of ignorance, so it is characteristic of Plato's dialogues to fall short of expressing the final truth; instead, it is brought into view as from a distance.[61]

This bringing the truth into view as from a distance, somewhat tempers Denning-Bolle's assertion that Plato's dialogues offer solutions. Thus, it is not that Plato himself offers solutions in his dialogues. Rather, using dialectic, Plato sees the conversation acting as a midwife through whom the pupil finds the way to truth through a process of questions.[62] In other words, "the dialectician is like the gardener who aids his plants but is unable to do for them what they must do for themselves."[63]

III. *Justin's* Dialogue *and the Genre of Dialogue*

A. *Similarity to Platonic Dialogue*

When this foundational understanding of the Platonic dialogues is brought into view with Justin's *Dialogue with Trypho*, the Platonic

---

[59] Friedländer, *Plato*, 168–169.
[60] Aristotle, *De soph. el.* 183^b 7. Friedländer, *Plato*, 157.
[61] Friedländer, *Plato*, 169–170.
[62] Plato, *Theaet.* 150C.
[63] Cairns, "Introduction," xiv–xv.

influence becomes apparent. Throughout chaps. 1–8 four main things stand out:[64] (1) the chance encounter setting the stage for the dialogue; (2) an old man à la Socrates, engaging in serious discussion; (3) the question and answer format; (4) the realization on the part of Justin that he did not really know all that he thought he did. In so doing, Justin uses a Platonic form and Platonic methods to discredit, eventually, Platonic truths.

B. *Divergence from Platonic Dialogue*

However, as much as these opening chapters indicate a close connection with Platonic dialogues, it is much more difficult to see this connection as the conversation in the *Dialogue* progresses. Reading the *Dialogue with Trypho* is no easy task. The modern reader is distracted by the apparent planlessness of it, and is constantly wondering where the thread of the argument is leading, or even if there is a thread at all.[65] It is this wondering that causes Chadwick to state, "As a writer he lacks the organizing power to arrange his material with desirable clarity. Were he writing today, he would be one of those scholars who place one line of text at the head of the page and cover the rest with lumpy footnotes."[66]

As one progresses past the opening nine chapters of the *Dialogue* the less dialogic it becomes. In many ways it could rather be described as Justin's *Monologue with Trypho*, considering the paucity of any significant dialogue in the writing. Denning-Bolle states that this is because Justin is being carried away by his own apology for Christianity. She notes that at around the middle point of the *Dialogue* an actual exchange does occur between the two men and Trypho even begins to lose his temper, returning Justin's comments with an irritation that was undetectable earlier than this point (*Dial.* 79–80). However, once this high point is reached, Justin's speeches become longer and any resemblance of a true dialogue virtually vanishes.[67]

But consider this in light of how the *Dialogue with Trypho* progresses. As stated above, the opening prologue of chaps. 1–9 truly can be compared with the Platonic dialogue. Many of the same settings and devices are present. But the remaining 133 chaps. are concerned with issues that Justin believes center around his attainment of the

---

[64] Denning-Bolle, "Christian Dialogue as Apologetic," 500–501.
[65] H. Chadwick, "Justin Martyr's Defence of Christianity," *BJRL* 47 (1965) 281.
[66] Chadwick, "Justin Martyr's Defence of Christianity," 276.
[67] Denning-Bolle, "Christian Dialogue as Apologetic," 504.

truth. In recounting his conversion in truly dialogue form Justin is able to go beyond the Platonic dialogue and add a dimension which exists because he believes he has attained truth. Because he is convinced of the truth of this philosophy of Christianity, he is not really interested in "dialogue." Chaps. 1–9 recount Justin's search and attainment of truth, after that point there is no longer any *search* for the truth. Chaps. 10–142 are the explanation of the truth that Justin has found. Thus the dialogue becomes a tool for apologetic.[68]

This understanding of the dialogue genre when compared to Justin's *Dialogue with Trypho* thus raises an important question: Can it still be maintained that that Justin chose the dialogue genre as a presentation of his search for truth when the vast majority of the *Dialogue* is not suited to the dialogue genre?

This question can be answered by returning to the purpose of the dialogue genre. While the *Dialogue* certainly contains elements that go beyond that of the basic understanding of the dialogue genre, it must also be understood that Justin's search resulted in something that went beyond the dialogue. Platonic dialogues, it may be recalled, did not result in the attainment of truth, the conversation acted more like a midwife of words through which the pupil was led to find truth for himself, but, ultimately, the Platonic dialogues fall short of expressing final truth.[69] Justin, therefore, had to add a new twist to the Platonic dialogue. So, whereas the Platonic dialogues led the pupil to discover truth, Justin, in his *Dialogue*, knew the truth and wanted to explain it. This allowed Justin to use the Platonic dialogue form, to a certain degree, and then ultimately add a new dimension because the newly discovered Christian philosophy contained the truth which Justin was seeking but could not find in Platonism. So while we may conclude that Justin chose the dialogue genre for a reason, we may also conclude that the dialogue genre ultimately fell short of Justin's goal or purpose. He was therefore obliged to go beyond the genre's original purpose and present his case as an attainment of truth rather than falling short of the attainment and merely presenting a search.

---

[68] Denning-Bolle, "Christian Dialogue as Apologetic," 505. E. F. Osborn ("From Justin to Origen: The Pattern of Apologetic," *Prudentia* 4 [1972] 1) states, "The business of apologetic is argument and its terms cannot be understood apart from the framework of argument." See also, M. J. Edwards, "On the Platonic Schooling of Justin Martyr," *JTS* ns 42 (1991) 20.

[69] Cairns, "Introduction," xiv–xv; Friedländer, *Plato*, 169–170.

IV. *Philosophy as a Search for Truth*

A. *Justin's Post-Conversion View of Philosophy*

Justin Martyr considered himself a philosopher. Upon his meeting
with Justin, Trypho noted that he wore the philosopher's cloak.
Trypho was apparently taught by Corinthus the Socratic that he
should take every occasion possible to converse with philosophers.
But Justin wonders why Trypho, a Jew, would expect to gain more
from philosophy than from his own "lawgiver and prophets."[70]

1. *Ethical Behavior*

Trypho's reply immediately steers the ensuing discussion toward philosophy. Trypho states, "does not the entire substance of what philosophers say concern God? And do they not always form questions
concerning his unity and providence? Is this not the task of philosophy—to inquire concerning God?"[71] Justin agrees with Trypho here
but is clear in expressing that he thinks most philosophers are not
interested in this task.

In response to Trypho, Justin makes two statements. First, philosophers are neither concerned to inquire whether there is one or even
several gods, nor whether all of mankind is watched over by divine
providence. For, according to them, such knowledge contributes nothing to happiness.[72] Second, the philosophers try to convince us that
God takes care of the universe with its genera and species, but not
for individuals.[73]

The general point of the passage here is quite clear—the majority of philosophers are not concerned with the relationship between
God and humanity. Justin's concerns for this neglect are present
because he believes it to have an effect on ethical behavior. Thus,
for Justin, both types of reasoning lead down the same road,

> But it is not difficult to see where they end up. It gives them an
> absence of fear and freedom to speak, doing and saying whatever they
> wish, neither fearing punishment nor having hope for any sort of

---

[70] *Dial.* 1.3 νομοθέτου καὶ τῶν προφητῶν.

[71] *Dial.* 1.3 οὐχ οἱ φιλόσοφοι περὶ θεοῦ τὸν ἅπαντα ποιοῦνται λόγον, ἐκεῖνος ἔλεγε,
καὶ περὶ μοναρχίας αὐτοῖς καὶ προνοίας αἱ ζητήσεις γίνονται ἑκάστοτε; ἢ οὐ τοῦτο
ἔργον ἐστὶ φιλοσοφίας, ἐξετάζειν περὶ τοῦ θείου;

[72] See above, Chapter 2, FN 148.

[73] *Dial.* 1.4.

benefit from God. For how could it be otherwise? They say these things will always be, that you and I will again live in a similar manner, becoming neither better nor worse. But there are some others who, supposing the soul immortal and incorporeal, believe that even though they have done evil they will not be given punishment (for the incorporeal is incapable of suffering), and if the soul is immortal it still needs nothing from God.[74]

2. *Diversification of Philosophy*

Following this initial exchange, the conversation continues with Trypho's next request, "What is your opinion concerning these things, and what judgment do you have concerning God, and tell us, what is your philosophy?"[75] Already the subject has been steered to the issues that will dominate the entire *Dialogue*—God and philosophy. But it is apparently neither the same God nor the same philosophy as the majority of philosophers have investigated. This is confirmed in *Dial.* 2.

In *Dial.* 2.1–2 Justin explains that philosophy is one's greatest possession and is most precious in the sight of God. He also explains that philosophy alone unites us to God, that philosophers (or men who have applied themselves to philosophy) are holy, that philosophy was sent down (κατεπέμφθη) by God to men, and that philosophy was originally one but has now become diversified or many-headed (πολύκρανος).

It is immediately apparent that Justin does not have a problem with philosophy per se, just with the path that philosophy has taken. The context in which Justin uses the terms καταπέμπω and πολύκρανος thus take on special significance in relation to Justin's concept of philosophy.

This is the only occurrence of καταπέμπω[76] in Justin's extant writings. He does, however, employ the term πέμπω without the prefixed

---

[74] *Dial.* 1.5 τοῦτο δὲ ὅπη αὐτοῖς τελευτᾷ, οὐ χαλεπὸν συννοῆσαι· ἄδεια γὰρ καὶ ἐλευθερία λέγειν καὶ ἔπεσθαι τοῖς δοξάζουσι ταῦτα, ποιεῖν τε ὅ τι βούλονται καὶ λέγειν, μήτε κόλασιν φοβουμένοις μήτε ἀγαθὸν ἐλπίζουσί τι ἐκ θεοῦ. πῶς γάρ; οἵ γε ἀεὶ ταὐτὰ ἔσεσθαι λέγουσι, καὶ ἔτι ἐμὲ καὶ σὲ ἔμπαλιν βιώσεσθαι ὁμοίως, μήτε κρείσσονας μήτε χείρους γεγονότας. ἄλλοι δέ τινες, ὑποστησάμενοι ἀθάνατον καὶ ἀσώματον τὴν ψυχήν, οὔτε κακόν τι δράσαντες ἡγοῦνται δώσειν δίκην (ἀπαθὲς γὰρ τὸ ἀσώματον), οὔτε, ἀθανάτου αὐτῆς ὑπαρχούσης, δέονταί τι τοῦ θεοῦ ἔτι.

[75] *Dial.* 1.6 Καὶ ὃς ἀστεῖον ὑπομειδιάσας· Σὺ δὲ πῶς, ἔφη, περὶ τούτων φρονεῖς καὶ τίνα γνώμην περὶ θεοῦ ἔχεις καὶ τίς ἡ σὴ φιλοσοφία, εἰπὲ ἡμῖν.

[76] In patristic literature this word is used in four basic ways: (1) Of the Father sending the Son in incarnation (Clement of Alexandria, *Paed.* 1.9; Methodius of

preposition κατά.[77] From the *Dialogue* we get a hint of Justin's meaning here. In *Dial.* 17.3 he explains that the Jews persecuted Jesus
who was the only blameless and righteous light sent (πεμφθέντος) by
God. Similarly, in *Dial.* 116.1 he explains that the power of God
was sent to us through Jesus Christ. The obvious agent in sending
Jesus Christ was God the Father. By stating that philosophy "was
sent down to men,"[78] the implication in this context is that it was
sent down by God, to whom it leads and unites us. Thus, in some
sense in Justin's mind, philosophy originated with God.

But still more can be said about the possible implications of Justin's
use of these terms as they relate to the *Logos*. Justin's definition of
philosophy is based upon certain negative qualities which he believes
must be corrected. The negative qualities are explained under the
assertion that philosophy has become "many-headed" (πολύκρανος).
In *Dial.* 1.4 he states that philosophers neglected God, and thus their
ethical conduct was contaminated. Now, in *Dial.* 2, Justin reiterates
his belief that philosophy has taken a wrong turn. Since this science
of philosophy is always one and the same,[79] there should not be a
plethora of philosophies. He continues,

> It happened that the first ones who were concerned with it [philoso-
> phy], and were considered illustrious men, were followed by men who
> made no investigation concerning truth, but only being impressed by
> their perseverance and self-control, and by the novelty of their doc-
> trines—each one presumed worthy of credit that which he had learned
> from his teacher. Then, the ones after that handed down to their fol-
> lowers such things and others like them, these then came to be named
> after the one who was the father of the doctrine.[80]

Olympus, *Symp.* 1.4); (2) Of the Father sending the Holy Spirit at Pentecost (John
Chrysostom, *Hom. 4 in principium Act Apost.*); (3) Of God sending spiritual gifts and
graces (Origen, *Joh.* 20.17; Methodius, *Symp.* 1.2, 4.2); Of the soul, in reference to
transmigration of souls (Justinianus Imperator, *liber adversus Origenem*; Theophilus of
Alexandria, *Frag. Origen*; Nemesius of Emesa, *de natura hominis* 2.). See G. W. H.
Lampe, *A Patristic Greek Lexicon* (Oxford: Clarendon, 1995) 714.

[77] It is difficult to determine if Justin was trying to emphasize the idea that philosophy was sent by God by compounding κατά with πέμπω. S. E. Porter (*Idioms of
the Greek New Testament* [Sheffield: Sheffield Academic Press, 1992] 140–143) indicates that there are three functions a preposition serves when prefixed to a verb:
(1) It may preserve but intensify the meaning of the verb; (2) It may transform the
meaning of the verb into a new meaning; (3) It may retain its basic or local meaning. Since the basic meaning of the preposition κατά is "direction downward" (Porter,
p. 162), it is probable here that either the first or third of the options are viable.

[78] *Dial.* 2.1 κατεπέμφθη εἰς τοὺς ἀνθρώπους.

[79] *Dial.* 2.1.

[80] *Dial.* 2.2 συνέβη τοῖς πρώτοις ἁψαμένοις αὐτῆς καὶ διὰ τοῦτο ἐνδόξοις γενομένοις

a. *Primordial Philosophy*

The idea that philosophy was originally given at an early time as one and then became contaminated evokes the concept of a primordial philosophy. The concept of a primordial philosophy may stem from the *Protrepticus*, written by the Stoic philosopher Posidonius of Apamaea (ca. 135–151 BCE).[81] Posidonius held that philosophy was given to humanity in primordial times, but later became corrupt when it split up into various schools. Hyldahl connected this with Justin and contended that Justin adopted the Posidonian view in order to criticize the decadence of recent philosophy. Thus, the primordial philosophy has not only degenerated, it has been lost, and it is now to be found in the books of the Prophets[82]—this is the conception that Justin has in mind when he calls Christianity a philosophy.[83]

This conception of a primordial philosophy can also be found in Antiochus of Ascalon (*d.* ca. 68 BCE).[84] Antiochus believed that all philosophy after Aristotle was decadent and that it was necessary to return to the "ancients".[85] The original philosophy was not broken until Zeno diverged from the teachings of his predecessors and

---

ἀκολουθῆσαι τοὺς ἔπειτα μηδὲν ἐξετάσαντας ἀληθείας πέρι, καταπλαγέντας δὲ μόνον τὴν καρτερίαν αὐτῶν καὶ τὴν ἐγκράτειαν καὶ τὸ ξένον τῶν λόγων ταῦτα ἀληθῆ νομίσαι ἃ παρὰ τοῦ διδασκάλου ἕκαστος ἔμαθεν, εἶτα καὶ αὐτούς, τοῖς ἔπειτα παραδόντας τοιαῦτα ἄττα καὶ ἄλλα τούτοις προσεοικότα, τοῦτο κληθῆναι τοὔνομα, ὅπερ ἐκαλεῖτο ὁ πατὴρ τοῦ λόγου.

[81] The impetus for relating Poseidonius's concept of a Primordial philosophy to this passage in the *Dialogue* originated with N. Hyldahl, *Philosophie und Christentum. Eine Interpretation der Einleitung zum Dialog Justins* (Acta Theologica Danica 9; Copenhagen: Munksgaard, 1966) 119–140. Hyldahl is supported by A. J. Droge, "Justin Martyr and the Restoration of Philosophy," *CH* 56 (1987) 317–319; O. Skarsaune, "The Conversion of Justin Martyr," *ST* 30 (1976) 63–65; van Winden, *An Early Christian Philosopher*, 42–48. Posidonius's writings are extant only in fragments so it is only through an investigation of the literature that refers to Posidonius that we are able to reconstruct his ideas. These fragments are conveniently compiled in L. Edelstein & I. G. Kidd (eds.), *Posidonius Volume I: The Fragments* (Cambridge Classical Texts and Commentaries; Cambridge: Cambridge University Press, 1972). ET of the Fragments in I. G. Kidd (eds.), *Posidonius Volume III: The Translation of the Fragments* (Cambridge Classical Texts and Commentaries; Cambridge: Cambridge University Press, 1999). For more on Posidonius see Copleston, *A History of Philosophy*, 1.2.166–169.

[82] Hyldahl connects *Dial.* 7 with *Dial.* 2.1 here.

[83] Hyldahl, *Philosophie und Christentum*, 112–140; 227–255.

[84] Droge, "Justin Martyr and the Restoration of Philosophy," 317. Antiochus's lectures were heard by Cicero. Thus, his ideas are quoted from Cicero. For a list of Cicero's works that cite Antiochus see, J. Dillon, *The Middle Platonists: A Study of Platonism 80 BC to AD 220* (London: Duckworth, 1977) 62–63.

[85] Cicero, *De fin.* 5.14. Antiochus thought that the true philosophy was maintained by the early Academics and Peripatetics (the "ancients") as late as the time of Polemo (315–270 BCE) (Cicero, *De fin.* 4.3; 5.7; *Acad. Pr.* 1.34–35).

established the Stoic school.[86] This view was taken up and modified
in the late second century CE by the Pythagorean philosopher Numenius
of Apamaea in his *On the Revolt of the Academics Against Plato*.[87] Numenius
claimed that genuine Platonic doctrine had been abandoned by
Speusippus, Xenocrates, and Polemo, "they did not abide by the
original tradition, but partly weakened it in many ways, and partly
distorting it: and beginning from his time, sooner or later they
diverged purposely or unconsciously, and partly from some other
cause perhaps other than rivalry."[88] What this shows is that the idea
of a pure primordial philosophy was current both before, during,
and after Justin's life.

b. *Primordial Philosophy in Justin Martyr*

Justin parallels this idea in two passages. In the first, *Dialogue* 35, he
makes reference to certain men who call themselves Christians but
who are really not. They are confessors of Jesus in name only, instead
of worshippers of him—in other words, they say they are Christians,
but they really are not. "Some are called Marcians, and some Valen-
tinians, and some Basilidians, and some Saturnillians and others by
other names; each called after the originator of the individual opinion, just as each one of those who consider themselves philosophers,
as I said before, thinks he must bear the name of the philosophy which
he follows, from the name of the father of the particular doctrine."[89]

In the second passage, *1 Apol.* 26, Justin mentions certain men
who operated by virtue of the devils within them. Included in this
list are Simon, Meander and Marcion. "All who take their opinions
from these men, are, as we said before [cf. *1 Apol.* 4.8;7.3], called
Christians; just as those also who do not agree with the philosophers
in their doctrines, have yet in common with them the name of philosophers given to them."[90] These texts can be compared as follows:[91]

---

[86] Cicero, *De fin.* 4.3.

[87] Relevant passages are quoted in Eusebius, *P.e.* 14.5–9. ET E. H. Gifford,
Preparation for the Gospel (2 vols.; Grand Rapids: Baker, 1981) 2.727–740.

[88] Eusebius, *P.e.* 14.5b-c.

[89] *Dial.* 35.6, italics mine. καί εἰσιν αὐτῶν οἱ μέν τινες καλούμενοι Μαρκιανοί, οἱ
δὲ Οὐαλεντινιανοί, οἱ δὲ Βασιλειδιανοί, οἱ δὲ Σατορνιλιανοί, καὶ ἄλλοι ἄλλῳ ὀνόματι,
ἀπὸ τοῦ ἀρχηγέτου τῆς γνώμης ἕκαστος ὀνομαζόμενος, ὃν τρόπον καὶ ἕκαστος τῶν
φιλοσοφεῖν νομιζόντων, ὡς ἐν ἀρχῇ προεῖπον, ἀπὸ τοῦ πατρὸς τοῦ λόγου τὸ ὄνομα ἧς
φιλοσοφεῖ φιλοσοφίας ἡγεῖται φέρειν.

[90] *1 Apol.* 26.6. πάντες οἱ ἀπὸ τούτων ὁρμώμενοι, ὡς ἔφημεν, Χριστιανοὶ καλοῦνται,
ὃν τρόπον καὶ οἱ οὐ κοινωνοῦντες τῶν αὐτῶν δογμάτων τοῖς φιλοσόφοις τὸ ἐπικατη-
γορούμενον ὄνομα τῆς φιλοσοφίας κοινὸν ἔχουσιν.

[91] van Winden, *An Early Christian Philosopher*, 43.

Philosophy	*Christianity*
one science	one faith
various schools	various sects or heresies
adherents named after	adherents named after
the "father of the doctrine"	the "father of the doctrine"
(πατὴρ τοῦ λόγου)	(ἀρχηγέτης τῆς γνώμης)
they call themselves philosophers	they call themselves Christians
but are not	but are not

This comparison leads us to two important conclusions.[92] First, Justin is clear that the adherents of these schools did not possess the true philosophy, that they wrongly called themselves philosophers, Platonists included.[93] Thus, in the above comparison, the philosophical founders are on the same level as the heretical founders—though they were in contact with the true philosophy, they still are not philosophers in the true sense. This is why Justin distinguishes the Prophets from *all* philosophers, founders included.[94] And since adherents directed their attention to the philosophers rather than at truth (the one philosophy) they went astray.

The above comparison also affords us a second conclusion. The "first ones"[95] of *Dial.* 2.2 are a reference to these fathers of the several philosophical schools. These first ones are only relatively first because "There were some men who existed long before the time of all these reputed philosophers, men who are ancient, blessed, and just, and loved by God . . . We call these men Prophets."[96] It is the Prophets, according to Justin, who possess and communicate the one true philosophy.

For Justin, Christians are in possession of the whole truth.[97] Greek philosophy has only an imperfect understanding of the truth because it is rife with contradictions and errors.[98] The Prophets are older

---

[92] van Winden, *An Early Christian Philosopher*, 44.

[93] *Dial.* 2.2, "Otherwise there would be neither Platonists, nor Stoics, nor Peropatetics, nor Theoretics, nor Pythagoreans, this knowledge being *one*."

[94] *Dial.* 7.1, Ἐγένοντό τινες πρὸ πολλοῦ χρόνου πάντων τούτων τῶν νομιζομένων φιλοσόφων παλαιότεροι . . .

[95] πρώτοις

[96] *Dial.* 7.1. Ἐγένοντό τινες πρὸ πολλοῦ χρόνου πάντων τούτων τῶν νομιζομένων φιλοσόφων παλαιότεροι, μακάριοι καὶ δίκαιοι καὶ θεοφιλεῖς . . . προφήτας δὲ αὐτοὺς καλοῦσιν.

[97] *Dial.* 39.5.

[98] *Dial.* 2; *1 Apol.* 13.2–4.

than the all the philosophers and it is they who communicate the
true philosophy. Since Justin has already placed the philosophers as
the "first ones" he quite naturally sees them as distorting the original philosophy of the Prophets. Thus, this relationship between
Christianity and philosophy is one of completion and correction.[99]

This relationship requires further explanation. Justin presents a
theory to account for the similarities he sees between Christianity
and Greek philosophy[100] which harmonizes with his conception of
the Prophets as possessors of the one true philosophy. He does so
by an appeal to the writings of Moses, from which the Greeks
acquired their knowledge, or through the *Logos*.[101]

c. *The Writings of Moses (Prophets)*
The idea of the antiquity of Moses and the Greek dependence on
him is well-attested in Hellenistic Judaism.[102] Justin extends this to
insist that not only Moses, but all the Prophets are older than Greek
poets, wise men, or philosophers.[103] Justin's arguments for the priority of Moses over Plato do have a precedent.[104] The idea that Plato
had also read Moses was well-known. According to widespread tradition, Plato had visited Egypt,[105] and Justin theorizes that while in
Egypt Plato had read a copy of the Pentateuch left behind by Moses.

d. Logos
But Justin's argument for historical priority and superiority of the
Prophets still did not account for Christ who has appeared on the
stage of history later than all these mentioned. After all, Christ was
born "one hundred and fifty years ago under Cyrenius and subse-

---

[99] Droge, "Justin Martyr and the Restoration of Philosophy," 307.
[100] For a complete list of points of agreement between Greek philosophy and
Christianity see, H. Chadwick, *Early Christian Thought and the Classical Tradition: Studies
in Justin, Clement, and Origen* (Oxford/New York: Clarendon, 1984) 11–13.
[101] Droge, "Justin Martyr and the Restoration of Philosophy," 307–316.
[102] See, A. J. Droge, *Homer or Moses? Early Christian Interpretations of the History of
Culture* (Hermeneutische Untersuchungen zur Theologie 26; Tübingen: J. C. B.
Mohr, 1989).
[103] *1 Apol.* 1.23; 54–60. Justin carries out his arguments for the priority of Moses
mainly with respect to Plato. These can be found in *1 Apol.* 44; 59; 60.
[104] See examples given in Droge, "Justin Martyr and the Restoration of Philosophy,"
310–311.
[105] Hecataeus of Abdera, *FGrHist* 264 F 25 (= Diodorus Siculus 1.96.2). Compare
Cicero. *De fin.* 5.87; Plutarch, *De Is. Et Osir.* 354e; Apuleius, *De Platone* 1.3; Diogenes
Laertius 3.6; Philostratus, *Vita Apollonii* 1.2; see also Cement, *Str.* 1.66.3; Origen, *C.
Cels.* 4.39.

quently, in the time of Pontius Pilate."[106] Justin's answer to this was to assert the historical Jesus as the embodiment of the eternal *Logos*. "He is the Word of whom every race of men were partakers; and those who lived reasonably (μετὰ λόγου) are Christians even though they have been thought atheists."[107] Christianity, therefore, is as ancient as the *Logos* itself.

This passage turns on the idea of the *spermatic Logos*. According to Justin's *2 Apol.* a share of the *Logos* has always been present in humankind. A germ (σπέρμα) was seen as existing in every rational mind that testified to the divine. Justin states that the moral teachings of the philosophers and poets were admirable because of the seed of reason planted in every race of men.[108] Justin can therefore agree with certain teachings of Plato, Socrates, and other philosophers because they had a share of the *spermatic Logos* (σπερματικοῦ λόγου). But the possessors of the *spermatic Logos* often contradicted themselves. They had only incomplete or partial knowledge because they did not have the whole of the Word, which is Jesus. "For whatever the philosophers or lawgivers continually uttered well, they achieved by finding and contemplating part of the Word. But since they did not know all of the Word, which is Christ, they often contradicted themselves in what they said."[109]

Despite this innate capacity, Justin realizes that only a relatively few individuals actually lived in accordance with the *Logos*.[110] The reason for this is that demons have so enslaved humanity that little can be expected from human reason.[111] So, the truth that does exist in the Philosophers is the result of their dependence on Moses and the Prophets. But Justin also identifies Christ with the eternal *Logos* of old and credits him with being the inspiration of Moses and the Prophets.[112] Thus, if Christ is identified both as the eternal *Logos* and the incarnate *Logos* this accounts for his pivotal significance in history.

[106] *1 Apol.* 46.1.
[107] *1 Apol.* 46.2–3. λόγον ὄντα, οὗ πᾶν γένος ἀνθρώπων μετέσχε. Καὶ οἱ μετὰ λόγου βιώσαντες Χριστιανοί εἰσι, κἂν ἄθεοι ἐνομίσθησαν.
[108] *2 Apol.* 8.1–2.
[109] *2 Apol.* 10.2 ὅσα γὰρ καλῶς ἀεὶ ἐφθέγξαντο καὶ εὗρον οἱ φιλοσοφήσαντες ἢ νομοθετήσαντες, κατὰ λόγου μέρος δι᾽ εὑρέσεως καὶ θεωρίας ἐστὶ πονηθέντα αὐτοῖς. ἐπειδὴ δὲ οὐ πάντα τὰ τοῦ λόγου ἐγνώρισαν, ὅς ἐστι Χριστός, καὶ ἐναντία ἑαυτοῖς πολλάκις εἶπον.
[110] *1 Apol.* 46.3.
[111] *1 Apol.* 5.2–6.1; *2 Apol.* 5.2–5.
[112] *1 Apol.* 63.10, 16.

Since Greek philosophy is dependent on Moses and the Prophets, who were inspired by the *Logos*, Christ has been active agent since the beginning. Indeed, it was he who appeared to Moses who is older than the Greek philosophers.[113] So, for Justin, the theory of dependence and the *Logos* theory serve to show that Christianity is responsible for whatever truth exists in Greek philosophy. In fact, Christianity is really the sole bearer of truth.

e. καταπέμπω

This leads us to a better position to comment on Justin's statement that philosophy was "sent down" to men. The idea of a primordial philosophy in Justin is clear. That primordial philosophy is ultimately identified as being one and as residing in the eternal *Logos*. Departure from this originally unified philosophy has corrupted philosophy. Moses and the Prophets are purveyors of the original philosophy, and everything that the philosophers knew is credited to the Prophets and the *spermatic Logos*. The *Logos* becomes the common denominator because it is he who inspired the Prophets.

It is clear, then, why Justin clams that philosophy was "sent down". Philosophy is one's greatest possession and it unites humanity to God.[114] The pure philosophy is not the many-headed version but the one revelation of the *Logos* to Moses and the Prophets which is witnessed to in scripture. This is the only philosophy. Further, it was sent down to men in the person of the incarnate *Logos*—the true philosophy appeared to humanity. It is the incarnate *Logos* who unites humanity to God.[115]

As an example of the problems with contemporary philosophy, Justin briefly recounts his own search through the philosophical systems of his day.[116] The progress is well-known. His first stop, with

---

[113] Droge, "Justin Martyr and the Restoration of Philosophy," 315.

[114] *Dial.* 2.1–2.

[115] The concept of wisdom being a gift from the gods was known in ancient philosophy (see Plato *Philebus* 16C). The verb καταπέμπω gets its explanation only in light of the comparison between philosophy and Christianity. Just as Christianity, in the person of Christ, was *sent down* to mankind, so true philosophy appeared among men. See van Winden, *An Early Christian Philosopher*, 45. The concept of *Logos* in Greek thought is long and complicated. See e.g., Copleston, *A History of Philosophy*; Hatch, E., *The Influence of Greek Ideas and Usages Upon the Christian Church* (repr.; Peabody, MA: Hendrickson, 1995 [London: Williams and Norgate, 1895]); G. B. Kerford, "*Logos*," in P. Edwards (ed.), *The Encyclopedia of Philosophy* (8 vols.; New York: Macmillan/The Free Press, 1967) 5.83–84; Zeller, *Outlines of the History of Greek Philosophy*.

[116] *Dial.* 2.3–6.

a Stoic, was a failure because after spending some time with him
he realized that his instructor had no knowledge about God, nor
did he consider this knowledge necessary. Next, the Peripatetic was
so concerned about tuition fee that Justin did not believe him to be
a real philosopher. He was dismissed by the Pythagorean because
of his lack of knowledge about music, astronomy, and geometry.
Finally, in a troubled state of mind he decided to consult a Platonist.
Under this philosopher Justin claims that he learned so much that
in a short time he considered himself a wise man.

Consider his search through these philosophical systems in the
context of Justin's contention that philosophy has become many-
headed. In so doing we can see that Justin was searching for two
things: truth and God. The main emphasis here is that "philosophy
is essentially the message of truth, that it proceeds from God to man,
that it demands from man continuous and total commitment (cf.
προσεσχηκέναι in D. 2:1) and careful investigation (cf. ἐξετάσαι
in D. 2:2), and that it introduces man to ultimate reality, i.e. God
(D. 2:1)."[117]

B. *Justin's Pre-Conversion View of Philosophy*

That this was Justin's emphasis is confirmed in his conversion account
of *Dial.* 3–8. In *Dial.* 3 Justin, the Platonist, meets the "respectable
old man" who would eventually convince him of the respectability
of Christianity. During the beginning of their conversation the old
man asks Justin to define philosophy. Justin's reply is that philosophy "is the knowledge of that which is, and knowledge based on
truth".[118] The parallels here with the Platonic concept of truth[119] are
apparent. Since it is Justin the Platonist speaking here this should
come as no surprise. "Knowledge of that which is," is in the realm
of Forms, of which the Good is the highest reality. "Knowledge
based on truth," is intimately related to this highest Form because
if it is the Good who is the ultimate giver and goal of knowledge,
then this is also where truth resides. Thus, both truth and knowledge are based on the ultimate Form—the Good. Since the Good
resides in the realm of being, true knowledge of the Good cannot

---

[117] C. I. K. Story, *The Nature of Truth in "The Gospel of Truth" and in the Writings
of Justin Martyr* (NovTSup 25; Leiden: E. J. Brill, 1970) 54.
[118] *Dial.* 3.4 ἐπιστήμη ἐστὶ τοῦ ὄντος καὶ τοῦ ἀληθοῦς ἐπίγνωσις.
[119] See section I.A-B.

be apprehended by the senses, but only through the mind. So truth is not found in an event since an event is in the realm of becoming and apprehended by the senses. There is neither knowledge of what is real nor ultimate truth found in the realm of Becoming. As a Middle Platonist, this is what Justin is claiming.

Following this definition the old man asks Justin to define God. To this request Justin answers, "That which always has the same manner and existence and is the cause of all other things—this indeed is God".[120] Why the old man asks this question is unknown. Perhaps he was trying to be sure of Justin's Platonic understanding before proceeding. Clearly the answer has confirmed this in the old man's mind. That which always has the same manner and that which is the cause of all other things is the Good. The Good resides in the realm of Being and is the ultimate Form.

Justin indicates that these Platonic definitions were given hearing by the old man "with pleasure."[121] Exactly why this was so we can not be sure. Perhaps the old man knew some common ground upon which he may steer the ensuing discussion. He was asking probing questions of Justin to be sure of where Justin was coming from. He certainly got Justin to clearly state that he was concerned with truth and the divine. I would suggest that this is the most likely reason why the old man showed pleasure at Justin's answers. He now knows where he will direct the conversation based on the common ground the two share—truth and God. Of course, certain presuppositions and conclusions are not common, but the fact that both are searching for truth and God is enough for the old man to progress. Through this progression, Justin's concept of truth is quite literally radically transformed.

The discussion following this exchange centers on God as the ultimate reality that the philosophers do not know. We must not miss the fact here that each are approaching this issue from radically different presuppositions. Justin is claiming that the ultimate reality is known through the mind. But the old man is making the radical claim that the philosophers do not and can not know the ultimate reality through the mind. This opens the door for the old man to introduce the truth that will grip Justin until his dying day—Christianity.

---

[120] *Dial.* 3.5 Τὸ κατὰ τὰ αὐτὰ καὶ ὡσαύτως ἀεὶ ἔχον καὶ τοῦ εἶναι πᾶσι τοῖς ἄλλοις αἴτιον, τοῦτο δή ἐστιν ὁ θεός.
[121] *Dial.* 3.5.

The fact that the statements concerning truth and God were expressed by Justin as a Middle Platonist should in no way diminish the fact that his purpose in searching the philosophies of his day was essentially a search for the ultimate truth—a truth which he eventually found in Christianity. It is important to keep in mind the fact that Justin still considers himself a philosopher after his conversion. Following his surrender to the old man's argument and realization of the truth in it Justin states, "But immediately my soul was set on fire and a love for the Prophets took hold of me as well as [a love for] these individuals who are friends of Christ. While pondering on his words I discovered that this was the only sure and profitable philosophy. Thus indeed, it is because of these things that I am a philosopher."[122] Justin's pre-conversion understanding of philosophy as a search for truth and the fact that he believed to have found this truth in Christianity, shows that Justin's pre-Christian and Christian concept of the task of philosophy had not changed. Justin could still consider himself a philosopher because he discovered in Christianity the ultimate reality.

After Justin responds to the old man's request to define philosophy and God he then presses Justin on the issue of epistemology.[123] The old man asks Justin if knowledge is not a word applied commonly to different matters. Some knowledge, such as military strategy, navigation, and medicine comes from study and practice. But some knowledge cannot be gained in this way, it must be gained by sight or hearing from someone who has seen. Justin agrees with the old man's reasoning, and upon this agreement the old man drives the point home. " 'Then how,' " he [the old man] said, 'can philosophers set forth truthfully or speak that which is true concerning God when they have no knowledge of Him, having never seen or heard him?' "[124] Upon this question Justin states that he is in agreement with Plato who asserts that God cannot be perceived by the eyes, but is to be perceived by the mind alone.[125] As Story points out, the

---

[122] *Dial.* 8.1–2 ἐμοῦ δὲ παραχρῆμα πῦρ ἐν τῇ ψυχῇ ἀνήφθη, καὶ ἔρως ἔχει με τῶν προφητῶν καὶ ἀνδρῶν ἐκείνων, οἵ εἰσι Χριστοῦ φίλοι· διαλογιζόμενός τε πρὸς ἐμαυτὸν τοὺς λόγους αὐτοῦ ταύτην μόνην εὕρισκον φιλοσοφίαν ἀσφαλῆ τε καὶ σύμφορον. οὕτως δὴ καὶ διὰ ταῦτα φιλόσοφος ἐγώ.

[123] *Dial.* 3.5–7.

[124] *Dial.* 3.7 Πῶς οὖν ἄν, ἔφη, περὶ θεοῦ ὀρθῶς φρονοῖεν οἱ φιλόσοφοι ἢ λέγοιέν τι ἀληθές, ἐπιστήμην αὐτοῦ αὐτοῦ μὴ ἔχοντες, μηδὲ ἰδόντες ποτὲ ἢ ἀκούσαντες;

[125] *Dial.* 3.7.

entire structure of the discussion between the old man and Justin
the Platonist revolves around the question, "How can man know the
Ultimate Truth, i.e., God?"[126] By way of summary, since God is the
ultimate truth, the discussion naturally centers on God and, as we
have seen above, Justin presents God in three ways: First, God is
that which is, that which is true.[127] Second, God is that which "always
has the same manner and existence and is the cause of all other
things."[128] Third, God can only be perceived by the mind alone.[129]

Dial. 4–7 continues to discuss certain Middle Platonic understandings of the mind and the soul, which the old man challenges
and ultimately refutes.[130] Justin has implied that, with the help of
philosophers and through the affinity that souls have with God,
humankind can know God. Both of these implications are questioned
by the old man. Thus, the possibility of any person (including philosophers) having knowledge of God through the mind is denied particularly because that mind is "unadorned" by the Holy Spirit.[131]
Further, Justin's assertion of the soul's kinship with God is corrected
by the old man. By way of correction, the soul is not immortal, but
is rather begotten just as the world is begotten.[132] However, the soul
will not die but will live on in a better or worse place.[133] The soul
lives not because it is life, but because it shares in life, it is entirely
different from that in which it partakes.[134] Then, in *Dial.* 7 Justin
asks the old man what teacher or method he should follow if these
philosophers do not know the truth. The discussion is then brought
around full circle to the issue of epistemology initiated in *Dial.* 3.
With the old man's distinction between the two kinds of knowledge
in mind, one by study and practice and the other by sight and hearing, the old man states,

---

[126] Story, *The Nature of Truth in "The Gospel of Truth" and in the Writings of Justin Martyr*, 65.

[127] *Dial.* 3.4.

[128] *Dial.* 3.5.

[129] *Dial.* 3.7.

[130] Justin has interpreted and synthesized certain aspects of Albinus' philosophy. Justin had a certain predilection for using the term ἄρρητος in reference to the unity and incomprehensibility of God. This coincides with Albinus' use of the same term for the same description (*Didask.* 10.4). Further, Albinus states that God is com-
prehensible by the mind alone. This idea is virtually the same as that stated by the pre-Christian Justin in *Dial.* 4.1. See Story, *The Nature of Truth in "The Gospel of Truth" and in the Writings of Justin Martyr*, 62–63.

[131] *Dial.* 4.1.

[132] *Dial.* 5.1–2.

[133] *Dial.* 5.3.

[134] *Dial.* 6.

There were some men who existed long before the time of all these
reputed philosophers, men who are ancient, blessed, just, and loved
by God, speaking by the spirit of God and prophesying things which
were about to take place which, indeed, are now taking place. We call
these men Prophets. They alone both saw and announced the truth
to men, neither fearing nor reverencing anyone, and not overcome
with a desire for glory. But they alone, being filled with the Holy
Spirit, communicated that which they heard and saw. Their writings
are still now unchanged, and the one reading them is greatly aided
concerning the beginning and end of all things, and that which the
philosopher needs to know, believing these things. For they did not
give proof at that time of their words, for they were above all proof,
being higher witnesses to the truth. And these things which have happened and are now happening force you to agree with what they are
saying. Indeed, because of the powers which they displayed they are
worthy of belief, since they glorified God, the creator and father of
all, and also announced the Christ, his son.[135]

Seeing and hearing, the second type of knowledge of which the old
man speaks, is here presented as occurring in the Prophets. The Prophets differ from the philosophers because, through the filling of the
Holy Spirit, they were witnesses to the truth, they had seen and heard
and did not need to use argument in their presentation of truth.
Further, the writings of the Prophets are extant, and in these writings are recorded events that have taken place and are now taking
place, forcing readers to believe their words.

In being lead to the Prophets and to Christianity as the one true
philosophy Justin came to the realization that contemporary philosophy cannot give knowledge of the truth directly. God as the ultimate reality cannot be known through the philosophers because they
have neither seen him nor heard from someone who has seen or
heard him. This is a radical departure from his Middle Platonic

---

[135] *Dial.* 7.1–3 Ἐγένοντό τινες πρὸ πολλοῦ χρόνου πάντων τούτων τῶν νομιζομένων
φιλοσόφων παλαιότεροι, μακάριοι καὶ δίκαιοι καὶ θεοφιλεῖς, θείῳ πνεύματι λαλήσαντες
καὶ τὰ μέλλοντα θεσπίσαντες, ἃ δὴ νῦν γίνεται· προφήτας δὲ αὐτοὺς καλοῦσιν. οὗτοι
μόνοι τὸ ἀληθὲς καὶ εἶδον καὶ ἐξεῖπον ἀνθρώποις, μήτ᾽ εὐλαβηθέντες μήτε δυσωπηθέντες τινά, μὴ ἡττημένοι δόξης, ἀλλὰ μόνα ταῦτα εἰπόντες ἃ ἤκουσαν καὶ ἃ εἶδον
ἁγίῳ πληρωθέντες πνεύματι. συγγράμματα δὲ αὐτῶν ἔτι καὶ νῦν διαμένει, καὶ ἔστιν
ἐντυχόντα τούτοις πλεῖστον ὠφεληθῆναι καὶ περὶ ἀρχῶν καὶ περὶ τέλους καὶ ὧν χρὴ
εἰδέναι τὸν φιλόσοφον, πιστεύσαντα ἐκείνοις. οὐ γὰρ μετὰ ἀποδείξεως πεποίηνται τότε
τοὺς λόγους, ἅτε ἀνωτέρω πάσης ἀποδείξεως ὄντες ἀξιόπιστοι μάρτυρες τῆς ἀληθείας·
τὰ δὲ ἀποβάντα καὶ ἀποβαίνοντα ἐξαναγκάζει συντίθεσθαι τοῖς λελαλημένοις δι᾽
αὐτῶν. καίτοι γε καὶ διὰ τὰς δυνάμεις, ἃς ἐπετέλουν, πιστεύεσθαι δίκαιοι ἦσαν, ἐπειδὴ
καὶ τὸν ποιητὴν τῶν ὅλων θεὸν καὶ πατέρα ἐδόξαζον καὶ τὸν παρ᾽ αὐτοῦ Χριστὸν υἱὸν
αὐτοῦ κατήγγελλον·

understandings. It clearly indicates a new way of thinking for Justin
because he has accepted that sensible perception is actually valid in
a search for truth. This, however, must be understood in the context of a filling of the Holy Spirit.

C. *The Spirit*

We have now come full circle with the old man's argument. In *Dial.*
4.1, the old man begins his assault on Platonic philosophy by asking Justin how the mind may ever see God if it is unadorned by
the Holy Spirit. Now, at the climax of the argument in *Dial.* 7.1–3,
we read of those who existed before the reputed philosophers who
are ancient, blessed, just and loved by God. These are called the
Prophets who actually were adorned by the Holy Spirit.[136] The point
here is that the old man introduces a problem into Justin's Middle
Platonic epistemology—the mind cannot possibly know God because
it has no kinship with God. The mind belongs to the created realm,
the realm of becoming. The only way a mind may know God is if
it is adorned by the Holy Spirit.

The filling of the Spirit appears to be the key in the old man's
argument against the philosophers attaining true knowledge of God.
And because Justin eventually accepts the old man's argument, it
becomes a key in the entire *Dialogue with Trypho*. The Prophets and
the prophecies which the Prophets uttered were believed by Justin
to have been given by God. Thus, the Prophets are stated to express
the words of God[137] and to speak for God.[138] The Prophets are also
said to speak by the Spirit of prophecy.[139] These ways of expressing
the Spirit's influence upon the Prophets are to be understood in the
context of the Father being the originator and the controller of the
process[140]—the revealer of the process. Therefore, any statement of
David, Isaiah, Moses, or any other Prophet foretelling by the Spirit
of prophecy, or the Spirit of prophecy speaking from the person of

---

[136] The term is not "adorned" (κεκοσμημένος) as in 4.1, but rather, speaking and
prophesying by the Spirit of God (θείῳ πνεύματι λαλήσαντες καὶ τὰ μέλλοντα
θεσπίσαντες, ἃ δὴ νῦν γίνεται).

[137] *Dial.* 15; 62; 65.

[138] *Dial.* 16; 17; 20; 21; 26; 41; 44; 46; 63; 65; 77; 80; 82.

[139] *Dial.* 25; 32; 38; 43; 53; 73; 74; 77; 78; 84; 91; 114; 124; 139. In *1 Apol.*
33–37 this Spirit of prophecy is actually identified with the *Logos*.

[140] *Dial.* 3; 127.

Christ[141] is viewed as coming ultimately from God because it was all done through the Spirit of prophecy.[142]

The trinitarian element of Justin's thinking here is not difficult to see. He had no developed doctrine of the Trinity,[143] yet the relationship between the Father, the *Logos* and the Spirit is implicit in the above explanation of the Spirit's role of inspiring the Prophets. The Father is shown to be the original possessor of the utterances of the Prophets and the controller/revealer of the process. The Prophets, who speak by this Spirit, communicate the *Logos*.

It appears as though the Prophets are viewed by Justin as receiving their message/knowledge through an ecstatic experience wherein the normal activity of the Prophet is submerged. Justin does indicate this in two places in the *Dialogue*. He recounts the vision of Daniel in Dan 7 which is quite obviously an ecstatic revelation.[144] And he also explains that Zechariah prophesied under a spirit of ecstasy when the revelation of Jesus was made known to him.[145] If Daniel and Zecharaiah received their revelations in an ecstatic state there is no indication in Justin that he believed otherwise of the other Prophets.[146] The point, however, must not be missed that it is God, through the Spirit, who reveals to the Prophets that which they proclaim.

The importance of the Spirit's influence on the Prophets comes to the fore in the climax of the old man's argument against Justin's Middle Platonic epistemology in *Dial.* 7. The Prophets, speaking by the Spirit of God, actually heard (ἤκουσαν) and saw (εἶδον) the things of which they spoke. This should be seen as a direct response and contradiction to the Middle Platonic idea that God may be seen through the powers of the mind.[147] To see the truth with the eye of

---

[141] *Dial.* 88.

[142] See also passages where God is said to speak by the Spirit of prophecy, e.g., *Dial.* 80. This is why Justin, in his *Apology*, can speak of the Prophets being inspired by the divine *Logos* (*1 Apol.* 33.9), by the prophetic Spirit (*1 Apol.* 35.3), and by God himself (*1 Apol.* 60.3). So it is not the Prophets themselves who speak or write, but the divine *Logos*, according to the will of the Father, who moves in them.

[143] L. W. Barnard, *Justin Martyr. His Life and Thought* (Cambridge: Cambridge University Press, 1967) 105.

[144] *Dial.* 31.

[145] *Dial.* 115.3.

[146] Goodenough, *The Theology of Justin Martyr*, 178; R. M. Grant, *The Letter and the Spirit* (London: SPCK, 1957) 75.

[147] *Dial.* 2.6. For more on Justin's Middle Platonism see above, Chapter 2.III.A.1. For the relationship between Justin's Platonism and Middle Platonism see also, C. Andresen, "Justin und der mittlere Platonismus," *ZNW* 44 (1952/53) 157–195;

the mind was the aim and goal of Platonic philosophy. But, as Justin
(through the old man) points out, Biblical revelation has another
emphasis. The Prophets do speak of "seeing God" (Exod 24:10; Job
42:5–6), but the vision is not related to the power of the mind, but
to God's presence or glory, for example, that filled the tabernacle
(Exod 40:43) and the temple (I Kgs 8:10), and especially to God's
presence in Jesus Christ (John 14:9).[148] Thus, it is through the Holy
Spirit that Prophets saw and heard, not through the Middle Platonic
nous. This is the difference between Middle Platonic epistemology
and Christian epistemology. The Prophets, through the prophetic
Spirit, revealed divine truth which concerns events which have happened (ἀποβάντα) and are still happening (ἀποβαίνοντα), just as the
Prophets predicted.[149]

With this Justin took the old man's words to heart and an affection
for the Prophets took hold of him, so much so that he considered
the message of the Prophets the only true philosophy. It thus became
his desire to convince everyone of the same belief.[150] At the center
of the message of the Prophets was Jesus the Christ and salvation
through him based on the events and actions of God. Justin's insistence on Christ as the essential message of the Prophets caused
Trypho's friends to laugh and state that he would have been better
to remain a Platonist or adhere to some other philosophy. They
believed that by putting his hope in Jesus Justin was turning from
God and losing any hope of salvation. Better for Justin to observe
the Law because the Messiah is not yet known, for the Christians
have simply believed a foolish rumor that Jesus is the Messiah.[151]

This, in turn, becomes the foundation upon which Justin proceeds
in the *Dialogue with Trypho*. Immediately following Justin's account of
his conversion he thus states, "For I will show proof that we believe

---

Barnard, *Justin Martyr*, 34–37; J. Daniélou, *Gospel Message and Hellenistic Culture*. (The
Development of Christian Doctrine Before the Council of Nicaea Vol 2; ET J. A.
Baker; London: Darton, Longman & Todd, 1973) 107–113; Droge, "Justin Martyr
and the Restoration of Philosophy," 304–307; G. May, *Creatio Ex Nihilo: The Doctrine
of 'Creation out of Nothing' in Early Christian Thought* (ET A. S. Worall; Edinburgh:
T&T Clark, 1994) 1–5; Story, *The Nature of Truth in "The Gospel of Truth" and in the
Writings of Justin Martyr*, 58–59.

[148] Story, *The Nature of Truth in "The Gospel of Truth" and in the Writings of Justin
Martyr*, 67.

[149] Story, *The Nature of Truth in "The Gospel of Truth" and in the Writings of Justin
Martyr*, 67.

[150] *Dial.* 8.1.

[151] *Dial.* 8.3.

in neither fables nor doctrines without proof, but in doctrines full of the spirit of God, emitting power and flourishing with grace."[152] Trypho agrees that the progress of the conversation will thus focus on why Justin places his hope in a crucified man yet still expects to receive favor from God when his commandments are ignored.[153] On the one hand, Trypho states that Justin does not really know God, while, on the other hand, Justin asserts that he does. The discourse is thus set. Justin will prove from the Prophets that what he states concerning Jesus as Messiah is true.

V. *Justin's Presentation of Truth*

Dial. 39 describes Christians as "instructed in all truth".[154] In the context, all truth centers on Jesus as the Christ. Jesus as the whole truth thus becomes the center of Justin's message, it revolves around Jesus. It is through Jesus that God is known and man attains salvation. Therefore, this examination of Justin's presentation of truth will also center on Jesus as the pivotal figure in Justin's presentation of truth—Christ himself is truth.

A. *The Argument From Prophecy*

1. *The Prophets and Jesus*

It has been shown above that Justin was converted to Christianity through an understanding of the Prophets and their message of truth.[155] Immediately upon commencing the dialogue proper (chap. 11) we get a hint of how Justin will use scripture in his explanation of truth. In discussing the Law he bases his assertions of a New Covenant upon quotations from Isaiah and Jeremiah. This type of argument is indicative of the entire *Dialogue* where Justin is dependent on the Old Testament scriptures, a fact that does not go unnoticed by Trypho. At one point in the *Dialogue* Trypho states that the only reason he has tolerated the conversation with Justin is because Justin has referred everything to the scriptures.[156] Later Trypho also remarks

---

[152] *Dial.* 9.1 παρεστῶτι γὰρ δείξω ὅτι οὐ κενοῖς ἐπιστεύσαμεν μύθοις οὐδὲ ἀναποδείκτοις λόγοις, ἀλλὰ μεστοῖς πνεύματος θείου καὶ δυνάμει βρύουσι καὶ τεθηλόσι χάριτι.

[153] *Dial.* 10.2–4.

[154] *Dial.* 39.5 οἱ ἐκ πάσης τῆς ἀληθείας μεμαθητευμένοι τιμῶμεν.

[155] See section IV.

[156] *Dial.* 56.16.

that Justin is very careful to keep close to the scriptures in all his statements.[157]

Even a cursory reading of the *Dialogue with Trypho* reveals Justin's reference to the OT. He explicitly alludes to and quotes from the OT (LXX) more than seven hundred times[158] from no less than nineteen different OT documents.[159] When Justin refers to the Prophets either prophesying, foretelling, or predicting he does not merely mean the major and minor Prophets of the OT, the whole of the OT writings are seen as prophetic. This is illustrated in *Dial.* 126.2 where Justin says to Trypho, "For if you had understood the words of the Prophets, you would not have denied that He [Jesus] was God, Son of the only, unbegotten and ineffable God."[160] In the context there exists the usual mention of the Prophets; Ezekiel, Daniel, Isaiah, and Zechariah. But also included among them are writings of the Old Testament (or persons contained in OT books) commonly referred to as Law and Writings, i.e. Moses and Solomon. Further, as we saw above, Justin also places the words of these OT Prophets and personalities on the same level as the words of God. This is because the Prophets spoke by "the prophetic spirit,"[161] and "the (holy) spirit of prophecy"[162] Many times Justin equates the words of an OT personality with the words of God,[163] thus indicating his belief that the Prophets spoke God's message.[164]

For Justin the OT scriptures are necessary not only because they are the words and message of God, but, perhaps most importantly,

---

[157] *Dial.* 80.1.

[158] E. J. Goodspeed, *The Formation of the New Testament* (Chicago: University of Chicago Press, 1962) 51.

[159] Gen, Exod, Lev, Num, Deut, 1–2 Kgs, Job, Pss, Isa, Jer, Ezek, Dan, Hos, Amos, Mic, Zech, and Mal.

[160] *Dial.* 126.2 ἐπεὶ εἰ νενοήκατε τὰ εἰρημένα ὑπὸ τῶν προφητῶν, οὐκ ἂν ἐξηρνεῖσθε αὐτὸν εἶναι θεόν, τοῦ μόνου καὶ ἀγεννήτου καὶ ἀρρήτου θεοῦ υἱόν.

[161] τὸ προφητικὸν πνεῦμα *Dial.* 43.3; 53.4; 77.3; 91.4.

[162] τοῦ (ἁγίου) προφητικοῦ πνεύματος *Dial.* 32.3; 84.2; 139.1.

[163] See e.g., *Dial.* 41.2; 44.2, 3; 46.5; 78.8, cf. 80.4–5; 84.1; 94.1; 133.2.

[164] Justin's reference to the Law and Writings was the Jewish way of speaking of what we now call the canon. The Jewish Bible today is made up three divisions, whose titles are combined to form the current Hebrew name for the complete writings of Judaism: *Torah, Nebiim, Kethubim = Tanak*. This trilication is ancient; it is supposed as long established in the Mishnah, the Jewish code of unwritten sacred laws, reduced to writing, ca. 200 CE. A grouping closely akin to it occurs in the NT in Christ's own words (Luke 24:44). In the prologue of Ecclesiasticus (prefixed ca. 132 BCE) we find mentioned "the Law, and the Prophets, and others that have followed them."

because they prophesy and testify concerning the life of Jesus. And
it is this testimony contained in the Prophets upon which Justin
focuses throughout the *Dialogue*. His reasoning is quite clear—the
Jews are at fault for being ignorant of the coming of Jesus as Messiah,
this is because it is all recorded in the Prophets.

> For you [the Jews] did not offer sacrifice to Baal, as your fathers, nor
> did you place cakes in groves and on the high places for the host of
> heavens. Yet, you have not accepted his [God's] Christ. For the one
> who is ignorant of this one [Christ] is also ignorant of the purpose of
> God, and the one who insults and hates this one [Christ] clearly hates
> and insults the one who sent him. And he who does not believe in
> him does not believe the Prophets, who offered the good news and
> proclaimed it to all.[165]

Justin's point here is that everything asserted about Jesus in the
Christian tradition was spoken of in the Prophets before he came
and was born a man. For Justin the OT scriptures were Christian
writings.[166] As Christian writings they needed to be interpreted
by the Christian tradition, and this is indeed what Justin does. For
this reason the prophecies, which are delivered or handed down
(παραδίδωμι) by the Prophets, are recalled to prove the event of Jesus
Christ.

Justin's use of the prophetic scriptures in this manner has been
commonly referred to as the argument (or proof) from prophecy.[167]
Because the *Dialogue* was set within a conversation with a Jew, Justin
was working from the same respect for the OT scriptures. In this
setting the appeal to scripture was entirely legitimate. The Jewish
and Christian frame of mind meant that world history and God's purposes were connected in some way and this is the way they approached
scripture. In the historical books of the OT the connection between

---

[165] *Dial.* 136.3 οὐ γὰρ καὶ ὑμεῖς τῇ Βάαλ ἐθύετε, ὡς οἱ πατέρες ὑμῶν, οὐδὲ ἐν συσκίοις
ἢ μετεώροις τόποις πέμματα ἐποιεῖτε τῇ στρατιᾷ τοῦ οὐρανοῦ, ἀλλ' ὅτι οὐκ ἐδέξασθε
τὸν Χριστὸν αὐτοῦ. ὁ γὰρ τοῦτον ἀγνοῶν ἀγνοεῖ καὶ τὴν βουλὴν τοῦ θεοῦ, καὶ ὁ τοῦτον
ὑβρίζων καὶ μισῶν καὶ τὸν πέμψαντα δῆλον ὅτι καὶ μισεῖ καὶ ὑβρίζει· καὶ εἰ οὐ πιστεύει
τις εἰς αὐτόν, οὐ πιστεύει τοῖς τῶν προφητῶν κηρύγμασι τοῖς αὐτὸν εὐαγγελισαμένοις
καὶ κηρύξασιν εἰς πάντας.

[166] *Dial.* 28–30. See also, D. E. Aune, "Justin Martyr's Use of the Old Testament,"
BETS 9 (1966) 179; J. N. D. Kelly, *Early Christian Doctrines* (rev. ed.; San Francisco:
Harper, 1978) 32.

[167] See, J. Daniélou, *Gospel Message and Hellenistic Culture* (A History of Early
Christian Doctrine Before the Council of Nicaea Volume 2; ET J. A. Baker; London:
Darton, Longman & Todd/Philadelphia: The Westminster Press, 1973) 211–220;
T. W. Manson, "The Argument From Prophecy," *JTS* 46 (1945) 129–130.

history and God's purposes was plain, but there was a large portion
of prophecy to which nothing in the history of the world appeared
to correspond, or—to put it the other way around—a large part of
world history whose place in the divine purpose was not obvious.
Therefore, the task was two-fold: (1) to study the oracles of God to
better understand the nature of God's purpose; (2) to study the events
in order to locate any indication that God was working his purposes
out in history. This is the basis upon which the argument from
prophecy rested and proceeded.

2. *The Argument Proper*

A large part of the argument from prophecy rested on interpretation and exegesis. Thus, the argument from prophecy was the result
of "correctly" interpreting scripture in light of "correctly" understanding the event. In order to rebut this, then, one had to challenge the correctness of exegesis, or the justice of the interpretation
of the event, or both.[168] This challenge to produce scriptural evidence for events such as the cross or the virgin birth naturally led
to some rather forced exegesis as well as some interesting literal and
allegorical interpretations of prophecies. As interesting as the exegetical issue is, however, the present purpose does not lie there. The
purpose here is simply to explain Justin's use of the argument from
prophecy as he presents it as truth.

Perhaps the best way to understand how the argument from
prophecy is employed by Justin is through the use of the following
schematic.

Agreed Basis of Argument:	The Messiah is he who corresponds to the picture given of him in the OT. A is B.
Justin:	The picture of the Messiah in the OT is *X. Y. Z.* All this is applicable to Jesus, as the parallel events from his life to the following texts from the OT prove. B is C.

---

[168] Manson, "The Argument From Prophecy," 130.

| Trypho: | Even if we agree with a certain like-ness of the Messianic picture from the OT to Jesus, *Y. Z.* aspects of your OT Messianic picture have other applications. Further, there are *K. L. M.* aspects of the OT picture of the Messiah which are obviously not applicable to Jesus.
Most of B is not C.
Therefore Jesus is not the Messiah.
C is not A.[169] |

The argument from prophecy generally takes form in one of the four following lines of argument:[170]

1) Sometimes an issue over whether a prophecy applies to Jesus takes the form of a philological or textual discussion. In this case Trypho would accuse Justin of assigning the wrong meaning to the text he quotes. When Trypho states that the prophecy of Isa 7:10–16[171] is misquoted by Justin, the issue rests on text and interpretation. Trypho believes the correct way to understand the prophecy is to apply it to Hezekiah, while Justin applies it to the birth of Jesus.[172] Justin does state that he will prove to Trypho that this prophecy refers to Jesus,[173] but his proofs amount to textual issues that are far from convincing. Justin even goes so far as to state that the Jews removed or changed parts of scripture that were obvious prophecies of Jesus.

> But I am not persuaded by your teachers, the ones refusing to admit that the interpretation provided by the seventy elders who were with Ptolemy King of the Egyptians is good, and they thus try to make their own interpretation. And I want you to see that they have taken away many of the writings from the interpretation by the elders with Ptolemy, from which this one who was crucified is shown to be proclaimed as God and man, and as being crucified and dying.[174]

---

[169] H. P. Schneider, "Some Reflections on the Dialogue of Justin Martyr With Trypho," *SJT* 15 (1962) 167.

[170] M. Wiles, "The Old Testament in Controversy with the Jews," *SJT* 8 (1955) 115.

[171] Trypho = "Behold a young woman shall conceive". Justin = "Behold a virgin shall conceive".

[172] *Dial.* 43; 66–73; 84; 124.

[173] *Dial.* 43.7.

[174] *Dial.* 71.1–2 Ἀλλ᾽ οὐχὶ τοῖς διδασκάλοις ὑμῶν πείθομαι, μὴ συντεθειμένοις καλῶς

At Trypho's request Justin proceeds to list, in *Dial.* 72–73, some of the passages that Justin claims were entirely omitted from the elders' interpretation (ἐξηγεῖσθαι). The list produced by Justin, however, no longer appears in our edition of the Septuagint. Nor do they appear in the original Hebrew.[175]

The most likely explanation here is that early Christian writers probably did not draw their arguments from the text of the OT itself. A number of scholars have shown that many early Christian writings include groups of quotations from Jewish sources that occur in textual forms that often do not agree with readings of the MT or the LXX. Further, these are given interpretations and applications uncommon or unknown in Judaism. This has given rise to the *testimonia* hypothesis.[176] This states that in the early church there was a collection (or collections) of "testimonies" of texts that had been extracted from Jewish scriptures and put together as proof-texts for Christian claims and that early Christian writers were indebted to these *testimonia* for their quotations.[177]

Evidence for *testimonia* is actually fairly widespread in literature. Both Graeco-Roman rhetoric and literary genre collections have been found.[178] Collections have also been seen in extant patristic writings where scriptural *testimonia* were indeed topically arranged.[179] More recently, some literature at Qumran provides concrete evidence that a variety of Jewish scriptural collections were used at a time contemporary with earliest Christianity.[180] The conclusion that is widely

---

ἐξηγεῖσθαι τὰ ὑπὸ τῶν παρὰ Πτολεμαίῳ τῷ Αἰγυπτίων γενομένῳ βασιλεῖ ἑβδομήκοντα πρεσβυτέρων, ἀλλ' αὐτοὶ ἐξηγεῖσθαι πειρῶνται. καὶ ὅτι πολλὰς γραφὰς τέλεον περιεῖλον ἀπὸ τῶν ἐξηγήσεων τῶν γεγενημένων ὑπὸ τῶν παρὰ Πτολεμαίῳ γεγενημένων πρεσ-βυτέρων, ἐξ ὧν διαρρήδην οὗτος αὐτὸς ὁ σταυρωθεὶς ὅτι θεὸς καὶ ἄνθρωπος καὶ σταυρούμενος καὶ ἀποθνῄσκων κεκηρυγμένος ἀποδείκνυται, εἰδέναι ὑμᾶς βούλομαι·

[175] M. Simon, *Verus Israel: A Study of the Relations Between Christians and Jews in the Roman Empire (135–425)* (ET H. McKeating; The Littman Library of Jewish Civilization; Oxford: Oxford University Press, 1986) 155.

[176] J. R. Harris, *Testimonies* (2 vols.; Cambridge: Cambridge University Press, 1916, 1920); E. Hatch, *Essays in Biblical Greek* (Oxford: Oxford University Press, 1889). For extensive historiography and bibliography see, M. C. Albl, *"And Scripture Cannot Be Broken": The Form and Function of the Early Christian* Testimonia *Collections* (NovTSup 96; Leiden: E. J. Brill, 1999); R. Hodgson, "The Testimony Hypothesis," *JBL* 98 (1979) 361–378.

[177] H. Y. Gamble, *Books and Readers in the Early Church: A History of Early Christian Texts* (New Haven and London: Yale University Press, 1995) 25.

[178] See Albl, *"And Scripture Cannot Be Broken"*, 70–96.

[179] Esp. Cyprian, *To Quirinus*; Ps.-Gregory of Nyssa, *Against the Jews*.

[180] *4QTestimonia*; *4QFlorilegium*. See, M. J. Allegro, *Qumran Cave 4: I (4Q158–4Q186)* (DJD 5; Oxford: Clarendon, 1968).

accepted from this evidence is that there is strong probability that *testimonia* were used in the early church and "should be reckoned among the lost items of the earliest Christian literature."[181]

The significance of this for our study is that Justin Martyr belongs to this era when *testimonia* were widely used. In fact, the prevailing understanding is that Justin did employ a collection of testimonies.[182] Justin was relying on *testimonia* that were apparently accompanied by interpretation and arguments.[183] This forms the basis of his argument.

2) Sometimes Trypho believes that the words Justin quotes are either an historical statement about person *D* or a prediction fulfilled by personage *E*. The determination of the issue then requires historical knowledge and a consideration of the context. In *Dial.* 32–33 Justin recognizes that the Jews recognize Hezekiah as the historical fulfillment of Ps 109:1–7. Justin, of course asserts that the prophecy is fulfilled in Jesus. For proof Justin refers to the very words of the Psalm to show that Trypho is wrong. In so doing Justin refers to the statement, "You art a high priest forever according to the order of Melchizedek". Justin then appeals to historical knowledge and states that Trypho must admit that Hezekiah was never an everlasting priest of God, therefore, the prophecy refers to Jesus.[184]

3) Sometimes Trypho believes that the words Justin quotes may seem to have a fulfillment in Jesus, but the immediate surrounding context does not, and therefore whatever the correct interpretation of the passage, it cannot refer to Jesus. The determination of the issue will again require consideration of the context. An example of this line of argument is found in *Dial.* 65, "And Trypho said, 'Being puzzled by so many scriptures, I do not know what to say concerning the scripture in Isaiah in which God says that he gives his

---

[181] Gamble, *Books and Readers in the Early Church*, 27.

[182] This was first established by A. Benoit, *Saint Irénée: Introduction à l'Étude de sa théologie* (Paris: Presses Universities de France, 1960) 82–87; 96–101. Daniélou (*Gospel Message and Hellenistic Culture*, 199) states, "Justin and Irenaeus made use of these collections may be taken as definitively established; cf. the convincing demonstration by A. Benoit . . .". More recent and detailed monographs arguing the position include, Albl, *"And Scripture Cannot Be Broken"*; O. Skarsaune, *The Proof from Prophecy. A Study in Justin Martyr's Proof-Text Tradition: Text-Type, Provenance, Theological Profile.* NovTSup 56; Leiden: E. J. Brill, 1987. Osborn also devotes a very helpful chapter on the issue, E. F. Osborn, *Justin Martyr* (BHT Gerhard Ebeling; Tübingen: J. C. B. Mohr [Paul Siebeck], 1973) 111–119.

[183] Skarsaune, *The Proof From Prophecy*, 91.

[184] Another example of this line of argument can also be found in *Dial.* 76–77.

glory to no other, saying this,' *I am the Lord God, this is my name. Neither my glory nor my virtues will I ever give to any other.*"[185]

Trypho's comment and quotation of Isa 42:8 arises because of Justin's citation of a number of Psalms which he believes testify to the deity of Christ.[186] Justin's reply to Trypho's comment relies on the context of Isa 42:8 alone. Justin thus quotes Isa 42:5–13 and simply states that therein God affirms that he will give his glory to him alone whom he has appointed to be the light of the Gentiles, and not, as Trypho claims, that he will reserve his glory for himself only. Thus, from the context Justin argues that the passage refers to Jesus.

4) Sometimes Trypho believes that Justin quotes words that seem to have a fulfillment in Jesus, but there are other facts about Jesus which do not correspond with prophecy and other Messianic prophecies which have no fulfillment in Jesus. The argument then requires, on the one hand, the production of further appropriate testimonies, and on the other hand, an answer in terms of the two advents. The application of this argument rested on the Jewish claims that the grandeur of the OT prophecies did not correspond to the humility of Jesus. This is well-illustrated in *Dial.* 32 where Trypho states that the OT prophecies claim a glorious and great Messiah but the Christians' Messiah was without glory—even to the extent that he incurred the last curse of God's law, crucifixion. Justin's reply was to refer to the two advents of Christ, the first in which he would be pierced by the Jews, and the second in which the Jews will look up and recognize him as Messiah.[187]

3. *The Interpretation of Events and Truth*

It is a truism that the crux of the argument from prophecy is the fulfillment of any prophecy offered in the argument. In Justin's case, his goal is to show that the prophecies he puts forth were foretold about and fulfilled in Christ. It has been shown above that the lines of argument in the argument from prophecy centered on textual, historical, and contextual issues. It is apparent, however, that the historical issues receive paramount treatment.

---

[185] *Dial.* 65.1 Καὶ ὁ Τρύφων ἔφη· Ὑπὸ τῶν τοσούτων γραφῶν δυσωπούμενος οὐκ οἶδα τί φῶ περὶ τῆς γραφῆς ἣν ἔφη Ἡσαίας, καθ' ἣν ὁ θεὸς οὐδενὶ ἑτέρῳ δοῦναι τὴν δόξαν αὐτοῦ λέγει, οὕτως εἰπών· Ἐγὼ κύριος ὁ θεός, τοῦτό μου ὄνομα, τὴν δόξαν μου ἑτέρῳ οὐ μὴ δώσω οὐδὲ τὰς ἀρετάς μου.

[186] *Dial.* 64. The Psalms quoted are 98:1–7; 71:1–5; 71:17–19; 18:1–6.

[187] A further example of this line of argument can be found in *Dial.* 51–52.

Justin primarily shows that the prophecies are true and that they were fulfilled in Jesus through an appeal to events. This is more than simply an appeal to the context of a particular prophecy, it is an appeal to reality. In this vein Justin claims that the doctrines which he states concerning Jesus are true because even in the face of persecution Christians do not deny the name of Jesus. It is significant in this case that Justin uses the term φαίνω (visible) in this context to indicate that it is plain for all to see.[188] The same idea is present in *Dial.* 110. 4 where Justin states, "Though being beheaded, and crucified, and exposed to wild beasts, and chains, and fire, and all other tortures, it is clear that we have not fallen away from the confession."[189] Here, the use of δῆλον (δῆλος) is also used in the sense of something that is clearly visible, evident, or plain to see. This appeal to sensible reality is, for Justin, an indication that the things prefigured in the OT are fulfilled in Jesus. They are so firm in the minds of Christians that they are willing to endure persecution, even unto death, for the truth of that proclamation.

The appeal to events does not stop there. Based again on the fact that scripture foretold events, Justin also gives specific examples in this appeal to events. One such example is in the context about the discussion of circumcision in *Dial.* 23. In trying to convince Trypho of the needlessness of circumcision for righteousness, Justin states that Abraham was not circumcised when he was blessed by God. Therefore, "he received circumcision as a sign, not for righteousness—just as the scriptures and the realities (πράγματα) compel us to confess."[190] It is the plain reality that proves circumcision to be unnecessary.

The appeal to reality is best exemplified in instances where Justin claims that things predicted in scripture are actually taking place before the eyes of humankind. Thus, in *Dial.* 53 Justin quotes Gen 49:11[191] to show that this was a prophecy of Jesus' triumphal entry into Jerusalem. This is then used to explain that since it had been foretold in scripture that Christ would do this, and since he did this in the sight of all, he furnished clear proof that he was the Christ.[192]

---

[188] *Dial.* 30.2.
[189] *Dial.* 110.4 κεφαλοτομούμενοι γὰρ καὶ σταυρούμενοι καὶ θηρίοις παραβαλλόμενοι καὶ δεσμοῖς καὶ πυρὶ καὶ πάσαις ταῖς ἄλλαις βασάνοις ὅτι οὐκ ἀφιστάμεθα τῆς ὁμολογίας, δῆλόν ἐστιν.
[190] *Dial.* 23.4 τὴν δὲ περιτομὴν εἰς σημεῖον, ἀλλ᾽ οὐκ εἰς δικαιοσύνην ἔλαβεν, ὡς καὶ αἱ γραφαὶ καὶ τὰ πράγματα ἀναγκάζει ἡμᾶς ὁμολογεῖν.
[191] "Tying his ass to the vine, and the foal's ass to the tendril of the vine."
[192] *Dial.* 53.2.

Later, in the same chapter, he makes the same type of appeal using a prophecy from Zech 9:9, with the conclusion that ". . . the Prophet Zechariah prophesied that this same Christ would be killed and his disciples scattered—and it actually happened."[193] Several other passages in the *Dialogue* employ the same type of argument.[194] In each case Justin appeals to scripture for a prophecy, he interprets it christologically, then he states that the fulfillment has taken place or is taking place before the eyes of the world. In other words the reality of the event is proof that the prophecy (as interpreted by Justin) is true.

Here is where the Memoirs of the Apostles become important. Each of the instances of the argument from events mentioned in the preceding paragraph uses non-OT narratives or accounts as proof. In other words, Justin either alludes to or quotes from a source (or sources) which evidently record the life and words of Jesus. These sources are the Memoirs of the Apostles.[195] Because Justin was dealing with unbelievers in his extant works he could make limited use of Christian writings. But Justin does make use of these writings, and they form a strong part of his argument. By calling these Christian writings "Memoirs of the Apostles"[196] it is apparent that Justin is presenting them to his readers as trustworthy documents.

Justin explicitly refers to the Memoirs of the Apostles thirteen times in *Dial.* 99–107. In each instance the term serves to quote, or refer to, Christian writings which demonstrate that the prophecy of Ps 22

---

[193] *Dial.* 53.5 ἀλλὰ καὶ διὰ τοῦ προφήτου Ζαχαρίου, ὅτι παταχθήσεται αὐτὸς οὗτος ὁ Χριστὸς καὶ διασκορπισθήσονται οἱ μαθηταὶ αὐτοῦ, προεφητεύθη· ὥσπερ καὶ γέγονε.

[194] *Dial.* 35; 51; 78; 82; 85; 96.

[195] A detailed treatment of the Memoirs of the Apostles is presented below in Chapter 4.

[196] ἀπομνημονεύματα τῶν ἀποστόλων. There has been some discussion about the origin of this term. Some (B. M. Metzger, *The Canon of the New Testament: Its Origin, Development, and Significance* [Oxford: Clarendon, 1987] 145; Barnard, *Justin Martyr*, 56) believe that the term was taken by Justin from Xenophon's Ἀπομνημονεύματα Σωκράτους which was well-known during the time. Others (R. G. Heard, "The ΑΠΟΜΝΗΜΟΝΕΥΜΑΤΑ in Papias, Justin, and Irenaeus," *NTS* 1 [1954–55] 125; H. Koester, *Ancient Christian Gospels. Their History and Development* [London: SCM/ Philadelphia: Trinity Press International, 1990] 38–39) believes that the term is not derived from Xenophon because the Greek term does not appear in his writings, but only as a title of his work in later manuscripts. To argue that Justin used the term in order to raise the Gospels to the rank of historical sources is incorrect because the term did not have such a meaning in Justin's time. Rather, the term was most likely derived from the verb "to remember" (ἀπομνημονεύειν). The term had been used by Papias as a technical term for the transmission of oral materials about Jesus. If Justin's use is derived from this usage it would designate the "Memoirs" as trustworthy written documents.

has been fulfilled in Jesus. But many times Justin makes reference to events in the life of Jesus or words which Jesus spoke but neglects to give any indication of how or where he came upon them.[197] It is a valid conclusion that references to the words and life of Jesus were most likely found in the Memoirs of the Apostles. The point here is that the Memoirs are thus used as reliable historical records, as written documents that are accessible to all. The authors of these documents were men who lived with Jesus, or, as their followers, received their information from them as reliable witnesses.[198] So, as reliable historical records of the words and life of Jesus they complement Justin's appeal to reality. They are used as records of fact, as proof for Justin's christological interpretations of prophecies.

The Memoirs, for Justin, are witnesses to the life, death, and resurrection of Jesus. This is significant because the knowledge Justin has of these events explains the OT prophecies. This is how the OT scriptures can be described as Christian writings,[199] because they needed to be interpreted by the Christian tradition.[200] Justin claims that the teachings of Jesus have been preserved by the Apostles and proclaimed in the churches.[201] There is thus an intimate link between Tradition, scripture, and the Memoirs. For Justin, παραδίδωμι[202] is often used in a technical sense to refer to the teaching of Jesus, the Apostles, and the Church.[203] Justin views Tradition as controlling but still substantiates his claim using written documents. The documents written by eyewitnesses or their nearest associates are therefore becoming just as reliable in Justin's proof than stories passed on orally for more than a century. The written Tradition and the oral Tradition are held together by Justin as equal. It is irrelevant to Justin whether the παράδοσις is passed on orally or in writing. The important thing is the content of the παράδοσις. He often refers to things which are taught, or teachings that are common knowledge to Christians, but

---

[197] See e.g., *Dial.* 35; 48–49; 53; 78; 80; 82; 85; 120.

[198] *Dial.* 103.

[199] *Dial.* 28–30.

[200] D. E. Aune, "Justin Martyr's Use of the Old Testament," *BETS* 9 (1966) 179; J. N. D. Kelly, *Early Christian Doctrines* (rev. ed.; San Francisco: Harper, 1978) 32.

[201] *1 Apol.* 66; *Dial.* 48.

[202] παραδίδωμι = to teach, transmit, or hand on as instruction or tradition. παράδοσις = handing over, delivery, hence teaching committed to a pupil, transmission, or handing down. See G. W. H. Lampe (ed.), *A Patristic Greek Lexicon* (Oxford: Clarendon, 1995) 1013; 1014–1016.

[203] *1 Apol.* 6.2; 46; 49.5; 66.1; 66.3; *Dial.* 49.1; 69.7; 70.4; 117.1.

this common knowledge was gathered from both oral Tradition and written Tradition. Therefore, on the one hand, he can view both the message proclaimed (κηρυχθεῖσιν) by the Apostles in all the nations,[204] or the Gentiles learning doctrine which was preached (κηρυχθέντα) by the Apostles[205] as of paramount importance. On the other hand, he views the written Christian message which was contained in the Memoirs written (γενομένοις) by the Apostles[206] as just as important. The reason for this is not necessarily the medium (aside from the fact that it was passed down through reliable accounts), but rather, the message. The message that is proclaimed is the same message that is written—this is the important thing.[207]

If the knowledge about the events of Jesus' life, death, and resurrection is found in the Memoirs then it is clear that the Memoirs are where the remembrance of Jesus takes place. It is not the textual form of the documents that are important, the important thing is that Jesus is remembered in the Memoirs. The same is true of other remembrances of Jesus like the Rule of Faith,[208] baptism,[209] and the Eucharist.[210] Illustrative of this point is *1 Apol.* 61 and 65–67.[211]

1 Apol. 61–67 is perhaps the best known passage from Justin's extant writings. In his defense of Christianity as non-threatening to the Empire, Justin describes what may be seen as a fairly typical representation of second century Christian rites. He thus describes the rite of baptism with the claim that it was "learned from the Apostles,"[212] a clear indication of a Traditioning that was discussed above. Following his description of the baptismal rite, Justin describes the administering of prayers and the Eucharist.[213] The only persons

---

[204] *1 Apol.* 42.4.

[205] *Dial.* 109.1.

[206] *1 Apol.* 66.3; *Dial.* 88; 105.

[207] See also, C. I. K. Story, *The Nature of Truth in "The Gospel of Truth" and in the Writings of Justin Martyr* (NovTSup 25; Leiden: E. J. Brill, 1970) 111.

[208] *1 Apol.* 13; 42; 46; 63; *2 Apol.* 6; *Dial.* 30; 51; 85; 95. Justin, unlike Irenaeus and Tertullian a few years later, does not explicitly refer to the Rule of Faith. The passages cited here, however, are meant to point out the content therein is consistent with the explicit citations of the Rule of Faith in Irenaeus and Tertullian. For more of the Rule of Faith see Chapter 4.II.

[209] *1 Apol.* 61–66; *Dial.* 13; 14; 19; 43; 44; 86. For more on baptism see Chapter 5.III.

[210] *1 Apol.* 61–67; *Dial.* 41; 70; 117; 118.

[211] Explanation of this passage as it relates specifically to baptism and illumination is discussed in detail below, Chapter 5.III.

[212] *1 Apol.* 61.9.

[213] *1 Apol.* 65–66.

eligible to partake in the Eucharist are those who believe "that the things we teach are true, and who has been washed with the washing that is for the remission of sins, and unto regeneration, and who is so living as Christ has enjoined (παρέδωκεν)."[214] This statement follows with the creed-like affirmation that the Eucharist is not received as common bread and common drink, "but in like manner as Jesus Christ our Saviour, having been made flesh by the Word of God, had both flesh and blood for our salvation."[215] This is reminiscent of the Rule of Faith. Following this, a strong connection is made with the Memoirs, "which are called Gospels,"[216] as a place where these things have been "delivered" (παρέδωκαν).

The point I am trying to make here is brought together in *1 Apol.* 67. So far, Justin has made a strong connection of Baptism, the Eucharist, the Rule of Faith, and the Memoirs as, not only important in the Christian rites, but also as being handed down through Christ and the Apostles. Justin now states that Christians "continually remind each other (ἀναμιμνήσκομεν) of these things."[217] He then continues on to describe the typical Sunday gathering of Christians where the Memoirs and the Prophets are read, prayers are offered, and the rites are administered. This description of the Christian rites and Sunday services is understood with the concluding statement that "He [Jesus] taught them [the Apostles] these things which we have submitted for your consideration."[218]

There are three things that are important to point out here. First, the idea of Tradition comes to the fore. There is the clear indication that what was being done has been handed down from Christ through the Apostles as controlling. Second, this traditioning, whether it be in the form of Baptism, the Eucharist, the Rule of Faith, or the Memoirs, is where Jesus is remembered. Third, because each of these Traditions is where Jesus is remembered, they are all bearers of the message, they allow the Christian to remember the event of Jesus Christ.

These points should temper any temptation to raise the written documents to a level that Justin did not. For him it is the message that is important, and because the Memoirs contain the message they are important. But they must be taken on an even plain with

---

[214] *1 Apol.* 66.1.
[215] *1 Apol.* 66.2.
[216] *1 Apol.* 66.3.
[217] *1 Apol.* 67.1.
[218] *1 Apol.* 67.

Baptism, Eucharist, and the Rule of Faith. It is the historical event
that is controlling and these events are remembered through Christian
rites and the service held on Sunday.

Thus, it is clear within Justin's Argument from Prophecy that his
concept of truth relied on events and history. In the Argument from
Prophecy we have a concrete example of the radical transformation
of his Middle Platonism. The argument shows that Justin no longer
believes truth to be resident in the realm of Being with the Good.
There is no longer any desire on the part of Justin to see God with
the powers of the mind. Rather, truth resides in the events that have
occurred and are occurring in the sensible realm. Their proof is
shown in their fulfillment.

In order to present his claims about Christianity as truth Justin
thus uses the argument from prophecy with Trypho. Working within
this familiar context Justin then uses OT scripture to show Trypho
two main truths, each having a christocentric focus: Jesus as the New
Testament or Law, and Jesus as the *Logos* of God.

B. *Jesus as the New Covenant or Law*

In Judaism the basis of the Law is found in the Covenant relationship into which Israel entered with God upon delivery from Egypt.
In this Covenant, God chose Israel to be his people through this
deliverance and this relationship finds its expression in the ethical
decalogue of Exodus 20.[219] The Law was given to make clear how
God's people might live within the Covenant. The Law was thus
given so that the people would know what was and what was not
a breach of the Covenant relationship. It was the way in which the
people could remain obedient and so remain in the Covenant.[220]

Thus, in Judaism, there was a close relationship between Law and
Covenant. From the time of Ezra onwards, it was believed that the
revelation of God found its supreme expression in the written code
of the Law contained in the Pentateuch. So, the word "Torah" comes
to be used with special reference to the Pentateuch. As the post-
exilic period dawned about two hundred years before the Christian

---

[219] D. S. Russell, *From Early Judaism to Early Church* (Philadelphia: Fortress, 1986) 55.
[220] The covenant and the Law were the foundation of Judaism. See, E. P. Sanders,
Jewish Law from Jesus to Mishnah (London: SCM Press/Philadelphia: Trinity Press
International, 1990); idem., *Judaism: Practice & Belief 63 BCE–63 CE* (London: SCM
Press/Philadelphia: Trinity Press International, 1992).

era a slight change of emphasis occurred within Judaism from faith-fulness within the Covenant to Obedience to the Torah. "Obedience to the Law of God was all important as the indispensable condition of their acceptance as heirs of the covenant; disobedience meant rejection of the covenant and the God-given promises that went with it."[221] This, again, points to the very close relationship between Law and Covenant in the mind of the Jew—to break the Law was to break the Covenant.

For Justin the Covenant and the Law belong together. He repeat-edly combines the terms "law" and "covenant."[222] The Law which was delivered at Sinai was valid for the Jewish people for a period of time. But this Law has now been surpassed and replaced by a New Covenant. This New Covenant is Christ himself and is uni-versal in scope and eternal in duration.[223] Justin recognizes that fulfillment of the Law is required in Jewish thought to remain in the Covenant. This is why he makes such a close relationship between Law and Covenant.

1. *The Problem of the Old Law*

The Mosaic Law is a problem for Justin. The reason for this is seen in chaps. 8–10 where Justin bids Trypho to convert. Trypho's reply includes a rejection of Justin's bid and the offer of a counter claim as the basis of salvation—the Mosaic Law. Further, Trypho claims that the Messiah is yet to come. In accepting Jesus as the Messiah Christians have believed a foolish rumor and have invented a Messiah for themselves.

The response of Trypho makes Justin's task two-fold:[224] Justin must show that Christ is not a matter of empty fantasy, but a divinely attested reality. This is done mainly in chaps. 31–118, the christo-logical section. But first Justin must also show Trypho how Christians can call themselves friends of God yet still not observe the Law.

---

[221] Russell, *From Early Judaism to Early Church*, 60.

[222] *Dial.* 11.2; 24.1; 34.1; 43.1; 122.

[223] E. Ferguson, "Justin Martyr on Jews, Christians and the Covenant," in F. Manns & E. Alliata (eds.), *Early Christianity in Context: Monuments and Documents* (Studium Biblicum Franciscanum Collectio Maior 38; Jerusalem: Franciscan Printing Press, 1993) 397.

[224] T. Stylianopoulos, *Justin Martyr and the Mosaic Law* (SBLDS 20; Missoula: Scholars Press, 1975) 9.

Justin does not define the Law anywhere in the *Dialogue with Trypho*, but the way in which he discusses it throughout indicates that it is the written Law of Moses. Even the first reference to the Law in the *Dialogue* shows that the discussion centers on the written Law of Moses.[225] The terminology which Justin employs when discussing the Law also indicates that it is the Mosaic Law.[226] Finally, Justin often refers to the Law by its specific ordinances.[227]

In *Dial.* 11.1–2 Justin summarizes what he will endeavor to show concerning the Law and truth,

> But we hope neither in Moses nor the Law. For then we would be doing the same things as you. But now I have read, O Trypho, that there shall be a final and highest covenant of all, of which is binding on all men to observe, as many as are seeking after the inheritance of God. For the Law given on Horeb is already old and belongs to you alone, but this new one is for all without discrimination. But law against law has abrogated that which stood before, and a covenant which occurs afterwards, in like manner, has put an end to the one before it.[228]

In this quotation we see that hope for the salvation of humankind is not through the Law, a new Law is here, the old Law is obsolete; the old Law was for the Jews only, the new Law is for all; the new Law is in opposition to the old. Therefore, the old Law is an inadequate Law. The old Law did come from God but it is now inadequate in three ways: in motive, content, and effect.[229]

a. *Old Law Inadequate in Motive*

The three motives of the Mosaic Law show its inadequacies. First, it was to soften hearts. It was imposed upon the Jews because of

---

[225] *Dial.* 8.4 τὰ ἐν τῷ νόμῳ γεγραμμένα πάντα.

[226] (ὁ) νόμος (*Dial.* 8.4; 10.4; 11.1; 45.3; 89.2; 96.1; 122.3–5). ὁ νόμος Μωϋσέως (*Dial.* 45.3; 52.3; 95.1). ὁ νόμος ὁ διαταχθεὶς διὰ Μωϋσέως (*Dial.* 34.1; 45.2; 47.3). ὁ νόμος θεοῦ (*Dial.* 32.4; 86.6). τὰ διὰ Μωϋσέως διαταχθέντα (*Dial.* 42.4; 46.1–2). τὰ ἐν τῷ νόμῳ γεγραμμένα (*Dial.* 8.4). ἔννομος πολιτεία (*Dial.* 47.4). νομοθεσία (*Dial.* 92.2). τὰ νόμιμα (*Dial.* 29.3; 52.3; 67.5). αἱ ἐντολαί (*Dial.* 10.3; 67.4). τὰ προστάγματα (*Dial.* 21.1–5; 86.6; 124.4). τὰ ἐντάλματα (*Dial.* 46.5; 67.10). τὰ δικαιώματα (*Dial.* 21.2–4; 46.2).

[227] περιτομή, σάββατον, ἄζυμα, νηστεῖαι, προσφοραί, θυσίαι, ἑορταί, ἔμμηνα, τὸ βαπτίζεσθαι, and ὁ ποδαί.

[228] *Dial.* 11.1–2 ἠλπίσαμεν δὲ οὐ διὰ Μωυσέως οὐδὲ διὰ τοῦ νόμου· ἦ γὰρ ἂν τὸ αὐτὸ ὑμῖν ἐποιοῦμεν. νυνὶ δὲ ἀνέγνων γάρ, ὦ Τρύφων, ὅτι ἔσοιτο καὶ τελευταῖος νόμος καὶ διαθήκη κυριωτάτη πασῶν, ἣν νῦν δέον φυλάσσειν πάντας ἀνθρώπους, ὅσοι τῆς τοῦ θεοῦ κληρονομίας ἀντιποιοῦνται. ὁ γὰρ ἐν Χωρὴβ παλαιὸς ἤδη νόμος καὶ ὑμῶν μόνων, ὁ δὲ πάντων ἁπλῶς· νόμος δὲ κατὰ νόμου τεθεὶς τὸν πρὸ αὐτοῦ ἔπαυσε, καὶ διαθήκη μετέπειτα γενομένη τὴν προτέραν ὁμοίως ἔστησεν.

[229] E. F. Osborn, *Justin Martyr*, 157–158.

the hardness of their hearts.[230] Second, it was to set right what had
gone wrong. The Law was only given when Moses discovered the
worship of the golden calf. The patriarchs had done well without
it.[231] Third, the Law was given for the sins of the people, but the
sins still persisted.[232]

b. *Old Law Inadequate in Content*
The content of the Law was inadequate because it was restricted in
scope and outlook—it was only for the Jews.[233]

c. *Old Law Inadequate in Effect*
The effect of the Law was also inadequate. It did fulfill a temporary purpose by hindering the hardness of human hearts but it has
also prefigured the future realities of the new Law by preparing
human minds for those future realities.[234]

2. *Necessity of a New Law*

Justin insists that a new Law has been foretold, a Law that could
truly give righteousness before God and salvation.[235] Because the old
Law was for the Jews it did not have the power to save Gentiles.
This necessitated a new Law which was foretold throughout scripture. The new Law is eternal and has the power to save all humankind.
"For if the law was able to enlighten the nations and the ones possessing it, why is there a need of a new covenant? But since God
foretold that he would send a new covenant, and an eternal law and
commandment, we will not understand this [the above quoted pas-
sages] as of the old law and its proselytes, but of Christ and his
proselytes—us Gentiles, whom he has enlightened . . ."[236]

---

[230] *Dial.* 18.2; 22; 27.2; 43.1; 44.2; 46.5; 47.2; 67.8.
[231] *Dial.* 19.5; 20.4.
[232] *Dial.* 27.2.
[233] *Dial.* 11.2; 19.6.
[234] B. de Margerie. *An Introduction to the History of Exegesis Vol. I: The Greek Fathers*
(ET L. Maluf; Petersham: St. Bede's, 1993) 31.
[235] See e.g., *Dial.* 11; 24; 34; 67.
[236] *Dial.* 122.5 ἐπεὶ εἰ νόμος εἶχε τὸ φωτίζειν τὰ ἔθνη καὶ τοὺς ἔχοντας αὐτόν, τίς
χρεία καινῆς διαθήκης; ἐπεὶ δὲ καινὴν διαθήκην καὶ νόμον αἰώνιον καὶ πρόσταγμα ὁ
θεὸς προεκήρυσσε πέμψειν, οὐχὶ τὸν παλαιὸν νόμον ἀκουσόμεθα καὶ τοὺς προσηλύτους
αὐτοῦ, ἀλλὰ τὸν Χριστὸν καὶ τοὺς προσηλύτους αὐτοῦ, ἡμᾶς τὰ ἔθνη, οὓς ἐφώτισεν.
For a discussion on the relationship between baptism, enlightenment, and Christ
see Chapter 5.

3. *Supremacy of the New Law*

The new Law surpasses or fulfils the old Law. The whole of the old Law is seen as a collection of symbols to prepare humankind's minds for Christ.[237] The Law, therefore, has a "true" or "real" meaning which surpasses the original intention.[238] It is by means of these precepts that, in prefiguring Jesus, God calls the Jews to know and remember God.[239] In each precept and prophecy there was a hidden meaning[240] which ultimately would have their fulfillment in Jesus the Christ.[241] As Justin succinctly states, ". . . from each such action certain great mysteries were accomplished."[242]

This new Law is based neither on fulfilling the precepts of the old Law, nor on the fact that the Jews are descendants of Abraham. The first point is made clear by Justin in his various discussions concerning Abraham's justification. In explaining that Abraham received circumcision as a sign the main point is that he was justified because of his faith. Indeed, he was justified *before* he was circumcised.[243] Thus, justification is not based on doing the Law but on faith in God. The second point is made clear when Justin makes clear to Trypho, in no uncertain terms, that no Jew will participate in the legacy of benefits promised by Christ simply because they are descendants of Abraham. The only participants will be those who have the same ardent faith as Abraham.[244] Therefore, the new Law is not for Jews only but also for those who display this same faith. This is the true spiritual Israel. The issue of faith and the true spiritual Israel is well summarized near the end of the *Dialogue* where Justin states,

> What, therefore, did Christ bestow on Abraham? That he, through a similar calling [to our own], called him with his own voice, telling him to leave the land where he lived. And with this voice he called all of us, and we have now come out of that way of life which we lived in common with the rest of the world—living wickedly. And we will, therefore, inherit the holy land with Abraham, receiving the inheritance for an unlimited age, being children of Abraham through the

[237] *Dial.* 42.4; 111.2.
[238] *Dial.* 12; 14; 27; 34; 40; 41; 42; 43; 44; 52; 54; 67; 86; 110; 111; 112; 118; 134.
[239] *Dial.* 27.4.
[240] *Dial.* 112.3.
[241] *Dial.* 43.1–2.
[242] *Dial.* 134.2 οἰκονομίαι τινὲς μεγάλων μυστηρίων ἐν ἑκάστῃ τινὶ τοιαύτῃ πράξει ἀπετελοῦντο.
[243] *Dial.* 11.5; 23.4–5.
[244] *Dial.* 44.2; 119.5–120.1.

same faith. For the manner in which he believed the voice of God, and as it was reckoned to him as righteousness, in this manner also we have believed the voice of God which was being spoken through the Apostles of Christ and through which it was proclaimed to us through the Prophets. And we renounce unto death all the things in the world. Therefore, he promises to him a nation of similar faith— God-fearing, righteous, and delighting in the father. But it is not you [Jews], "in whom there is no faith."[245]

These appeals to justification before circumcision and Christians as the true Israel are similar to some Pauline arguments in Paul's epistles to the Romans and to the Galatians.[246] Both *Dial.* 11 and Rom 4 refer to Genesis for support that Abraham was declared righteous by God before his circumcision.[247] In *Dial.* 11 and 23 Justin uses the Abraham story to argue that both the Jews and the Gentiles trace their lineage back to Abraham. But while Justin initially uses the Abraham story in the same way as Paul that Abraham received circumcision as a sign that he was already justified by God, he soon moves away from Paul by declaring that the church has replaced the Jews as the true Israel. So here the Pauline material stands alongside the prophetic announcements that the Jews would reject Jesus and the Gentiles accept him.[248]

A further similarity to a Pauline argument is found in *Dial.* 119.5 where there is a citation of Gen 15:6 that is used by Justin to claim that uncircumcised Gentiles who believe are like their spiritual father Abraham.[249] Abraham's call parallels the call of the Gentiles in Justin's day. Because the Gentiles are children of Abraham through faith,

---

[245] *Dial.* 119.5–6 τί οὖν πλέον ἐνθάδε ὁ Χριστὸς χαρίζεται τῷ Ἀβραάμ; ὅτι διὰ τῆς ὁμοίας κλήσεως φωνῇ ἐκάλεσεν αὐτόν, εἰπὼν ἐξελθεῖν ἀπὸ τῆς γῆς ἐν ᾗ ᾤκει. καὶ ἡμᾶς δὲ ἅπαντας δι᾽ ἐκείνης τῆς φωνῆς ἐκάλεσε, καὶ ἐξήλθομεν ἤδη ἀπὸ τῆς πολιτείας, ἐν ᾗ ἐζῶμεν κατὰ τὰ κοινὰ τῶν ἄλλων τῆς γῆς οἰκητόρων κακῶς ζῶντες· καὶ σὺν τῷ Ἀβραὰμ τὴν ἁγίαν κληρονομήσομεν γῆν, εἰς τὸν ἀπέραντον αἰῶνα τὴν κληρονομίαν ληψόμενοι, τέκνα τοῦ Ἀβραὰμ διὰ τὴν ὁμοίαν πίστιν ὄντες. ὃν γὰρ τρόπον ἐκεῖνος τῇ φωνῇ τοῦ θεοῦ ἐπίστευσε καὶ ἐλογίσθη αὐτῷ εἰς δικαιοσύνην, τὸν αὐτὸν τρόπον καὶ ἡμεῖς τῇ φωνῇ τοῦ θεοῦ, τῇ διά τε τῶν ἀποστόλων τοῦ Χριστοῦ λαληθείσῃ πάλιν καὶ τῇ διὰ τῶν προφητῶν κηρυχθείσῃ ἡμῖν, πιστεύσαντες μέχρι τοῦ ἀποθνῄσκειν πᾶσι τοῖς ἐν τῷ κόσμῳ ἀπεταξάμεθα. ὁμοιόπιστον οὖν τὸ ἔθνος καὶ θεοσεβὲς καὶ δίκαιον, εὐφραῖνον τὸν πατέρα, ὑπισχνεῖται αὐτῷ, ἀλλ᾽ οὐχ ὑμᾶς, οἷς οὐκ ἔστι πίστις ἐν αὐτοῖς.

[246] On the argument for Abraham's justification before circumcision see Rom 4:10–12, cf. *Dial.* 11.5; 23.4–5. On the argument for Christians as the true Israel see Gal 3:8–9, cf. *Dial.* 44.2; 119.5–120.1.

[247] Both passages refer to Gen 12:3; 15:6; 17:24.

[248] Cf. *Dial.* 93. See also R. Werline, "The Transformation of Pauline Arguments in Justin Martyr's *Dialogue with Trypho*," *HTR* 92 (1999) 84.

[249] Cf. Gal 3:8–9.

the inheritance belongs to them. Both Justin and Paul quote the passage from Genesis to declare that Gentle Christians are justified like Abraham.

Justin's use here of the Abraham story in *Dial.* 11, 23, and 119 and their contexts indicate that Justin has drifted away from the original purposes of Paul's arguments.[250] The passage in Romans is used by Paul to show that both Jew and Gentile share equal standing before God because both have the same faith as Abraham. The passage in Galatians is used in much the same way. In neither passage does Paul use Abraham to argue for the exclusion of the Jews, but rather, to show that both Jew and Gentile inherit the promise to Abraham. But Justin has taken this argument and transformed it by placing it with ideas of the new covenant, new people, and understanding of the Prophets as witnesses to Jewish unfaithfulness and rejection.[251] Thus, the Abraham material is linked with prophetic material to substantiate his claim that Christians are the true Israel.

The explanation for this transformation of Pauline arguments is quite logical.[252] Since Paul's death Palestinian Jews had fought two wars with Rome.[253] Further, by Justin's time, the church had become predominantly Gentile since the Jews had, in general, not embraced the gospel. Thus, the church in Justin's era had a different character than it had in Paul's era. The more Gentiles that entered the church, the more the Law faded into the background. The church became a Gentile phenomenon rather than a Jewish sect.[254]

Ultimately the necessity of faith and the expectation of an eternal Law is fulfilled in Jesus. He is the new and eternal Law whom the Prophets predicted. In many places throughout the *Dialogue* Justin makes this explicit claim.[255] Perhaps the best example of these claims

---

[250] Werline, "The Transformation of Pauline Arguments in Justin Martyr's *Dialogue with Trypho*," 86.

[251] Cf. *Dial.* 7 where Justin claims that the Prophets announce (καταγγέλλω) the Christ. The Prophets also knew about the Jews' rejection of the Messiah. Further, the Prophets also testify to the fact that God will create a new people from among the Gentiles with whom he makes a new covenant and through which they become the new Israel (*Dial.* 39.1). See also Werline, "The Transformation of Pauline Arguments in Justin Martyr's *Dialogue with Trypho*," 82; 86.

[252] Werline, "The Transformation of Pauline Arguments in Justin Martyr's *Dialogue with Trypho*," 80–81.

[253] This, obviously, had a negative effect on Jewish-Christian relations and identity. See P. Richardson, *Israel in the Apostolic Church* (SNTSMS 10; Cambridge: Cambridge University Press, 1969) 33–38.

[254] Simon, *Verus Israel*, 68.

[255] *Dial.* 24; 34; 43; 51; 67; 110; 118; 121; 122.

is *Dial.* 43 where Justin states that, according to the will of the Father, circumcision, sabbaths, sacrifices, oblations and festivals originating with Abraham and Moses have their end in Him who was born of the virgin, of the race of Abraham, of the tribe of Judah, and of the family of David. Justin continues, ". . . in Christ, the Son of God, who was proclaimed as coming to the whole world to be an eternal law and a new covenant, just as the prophecies which were mentioned before show."[256]

C. *Jesus as the Logos of God*

The understanding of Jesus as the new and eternal Covenant is an important concept in the *Dialogue* as a point of contact with the Jews in his presentation of truth. Justin's *Logos* concept, however, also remains an integral part of his presentation of truth. In Justin's hands the *Logos* theology was able to explain to Trypho Christ's deity (pre-existence with the Father) and his incarnation.

1. *God*

It is necessary to view Justin's *Logos* theology in light of a necessary progression from his concept of God.[257] In summary form Justin's basic concept is that God, the Creator of the universe, is unlike any other being. He resides in the super-celestial realms and is unseen by humankind. He is without beginning and end and is the cause through whom all else exists. Everything that exists does so through his purposes and will.

The connection of this with Justin's *Logos* theology is hinted at in *Dial.* 59 where Justin explains to Trypho that the theophanies which appeared to Abraham, Jacob, and Moses were not God the Creator. Then, in the next chapter, he states that his reason for this understanding is because he believes it absurd to assert that the Creator and Father of all things would leave the super-celestial realms to make himself visible in a little spot on the earth. This argument was hinted at in chap. 56 where Justin tells us that God ". . . remains forever in the super-celestial realms, having never been seen or ever conversing with anyone, whom we understand to be creator and

---

[256] *Dial.* 43.1 υἱὸν τοῦ θεοῦ Χριστόν, ὅστις καὶ αἰώνιος νόμος καὶ καινὴ διαθήκη τῷ παντὶ κόσμῳ ἐκηρύσσετο προελευσόμενος, ὡς αἱ προλελεγμέναι προφητεῖαι σημαίνουσι.
[257] For a detailed treatment of Justin's concept of God see above, Chapter 2.III.

father of all."[258] And this argument appears again in chap. 114 where
Justin criticizes Trypho's teachers for believing that the unbegotten
God has hands and feet and fingers and a soul like a compound
creature. This belief causes the Jews to assert that God himself
appeared to Abraham and Jacob. But in Justin's Middle Platonic
influenced concept of God it is the *Logos* who appears to reveal the
Father to humanity.

2. *The Logos as God's Mode of Expression*

Rather than leaving it to rest here Justin builds upon this foundation to express what is perhaps the most pivotal doctrine in all of
Justin's writings.[259] Because Justin's concept of God does not allow
that the Father appear in space and time, Justin used the well-known
Logos concept as God's mode of expression in space and time. What
was hinted at in chaps. 56, 59, and 114 is made clear in chap. 127.
An extended quotation here well illustrates Justin's progression of
thought on this matter.

> Whenever God says, "God went up from Abraham," or "The Lord
> spoke to Moses," and "The Lord came down to see the tower which
> the sons of men had built," or when "God closed the ark of Noah
> from the outside," do not think that the unbegotten God himself came
> down or went up from or to his state. For the ineffable Father and
> lord of all neither comes to any place nor walks, nor sleeps, nor rises,
> but remains in his own environment, wherever that is. Keenly seeing
> and keenly hearing, not with eyes or ears, but with an indescribable
> power. And he bears and knows all things and none of us escapes his
> notice. Nor is this one moved or confined to a locality in the whole
> world, for he was existing even before the creation of the world! How,
> therefore, could he be talking to someone, or be seen by someone, or
> to appear in an insignificant place on the earth . . .? Therefore, nei-
> ther Abraham, nor Isaac, nor Jacob, nor any other man really saw
> the Father and ineffable Lord of all and of Christ himself. But [they
> saw] him who was according to his will his son, being God, and angel
> because he ministered to his purpose—the one who, by his (God's)
> will, became man through a virgin; the one who also became fire when
> he conversed with Moses from the bush. If we do not thus understand
> the scriptures, we must conclude that the Father and Lord of all was
> not in heaven when what Moses wrote took place.[260]

---

[258] *Dial.* 56.1 τοῦ ἐν τοῖς ὑπερουρανίοις ἀεὶ μένοντος καὶ οὐδενὶ ὀφθέντος ἢ ὁμιλήσαντος
δι᾽ ἑαυτοῦ ποτε, ὃν ποιητὴν τῶν ὅλων καὶ πατέρα νοοῦμεν.

[259] I disagree with Goodenough (*The Theology of Justin Martyr*, 140) who states that
"the *Logos* is not fundamental for the theology of Justin . . ."

[260] *Dial.* 127.1–5 ὅταν μου ὁ θεὸς λέγῃ· Ἀνέβη ὁ θεὸς ἀπὸ Ἀβραάμ, ἢ Ἐλάλησε

The progression of thought is plain here. The understanding of God being unbegotten is used to differentiate between God and all other beings.[261] Thus, the Middle Platonic concept of God being unbegotten and not himself desiring to leave the heavens to make himself visible is moved to the next logical step. The *Logos* incarnate, Jesus, is the one who appeared to the OT patriarchs and ultimately became manifest to all humankind under the auspices of the Father's will.[262] Thus we see that Justin's reliance and dependence upon his *Logos* theology is necessary because of his Middle Platonic understanding of God being unbegotten. The progression is natural for Justin as he uses the *Logos* concept to show that the Son existed with the Father before the creation of the world and played a significant role in carrying out the plan of the Father.

3. *The Logos and John's Gospel*

It is well known that out of all the NT documents only the Gospel of John refers to Jesus as λόγος. But Justin develops his doctrine of the *Logos* beyond anything found in the fourth Gospel. A number of aspects of his *Logos* theology have no NT parallel:[263] the *Logos* as the speech and fire of God,[264] the *Logos* as a "rational power,"[265] and as the angel of the Lord in the OT theophanies.[266] Many studies have been undertaken in an attempt to discern the source of Justin's

κύριος πρὸς Μωυσῆν, καὶ Κατέβη κύριος τὸν πύργον ἰδεῖν ὃν ᾠκοδόμησαν οἱ υἱοὶ τῶν ἀνθρώπων ἢ ὅτε Ἔκλεισεν ὁ θεὸς τὴν κιβωτὸν Νῶε ἔξωθεν, μὴ ἡγεῖσθε αὐτὸν τὸν ἀγέννητον θεὸν καταβεβηκέναι ἢ ἀναβεβηκέναι ποθέν. ὁ γὰρ ἄρρητος πατὴρ καὶ κύριος τῶν πάντων οὔτε ποι ἀφῖκται οὔτε περιπατεῖ οὔτε καθεύδει οὔτε ἀνίσταται, ἀλλ᾽ ἐν τῇ αὐτοῦ χώρᾳ, ὅπου ποτέ, μένει, ὀξὺ ὁρῶν καὶ ὀξὺ ἀκούων, οὐκ ὀφθαλμοῖς οὐδὲ ὠσὶν ἀλλὰ δυνάμει ἀλέκτῳ· καὶ πάντα ἐφορᾷ καὶ πάντα γινώσκει, καὶ οὐδεὶς ἡμῶν λέληθεν αὐτόν· οὔτε κινούμενος, ὁ τόπῳ τε ἀχώρητος καὶ τῷ κόσμῳ ὅλῳ, ὅς γε ἦν καὶ πρὶν τὸν κόσμον γενέσθαι. πῶς ἂν οὖν οὗτος ἢ λαλήσειε πρός τινα ἢ ὀφθείη τινὶ ἢ ἐν ἐλαχίστῳ μέρει γῆς φανείν ... οὔτε οὖν Ἀβραὰμ οὔτε Ἰσαὰκ οὔτε Ἰακὼβ οὔτε ἄλλος ἀνθρώπων εἶδε τὸν πατέρα καὶ ἄρρητον κύριον τῶν πάντων ἁπλῶς καὶ αὐτοῦ τοῦ Χριστοῦ, ἀλλ᾽ ἐκεῖνον τὸν κατὰ βουλὴν τὴν ἐκείνου καὶ θεὸν ὄντα, υἱὸν αὐτοῦ, καὶ ἄγγελον ἐκ τοῦ ὑπηρετεῖν τῇ γνώμῃ αὐτοῦ· ὃν καὶ ἄνθρωπον γεννηθῆναι διὰ τῆς παρθένου βεβούληται, ὃς καὶ πῦρ ποτε γέγονε τῇ πρὸς Μωυσέα ὁμιλίᾳ τῇ ἀπὸ τῆς βάτου. ἐπεὶ ἐὰν μὴ οὕτω νοήσωμεν τὰς γραφάς, συμβήσεται τὸν πατέρα καὶ κύριον τῶν ὅλων μὴ γεγενῆσθαι τότε ἐν τοῖς οὐρανοῖς, ὅτε διὰ Μωυσέως λέλεκται

[261] Osborn, *Justin Martyr*, 21.
[262] This is made clear in *Dial.* 128–129.
[263] J. W. Pryor, "Justin Martyr and the Fourth Gospel," *SecCent* 9 (1992) 160.
[264] *Dial.* 61.
[265] *Dial.* 61.1 δύναμις λόγικη.
[266] *Dial.* 56; 58; 59; etc.

doctrine of the *Logos*. From these studies five main sources or possible influences have been suggested: Philo,[267] Stoicism,[268] Neo-Platonism,[269] Christian tradition,[270] or a mixture of all four.[271] To state the matter in a different way, one could ask, "Did Justin argue his *Logos* theology independent of John's Gospel[272] or was the fourth Gospel the springboard upon which Justin progressed?"[273]

The most balanced and fair assessment of the issue appears to be the last of the five, but this must be balanced by a distinction between a total dependence on the fourth Gospel and using the same Gospel as a starting point. The idea of the *Logos* was a widespread concept preceding and during Justin's era. But over against all the theories concerning influence upon Justin's doctrine is the fact that he ultimately regarded the *Logos* as the manifestation of the Father in space and time, that is, Justin identified the *Logos* with the incarnate Son.[274] Therefore, in attempting an understanding of Justin's dependence on John's Gospel five factors must be kept in mind.[275] First, other than the Johannine tradition there is no evidence of an explicit *Logos* christology in the first century.[276] Second, the philosophical *Logos* speculation present in Justin and other Apologists is not paralleled in John's Gospel. Third, Justin never explicitly quotes the prologue of John. Fourth, even though Justin never quotes from the Prologue,

---

[267] See e.g., L. Duschesne, *Early History of the Christian Church* (3 vols.; 4th ed.; London: John Murray, 1950) I.221–222; R. M. Price, "'Hellenization' and the *Logos* Doctrine in Justin Martyr," *VC* 42 (1988) 18–23; D. T. Runia, *Philo in Early Christian Literature: A Survey* (CRINT 3/3; Assen: Van Gorcum/Philadelphia: Fortress, 1993).

[268] See e.g., G. L. Prestige, *God in Patristic Thought* (London: SPCK, 1956).

[269] See e.g., Droge, "Justin Martyr and the Restoration of Philosophy"; C. Nahm, "The Debate on the 'Platonism' of Justin Martyr" *SecCent* 9 (1992) 129–151; T. F. Torrance, "Early Patristic Interpretation of the Holy Scriptures," in idem., *Divine Meaning: Studies in Patristic Hermeneutics* (Edinburgh: T&T Clark, 1995) 93–129.

[270] See e.g., Barnard, *Justin Martyr*; M. J. Edwards, "Justin's *Logos* and the Word of God," *J Early Chr St* 3 (1995) 261–290; Pryor, "Justin Martyr and the Fourth Gospel".

[271] See e.g., A. Grillmeier, *Christ in Christian Tradition Vol. I: From the Apostolic Age to Chalcedon (451)* (2nd ed. rev.; ET J. Bowden; Atlanta: John Knox, 1975) 89–113; J. N. D. Kelly, *Early Christian Doctrines*; W. Pannenberg, *Jesus—God and Man* (ET L. W. Wilkens & D. A. Priebe; Philadelphia: Westminster, 1968); D. F. Wright, "Christian Faith in the Greek World: Justin Martyr's Testimony" *EvQ* 54 (1982) 77–87.

[272] See, C. K. Barrett, *Gospel According to St. John* (London: SPCK, 1978) 65; J. N. Sanders, *The Fourth Gospel in the Early Church* (Cambridge: Cambridge University Press, 1943) 20.

[273] See, Osborn, *Justin Martyr*, 28–43; Pryor, "Justin Martyr and the Fourth Gospel," 160–163.

[274] Barnard, *Justin Martyr*, 87; Kelly, *Early Christian Doctrines*, 96; Torrance, "Early Patristic Interpretation of the Holy Scriptures," 94.

[275] Pryor, "Justin Martyr and the Fourth Gospel," 161–162,

[276] Even this is limited to three passages, John 1:1–14; Rev 19:3; 1 John 1:1.

verbal allusions are apparent.[277] Fifth, it was not in Justin's best interests to quote from the fourth Gospel. Trypho would not have been
impressed by this appeal.[278] But it must be remembered that failure
to cite and failure to make extensive use of a document are not the
same thing.

If the above five factors are taken into consideration it is not problematic to posit that Justin used the Johannine prologue as a starting point for his *Logos* christology. The belief that Justin did not
know the Prologue simply because he went beyond it is not proof
of Justin's teaching being independent of the fourth Gospel. In fact,
it is perhaps more probable that since he did go beyond the Gospel
Justin did derive his initial understanding from it.[279]

Justin is sometimes criticized for the apparent contradiction in his
theory which states that the *Logos* is with God, therefore numerically
distinct from the Father, yet is still designated "God".[280] But this corresponds to the fact that throughout John's Gospel the Son, on the
one hand, is described as being as one with the Father (10:30), and
as having equal power with the Father (5:18–24), but, on the other
hand, the Father is called greater than the Son (14:28), and the Son
is obedient to the Father in the execution of his will (5:30; 6:38).[281]
The writer of John's Gospel makes no attempt to clear up this apparent contradiction. Whatever the influences on Justin were in his
development of his *Logos* theology his originality lay in drawing out
further implications of the *Logos* idea in order to make plausible the
uneasy juxtaposition expressed in John's Gospel. In other words, he
wanted to explain the two-fold fact of Christ's pre-temporal oneness
with the Father and his manifestation in space and time.[282]

4. *Distinction Between the Logos and the Father*

Based upon the above mentioned Middle Platonic understanding of
God as apart from this mode of existence Justin makes use of the

---

[277] See, Osborn, *Justin Martyr*, 138.
[278] On the status of the fourth Gospel in the second century see, H. Y. Gamble,
The New Testament Canon: Its Making and Meaning (Guides to Biblical Scholarship;
Philadelphia: Fortress, 1985) 23–35.
[279] On the improbability of Justin's dependence on Philo for his starting point
see, Barnard, *Justin Martyr*, 85–100; Osborn, *Justin Martyr* 28–43; Pryor, "Justin
Martyr and the Fourth Gospel," 160–161.
[280] *Dial.* 56.1; 61.1, 3; 127.4; 128; 129.
[281] Pannenberg, *Jesus—God and Man*, 160–161.
[282] Kelly, *Early Christian Doctrines*, 96.

ambiguity of the term λόγος. The term has basically two meanings subsumed under the two main heads of inward thought and outward expression of that thought. *Logos*, therefore, in Justin is not merely "word" or "speech", but the divine Mind or Reason expressing itself and acting upon us as Word.[283] In reference to Christ as the pre-existent *Logos* of God, Christ was the Father's thought or mind, and Jesus, as manifested in creation, was the outward expression of that thought or mind.

In developing the theory of the *Logos* as the Father's intelligence or rational thought Justin was sure to show that the *Logos* was a separate person, distinct from the Father.[284] The proof that Justin offered of the numerical distinction of the *Logos* was three-fold.[285] First, he argued that the appearances of God in the Old Testament writings were not actual appearances of the Father. Because the Father is ineffable,[286] unbegotten,[287] unseen and unheard,[288] and does not come or go to any place, does not walk, sleep, rise up and is not confined to any one spot in the whole world,[289] there must be some explanation for the Old Testament expressions of God doing such things. Justin's explanation is found in the *Logos*. Concerning these appearances of God Justin states, "Therefore, neither Abraham, nor Isaac, nor Jacob, nor any other man really saw the Father and ineffable Lord of all, and of Christ himself, but [they saw] him who was according to his will his son, being God, and angel because he ministered to his purpose—the one who, by his will, became man through a virgin."[290] The alleged appearances of the Father are therefore described as appearances of the *Logos*.

The second proof offered for the numerical distinction of the Father and the *Logos* was the OT passages which presented God as conversing with another rational being. Justin argues that passages like Gen 1:26 ("Let *us* make man in *our* image . . .") are evidence, not only of the thought or reason (λόγος) of God being pre-tempo-

---

[283] Torrance, "Early Patristic Interpretation of the Holy Scriptures," 94.
[284] *Dial.* 41; 42; 128; 129.
[285] Adapted from Kelly, *Early Christian Doctrines*, 96–97.
[286] *Dial.* 127.1.
[287] *Dial.* 127.1.
[288] *Dial.* 3.7.
[289] *Dial.* 127.1–2.
[290] *Dial.* 127.4 οὔτε οὖν Ἀβραὰμ οὔτε Ἰσαὰκ οὔτε Ἰακὼβ οὔτε ἄλλος ἀνθρώπων εἶδε τὸν πατέρα καὶ ἄρρητον κύριον τῶν πάντων ἁπλῶς καὶ αὐτοῦ τοῦ Χριστοῦ, ἀλλ' ἐκεῖνον τὸν κατὰ βουλὴν τὴν ἐκείνου καὶ θεὸν ὄντα, υἱὸν αὐτοῦ, καὶ ἄγγελον ἐκ τοῦ ὑπηρετεῖν τῇ γνώμῃ αὐτοῦ· ὃν καὶ ἄνθρωπον γεννηθῆναι διὰ τῆς παρθένου βεβούληται

rally existent with the Father before creation, but also of the otherness of this *Logos*. After quoting Gen 1:26, 27 to Trypho Justin states,

> I inquire by quoting again the words of Moses himself, from which we unhesitatingly learn that he [God] associated with someone who was different in number and a rational being. And these are the words [of Moses], "And God said, 'Behold, Adam has become like one of us, to know good and evil.'" Therefore, by saying, "like one of us," he [Moses] has called to mind that [there were] a number of persons being in company with each other, and that [there were] at least two . . . but this offspring, being brought forth by the Father, was with the Father before all creation, and the Father associated with this one before [all creation], just as the word through Solomon made known, that he whom Solomon called wisdom was begotten as a beginning before all creation and as offspring by God.[291]

The Third proof offered by Justin for the numerical distinction of the Father and the *Logos* is the great Wisdom texts such as Prov 8:22 ("The Lord created me a beginning of his ways"). In *Dial.* 129 Justin states that the only explanation for such texts is that "that which is begotten is numerically distinct from that which begets."[292]

5. *Generation of the Logos*

Since the *Logos* is numerically distinct from the Father in Justin's thought it is logical to ask about the generation of the *Logos*. With the numerical distinction of the Father and the *Logos* already in place we also see that the *Logos* is described by Justin as divine[293] and that we worship the *Logos* as God.[294] Is it logical to conclude, therefore, that Justin is speaking ditheistically about another God? A number of passages show that Justin's comments do not merit this conclusion. For example, in explaining that the *Logos* is not sent as an inanimate power, but as one begotten from the Father, Justin states,

---

[291] *Dial.* 62.2–4 λόγους τοὺς εἰρημένους ὑπ' αὐτοῦ τοῦ Μωυσέως πάλιν ἱστορήσω, ἐξ ὧν ἀναμφιλέκτως πρός τινα, καὶ ἀριθμῷ ὄντα ἕτερον καὶ λογικὸν ὑπάρχοντα, ὡμιληκέναι αὐτὸν ἐπιγνῶναι ἔχομεν. εἰσὶ δὲ οἱ λόγοι οὗτοι· Καὶ εἶπεν ὁ θεός· Ἰδοὺ Ἀδὰμ γέγονεν ὡς εἷς ἐξ ἡμῶν τοῦ γινώσκειν καλὸν καὶ πονηρόν. οὐκοῦν εἰπὼν Ὡς εἷς ἐξ ἡμῶν, καὶ ἀριθμὸν τῶν ἀλλήλοις συνόντων, καὶ τὸ ἐλάχιστον δύο μεμήνυκεν . . . ἀλλὰ τοῦτο τὸ τῷ ὄντι ἀπὸ τοῦ πατρὸς προβληθὲν γέννημα πρὸ πάντων τῶν ποιημάτων συνῆν τῷ πατρί, καὶ τούτῳ ὁ πατὴρ προσομιλεῖ, ὡς ὁ λόγος διὰ τοῦ Σολομῶνος ἐδήλωσεν, ὅτι καὶ ἀρχὴ πρὸ πάντων τῶν ποιημάτων τοῦτ' αὐτὸ καὶ γέννημα ὑπὸ τοῦ θεοῦ ἐγεγέννητο, ὃ σοφία διὰ Σολομῶνος καλεῖται.
[292] *Dial.* 129.4 cf. 61.3–7; 62.4.
[293] *Dial.* 56.1; 61.1, 3; 63.3; 127.4.
[294] *Dial.* 30.3; 34.2; 63.5; 116.3.

For he possesses all these names because he serves the Father's will and was begotten from the Father's will. Do we not see something of like manner occurring in us? For when we put forth a word, we beget the word; not by cutting it off, in the sense that by putting forth the word in us, it is made inferior. And we see this occurring in a similar manner in a fire, which is not made inferior when it has become kindled, but it remains the same; and that which has been kindled by it appears on its own, not being inferior to that from which it was kindled.[295]

So the *Logos* is not another God in the ditheistic sense. The *Logos* has always been with the Father and always ministers according to the Father's will.

6. *The Logos and the Will of the Father*

Justin's intent is to show that the *Logos* was present with God before creation, active throughout the dispensation of the old covenant and the manifestation of the new covenant. Any time Justin discusses the participation of the *Logos* in these contexts it is always with the understanding that the *Logos* is carrying out the will of the Father, that he is a manifestation of the Father's will. Thus, in speaking of creation Justin points out that the Father talked with him (the *Logos*) before all creation signifying, among other things, his participation in creation.[296] And the participation of the *Logos* during the dispensation of the old covenant is indicated by the various theophanies that Justin insists are not appearances of the Father, but rather, appearances of the *Logos*.

---

[295] *Dial.* 61.1–2 ἔχει γὰρ πάντα προσονομάζεσθαι ἔκ τε τοῦ ὑπηρετεῖν τῷ πατρικῷ βουλήματι καὶ ἐκ τοῦ ἀπὸ τοῦ πατρὸς θελήσει γεγεννῆσθαι. ἀλλ᾽ οὐ τοιοῦτον ὁποῖον καὶ ἐφ᾽ ἡμῶν γινόμενον ὁρῶμεν; λόγον γάρ τινα προβάλλοντες, λόγον γεννῶμεν, οὐ κατὰ ἀποτομήν, ὡς ἐλαττωθῆναι τὸν ἐν ἡμῖν λόγον, προβαλλόμενοι. καὶ ὁποῖον ἐπὶ πυρὸς ὁρῶμεν ἄλλο γινόμενον, οὐκ ἐλαττουμένου ἐκείνου ἐξ οὗ ἡ ἄναψις γέγονεν, ἀλλὰ τοῦ αὐτοῦ μένοντος, καὶ τὸ ἐξ αὐτοῦ ἀναφθὲν καὶ αὐτὸ ὂν φαίνεται, οὐκ ἐλαττῶσαν ἐκεῖνο ἐξ οὗ ἀνήφθη. Cf. also *Dial.* 128.4. "It has also been shown at length that this power which the prophetic word calls God and Angel not only is numbered as different by its name (as is the light of the sun), but is something distinct in real number, I have already briefly discussed. For I stated that this power was generated from the Father, by His power and will, but not by abscission, as if the substance of the Father were divided; as all other things, once they are divided and severed, are not the same as they were before the division. To illustrate this point, I cited the example of fires kindled from a fire; the enkindled fires are indeed distinct from the original fire which, though it ignites many other fires, still remains the same undiminished fire."

[296] *Dial.* 62.4.

But ultimately the importance of the *Logos* is seen in the incarnation. In making use of the ambiguity of the term λόγος as the expression of the Divine Mind or reason Justin claims that the *Logos* became incarnate through an act of the Father's will.[297] In the *Dialogue with Trypho* there is no mention of the spermatic *Logos* that is present in the *Apologies* of Justin.[298] In the *Apologies* Justin uses the concept of the spermatic *Logos* to show that Jesus completed the knowledge of the Father. Here, in the *Dialogue*, Justin still desires to show that the incarnate Word completes the knowledge of the Father but he does so in a different way.

Trypho and his friends are exhorted to follow Jesus because it is through him that people are enlightened[299] and saved.[300] Throughout the stress that Justin places on the ministry of Jesus there is the underlying assertion of the unity of his ministry with the will of the Father. Not only was Christ begotten by an act of the Father's will[301] but he also ministers according to the Father's will because of his generation from the Father.[302] It is this unity in the relationship with the Father that necessarily must be stressed in Justin's presentation of the truth. The *Logos* does nothing that is outside the plan and will of the Father.

VI. *Summary and Conclusion*

If we now reflect back to what was stated earlier concerning the second century context of truth,[303] we can place Justin's presentation of truth into a more understandable framework. With the merging of Hebrew and Greek concepts of truth the NT writers were seen to diverge from both thought forms. The NT presents a realized eschatology that the Hebrews only looked forward to in the OT, and still do in the second century. By affirming the historical reality of Jesus Christ the Greek thought form is also challenged. He is recognized

---

[297] *Dial.* 61.1–2; 101.1; 102.5.
[298] For more on the Spermatic *Logos* see below, Chapter 3.IV.A.2.c-d; 3.V.C.6; Chapter 5.III.B.
[299] *Dial.* 127.
[300] *Dial.* 102.
[301] *Dial.* 56.11; 127.4.
[302] *Dial.* 61.1.
[303] See above, Chapter 3.I.

and affirmed as being involved in the flow of history. Upon this realization, Justin's presentation of truth was investigated as philosophical and thoroughly christological.

That Justin desired to communicate something about the concept
of truth, or what he believed was truth, is seen from the very genre
that he chose. The genre of dialogue was thus chosen to present
truth. There are some similarities between Justin's *Dialogue* and the
Platonic dialogues, but it is the divergences which stand out. Justin's
Dialogue contains elements that go beyond the basic understanding
of dialogue genre. The most important of these elements is that the
Platonic dialogues did not result in the attainment of truth, they
acted more as a midwife leading the pupil to find truth himself. It
was left to Justin, in light of this "shortcoming," to add a new twist
to the dialogue genre. Because Justin believed he had found the
truth, he wanted to explain it. He therefore chose the dialogue genre
as the medium of his explanation.

Justin's presentation of truth is philosophical in that he believed
that the primary task of the philosopher was the investigation of truth.
Even after his conversion Justin considered himself to be a philosopher. Indeed, he thought of himself as more of a philosopher than
ever before because he had attained the ultimate reality in God, the
true philosophy. For Justin, truth was one of the main areas of investigation for the philosopher. Through the old man he learned that
the truth which philosophers seek cannot be attained through philosophers because they had neither seen nor heard God or from the
Prophets. Truth can only be known directly through someone who
had seen or heard God—the Prophets. Thus, philosophy was sent
down to men by God (καταπέμπω). But the philosophy that was sent
down to humanity by God was not the "many-headed" version of
contemporary philosophy. It was rather the philosophy which was
clearly shown by the Prophets who had seen and heard God himself. It is the message of the Prophets that is the true philosophy
and this is what should be investigated and understood.

Justin's presentation of truth is thoroughly christological in that it
is centered on the event of Jesus Christ. Foundational to this is the
fact that God is in control—everything functions according to his
will and purposes. This will and purpose is ultimately presented by
Justin in the historical figure of Jesus, the New covenant and the
Logos of God as the new covenant. Thus, since the search for truth
finds its fulfillment in Jesus Christ, and since the philosophical enter-

prise centers on this truth, truth is actually more christological than philosophical. Truth resides in the sensible realm in the form of the *Logos* incarnate. The Prophets predict this and the Apostles witness it.

In this vein, Justin uses the argument from prophecy to show that the Jewish way of justification before God is obsolete and has been surpassed. It is based upon Jewish and Christian mutual respect for the OT scriptures and the sovereignty of God in history. The argument proceeded by an appeal to a prophecy, a christological interpretation and a sign of fulfillment in Jesus. The crux of the argument rested in the reality of a fulfillment, in truth. This is done through an appeal to evidence and facts which are received through observation and the Memoirs of the Apostles as portraying history. Thus, it is the incarnate *Logos*, the historical Jesus, who is the key because he is the one who brings fulfillment to the Prophecies. Without the event, there is nothing to which the prophecies point, nothing that is fulfilled.

Justin also employs the argument from prophecy to argue that Jesus is the New Covenant or Law that was prophesied in scripture. The old Mosaic Law is rejected because of its lack of provision of salvation. Salvation can only be found in the predicted New Law, which surpasses or fulfils the Old. It is based on faith, the same faith that justified Abraham.

Finally, the *Logos* theology of Justin presents the truth of Christianity as a master plan in the will of the Father. Because the Father does not desire to leave the heavenly realm, the *Logos* is employed by Justin to show the partnership in performing and exemplifying the will of God. The *Logos* (Jesus) was therefore present with the Father before creation, was an active agent in creation, appeared in theophanies as a true representative of God, and ultimately became the *Logos* incarnate—God in human form. The key in understanding the incarnation of the *Logos* is that he always carries out the will of the Father, his will is the Father's will. Therefore, to see Jesus is to see the Father. He completed the knowledge of the Father.

From the foregoing understanding of Justin's presentation of truth we return to the question of concepts of truth. Did Justin hold to his old Platonic way of understanding truth, the Hebraic way, or, does he fall in line with the NT writers in creating a hybrid concept of truth? The answer should be clear that Justin rejects both the Hebraic and Greek concepts of truth for the NT concept. History is certainly central in his concept, a history that is centered in the prediction and the actual appearance of Jesus Christ. The Prophets predicted and the Apostles witnessed his coming. This is similar to the Hebraic concept, but the pivotal thing is that with the coming of Jesus there is a realized fulfillment of what the Prophets predicted. There can be no more waiting, the messiah had arrived. This is also similar to the Greek concept in that Justin's presentation of truth was seen as progressive. God had a will and a plan throughout history which would prepare humanity for the appearance of the messiah. But it was an actual appearance within the changing history.

In light of this we can conclude that Justin continues the NT understanding of truth. He is within the tradition of transforming Greek and Hebrew thinking to strengthen his presentation of the Gospel of Jesus Christ. There is no "watering down" due to undue influence of Platonic thought.

So we come full circle to the concept of truth in the *Dialogue*. That Jesus was an actual historical person is beyond question to Justin. He acted and spoke and these things are recorded in the historic writings of the Apostles. These writings testify to the reality of his appearing. These things have the ability to be tested. But Justin realizes that not everything he puts forward as truth is this clear.[304] Much of Justin's presentation of truth requires a further investigation into his foundations for exegesis or interpretation of scripture, and this will be done in chapter four of this work. The fact remains, however, that Justin's presentation of truth rested on his respect for the Prophets as hearers and observers of the ultimate reality—God.

The foundational understanding of *Dialogue with Trypho* is that it is a presentation of what Justin believed to be the ultimate truth— salvation for all men through Jesus Christ. His presentation of this truth includes the witness of scripture as well as philosophical underpinnings. But the key is that Justin sees these as realities originating with God.

---

[304] *Dial.* 48.

CHAPTER FOUR

THE NEW TESTAMENT CANON
AND THE *DIALOGUE WITH TRYPHO*

From the perspective of the emergence of the NT canon, Justin's *Dialogue with Trypho* is important and intriguing because of the time frame in which Justin lived and wrote. Justin remains the most important of all the second century apologists. He is the first post-apostolic writer whose writings are of considerable size. Further, he lived in and was acquainted with the church at Rome[1] during a time when Christian oral and written tradition still existed side by side, although, "slowly the written documents alone were coming to be held as authoritative."[2] It could be argued that this transition is best seen in the Apostolic Father Papias of Hieropolis (ca. 60–130), but since his extant writings are only fragmentary one is better served by the comparatively voluminous writings of Justin.[3]

As will be seen later in this chapter, the deliberate closing of a collection of Christian writings is an event that belongs to an age beyond Justin's. This being the case, it is more proper to speak of the *state* of the NT writings in Justin's *Dialogue with Trypho* rather than the NT canon itself.[4] In other words the direction pursued here is in the area of Justin's view of the writings that eventually became part of the NT canon. Did he precede Irenaeus in the conception of a four-fold gospel canon? Did he use any extra-canonical works in his *Dialogue*? These and other related questions will dominate the

---

[1] Eusebius, *H.e.* 4.11.7–11; 4.16.1–9.

[2] L. W. Barnard, *Justin Martyr: His Life and Thought* (Cambridge: Cambridge University Press, 1967) 53.

[3] Greek texts and English translations of the fragments of Papias of Hieropolis can be found in J. B. Lightfoot, *The Apostolic Fathers* (London: Macmillan, 1907) 513–535.

[4] Polemics concerning the "closing" of the canon have distracted constructive focus on the *process* of the canon closing. This is what I have in mind by using the term *state* of the NT canon at the time of the *Dialogue with Trypho*. The process or state of the canon does not presuppose a closed canon, but rather focuses on attitudes toward and uses of early Christian literature on the way to canonization. See, A. C. Outler, "The 'Logic' of Canon-Making and the Tasks of Canon-Criticism," in W. E. March (ed.), *Texts and Testaments: Critical Essays on the Bible and Early Church Fathers* (FS S. D. Currrie; San Antonio: Trinity University Press, 1980) 263–276.

discussion as Justin's quotations, references, and possible allusions to NT documents are examined.

Study of Justin Martyr in reference to the emerging NT writings has centered on the ἀπομνημονεύματα. It is with good reason that this has been the case, for Justin's conception and use of the "Memoirs"[5] and the "Memoirs of the Apostles"[6] give good indication about the attitude he had toward Christian writings of his time. This attitude is, of course, instructive in a study of the state of the emerging NT canon.

I. *The ἀπομνημονεύματα*

A. *Authorship, Reliability and Content*

1. *Written Documents*

Justin presents the Memoirs of the Apostles as written documents which were composed by the Apostles and those who followed them. It is apparent that they are written documents because Justin not only quotes from them,[7] but he also states that they were read (ἀναγινώσκεται), along with the writings of the Prophets, during the Sunday gathering for instruction and exhortation.[8] These Memoirs were literally created[9] or put together[10] by the Apostles and their followers. It is thus clear that the Memoirs were written by the Apostles and their followers.

2. *The Memoirs and the Argument From Prophecy*

Justin refers to the Memoirs of the Apostles a total of fifteen times in all his extant writings,[11] with the majority of references (13) con-

---

[5] ἀπομνημονεύματα.

[6] ἀπομνημονεύματα τῶν ἀποστόλων.

[7] Justin uses various introductory formulas to introduce quotations from written sources which he identifies as memoirs: *Dial.* 100.1 γέγραπται εἰπών, *Dial.* 101.3 ἐν τοῖς ἀπομνημονεύμασι τῶν ἀποστόλων αὐτοῦ γέγραπται, *Dial.* 103.6 ἐν τοῖς ἀπομνημονεύμασι τῶν ἀποστόλων γέγραπται, *Dial.* 104.1 ὅπερ καὶ ἐν τοῖς ἀπομνημονεύμασι τῶν ἀποστόλων αὐτοῦ γέγραπται γενόμενον, *Dial.* 105.6 ταῦτα εἰρηκέναι ἐν τοῖς ἀπομνημονεύμασι γέγραπται, *Dial.* 106.4 ὡς γέγραπται ἐν τοῖς ἀπομνημονεύμασι τῶν ἀποστόλων αὐτοῦ, *Dial.* 107.1 γέγραπται ἐν τοῖς ἀπομνημονεύμασιν.

[8] *1 Apol.* 67.3–4.

[9] *1 Apol.* 66.3 γενομένοις.

[10] *Dial.* 103.8 συντετάχθαι.

[11] *1 Apol.* 65.3; 67.3; *Dial.* 100.4; 101.3; 102.5; 103.6, 8; 104.1; 105.1, 5, 6; 106.1, 3, 4; 107.1.

centrated in chapters 99–107 of the *Dialogue with Trypho*. In each instance the term serves to quote, or refer to Christian writings which demonstrate that the prophecy of Ps 22 had been fulfilled in Jesus. It is here that the value of the Memoirs in Justin's argument from prophecy is seen.[12] It has already been pointed out that Justin was converted to Christianity through an appeal to the Prophets. This conversion, and the influence of the old man, sets the stage in the *Dialogue* for the framework which Justin would then follow throughout—a strong connection with the OT scriptures. As stated above, Trypho is clear in his appreciation of this fact.[13]

According to Justin, the Prophets spoke God's words, thus their words are perceived as being on the same level as the words of God.[14] This is because the Prophets spoke by "the prophetic spirit,"[15] and "the (holy) spirit of prophecy."[16] The prophetic writings are reliable because they are the words and message of God.

But this is not the only significance of the prophetic scriptures. Another, and perhaps more important, reason is that they prophesy and testify concerning the life, death, and resurrection of Jesus. Justin uses the life of Christ, as witnessed in the apostolic writings and the apostolic tradition, as a sort of proving ground for the prophetic scriptures. He therefore believes that Jesus was spoken of in the prophetic scriptures. The Jews, therefore, cannot use ignorance as an excuse,

> For you [the Jews] did not offer sacrifice to Baal, as your fathers, nor did you place cakes in groves and on the high places for the host of heavens. Yet, you have not accepted his [God's] Christ. For the one who is ignorant of this one [Christ] is also ignorant of the purpose of God, and the one who insults and hates this one [Christ] clearly hates and insults the one who sent him. And he who does not believe in him does not believe the Prophets, who offered the good news and proclaimed it to all.[17]

---

[12] Justin's argument from prophecy is discussed in more detail above, Chapter 3.V.A.

[13] *Dial.* 56.16; *Dial.* 80.1.

[14] See e.g., *Dial.* 41.2; 44.2, 3; 46.5; 78.8; cf. 80.4–5; 84.1; 94.1; 133.2.

[15] τὸ προφητικὸν πνεῦμα *Dial.* 43.3; 53.4; 77.3; 91.4.

[16] τοῦ (ἁγίου) προφητικοῦ πνεύματος *Dial.* 32.3; 84.2; 139.1.

[17] *Dial.* 136.3 οὐ γὰρ καὶ ὑμεῖς τῇ Βάαλ ἐθύετε, ὡς οἱ πατέρες ὑμῶν, οὐδὲ ἐν συσκίοις ἢ μετεώροις τόποις πέμματα ἐποιεῖτε τῇ στρατιᾷ τοῦ οὐρανοῦ, ἀλλ᾽ ὅτι οὐκ ἐδέξασθε τὸν Χριστὸν αὐτοῦ. ὁ γὰρ τοῦτον ἀγνοῶν ἀγνοεῖ καὶ τὴν βουλὴν τοῦ θεοῦ, καὶ ὁ τοῦτον ὑβρίζων καὶ μισῶν καὶ τὸν πέμψαντα δῆλον ὅτι καὶ μισεῖ καὶ ὑβρίζει· καὶ εἰ οὐ πιστεύει τις εἰς αὐτόν, οὐ πιστεύει τοῖς τῶν προφητῶν κηρύγμασι τοῖς αὐτὸν εὐαγγελισαμένοις καὶ κηρύξασιν εἰς πάντας.

This, in essence, is the argument from prophecy. Everything asserted about Jesus in the Christian tradition was predicted by the Prophets before he came and was born a man. For Justin the OT scriptures were Christian writings.[18] As Christian writings they needed to be interpreted by the Christian tradition.[19] For this reason, the prophecies which are delivered or handed down (παραδίδωμι) by the Prophets, are recalled to prove the event of Jesus Christ, the *Logos* incarnate in space and time.[20]

When the concentration of references to the Memoirs in *Dial.* 99–107 are examined in light of Justin's argument from prophecy we see that they are vital in his presentation. In this sense Justin uses the Memoirs as reliable written records, as documents that are accessible to all. Because these documents were written by men who lived with Jesus or, as followers of these men, received their information from them as reliable witnesses they are considered by Justin to be valuable in proving the fulfillment of prophecy.[21] And this is exactly what Justin does with the Memoirs in *Dial.* 99–107.

3. *The Memoirs and Psalm 22*

In *Dial.* 99.1 Justin states that he will show Trypho how the whole of Ps 22 referred to Christ. Following this assertion Justin makes the thirteen references mentioned above to the Memoirs which, in his mind, prove that what was stated in Ps 22 is fulfilled in the person of Jesus and the events of his incarnation. Contained in these Memoirs are many statements about Jesus and references to specific occurrences surrounding his life, death, and resurrection. Thus, from the memoirs we can learn about the generation, birth, life, crucifixion, and resurrection of Jesus.

a. *Generation*
From the Memoirs one can learn that Jesus is the Son of God and that he proceeded before all creatures from the Father by his power and will.[22] Jesus is the only-begotten of the Father of the universe, having been begotten of him as his Word (λόγος) and Power (δύναμις).[23]

---

[18] *Dial.* 28–30.
[19] See, D. E. Aune, "Justin Martyr's Use of the Old Testament," *BETS* 9 (1966) 179; J. N. D. Kelly, *Early Christian Doctrines* (rev. ed.; San Francisco: Harper, 1978) 32.
[20] See above, Chapter 3.V.A.3.
[21] *Dial.* 103.
[22] *Dial.* 100.4.
[23] *Dial.* 105.1.

b. *Birth*

From the Memoirs one can learn that Jesus was born of a virgin[24] in Bethlehem.[25] At his nativity a star arose causing the Magi from Arabia to come and worship him.[26] Further, King Herod plotted to kill him, so, at God's command, Joseph took Mary and the child and fled to Egypt.[27]

c. *Life*

From the Memoirs one can learn that as soon as Jesus came out of the River Jordan at his baptism a voice said to him, "You are my Son, today I have begotten you."[28] The devil came and tempted Jesus, even so far as to get Jesus to worship him. But Jesus replied, "Get behind me Satan! The Lord your God you will worship and him only will you serve."[29] Jesus also urged his disciples to excel the Pharisees way of living by stating, "Unless your righteousness far exceeds that of the Scribes and Pharisees, you will not enter into the kingdom of heaven."[30] Jesus changed the names of some of his disciples including Peter, and the sons of Zebedee.[31] When the Jews requested of him a sign, Jesus replied, "An evil and adulterous generation demands a sign, and a sign will not be given to them except the sign of Jonah."[32]

d. *Crucifixion*

From the Memoirs one can learn that the ones who saw Jesus on the cross wagged their heads, curled their lips in scorn, turned up their noses, and said, "He was calling Himself the Son of God, let him come down [from the cross] and walk! Let God save him!"[33] In his trial before Pilate Jesus remained silent and would not answer his accusers.[34] It is further recorded that on the night they came to capture him on the Mount of Olives that Jesus' perspiration poured

---

[24] *Dial.* 100.4; 105.1.
[25] *Dial.* 102.2.
[26] *Dial.* 106.4.
[27] *Dial.* 102.2.
[28] *Dial.* 103.6 Υἱός μου εἶ σύ, ἐγὼ σήμερον γεγέννηκά σε·
[29] *Dial.* 103.6 Ὕπαγε ὀπίσω μου, σατανᾶ· κύριον τὸν θεὸν σου προσκυνήσεις καὶ αὐτῷ μόνῳ λατρεύσεις.
[30] *Dial.* 105.6 Ἐὰν μὴ περισσεύσῃ ὑμῶν ἡ δικαιοσύνη πλεῖον τῶν γραμματέων καὶ Φαρισαίων, οὐ μὴ εἰσέλθητε εἰς τὴν βασιλείαν τῶν οὐρανῶν.
[31] *Dial.* 100.4; 106.3.
[32] *Dial.* 107.1 Γενεὰ πονηρὰ καὶ μοιχαλὶς σημεῖον ἐπιζητεῖ, καὶ σημεῖον οὐ δοθήσεται αὐτοῖς εἰ μὴ τὸ σημεῖον Ἰωνᾶ.
[33] *Dial.* 101.3 Υἱὸν θεοῦ ἑαυτὸν ἔλεγε, καταβὰς περιπατείτω· σωσάτω αὐτὸν ὁ θεός.
[34] *Dial.* 102.5.

out like blood as he prayed, "If possible, let this cup pass."[35] Jesus
was indeed crucified and that after the crucifixion those who crucified
him would divide his garments among themselves. During his trial
Jesus did not utter a word in his own defense.[36] As he was giving
up his spirit on the cross he said, "Father, into thy hands I commit
my spirit."[37] While Jesus was with the Apostles before his arrest, they
sang hymns to God.[38]

e. *Resurrection*

From the Memoirs one can learn that Jesus was resurrected from
the dead on the third day after the crucifixion.[39]

The above information is presented by Justin in *Dial.* 99–107 as
proof that the prophecies of Ps 22 had actually occurred in Jesus.
No argument for the reliability or the existence of the Memoirs is
offered, they are self-evidently presented as proving the occurrences
of certain events in the life of Jesus. Thus, it is quite clear that these
written Memoirs inform readers about Jesus and that the information which is related in these concentrated references (99–107) are
said to be contained in the Memoirs. But can these Memoirs be
more specifically identified? Much of the study about Justin Martyr
has centered on this very issue, i.e., what are the Memoirs?

B. *Identification of the Memoirs*

For our purposes, it is best to begin discussion of this issue with the
concentrated references to the Memoirs in *Dial.* 99–107. There Justin
actually identifies the source of one of Jesus' sayings as being written in the gospel (ἐν τῷ εὐαγγέλιῳ). Justin states, ". . . but also in the
gospel it is written that he [Jesus] said, 'Everything has been handed
over to me by the Father . . .' "[40] Here Justin uses the term εὐαγγέλιον
as a source where one may obtain sayings of Jesus in written form.
The use of the term is provocative in light of the fact that it is contained within those concentrated references to the Memoirs of the
Apostles. We know that the Memoirs are written documents, and

---

[35] *Dial.* 103.8 Παρελθέτω, εἰ δυνατόν, τὸ ποτήριον τοῦτο.
[36] *Dial.* 104.1–2.
[37] *Dial.* 105.5 Πάτερ, εἰς χεῖράς σου παρατίθεμαι τὸ πνεῦμά μου.
[38] *Dial.* 106.1.
[39] *Dial.* 107.1.
[40] *Dial.* 100.1 καὶ ἐν τῷ εὐαγγελίῳ δὲ γέγραπται εἰπών· Πάντα μοι παραδέδοται ὑπὸ
τοῦ πατρός.

Justin has just stated that the "gospel" is a written document as well. We also know that just as the εὐαγγέλιον contains sayings of Jesus in a written form, so do the Memoirs.[41] Could it be that the Memoirs and the εὐαγγέλιον are simply different terms for the same document(s)?

Justin does use the term εὐαγγέλιον two other times in his writings,

> For the Apostles, in the Memoirs created by them, which are also called gospels, have handed down that which he [Jesus] commanded . . .[42]

> Trypho said . . . But I believe your precepts in the so-called gospel to be so wonderful and so great that no one is able to keep them. For I have carefully read them.[43]

It does appear that these three occurrences of the term support the tentative conclusion above that when Justin refers to the εὐαγγέλιον he is referring to a written document—the Memoirs. This is indeed the scholarly consensus.[44]

If we know that in Justin the ἀπομνημονεύματα and the εὐαγγέλιον are written documents, that both contain sayings of Jesus in written form, and that both record events surrounding the life of Jesus, then it is quite probable that both the ἀπομνημονεύματα and the εὐαγγέλιον are references to the same writing(s). Justin often uses these as reliable demonstration that prophecies of the OT concerning Jesus had taken place. They are trustworthy records because the authors of these documents were men who lived with Jesus or, as their followers, received their information from them as reliable witnesses.[45]

---

[41] See, *Dial.* 103.6, 8; 105.5, 6; 107.1.

[42] *1 Apol.* 66.3 οἱ γὰρ ἀπόστολοι ἐν τοῖς γενομένοις ὑπ᾽ αὐτῶν ἀπομνημονεύμασιν, ἃ καλεῖται εὐαγγέλια, οὕτως παρέδωκαν ἐντετάλθαι αὐτοῖς.

[43] *Dial.* 10.2 ὑμῶν δὲ καὶ τὰ ἐν τῷ λεγομένῳ εὐαγγελίῳ παραγγέλματα θαυμαστὰ οὕτως καὶ μεγάλα ἐπίσταμαι εἶναι, ὡς ὑπολαμβάνειν μηδένα δύνασθαι φυλάξαι αὐτά· ἐμοὶ γὰρ ἐμέλησεν ἐντυχεῖν αὐτοῖς.

[44] See e.g., L. W. Barnard, *Justin Martyr*; H. Y. Gamble, *The New Testament Canon. Its Making and Meaning* (Guides to Biblical Scholarship; Philadelphia: Fortress, 1985) 28–29; G. M. Hahneman, *The Muratorian Fragment and the Development of the Canon* (Oxford Theological Monographs; Oxford: Clarendon, 1992) 96–98; C. E. Hill, "Justin and the New Testament Writings," *StudPat* 30 (1997) 42–48; H. Koester, *Ancient Christian Gospels. Their History and Development* (London: SCM/Philadelphia: Trinity Press International, 1990) 40–43; W. Sanday, *The Gospels in the Second Century* (London: Macmillan, 1876) 88–137; G. N. Stanton, "The Fourfold Gospel," *NTS* 43 (1997) 329–332; B. F. Westcott, *A General Survey of the History of the Canon of the New Testament* (5th ed.; Cambridge and London: Macmillan, 1881) 96–179.

[45] *Dial.* 103.

C. *Non-Referenced Material in the* Dialogue

But the *Dialogue with Trypho* contains additional appeals to this type of information. For example, throughout the rest of the *Dialogue* Justin relates much of the same of information that he did in *Dial.* 99–107 concerning the generation, birth, life, crucifixion and resurrection of Jesus.[46] It is only in the concentrated references, however, that Justin informs the reader that the information can be found in the Memoirs. In these other references the reader is not informed as to the source of the information which Justin communicates. But because this same information is later stated by Justin to be included in the Memoirs, we can safely conclude that wherever this information is given to the reader without indication of source, Justin most likely obtained it from the Memoirs. In other words, information that is given by Justin anywhere in the *Dialogue with Trypho* that is consistent with the information contained in the concentrated section of *Dial.* 99–107, is best understood as having its source in the Memoirs of the Apostles.

This leaves open the question as to the source(s) of the other information about Jesus: his life, information about John the Baptist, and sayings that are attributed to him by Justin. For example, in reference to Jesus' life, Justin informs his readers that Jesus ascended into heaven,[47] that there was no lodging place at Bethlehem at the time of Jesus' birth,[48] and that the soldiers cast lots for Jesus' garments at the cross.[49] In reference to John the Baptist, Justin informs his

---

[46] *Dial.* 17.1; 23.3; 30.3; 32.3; 40.1; 51.1–2; 53.5; 77.4; 78.1, 2, 3, 4, 5, 7; 85.2; 88.1, 3; 94.5; 97.1, 4.

[47] *Dial.* 17.1; 32.3; 85.2.

[48] *Dial.* 78.5.

[49] *Dial.* 97.4. Other events referred to by Justin with no reference to source include: that he was a descendant of Abraham (32.3); that Pilate was governor of Judea when Jesus was crucified (30.3); that Christ was placed at God's right hand after the resurrection (32.3); that Christ commanded us to offer the Eucharistic bread in remembrance of his passion (40.1); that Jesus ordered his disciples to get an ass and its foal when he was about to enter Jerusalem (53.2); that the Magi presented gifts of gold, frankincense, and myrrh to the child (78.2); that the Magi were admonished in a vision not to return to Herod (78.2); that Joseph received a vision commanding him not to put Mary away for her conception was of the Holy Spirit (78.3); that Joseph received another vision commanding him, Mary and the child to go into Egypt and remain there until another vision should advise them to return (78.4); that the Magi failed to return to Herod as a result of the vision they received (78.7); that Herod, because the Magi had not informed him who the child was, ordered every boy in Bethlehem to be killed (78.7); that Jesus was the son of a carpenter (88.8).

readers that Elijah is a forerunner of the Christ and that John the
Baptist is Elijah.[50] In reference to dominical sayings, one can deduce
that there are no less than twenty-three sayings in the *Dialogue* that
Justin attributes to Jesus.[51] The question at hand concerning the
information contained in these references in the *Dialogue* centers
around the source—where did Justin get this information?

We do know that all the information contained in the concentrated section of chapters 99–107 can be found in what later became
the canonical Synoptic Gospels. If we now compare the information
that Justin cites or alludes to with no source reference we can also
see that the majority of it is found in what later became the canonical Synoptic Gospels.[52] This is strong evidence that the source for
this material is also the Memoirs of the Apostles which, ultimately,
contain (at least) synoptic gospel material. Thus, one possible conclusion which might be reached that is Justin, in one form or another,
knew of the Synoptic Gospels, that he used them in his *Dialogue with
Trypho*, and that he referred to them as Memoirs of the Apostles.
But, it remains to be seen that this is the most likely conclusion.

D. *Source of the Non-Referenced Material in the Dialogue*

The fact is that Justin's *Dialogue with Trypho* contains passages reminiscent of passages from the canonical Gospels. Few would argue
with this conclusion, but the issue becomes a bit clouded when
research is devoted to attempting to identify the source(s) that Justin
quotes and alludes to. For the last two centuries scholars have been
trying to ascertain the exact relationship between the writings of
Justin and the canonical gospels.[53]

---

[50] *Dial.* 49.3–5; 51.1–2. Other events surrounding John the Baptist which Justin
relates with no reference to source include: a quotation of John the Baptist as he
sat by the Jordan (49.3); that John was imprisoned by Herod, and while in prison
the dancing of Herod's niece pleased Herod so much that he promised to give her
whatever she desired. At her mother's prompting the niece asked for the head of
John the Baptist (49.4); a description of John's clothing and diet, and a summary
of his preaching by the Jordan, saying that he was not the Christ (88.7).

[51] These include the following: *Dial.* 17.3, 4 (2x); 35.2–3; 48.8; 51.3; 76.4, 5 (2x),
6, 7; 81.4; 82.1–2; 88.8; 93.2; 96.3; 112.4; 120.6; 122.1; 125.1, 4; 130.4; 140.4.

[52] For a comparison of Justin's NT quotes or allusions with actual NT documents see the Appendix.

[53] For a detailed summary of the past and present research into this area see,
A. J. Bellinzoni, *The Sayings of Jesus in the Writings of Justin Martyr* (NovTSup 17;
Leiden: E. J. Brill, 1967); D. A. Hagner, "The Sayings of Jesus in the Apostolic

The investigation was initiated in 1814 by Johann Christian Zahn.[54] Zahn believed that the Gospel text from which Justin quoted was the *Gospel According to the Hebrews*. Further investigation into this Gospel caused Zahn to conclude that quotations from the *Gospel According to the Hebrews* in Epiphanius show that this now lost Jewish-Christian Gospel was a harmonized work, composed from three synoptic Gospels (or, more likely, early versions of them).[55] Since then Zahn's assertions have been echoed by many scholars.

Zahn's conclusions were based on both textual and circumstantial evidence. The textual evidence shows that the document used by Epiphanius shares several distinct readings with the source Justin is citing. For example, both report that a "fire" (πῦρ) or "light" (φῶς) shone in the Jordan at Jesus' baptism, and both have the full text of Ps 2:7 when Jesus is baptized, "this day I have begotten you."[56] Textual agreements such as this suggest a common source.

The circumstantial evidence shows two characteristics: First, the longer the citation in Justin, the more obviously it is harmonized; second, the harmonizations consist of passages drawn *only* from the synoptics, Johannine elements are absent. Because Zahn knew that the *Gospel According to the Hebrews* appeared to be a harmony which also incorporated synoptic texts he drew the conclusion that when Justin set about to write his *Apologies* and *Dialogue with Trypho*, his Gospel citations were taken from an already existing harmonized source known to Epiphanius as the *Gospel According to the Hebrews*.

Zahn's conclusions have led Petersen to draw a very important observation:[57] the Harmonized Gospel tradition antedates Tatian, and probably even Justin. Petersen then proceeds to show that there

---

Fathers and Justin Martyr," in D. Wenham (ed.), *Gospel Perspectives Vol. 5: The Jesus Tradition Outside the Gospels* (Sheffield: JSOT Press, 1984) 233–268; H. Koester, "The Text of the Synoptic Gospels in the Second Century," in W. L. Petersen (ed.), *Gospel Traditions in the Second Century. Origins, Rescensions, Text and Transmission* (Notre Dame: University of Notre Dame Press, 1989) 19–37; W. L. Petersen, "From Justin to Pepys: The History of the Harmonized Gospel Tradition" *StudPat* 30 (1997) 71–76; idem, "Textual Evidence of Tatian's Dependence upon Justin's ΑΠΟΜΝΗΜΟΝΕΥΜΑΤΑ," *NTS* 36 (1990) 512–534.

[54] Peterson, "From Justin to Pepys," 71.

[55] J. C. Zahn, "Ist Ammon oder Tatian Verfasser der ins Lateinische, Altfrankische und Arabische übersetzten Evangelien-Harmonie? und was hat Tatian bei seinem bekannten Diatessaron oder Diapente vor sich gehabt und zum Grunde gelegt?" in C. A. G. Keil and H. G. Tzschirner, *Analekten für das Studium der exegetischen und systematischen Theologie* 2/1 (Leipzig, 1814), 206–207.

[56] Epiphanius, *Panarion* 30.13.7; Justin, *Dial.* 88.3.

[57] Petersen, "From Justin to Pepys," 73.

is good evidence for three other harmonies that antedate Tatian's *Diatessaron*. First, it is clear that the canonical Gospels are, in the strict sense, harmonies of earlier material. It does not matter if one argues that the Gospel of Matthew came first followed by Luke, and finally Mark, who harmonized Matthew and Luke. Nor does it matter if one argues that Luke and Matthew harmonized "Q" with Mark, as well as their own special traditions. The fact remains, in each of these hypotheses a harmony of an earlier Gospel(s) is apparent. Second, Eusebius mentions a man named Ammonius of Alexandria. Knowledge of this individual is very scarce. But Altaner believes him to be a contemporary of Origen.[58] If this is so, then he would be a contemporary of Tatian. Eusebius claims that Ammonius created a Gospel "diatessaron" where he set running beside a section of Matthew the same pericope from other Gospels.[59] Third, According to Jerome, Theophilus of Antioch composed a harmony.[60] As an opponent of Marcion, Theophilus would have been a contemporary of Justin. Nothing more is said of the work.

The idea of a pre-Tatianic harmony is, therefore, very probable. Because of this scholars have taken Zahn's conclusions as a starting point from which to proceed and identify the source of Justin's quotations. An informative exercise in this vein is collecting Justin's citations and allusions to sources other than from OT scripture.[61] Once this is done it is evident that the citations and allusions contain numerous variant readings and are frequently harmonized versions of other documents.[62]

For example, *Dial.* 78.4 contains a description of the Judean census and the revelation to Joseph and Mary to go into Egypt after Jesus' birth,

---

[58] B. Altaner, *Patrology* (Frieburg: Herder, 1960) 210.
[59] Eusebius, *Ep. ad Carpianum* 1.
[60] Jerome, *Ep. ad Algasiam* 6.
[61] This is done for the *Dialogue with Trypho* in the Appendix.
[62] For a complete discussion concerning the harmonizing tendencies in Justin see, A. Baker, "Justin's Agraphon in the Dialogue With Trypho," *JBL* 87 (1968) 277–287; A. J. Bellinzoni, "The Source of the Agraphon in Justin Martyr's Dialogue With Trypho 47:5," *VC* 17 (1963) 65–70; idem, *The Sayings of Jesus in the Writings of Justin Martyr*; Hagner, "The Sayings of Jesus in the Apostolic Fathers and Justin Martyr"; L. K. Kline, "Harmonized Sayings of Jesus in the Pseudo-Clementine Homilies and Justin Martyr," *ZNW* 66 (1975) 223–241; Koester, *Ancient Christian Gospels*; Petersen, "Textual Evidence of Tatian's Dependence Upon Justin's ΑΠΟΜΝΗΜΟΝΕΥΜΑΤΑ".

Therefore, being afraid, he [Joseph] did not reject her [Mary]. But
at the time when the first census was being taken by Quirinius, he
[Joseph] went up from Nazareth, where he lived, to Bethlehem, to
which he belonged, in order to register. For he was by birth of the
people of Judah, which inhabited that land. And he was directed to
go with Mary into Egypt and stay there with the child until again it
was revealed to them to return to Judea.[63]

This is a good example of the harmonizing tendency in *Dialogue with
Trypho*. The events referred to here can be found in both Matt 2:13
and Luke 2:1–5. The interesting thing when the three passages are
compared is that neither of the canonical passages contain every element in the passage from the *Dialogue*. The first part of the passage,
which refers to the census, is found only in the Lukan passage. While
the second part of the passage, which refers to the escape into Egypt,
is found only in the Matthean passage. This amounts to strong evidence that Justin, or the source which Justin was using, harmonized
the two passages.

Another example that strongly suggests that Justin harmonized
passages or that he used a harmony is found in *Dial.* 88.7,

> For John was sitting by the Jordan proclaiming a baptism of repen-
> tance, wearing only a belt made of skin and a garment of camel hairs,
> and eating nothing except locusts and wild honey. Men thought him
> to be the Christ—to which he cried out, "I am not the Christ, but
> the voice of one crying out. For one will come who is stronger than
> me, whose sandals I am not worthy to carry.[64]

This appears to be a harmonization of a number of verses found in
the synoptics: Matt 3:1–6, 11; Mark 1:4–7; Luke 3:3, 15–16. The
fact that the canonical versions are ordered differently and the fact
that the canonical versions are not one continuous narrative, while
Justin's version is, suggests harmonization.

---

[63] φοβηθεὶς οὖν οὐκ ἐκβέβληκεν αὐτήν, ἀλλά, ἀπογραφῆς οὔσης ἐν τῇ Ἰουδαίᾳ τότε
πρώτης ἐπὶ Κυρηνίου, ἀνεληλύθει ἀπὸ Ναζαρέτ, ἔνθα ᾤκει, εἰς Βηθλεέμ, ὅθεν ἦν,
ἀπογράψασθαι· ἀπὸ γὰρ τῆς κατοικούσης τὴν γῆν ἐκείνην φυλῆς Ἰούδα τὸ γένος ἦν.
καὶ αὐτὸς ἅμα τῇ Μαρίᾳ κελεύεται ἐξελθεῖν εἰς Αἴγυπτον καὶ εἶναι ἐκεῖ ἅμα τῷ παιδίῳ,
ἄχρις ἂν αὐτοῖς πάλιν ἀποκαλυφθῇ ἐπανελθεῖν εἰς τὴν Ἰουδαίαν.

[64] Ἰωάννου γὰρ καθεζομένου ἐπὶ τοῦ Ἰορδάνου καὶ κηρύσσοντος Βάπτισμα μετανοίας,
καὶ ζώνην δερματίνην καὶ ἔνδυμα ἀπὸ τριχῶν καμήλου μόνον φοροῦντος καὶ μηδὲν
ἐσθίοντος πλὴν ἀκρίδας καὶ μέλι ἄγριον, οἱ ἄνθρωποι ὑπελάμβανον αὐτὸν εἶναι τὸν
Χριστόν· πρὸς οὓς καὶ αὐτὸς ἐβόα· Οὐκ εἰμὶ ὁ Χριστός, ἀλλὰ φωνὴ βοῶντος· ἥξει γὰρ
ὁ ἰσχυρότερός μου, οὗ οὐκ εἰμὶ ἱκανὸς τὰ ὑποδήματα βαστάσαι.

The examples presented above suggest that the source(s) for the harmony (whether it be Justin himself who is harmonizing or whether Justin is using a harmony) are the Synoptic Gospels.[65] But there are also examples of this harmonizing tendency with variants that are not found in any of the Gospels. For example, when relating the event of the birth of Jesus, Justin states,

> But when the child was born in Bethlehem, since Joseph did not have ready somewhere to stop for the night in the village, they stopped for the night in a cave which was near the village. And while they were there, Mary brought forth the Christ and laid him in a manger, where the Magi who came from Arabia found him.[66]

Here we have very much the same events recorded in Matt 2:1–25 and Luke 2:7. Evidence of harmony exists by the fact that the event of laying the child in the manger, which is peculiar to Luke, is mentioned along with other material that is included in Matthew. But there are also two very important differences between Justin's citation and the two evangelists. First, Justin states that Jesus was born in a "cave" (σπήλαιον) while Matthew states that the Magi found the child in a "house" (οἰκία). Second, Justin mentions here (and several other places[67]) that the Magi were from Arabia, but none of the canonical accounts includes this detail. This supports the previous assertion that Justin probably harmonized sources himself or that he used a harmonized source. Further, because some of the information that Justin includes is not found in our canonical documents this indicates that Justin used sources in addition to the Synoptic Gospels.

Another example of a harmonizing tendency which includes information not found in any of the synoptics is *Dial.* 88.3,

> And when Jesus came to the Jordan River, where John was baptizing, he stepped down into the water and a fire ignited in the Jordan. And as he was coming up from the water, the Holy Spirit alighted upon him like a dove [as] the Apostles of this very Christ of ours wrote.[68]

---

[65] They also point out the fact that the verbal agreement suggests written formula as opposed to merely oral.

[66] *Dial.* 78.5 γεννηθέντος δὲ τότε τοῦ παιδίου ἐν Βεθλεέμ, ἐπειδὴ Ἰωσὴφ οὐκ εἶχεν ἐν τῇ κώμῃ ἐκείνῃ ποῦ καταλῦσαι, ἐν σπηλαίῳ τινὶ σύνεγγυς τῆς κώμης κατέλυσε· καὶ τότε, αὐτῶν ὄντων ἐκεῖ, ἐτετόκει ἡ Μαρία τὸν Χριστὸν καὶ ἐν φάτνῃ αὐτὸν ἐτεθείκει, ὅπου ἐλθόντες οἱ ἀπὸ Ἀρραβίας μάγοι εὗρον αὐτόν.

[67] *Dial.* 77.4; 78.1, 2, 5, 7; 88.1.

[68] καὶ τότε ἐλθόντος τοῦ Ἰησοῦ ἐπὶ τὸν Ἰορδάνην ποταμόν, ἔνθα ὁ Ἰωάννης ἐβάπτιζε,

The mention of the fire igniting the waters of the Jordan is mentioned in no canonical document, yet Justin accepts the handing
down of this tradition through that which the Apostles wrote (ἔγραψαν).

When Justin's references are compared to the documents which
later became canonical, three observations can be made. First, in all
likelihood a harmony was employed by Justin. He may have harmonized the texts himself, or he may have used an already existing
harmony. Second, the harmony is based on the synoptics, with most
of the information paralleled there. Third, the harmony also employed
some extra-canonical source(s).

For many years debate has centered on how best to understand
these phenomena. In this vein, Justin's divergences from or additions
to the text of our canonical Gospels has been explained from five
perspectives. (1) *Failure of memory*. This perspective believes that when
Justin quotes variations and diverges from canonical sources it is
because he relies on his memory rather than referring directly to
the document for his source.[69] (2) *The use of one or more extra-canonical
source*. This perspective sees Justin as dependent on a source that was
not later included in the NT canon. However, the source is most
likely a harmony of documents that were later included in the canon.[70]
(3) *The use of pre-synoptic harmony*. This perspective argues that the variations in Justin are due to the fact that Justin used harmonized
sources that were prior to the synoptics.[71] (4) *The use of a post-synoptic
harmony*. This perspective holds that the variations are explained by

---

κατελθόντος τοῦ Ἰησοῦ ἐπὶ τὸ ὕδωρ καὶ πῦρ ἀνήφθη ἐν τῷ Ἰορδάνῃ, καὶ ἀναδύντος
αὐτοῦ ἀπὸ τοῦ ὕδατος ὡς περιστερὰν τὸ ἅγιον πνεῦμα ἐπιπτῆναι ἐπ᾽ αὐτὸν ἔγραψαν οἱ
ἀπόστολοι αὐτοῦ τούτου τοῦ Χριστοῦ ἡμῶν.

[69] See e.g., K. Semisch, *Die apostolischen Denkwürdigkeiten des Märtyrers Justinus*
(Hamburg, 1848) 389–392; T. Zahn, *Geschichte des neutestamentlichen Kanons*, I.2 (Erlangen:
Andreas Deichert, 1881) 114–116; 463–585; W. A. Shotwell, *The Biblical Exegesis of
Justin Martyr* (London: SPCK, 1965) 24–25.

[70] See e.g., E. R. Buckley, "Justin Martyr's Quotations from the Synoptic Tradition,"
JTS 36 (1935) 175; C. A. Credner, *Beiträge zur Einleitung in die biblischen Schriften*
(Halle, 1832) 133–149, 266–267; A. Hilgenfeld, *Kristische Untersuchungen über die
Evangelien Justin's, der Clementinischen Homilien und Marcion's* (Halle, 1850); O. A. Piper,
"The Nature of the Gospel According to Justin Martyr," *JR* 41 (1961) 155–168;
A. Thoma, "Justins literarisches Verhältnis zu Paulus und zum Johannesevangelium,"
Zeitschrift für wissenschaftliche Theologie 18 (1875) 383–412; G. Volkmar, *Über Justin den
Märtyrer und sein Verhältnis zu unsern Evangelien* (Zurich, 1853); Zahn, "Ist Ammon oder
Tatian Verfasser der ins Lateinische, Altfrankische und Arabische überstetzen
Evangelien-Harmonie?" 206–207.

[71] See e.g., W. Bousset, *Die Evangeliencitate Justins des Märtyrers in ihrem Wert für die
Evangelienkritik* (Göttingen: Vandenhoeck & Ruprecht, 1891) 114–116.

the fact that Justin used a harmony that was based upon the synoptics and other extra-canonical material.[72] (5) *The use of only the canonical gospels.* This position argues that Justin used only the canonical gospels, which he sometimes quoted exactly, sometimes harmonized, and sometimes modified for dogmatic or catechetical reasons.[73]

A. J. Bellinzoni, in his monograph *The Sayings of Jesus in the Writings of Justin Martyr*, has carefully examined the variations of the sayings of Jesus in Justin's writings. In light of the above explanations for their occurrence Bellinzoni examines each position and concludes that the best solution is that Justin relied on a post-synoptic harmony.[74]

Bellinzoni concludes that there is no basis for the position that Justin's variations were the result of a failure of memory. The position that Justin is dependent upon pre-synoptic material is also seen as without foundation because the evidence overwhelmingly points to a post-synoptic source. The thesis that Justin used only the canonical gospels is also given little credence because, even though the majority of Justin's sources were based upon canonical sources, there is considerable evidence that Justin's sources were not always the canonical gospels themselves but rather post-canonical sources based on the synoptics. Bellinzoni also concludes that the idea that Justin is dependent on one or more non-canonical gospels is also lacking in evidence. Not only are the parallels between the specific non-canonical gospel mentioned by adherents different, but ultimately all the sayings in Justin are based in the synoptics.

Bellinzoni places his agreement with the solution that Justin used a post-synoptic harmony of Matthew, Mark, and Luke. His evidence for such a conclusion includes the following:[75]

---

[72] See e.g., Bellinzoni, *The Sayings of Jesus in the Writings of Justin Martyr*; M. von Englehardt, *Das Christenthum Justins Märtyrers, Eine Untersuchung über die Anfänge katholischen Glaubenslehre* (Erlangen, 1878) 335–348; E. Lippelt, *Quae fuerint Justini Martyris APOMNHMONEUMATA quaque ratione cum forma Evangeliorum syro-latina cohaeserint* (Halle, 1901) 35; E. F. Osborn, *Justin Martyr* (BHT Gerhard Ebeling; Tübingen: J. C. B. Mohr [Paul Siebeck], 1973) 120–138; W. Sanday, *The Gospels in the Second Century*, 136–138.

[73] See e.g., A. Baldus, *Das Verhältnis Justins des Märtyrers zu unsern synoptischen Evangelien* (Münster, 1895) 98ff.; F. Massaux, *The Influence of the Gospel of Saint Matthew on Christian Literature Before Saint Irenaeus. Book 3: The Apologists and the Didache* (ET N. J. Belval & S. Hecht; New Gospel Studies 5/2; Leuven: Peeters, 1986); idem, "La Texte du Sermone sur la Montagne de Mattieu utilisé par Saint Justin," *EThL* 28 (1952) 411–448; B. F. Westcott, *A General Survey of the Canon of the New Testament*, 96–179.

[74] Bellinzoni, *The Sayings of Jesus in the Writings of Justin Martyr*, 139–142.

[75] Bellinzoni, *The Sayings of Jesus in the Writings of Justin Martyr*, 140.

1) It is easily demonstrated that Justin used more than one source.
2) Justin generally used as his source written tradition.
3) Justin's written sources harmonized parallel material from Matthew, Mark, and Luke.
4) In the case of Matthew and Luke, related material from different parts of a single gospel were often combined into a single saying.
5) Justin's sources often derived material from a single gospel (either Matthew or Luke, never Mark or John).
6) Justin's quotations of the sayings of Jesus show absolutely no dependence on the Gospel of John.

It should be pointed out that Bellinzoni purposed only to examine the sayings of Jesus contained in the writings of Justin. He did not examine the narrative material. But with respect to the narrative material, I agree with many scholars who say virtually the same thing, i.e., that Justin's source was a harmonized account.[76]

The point in this brief recount of explanations of variants in Justin is to center on the fact that Justin's use of, or even composition of, a harmony is undeniable. It is apparent that each of the above explanations somehow allows for a harmony as a source for Justin's citations. Agreement on this point is quite significant when we bring it into the subject of the shape or state of the NT canon at the time of Justin's *Dialogue with Trypho*.

II. *The New Testament Canon*

"When we follow the process of the formation of the canon in detail, we can hardly avoid the impression that the second century really had no need of a canon."[77] This provocative statement by Kurt Aland summarizes Justin Martyr's relationship to the NT canon. Once we understand that the source of some his content and quotations was a harmony we are in the proper position to understand how Justin viewed these Christian writings, thus leading to a clearer understanding of the state of the NT canon in Justin's *Dialogue with Trypho*.

---

[76] See e.g., Koester, *Ancient Christian Gospels*, 360–402; idem, "The Text of the Synoptic Gospels in the Second Century"; Petersen, "From Justin to Pepys"; idem, "Textual Evidence of Tatian's Dependence Upon Justin's ΑΠΟΜΝΗΜΟΝΕΥΜΑΤΑ"; G. N. Stanton, "The Fourfold Gospel," *NTS* 43 (1997) 329–332.

[77] K. Aland, *A History of Christianity* (2 vols.; ET J. L. Schaaf; Philadelphia: Fortress, 1985) 1.114.

Justin lived in and was acquainted with the church at Rome during a time when Christian oral and written tradition still existed side by side, although, "slowly the written documents alone were coming to held as authoritative."[78] Just as this relationship between oral and written tradition must be placed in its proper perspective in the second century, so must the relationship between scripture and canon. In other words, if the written documents were slowly coming to gain popularity and prestige, one must take care in describing or assuming how these writings were perceived and used. This care must be manifested in the employ of specific terms to describe Christian literature used during the mid-second century. Specifically, a proper definition of the terms "scripture" and "canon" are essential if one is to understand Justin's view of and possible contribution to the formation of the NT canon. This is precisely where Aland's statement above must come into focus because the only "canon" in existence during Justin's era was the canon or rule of faith.

A. *The Rule of Faith*[79]

The earliest reference to the rule of faith is found in the writings of Irenaeus.[80] Because most of Irenaeus's works survive only in Latin the exact language used by him is uncertain. We know that he did use the phrase "rule of truth" (κανὼν τῆς ἀληθείας) among his other expressions, because this phrase occurs in one extant Greek fragment.[81] Irenaeus also uses the words "preaching" (κήρυγμα), "the

---

[78] Barnard, *Justin Martyr*, 53.

[79] The following is meant only as a brief summary. For a convenient listing of the ante-Nicene rules of faith see P. Schaff, *The Creeds of Christendom* (rev. ed. by D. S. Schaff; 3 Vols.; Grand Rapids: Baker, 1996) 2.9–41. For a more detailed discussion on the rule of faith see O. Cullmann, *The Earliest Christian Confessions* (ET J. K. S. Reid; London: Lutterworth, 1949); R. P. C. Hanson, *Tradition in the Early Church* (Library of History and Doctrine; London: SCM, 1962); J. N. D. Kelly, *Early Christian Creeds* (London/New York/Toronto: Longmans, Green & Co., 1950) 30–99; idem, *Early Christian Doctrines*, 29–108; J. T. Lienhard, *The Bible, the Church, and Authority. The Canon of the Christian Bible in History and Theology* (Collegeville, Minn.: The Liturgical Press, 1995); B. M. Metzger, *Canon of the New Testament. Its Origin, Development, Significance.* (Oxford: Clarendon, 1992) 251–253; H. A. Oberman, "*Quo Vadis, Petre?* Tradition from Irenaeus to *Humani Generis*," in idem, *The Dawn of the Reformation. Essays in Late Medieval and Early Reformation Thought* (Edinburgh: T. & T. Clark, 1986) 269–296; E. F. Osborn, "Reason and the Rule of Faith in the Second Century AD," in R. R. Williams, *The Making of Orthodoxy* (Cambridge: Cambridge University Press, 1989) 40–61.

[80] This paragraph is dependent on Hanson, *Tradition in the Early Church*, 75.

[81] *Haer.* 1.1.20.

faith" (ἡ πίστις), and "the tradition" (παράδοσις) to express the same
thing. His Latin translator seems to have regularly translated all
words used for the rule of faith by the phrase "rule of truth" (*regula
veritatis*). Tertullian prefers to use the phrase "rule of faith".

The rule of faith was not a fixed formula or creed. This is evidenced in the fact that no two writers of the early church express
the rule in exactly the same way.[82] Further, not even the same writer
in the same document states it in exactly the same way either.[83]
Thus, the rule of faith was expressed in a more fluid way. Its content was broadly the same as most later creeds, which included one
God the creator, Jesus Christ and his coming, the Holy Spirit, the
Church, and the future judgment.[84] Perhaps the best way to define
or show the content of the rule of faith is to examine its use by its
two main representatives, Irenaeus and Tertullian.

1. *Irenaeus and the Rule of Faith*

Irenaeus is well known for his major work directed against the
Gnostics, *Against Heresies*. While this work is certainly valuable for
gaining information about the Gnostic system and how Irenaeus
viewed it, it is also valuable simply because it contains much positive exposition of contemporary orthodoxy. In his exposition of the
true faith in contrast to the élitism of secret gnostic revelations
Irenaeus posits the "gift of truth". He states, "Wherefore it is incumbent to obey the presbyters who are in the Church,—those who, as
I have shown, possess the succession from the apostles; those who,
together with the episcopate, have received the certain gift of truth
[*charisma veritatis certum*], according to the good pleasure of the Father."[85]

---

[82] G. W. H. Lampe, "Christian Theology in the Patristic Period," in H. Cunliffe-
Jones with B. Drewery (eds.), *A History of Christian Doctrine* (Edinburgh: T. & T.
Clark, 1978) 42. Perhaps a better way to state this would be to say that the rule
of faith was a fixed form for every local church, and that is why no two writers
express it in the same way.

[83] For example, compare the three delineations of the Rule of Faith in Irenaeus
in *Haer.* 1.9.4; 1.10.1; 5.20.1. See also, H. Lietzmann, *A History of the Early Church*
(4 vols.; ET B. L. Woolf; Cleveland and New York: The World Publishing Company,
1961) 2.114–115.

[84] W. H. C. Frend, *The Early Church* (Knowing Christianity; London: Hodder and
Stoughton, 1965) 77; S. G. Hall, *Doctrine and Practice in the Early Church* (Grand
Rapids: Eerdmans, 1991) 61.

[85] Irenaeus, *Haer.* 4.26.2. ET from A. Roberts & J. Donaldson, *Ante-Nicene Fathers*
(10 vols.; Peabody: Hendrickson, 1994 [Buffalo: Christian Literature Publishing
Company, 1885]) 1.315–567.

In the context Irenaeus makes reference to a process of succession from the Apostles to the contemporary church leadership safeguarding this gift of truth. The succession of which Irenaeus speaks, in his opinion, maintains the true faith. The succession safeguards the faith which is the tradition derived from the Apostles, or the apostolic tradition.[86] In opposition to those who are forming wrong doctrines concerning the Father and the Son Irenaeus claims that,

> ... the preaching of the Church is everywhere consistent, and continues in an even course, and receives testimony from the prophets, apostles, and all the disciples—as I have proved—through [those in] the beginning, the middle, and the end, and through the entire dispensation of God, and that well-grounded system which tends to man's salvation, namely, our faith; which, having been received from the Church, we do preserve, and which always, by the Spirit of God, renewing its youth, as if it were some precious deposit in an excellent vessel, causes the vessel itself containing it to renew its youth also. For this gift of God has been entrusted to the Church, as breath was to the first created man, for this purpose, that all the members receiving it may be vivified.[87]

In Irenaeus's thinking, church leaders are both representatives and spokesmen—defenders of the apostolic tradition which is consistent everywhere the church is present. This is in direct contrast to the secret revelations of the Gnostics whom Irenaeus was combating. It is apparent that this sure gift of truth which was entrusted to the church is the faith, or apostolic tradition, or doctrine.

The faith which was entrusted to the church is often delineated by Irenaeus as the Rule of Truth.[88] A good example of Irenaeus delineating the rule is found in *Haer.* 1.10.1,

> The Church, though dispersed throughout the whole world, even to the ends of the earth, has received from the apostles and their disciples this faith: [She believes] in one God, the Father Almighty, Maker of heaven, and earth, and the sea, and all things that are in them, and in one Christ Jesus, the Son of God, who became incarnate for our salvation; and in the Holy Spirit, who proclaimed through the prophets the dispensations of God, and the advents, and the birth from a virgin, and the passion, and the resurrection from the dead, and the ascension into heaven in the flesh of the beloved Christ Jesus, our Lord and His

---

[86] Irenaeus, *Haer.* 3.3.2.
[87] Irenaeus, *Haer.* 3.24.1.
[88] See the three explicit delineations of the content of the rule in *Haer.* 1.9.4; 1.10.1; 5.20.1.

[future] manifestation from heaven in the glory of the Father "to gather all things in one" and to raise up anew all flesh of the whole human race ... As I have already observed, the Church having received this preaching and this faith, although scattered throughout the whole world, yet, as if occupying but one house, carefully preserves it.[89]

Here we see reference to the churches as receiving the faith from the Apostles. This represents a certain consistency of belief, a universal acceptance which guarantees the maintenance of the true faith in contrast to Gnostic systems of belief.

2. *Tertullian and the Rule of Faith*

Tertullian also appeals to a tradition that is handed down from the Apostles. This faith was first delivered by Christ, spread by the Apostles and finally deposited and safeguarded by the apostolic church.[90] Tertullian expresses the rule of faith in a number of places,[91] of which his expression in *Prescription of Heretics* is exemplary.

The Rule of faith is ... namely, that by which we believe that there is one God, and no other besides the Maker of the world, who produced the universe out of nothing, by his Word sent forth first of all; that this Word, called his Son, was seen in the name of God in various ways by the patriarchs, was always heard in the prophets, at last was sent down, from the Spirit and power of God the Father, into the Virgin Mary, was made flesh in her womb, and born of her, lived as Jesus Christ; that then he preached the new law and the new promise of the kingdom of heaven; wrought miracles; was nailed to the cross; rose again on the third day; was caught up to the heavens; and sat down at the right hand of the Father; sent in his place the power of the Holy Ghost, to guide the believers; he will come again

---

[89] Irenaeus, *Haer.* 1.10.1–2. ET from Roberts & Donaldson, *Ante-Nicene Fathers*. Ἡ μὲν γὰρ ἐκκλησία, καίπερ καθ᾽ ὅλης τῆς οἰκουμένης ἕως περάτων τῆς γῆς διεσπαρμένη, παρὰ δὲ τῶν Ἀποστόλων καὶ τῶν ἐκείνων μαθητῶν παραλαβοῦσα τὴν [πίστιν] εἰς ἕνα Θεὸν, Πατέρα παντοκράτορα, τὸν πεποιηκότα τὸν οὐρανὸν, καὶ τὴν γῆν, καὶ τὰς θαλάσσας, καὶ πάντα τὰ ἐν αὐτοῖς, πίστιν· καὶ εἰς ἕνα Χριστὸν Ἰησοῦν, τὸν Υἱὸν τοῦ Θεοῦ, τὸν σαρκωθέντα ὑπὲρ τῆς ἡμετέρας σωτηρίας· καὶ εἰς Πνεῦμα ἅγιον, τὸ διὰ τῶν προφητῶν κεκηρυχὸς τὰς οἰκονομίας καὶ τὰς ἐλεύσεις [τὴν ἔλευσιν, *adventum*], καὶ τὴν ἐκ Παρθένου γέννησιν, καὶ τὸ πάθος, καὶ τὴν ἔγερσιν ἐκ νεκρῶν, καὶ τὴν ἔνσαρκον εἰς τοὺς οὐρανοὺς ἀνάληψιν τοῦ ἠγαπημένου Χριστοῦ Ἰησοῦ, τοῦ Κυρίου ἡμῶν, καὶ τὴν ἐκ τῶν οὐρανῶν ἐν τῇ δόξῃ τοῦ Πατρὸς παρουσίαν αὐτοῦ, ἐπὶ τὸ ἀνακεφαλαιώσασθαι τὰ πάντα, καὶ ἀναστῆσαι πᾶσαν σάρκα πάσης ἀνθρωπότητος.

[90] This sequence and defence of its accuracy is clearly laid out by Tertullian in *Praescip.* 20–29.

[91] *Virg. Vel.* 1; *Prax.* 2.

with glory to take the saints into the enjoyment of eternal life and the celestial promises, and to judge the wicked with eternal fire, after the resuscitation of both, with the restitution of the flesh.[92]

The rule of faith in Tertullian is not the same as Irenaeus in wording, but it is very similar in content. The key here is that the rule of faith was a guide or standard of right belief. Its general content was seen as flowing directly from Christ, through the Apostles and to the church. This was the content of the true faith. In this light Aland's statement[93] that the second century church had no need for a written canon is better understood. The church believed that it already possessed a reliable exposition of the faith. Tradition had handed down the content and it was thus safeguarded.

3. *The Rule of Faith and Canon*

A proper understanding of this rule of faith is foundational to a proper understanding of "canon" and "scripture". The term "canon" did not come to be used as an appellation for a collection or list of Christian writings (the New Testament) until the mid-fourth century in the writings of Athanasius.[94] Earlier in the second century, however, the word designated what the church acknowledged as having

---

[92] Tertullian, *Praescrip.* 13. Translation from Schaff, *Creeds of Christendom*, 2.19–20. *Regula est autem fidei, . . . illa scilicet qua creditur, Unum omnino Deum esse, nec alium præter mundi conditorem, qui universa de nihilo produxerit, per Verbum suum primo omnium demissum; id Verbum, Filium ejus appellatum, in nomine Dei varie visum a patriarchis, in prophetis semper auditum, postremo delatum, ex Spiritu Patris Dei et virtute, in Virginem Mariam, carnem factum in utero ejus, et ex ea natum, egisse Jesum Christum; exinde prædicasse novam legem et novam promissionem regni cælorum; virtutes fecisse; fixum cruci; tertia die resurrexisse; in cælos ereptum; sedisse ad dexteram Patris; misisse vicariam vim Spiritus Sancti, qui credentes agat; venturum cum claritate ad sumendos sanctos in vitæ æternæ et promissorum cælestium fructum, et ad profanos adjudicandos igni perpetuo, facta utriusque partis resuscitatione, cum carnis restitutione.*

[93] See above, section II.

[94] Athanasius of Alexandria, *Decr.* 5.18. Here Athanasius describes the *Shepherd of Hermas* as "not of the canon." See also Athanasius' famous *Ep. fest.* 39 of the year 367, wherein he describes certain Christian books as "canonical". "Again it is not tedious to speak of the [books] of the New Testament. These are, the four Gospels, according to Matthew, Mark, Luke, and John. Afterwards, the Acts of the Apostles and Epistles (called Catholic), seven, viz. Of James, one; of Peter, two; of John, three; after these, one of Jude. In addition, there are fourteen epistles of Paul, written in this order. The first, to the Romans; the two to the Corinthians; after these, to the Galatians; next, to the Ephesians; then to the Philippians; then to the Colossians; after these, two to the Thessalonians, and that to the Hebrews; and again, two to Timothy; one to Titus; and lastly, that to Philemon. And besides, the Revelation of John."

regulative control for its faith and life—the rule of faith.[95] It was
only after Athanasius that the term came to denote a closed collection of writings to which nothing could be added or from which
nothing could be taken away.

The idea that the church consciously discussed or contemplated
a closed or fixed collection of NT writings during the second and
third centuries lacks a strong foundation. This is well illustrated in
the church's answers to Marcionism, Gnosticism, and Montanism.
These three heterodox movements were not challenged by the fathers
of the era with a closed collection of Christian writings. Rather, the
fathers answered these challenges with a confession of faith which
was defended by an appeal to the apostolic writings. Both Irenaeus[96]
and Tertullian[97] are exemplary of this. Even as late as the third century Serapion shows this same appeal.[98] In writing to his church
Serapion wished to settle the question of whether the *Gospel of Peter*
could be read there. He had previously allowed its reading but subsequently reversed this decision on the basis that it contained denials
of the humanity of Jesus. The point here is that Serapion did not
revoke his permission to allow the *Gospel of Peter* to be read in the
church on the basis of an appeal to a closed collection of Christian
writings (a New Testament canon), but on the basis of an appeal to
a confession of faith, on the basis that certain doctrines contained
in that Gospel were at variance with what was handed down through
the Apostles and Bishops of the churches. The issue was dealt with
on the basis of an appeal to orthodoxy that is represented in the
rule of faith, not canonicity.[99]

This assertion is not meant to disparage the use of Christian writings (writings that later became canonical as well as other orthodox
documents) during Justin's era. It is meant simply to put the issue
of canonicity in its proper chronology. Before there was a New
Testament canon there existed a rule of faith which functioned as
the guardian of proper doctrine. There is a close relationship between

---

[95] In addition to the rule as expressed by Irenaeus and Tertullian see also, Clement
of Alexandria, *Str.* 7.15.90; Eusebius of Caesarea *H.e.* 6.13.3.
[96] *Haer.* 1.8.1; 1.9.1–4.
[97] *Praescrip.* 8–9.
[98] Eusebius, *H.e.* 6.12.3–6.
[99] L. M. McDonald, "The Integrity of the Biblical Canon in Light of Its Historical
Development," *BBR* 6 (1996) 118–119.

Christian writings and the rule of faith. But it is extremely important to place the relationship in its proper context. Again, Irenaeus and Tertullian best exemplify this context.

Irenaeus clearly shows the importance of the rule of faith in relation to apostolic writings. In *Haer.* 3.4.1 he speaks of the church guarding Christian doctrine like a rich man depositing his money in a bank. It is clear that the reference is to the rule of faith, which is the entrance to life (salvation). For Irenaeus only the church is in possession of these sacred truths. Persons who pervert this truth or add to it are thieves and robbers.

To stress the importance of this "tradition of truth," Irenaeus asks a question, "Suppose there arise a dispute relative to some important question among us, should we not have recourse to the most ancient Churches with which the apostles held constant intercourse, and learn from them what is certain and clear in regard to the present question?" We see here an appeal to the true doctrine which was faithfully safeguarded and handed down through the church universal to the contemporary church. Irenaeus then continues, "For how should it be if the apostles themselves had not left us writings? Would it not be necessary, [in that case,] to follow the course of the tradition which they handed down to those to whom they did commit the churches?" The question is rhetorical here. The rule of faith is a sufficient shepherd to salvation. In fact, Irenaeus makes explicit reference to people who are saved through it in the absence of written documents. In direct reference to the course of tradition stated in *Haer.* 3.4.1 Irenaeus continues,

> To which course [of tradition] many nations of those barbarians who believe in Christ do assent, having salvation written in their hearts by the Spirit, without paper or ink, and, carefully preserving the ancient tradition, believing in one God, the Creator of heaven and earth, and all things therein, by means of Jesus Christ, the Son of God; who, because of his surpassing love towards His creation, condescended to be born of the virgin, he Himself uniting man through Himself to God, and having suffered under Pontius Pilate, and rising again, and having been received up in splendor, shall come in glory, the Saviour of those who are saved, and the Judge of those who are judged, and sending into eternal fire those who transform the truth, and despise His Father and His advent. Those who, in the absence of written documents, have believed this faith, are barbarians, so far as regards our language; but as regards doctrine, manner, and tenor of life, they are because of faith, very wise indeed ... Thus, by means of that ancient tradition of

the apostles, they do not suffer their mind to conceive anything of the
[doctrines suggested by the] portentous language of these teachers, among
whom neither the Church nor doctrine has ever been established.[100]

The point here is clear, the true doctrine of the church has been
faithfully passed on and is sufficient to lead people to salvation.

A similar line of argument is found in Tertullian's *Prescription of
Heretics* 15–19. Here Tertullian deals with how one should conduct
an argument with heretics. In using scripture, the heretics were leading many astray. But Tertullian states that the heretics have no right
to do so because the scriptures do not belong to them, but to the
church.[101] He continues this line of argument by explaining that even
though the heretic may use scripture in his argument it is inadmissible
because the heretic has produced diverse interpretations. It is the
church which has possessed the scriptures since ancient times and it
is the church's ordained responsibility to correctly interpret scripture.[102]

The climax of Tertullian's argument appears in the nineteenth
chapter. It is in the interpretation of scripture that the apostolic tradition plays an important role. Tertullian states,

> Our appeal, therefore, must not be made to the Scriptures; nor must
> controversy be admitted on points in which victory will either be impos-
> sible, or uncertain, or not certain enough. But even if a discussion
> from the Scriptures should not turn out in such a way as to place
> both sides on par, (yet) the natural order of things would require that
> this point should be first proposed, which is now the only one which
> we must discuss: "With whom lies that very faith to which the Scriptures
> belong. From what and through whom, and when, and to whom, has
> been handed down that rule, by which men become Christians?" For
> wherever it shall be manifest that the true Christian rule and faith
> shall be, *there* will likewise be the true Scriptures and expositions thereof,
> and all the Christian traditions.[103]

For Tertullian the proper interpretation of scripture is found in adherence to the rule of faith which was handed down and safeguarded
by the church. It is in this rule where one finds the true faith and
one must adhere to this rule in discussions with heretics. Scripture
is open to many different interpretations. It is only the apostolic
faith, which is manifested in the rule of faith, where proper interpretation of scripture is manifested.

---

[100] *Haer.* 3.4.2.
[101] *Praescrip.* 15.
[102] *Praescrip.* 16–18.
[103] *Praescrip.* 19.

If we now return to the statement of K. Aland at the beginning of this section we may see its accuracy. It was against this rule of faith which everything was measured, even the writings of the developing NT.[104] The danger here may be in pressing this too far.[105] In other words, we must not, in view of the importance of the rule of faith, take this to mean that Christian writings were relatively unimportant in the early church. In fact, the later development of a collection of these writings speaks volumes to the contrary. The point here in stressing the importance of the rule of faith in the second and third centuries is simply get a proper chronology of the development of the NT canon. Once we understand that the rule of faith was actually one of the criteria in choosing the writings which eventually made up the NT canon[106] we have the proper perspective to understand Justin's place in its history. However, one important distinction remains to be discussed.

B. *Scripture and Canon*

About thirty years ago A. C. Sundberg Jr. called for a more precise definition of the terms "scripture" and "canon" in order to distinguish some very important features of each.[107] Sundberg believed that much of the discussion surrounding the history of the NT canon inappropriately applied the terms scripture and canon as synonyms. This, Sundberg believed, caused great confusion for those who sought to understand the state of the NT canon during the second century. Many simply moved from scripture to canon without realizing the inherent differences between the two terms.[108]

At the heart of the issue is discussions on canon which employ the two terms in a rather loose sense. Sundberg states, "It is necessary

---

[104] Aland, *A History of Christianity*, 1.114.

[105] H. F. von Campenhausen (*The Formation of the Christian Bible* [ET J. A. Baker; London: Adam & Charles Black, 1969], 329) very succinctly expresses the proper balance between scripture and the rule of faith.

[106] For discussions on this and other criteria of canonicity see, F. F. Bruce, *The Canon of Scripture* (Downers Grove: Inter-Varsity, 1988) 255–269; H. Y. Gamble, *The New Testament Canon*, 67–72; L. M. McDonald, *The Formation of the Christian Biblical Canon* (rev. ed.; Peabody, MA: Hendrickson, 1995) 228–249; Metzger, *The Canon of the New Testament*, 251–257; A. G. Patzia, *The Making of the New Testament. Origin, Collection, Text & Canon* (Leicester: Apollos, 1995) 102–107.

[107] A. C. Sundberg, Jr., "The Making of the New Testament Canon," in C. M. Laymon (ed.), *The Interpreter's One Volume Commentary on the Bible* (London: Collins, 1972) 1216–1224; idem, "Towards a Revised History of the New Testament Canon," *StudEv* 4 (1968) 452–461.

[108] Sundberg, "Towards a Revised History of the New Testament Canon," 452.

to distinguish between the terms 'scripture,' meaning writings which
are held in some sense as authoritative for religion and 'canon,'
meaning a defined collection that is held to be exclusively, i.e. with
respect to all other books, authoritative."[109] Sundberg objects to discussions which employ "canon" and "canonical" to written documents that were widely held as, in some sense, scripture without
regard to a definitive and exclusive determination of a closed group
of such documents (canon). The application of "canonical" to such
documents is viewed as anachronistic because a written canon, by
definition, is closed and no such canon existed in the second and
third centuries. In order to avoid this anachronistic perspective of
canon Sundberg stresses the importance of maintaining the above
distinctions between canon and scripture.

More recently, Sundberg's call for distinction have been echoed
by L. M. McDonald[110] and H. Y. Gamble.[111] Taking his cue from
G. T. Sheppard,[112] McDonald also calls for a distinction between
scripture and canon. McDonald, however, prefers to express it in
terms of "canon 1," and "canon 2".[113] Canon 1 is essentially a rule,
standard, or guide that functions in an controlling manner in a community. It is fluid or flexible and not yet fixed. Canon 1 is therefore present wherever there exists some respect for regulative control
within a community, either in a written or oral form. Canon 2 occurs
when canon 1 becomes fixed in a given community. Canon 2 thus
becomes so well-established in a given community of faith that very
little doubt arises about the status of a text thereafter. Canon 2,
therefore, is more fixed in the community.

Gamble also wishes to maintain a distinction but chooses a different
way to express it. His starting point is the perception that by its very
existence the NT canon "calls special attention to its form, i.e., a
fixed collection of precisely twenty-seven early Christian documents,

---

[109] Sundberg, "The Making of the New Testament Canon," 1216.
[110] McDonald, *The Formation of the Christian Biblical Canon*; idem, "The Integrity of
the Biblical Canon in Light of Its Historical Development".
[111] H. Y. Gamble, "Canon—New Testament," in N. D. Freedman (ed.), *ABD* (6
vols.; New York: Doubleday, 1992) 1.852–861; idem, "The Canon of the New
Testament," in E. J. Epp and G. W. MacRae (eds.), *The New Testament and Its Modern
Interpreters* (Atlanta: Scholars Press, 1989) 201–243; idem, *The New Testament Canon.*
[112] G. T. Sheppard, "Canon," in M. Eliade (ed.), *The Encyclopedia of Religion* (10
vols.; New York: MacMillan, 1987) 3.62–69.
[113] McDonald, *Formation of the Christian Biblical Canon*, 29; idem, "The Integrity of
the Biblical Canon," 101.

and to its function, i.e., literature that is normative for the faith and life of the Christian community."[114] Gamble employs the distinction with the terms "functional" and "fixed". Thus the importance of understanding canon as a *fixed* collection is emphasized. On the other hand, a functional canon is one which operated in the looser sense of a norm or standard, whether written or oral. Gamble stresses that a scrupulousness about such terminology is necessary so that these real distinctions are not blurred. The history of the NT canon is not only concerned with the normative use of Christian documents (scripture), but also with the delimitation of such documents and with its meaning and function *as a collection* (canon).[115]

What we are dealing with here is really three ways of saying the same thing. Canon is *not* synonymous with scripture. McDonald has pointed out that there is considerable overlap.[116] The overlap occurs in the normative status of a document, that is, both scriptural documents and documents that later became canonical were viewed as normative in the life of the community. However, a line of demarcation must be understood. This line occurs when a document is chosen to be placed between two distinct poles.[117] At one end of the pole is a rule, standard, ideal, norm, or regulative office or literature.[118] The focus here is on the internal signs of an elevated status within a community of faith. At the other end of the pole is a fixation, standardization, enumeration, listing, register, or catalog of exemplary writings.[119] The emphasis here rests on the precise boundary, limits, or measure of what, from some preunderstood standard, belongs within or falls outside of a specific canon.

In this light I again call attention to the fact that the term "canon" did not come to be used as an appellation for a collection or list of Christian writings until the mid-fourth century with Athanasius.[120]

---

[114] Gamble, "Canon—New Testament," 852.
[115] Gamble, "The Canon of the New Testament," 205.
[116] McDonald, *Formation of the Christian Biblical Canon*, 13.
[117] Sheppard, "Canon," 64.
[118] McDonald describes this as "canon 1" while Gamble calls it a "functional canon". It appears to me that some confusion could be avoided if Sundberg's description of it as "scripture" were consistently and properly maintained.
[119] McDonald describes this as "canon 2" while Gamble calls it a "fixed canon". Again, confusion could be avoided here as well if Sundberg's description of it as "canon" was also consistently and properly maintained.
[120] Athanasius, *Decr.* 5.18. Here Athanasius describes the *Shepherd of Hermas* as "not of the canon." See also Athanasius's famous *Ep. fest.* 39 of the year 367, wherein he describes certain Christian books as "canonical".

Before that time, as I have shown above, the word designated what the church acknowledged as having regulative control for its faith and life. Only after Athanasius did the term "canon" come to denote a closed collection of writings.

On the other hand, the term "scripture" designates writings which were religiously normative. They are used as such without regard to their systematic enumeration or limitation. This is, in fact, how Christian writings were used throughout the second century. The concept of canon presupposes scripture, but the concept of scripture does not necessarily entail the notion of canon.

C. *Rule of Faith, Scripture, and Canon in the Second Century*

The two sections above on the rule of faith and on the distinction between scripture and canon are intended as a warning against attributing canonical status to a document that attained only scriptural status. The section concerning the rule of faith does so by pointing out the chronology of the rule of faith in relation to a closed canon of Christian writings. The rule of faith was actually used as a criterion in the eventual collection of certain Christian documents into a closed canon. The section on the distinction between scripture and canon warns us not to apply canonical status to a document that had attained only scriptural status. This is particularly important when dealing with the reception of Christian literature during the second and third centuries. This is so because of the lack of evidence that the church consciously discussed or contemplated a closed or fixed collection of NT scriptures during this time. Being aware of the concept of the rule of faith and of the distinction between scripture and canon should act as a guard to an anachronistic understanding of canonicity in the second and third centuries.

At the very least, the discussions above show us that the NT canon was not a topic of discussion during the second and third centuries. Further, the very fact that discussions concerning canonicity were occurring well into the fourth century make it extremely difficult to apply canonical status to Christian documents in the second century. Eusebius's famous list of recognized, disputed, and rejected books is illustrative of this point.[121] Since the notion of a canon of scripture entails a fixity, discussions of this sort, by their very occur-

---

[121] Eusebius, *H.e.* 6.12.3–6.

rence, argue strongly against a closed canon. If this is the case in the early fourth century, it is most certainly the case in the second and third centuries as well.

The above understanding of the rule of faith and of the proper distinction between scripture and canon has implications for the study of Justin's *Dialogue with Trypho* and the NT canon. It is in this context that our discussion of Justin's understanding of and contribution to NT canonicity must be placed. One must remain aware of the function and importance of the rule of faith as well as the misunderstandings that may occur in using scripture and canon synonymously in reference to Christian literature of the second century.

III. *Justin's Memoirs and the NT "Canon"*

E. J. Goodspeed confidently asserts that the deliberate creation of the four-fold Gospel occurred in AD 115–125.[122] This date was chosen because Goodspeed believes the *Preaching of Peter*, 2 Peter, the *Gospel of Peter*, Papias, the *Epistle of the Apostles* and Justin Martyr all show acquaintance with or use of all four canonical documents. Similarly, R. L. Harris, in reference to the scriptures (apostolic writings) to which Justin refers, states, "Justin's importance lies in the fact that he refers to a well-defined corpus of sacred books."[123] Later, in specific reference to the four gospels, he claims that they are clearly a regulative corpus for Justin.[124] F. F. Bruce also indicates his belief that Justin knew of a gospel collection.[125]

All three of the above men have made statements about a fixed collection of Gospels based solely on Justin's use of or acquaintance with what later became canonical Gospels. But this confuses acquaintance with, and even use of, the Gospels with a conscious attempt to arrange them into a collection. A fixed collection necessarily entails a deliberate catalog of exemplary writings, a standard which requires or allows no alteration. But in Justin we see no indication that it was his purpose to form such a collection, nor was it his assumption

---

[122] E. J. Goodspeed, *Formation of the New Testament* (Chicago: University of Chicago Press, 1962) 37–38.

[123] R. L. Harris, *Inspiration and Canonicity of the Bible. An Historical and Exegetical Study* (Contemporary Evangelical Perspectives; Grand Rapids: Zondervan, 1969) 213.

[124] Harris, *Inspiration and Canonicity*, 213.

[125] Bruce, *The Canon of Scripture*, 126–127.

that this was already completed and accepted by him. In this respect, two issues merit attention here: The Apostolic Writings as Scripture; and, The Implications of Justin's use of a Harmony.

A. *The Apostolic Writings as Scripture*

There is no arguing that Justin held the Prophetic scriptures in high esteem.[126] He used and referred to them often. This esteem goes back to his conversion to Christianity when the respectable old man taught Justin that only those who had seen or heard from someone who had seen God can truly give knowledge concerning him. Philosophers have no qualification in this area, but the Prophets do because "they alone, being filled with the Holy Spirit, communicated that which they heard and saw."[127] This communication, which amounts to knowledge about God and his plan of salvation, is written down and still available for study.[128] When Justin accepted the old man's argument it changed the way he attained knowledge about God. Instead of inquiring from philosophers who had neither seen nor heard from someone who had seen, Justin appealed directly to those who had seen—the Prophets. The Prophets were, therefore, viewed as writings which were used as scripture by Justin.

But what about the Apostolic writings—the Memoirs? Reference has been made to the fact that Justin used the Memoirs as trustworthy documents which prove the prophecies concerning Jesus had actually occurred. This is certainly true. However, does this mean it is proper to speak of the Memoirs simply as "historical" records and viewed in a lesser light than the Prophets?

God can be known through the writings of the Prophets, they possess a special knowledge which was revealed by God. Because of this they were held in high esteem. But in Justin's appeal to the Prophets as a place to attain knowledge about God, he also mentions that his heart was set on fire and an affection for the "friends of Christ" took hold of him.[129] This appellation can be nothing less than a reference to the Apostles.[130] In several places in the *Dialogue* the Apostles figure quite prominently as equal to the Prophets because

---

[126] See above, Chapter 2.IV.A.

[127] *Dial.* 7.1 ἀλλὰ μόνα ταῦτα εἰπόντες ἃ ἤκουσαν καὶ ἃ εἶδον ἁγίῳ πληρωθέντες πνεύματι.

[128] *Dial.* 7.2.

[129] *Dial.* 7.2–3.

[130] See above, Chapter 2.IV.B.

they preach the same message.[131] Justin even states that the Prophets preached the gospel of Jesus and proclaimed him to all men[132]—a task performed also by the Apostles in their Memoirs.

But the crux of the relationship between the Prophets and the Apostles is located in the significance of seeing and hearing. In other words, the qualification of the Prophets for communicating knowledge of God rested in the fact that they had seen and heard God. The qualification of the Apostles also rested in the fact that they had seen and heard God, as well as reading the Prophets. This is shown in two ways. First, because knowledge about God required communication from someone who heard from someone who had seen,[133] the Apostles rested on the communication of the Prophets. The Prophets had seen and heard that which they communicated, therefore the Apostles were able to use their writings for gaining knowledge of God.

The second way in which the Apostles are qualified to communicate knowledge about God is because the Apostles witnessed the ultimate revelation of God in the incarnation of his *Logos*.[134] Thus the significance of the Memoirs does not lie solely in their function as "historical" records. It rests also in the fact that they saw and heard the ultimate revelation of God. The Apostles witnessed that to which the Prophets pointed. They thus fulfil the criteria by which knowledge of God may be attained and communicated.

The Prophets saw and heard. In Justin's eyes this qualified them to communicate knowledge about God. The Apostles read the writings of the Prophets who had seen God, but more importantly, they actually saw God's plan for salvation played out before their eyes. Through the incarnate *Logos*, the Apostles saw the fulfillment of God's will in his very being, and in his actions. As witness to this action the Apostles have the qualification to communicate this to humankind—this is the significance of their writings.

Thus, in a very real sense, the Prophets and the Memoirs must be viewed together in that they are witnesses to God. In this respect, the Memoirs can be viewed as scripture. They can be viewed as scripture because they were used by Justin as invaluable for gaining knowledge about God and his plan of salvation through his *Logos* incarnate.

---

[131] *Dial.* 42.1–2; 76.6; 88.3; 106.1; 109.1; 110.2; 119.6.
[132] *Dial.* 136.3.
[133] *Dial.* 3; 7; 8.
[134] This is discussed in detail above, Chapter 2.V.

B. *The Implications of Justin's Use of a Harmony*

If Justin's use of the memoirs can allow us to conclude that he used them as scripture can we take the next step, as Goodspeed, Harris and Bruce have done above, and conclude that they are a fixed collection? In light of the probability that he used a harmony the answer must be negative.

If the four Gospels were all included in a fixed collection at the time of Justin it is highly unlikely that he would choose to use a harmony. A fixed collection suggests a catalog of exemplary writings. If these writings were seen as exemplary one must ask why Justin saw fit to ignore this collection and employ a harmony which attempted to form an even better picture than the separate Gospels produced.[135] Even though the majority of the harmony was based on the synoptics, we still must understand that the very act of Justin employing a harmony indicates that a four-fold Gospel canon was not in existence, or, at the very least, not recognized. Even if we recognize the probability that Justin's harmony lent a certain amount of prestige to the Gospels it is a mistake to assume that this recognition shows that they were canonical. Perhaps the lines have become blurred because the main sources employed by Justin are known to us today as canonical. But the fact remains, Justin used the Gospels in much the same way that the Gospel writers employed their sources, but no one has ever argued that because Matthew used Mark and Luke used Mark that Mark was therefore canonical.

The text of what later became the canonical Gospels was apparently not free from major revision in wording and context. For in harmonization both these are done. This very act argues against a fixed collection of exemplary writings for the Gospels at the time of Justin. For Justin the Memoirs were scripture, but they were not canonical. Because of this Justin felt free to either construct a harmony himself or employ a harmony upon which to base his understanding of the coming of the *Logos* of God.

---

[135] For the motives of harmonization see, Tj. Baarda, "Διαφώνια—Συμφωνία. Factors in the Harmonization of the Gospels, especially in the Diatessaron of Tatian," in *Essays on the Diatessaron* (Contributions to Biblical Exegesis & Theology 11; Kampen: Kok Pharos, 1994) 29–47; O. Cullmann, "The Plurality of the Gospels as a Theological Problem in Antiquity," in *The Early Church* (London: SCM, 1956) 37–54; Petersen, "From Justin to Pepys".

IV. *Summary and Conclusion*

This chapter has focused on the Memoirs of the Apostles and the question of their canonical standing. The probability that the Memoirs were, in fact, the Synoptic Gospels is high. We know that they were documents written by the Apostles or those who followed them. We also know that the Memoirs contain information pertaining to the life of Jesus. As such they are treated as reliable in proving that the prophecies concerning Jesus actually occurred.

But it is not enough to simply state that the Memoirs are the Synoptic Gospels. Investigation into Justin's method of citing the memoirs reveals that the source Justin used (the memoirs) was a harmony. The harmony was based on the Synoptics, with some indication of the use of some source which did not later become part of the canon. Thus, while it may be accurate to say that Justin used the Synoptic Gospels in the *Dialogue with Trypho*, it must be clarified that he used a source that was based on the synoptics and not actually the separate synoptics.

This realization has implications for the emerging NT canon during Justin's era. And it is here that the proper distinction between scripture and canon must come into play. The temptation to form conclusions about canon based simply on the use of the synoptics must be resisted. Use or acquaintance of any document in a writer does not automatically imply that the writer had this in some sort of exemplary canon. At the most this may imply the scriptural status of a document, but even this must be measured by other indicators. There is indication in Justin that he held the Gospels (or at least a harmony of them) to be scripture. But there is no indication that canonical status was given to his source. In fact, the application of canonical status in Justin's day is anachronistic in light of later discussions concerning a NT canon.

The application of canonical status to Justin's source is further tempered by his use of a harmony. If a canon of the Gospels was accepted by Justin it would be highly unlikely that he would deviate from that accepted collection and use a different source which attempted to improve on the separated Gospels.

The study of Justin's contribution to the NT canon is best understood as a process toward a fixed collection Christian writings. This process should be understood as having occurred over a fairly long period of time. The Christian documents that were eventually accepted

into the NT canon underwent a period of use in the church before
the closure of the canon.[136] During this time it is not inaccurate to
say that the church viewed these writings as scripture, but it is inaccurate to say that these writings were canonical. The place of Justin
within the history of the NT canon is in the period where the church
was still in the position of sifting through and employing whatever
Christian document was useful to them.

---

[136] The history of the NT canon has been admirably presented in recent years
by J. Barton, *Holy Writings, Sacred Text. The Canon in Early Christianity* (Louisville, KY:
Westminster John Knox Press, 1997); Campenhausen, *The Formation of the Christian Bible*;
Gamble, *The New Testament Canon*; J. F. Kelly, *Why is There a New Testament?* (London:
Geoffrey Chapman, 1986); McDonald, *The Formation of the Christian Biblical Canon*.

CHAPTER FIVE

INTERPRETATIONAL FOUNDATIONS IN
DIALOGUE WITH TRYPHO

I. *Introduction*

The interpretation of scripture in the *Dialogue with Trypho* is a study that could lead in many directions. A natural tendency in such a chapter is to attempt to boil the *Dialogue* down to its core method and list the interpretive rules followed by Justin. By so doing, Justin is then described as following the rules of typological interpretation, or allegorical interpretation, or Hellenistic interpretation. But this kind of delineation tends to overlook important contextual and motivational issues involved in Justin's exegesis. Here we are speaking of the difference between the methods or forms of exegesis and the function of exegesis.[1] In other words, we must understand that the function of Justin's exegesis was not necessarily governed by any precise rules.[2] It followed, instead, the needs which Justin was required to meet, in situations that were apologetic rather than exegetical.[3]

This functional understanding of interpretation requires a clear understanding of the foundations and presuppositions of the exegete, in this case, Justin. For if the apologetic aspects of Justin's discussion with Trypho necessitated a certain explanation, it is incumbent on the historical theologian to uncover the presuppositions, polemics,

---

[1] The decisive feature of early Christian interpretation is found not in the methods or forms but in the function of the exegesis. See, J. L. Kugel & R. A. Greer, *Early Biblical Interpretation* (Library of Early Christianity 3; Philadelphia: Westminster, 1986) 126–128.

[2] This is not to say that Justin simply practiced a random interpretation of the scriptures. He did employ hermeneutical principles. It would, however, be inaccurate to assume that Justin made the same distinction modern scholars make between different exegetical practices. See H. M. Knapp, "Melito's Use of Scripture in *Peri Pascha*: Second Century Typology," *VC* 54 (2000) 348–352.

[3] M. Simonetti, *Biblical Interpretation in the Early Church. An Historical Introduction to Patristic Exegesis* (ET J. A. Hughes; Edinburgh: T. & T. Clark, 1994) 24–25. Simonetti speaks generally here of Justin, Irenaeus, and Tertullian. I have included only Justin here for the sake of brevity.

and resulting interpretation. All three aspects are required in an understanding of Justin's functional exegesis.[4]

A functional understanding of Justin's interpretation of scripture in the *Dialogue* will give a clear picture of the reasons why Justin employed certain arguments. Its basis is in the contextual framework of the *Dialogue* as a work directed toward Jews.[5] It is this contextual basis that governs Justin's use of scripture. Throughout the *Dialogue* he is dealing with issues that are of particular concern to the second century Jewish/Christian debate. This type of approach necessitates some clarification of the presuppositions of both participants in the *Dialogue* as the foundation upon which the discussion proceeds. When these presuppositions are clarified, the stage is set for a discussion of the interpretation of scripture in the *Dialogue*.

The chapter is divided into three main sections. First, the foundation of Justin's OT interpretation is presented under the explanatory headings of "Two Laws," and "Two Advents."[6] Without a clear understanding of this foundation, one is ill prepared to understand Justin's exegesis. The second section discusses two important concepts in Justin's presentation: baptism and illumination. These are both discussed in relation to his OT interpretation. The third section is an evaluation of Justin's OT interpretation. Here Justin is placed squarely in the typological tradition.

One main question has governed the approach set out in this chapter—"How is it possible that two different interpretations can arise from the same scriptural passage?" This is a vital question, especially in view of the fact that both Justin and Trypho accept the OT as containing knowledge of God.

---

[4] T. Stylianopoulos, *Justin Martyr and the Mosaic Law* (SBL Dissertations 20; Missoula: Scholars Press, 1975) 9.

[5] In spite of arguments to the contrary, I hold to an intended audience that is Jewish. While the Jews are most likely the main readers whom Justin had in mind, this does not negate the fact that any writing produced within the Christian community would be seen as valuable by the members of that community. In this respect, a Christian readership may also have been in Justin's mind. But this Christian readership was not primary in writing the *Dialogue*. A history of the discussion of the intended audience of the *Dialogue* is presented in Chapter 1. There, I offer a more detailed explanation of my reasons for accepting a Jewish/Christian readership.

[6] I would not describe theses categories as rules because they form the context through which Justin interprets scripture. They are the foundations upon which he proceeds to understand OT texts.

II. *Foundations for Interpretation*

In order to understand Justin's interpretational concerns in the *Dialogue* it is axiomatic that one should understand the audience to which Justin addresses the work. It has only been in this last century that scholars have seriously started to doubt a Jewish audience for the *Dialogue*. This is based on both internal and external evidence surrounding the document. There has been no consensus reached on this issue but this does not negate the fact that it is necessary to state my conclusion on the matter. Chapter One is devoted solely to a history of the discussion in this century, giving the main reasons for denying a Jewish readership. In spite of these denials, however, I believe that there is adequate evidence for an intended Jewish audience on the part of Justin. These, I would hold, are the main readers whom Justin had in mind upon writing his *Dialogue*. There is, however, a strong probability that an apologetic of this standard, written as it was within the Christian community, would lend itself as a valuable tool to that community in its proselytization of the Jews. In that respect I further conclude, in Chapter One, that a Christian readership may also have been in Justin's mind. But this Christian readership was not primary to Justin in writing the *Dialogue*.[7]

Justin's presuppositions must also be clarified if we are to get an accurate understanding of his exegesis. Just as Trypho approached the discussion with certain preconceived understandings upon which he argued, so did Justin. Justin follows a suggestive "pattern of twos"[8] in the *Dialogue*. This pattern is based on the two most important concepts with which he deals—the two Laws and the two advents of the Messiah. This "pattern of twos" is important because the two Laws and the two advents form the hermeneutical key to Justin's interpretation of OT scripture in the *Dialogue*.

A. *Two Laws*

For Trypho, the Law is all important. It is the means by which one is looked upon with favor by God, and is the only means by which

---

[7] This is also the position of Stylianopoulos, *Justin Martyr and the Mosaic Law*, 10–20; 169–175.

[8] My own designation, for lack of a better term.

one may attain salvation.[9] This creates a problem for Justin. He
believes that the salvific value of the Law has been negated by the
coming of Jesus the Messiah.[10] Hope for the salvation of humankind,
in Justin's mind, is no longer through the Law because a new and
eternal Law has been foretold, and only it can give salvation.[11] With
regard to the Law then, Justin must show why Christians do not
observe the Law and yet still claim to hold a privileged position
before God.[12]

The covenant idea was a central category in the Jewish faith.[13]
This can be seen in the importance placed in the Law by Trypho.
But Justin's position on the covenant had to be carefully presented,
for in accepting the Jewish scriptures as his own he had to explain
how he could thus reject the Law that was so clearly presented in
those scriptures.[14] Justin thus had to use the common ground of the
Jewish scriptures to show that the old Covenant had been surpassed
by a new Covenant. To do so Justin employed four arguments:[15] (1)
Prophecies of a new Covenant point to the cessation of the Law
through the coming of Christ; (2) The Law was for the Jews only;
(3) Patriarchs such as Noah, Job, Abraham, and others were justified
without keeping the Law; (4) The Prophets declared that God did
not really desire observance of the ritual Law but a spiritual obedience.

---

[9] *Dial.* 8.3–4; 10.4.

[10] *Dial.* 11.1–2.

[11] *Dial.* 11; 24; 34; 67. This new and eternal Law is Jesus Christ, see above,
Chapter 3.V.B.

[12] This will be shown as we progress.

[13] G. W. Buchanan, *The Consequences of the Covenant* (NovTSup; Leiden: E. J. Brill,
1970); E. A. Martens, *God's Design. A Focus on Old Testament Theology* (Grand Rapids:
Baker, 1981)65–80; T. H. McComiskey, *The Covenants of Promise. A Theology of the
Old Testament Covenants* (Grand Rapids: Baker, 1985); D. J. McGarthy, *Treaty and
Covenant* (Rome: Pontifical Biblical Institute, 1963); idem., *Old Testament Covenant*
(Richmond: John Knox, 1972).

[14] In Justin's thinking the Covenant and the Law went together. In other words,
in order to remain in the Covenant, the Jew had to fulfill the Law. See above,
Chapter 3.V.B.

[15] E. Ferguson, "The Covenant Idea in the Second Century," in W. E. March (ed.),
Text and Testaments: Critical Essays on the Bible and Early Church Fathers (FS S. D. Currie;
San Antonio: Trinity University Press, 1980) 139. Arguments 1, 3, and 4 are adapted
from Ferguson. I have added Argument #2. Marcel Simon (*Verus Israel: A Study of
the Relations Between Christians and Jews in the Roman Empire (135–425)* [ET H. McKeating;
The Littmen Library of Jewish Civilization; Oxford: Oxford University Press, 1986]
163–169) also includes the reasons for the Christian criticism of the Jewish Law.
His explanation, while similar, is explained under the main heads of a distinction
between the moral law and the ritual law, a distinction between circumcision and
the rest of the ritual provisions, and the transitory nature of the law itself.

1. *New Covenant Foretold*

Justin recognizes the fact that Christianity and Judaism would have the same rites and customs if Christianity's hope was through Moses or the Law.[16] So, in offering his reasons why Christians do not place their hope of salvation there, Justin claims that a "final Law and Covenant"[17] which is above all others has been prophesied. This new and everlasting Covenant is Jesus Christ himself, and as scriptural proof of his assertions Justin cites Isa 51:4–5, Jer 31:31–32,[18] Isa 55:3–5, and Isa 6:10.[19]

The difference between the old Covenant and the new Covenant is decisive in Justin's argument—it gets right down to the issue of salvation. This is seen in *Dial.* 24 where Justin states that "this blood of circumcision has been rendered useless, and we now have come to trust in the blood of salvation. [There is] now another covenant, and another law has come out of Zion."[20] In *Dial.* 12–24 Justin has been referring to circumcision as symbolizing the entire Mosaic Law. So, here when Justin states that the blood of circumcision is abolished he is unmistakably referring to the abolition of the Mosaic Law. But if the old Law has been abolished, why was it instituted in the first place? Justin answers why the Mosaic Law was initially instituted in the second of his four arguments.

2. *Old Law for Jews Only*

Justin believes that the old Law was for the Jews only.[21] In this context he gives four basic reasons for this belief. First, he states that circumcision was given to the Jews to mark them off for suffering.[22] The Sabbath, among other precepts, is also claimed by Justin to have been imposed as a sign.[23] Second, Justin claims that the sacrifices were commanded by God in order to keep the people from idolatry.[24]

---

[16] *Dial.* 11.1.

[17] *Dial.* 11.2. νυνὶ δὲ ἀνέγνων γάρ, ὦ Τρύφων, ὅτι ἔσοιτο καὶ τελευταῖος νόμος καὶ διαθήκη κυριωτάτη πασῶν. See also *Dial.* 34.1; 67.9.

[18] *Dial.* 11.2–3.

[19] *Dial.* 12.1–2.

[20] *Dial.* 24.1. τὸ αἷμα τῆς περιτομῆς ἐκείνης κατήργηται, καὶ αἵματι σωτηρίῳ πεπιστεύκαμεν· ἄλλη διαθήκη τὰ νῦν, καὶ ἄλλος ἐξῆλθεν ἐκ Σιὼν νόμος.

[21] *Dial.* 11.2.

[22] *Dial.* 19.2.

[23] *Dial.* 21.1.

[24] *Dial.* 19.6; 22.1; 67.8.

Third, the Law was given to the Jews so that they would remember God. In this respect, specific rites such as the Sabbaths[25] and
the eating of certain kinds of meat[26] were imposed so that the Jews
would always remember God. But commandments in general are
also stated by Justin to have been instituted so that the Jews may
always have God before their eyes.[27] The fourth reason why Justin
believes that the Law was given to the Jews is the one mentioned
the most in the *Dialogue*. Justin reasons that it was because of sin or
the hardness of hearts that God instituted the Law. He alludes to
this when he explains that God adapted his laws to a weak people,[28] but other passages make it clear that the weakness referred to
here is sin.[29]

3. *Justification of Patriarchs*

The third argument employed by Justin to show the obsolescence
of the old Law is the fact that the patriarchs were justified without
keeping the Law. Here again, circumcision functions as representative
of the old Law. In *Dial.* 19, Justin explicitly states that circumcision
is not necessary for salvation. If it was, God would neither have created Adam uncircumcised,[30] nor would he have accepted the sacrifice
of the uncircumcised Abel, nor would he have been pleased with
the uncircumcised Enoch (Gen 5:24). Further, Lot was led out of
Sodom, even though he was uncircumcised, and Noah, the uncircumcised father of the Jewish race, was safe in the ark. Even though
Melchisedech was uncircumcised, Abraham paid tithes to him and
was blessed by him. Indeed God, through David, announced that
he would make him a high priest forever according to the order of
Melchisedech. Justin also explains the keeping of the Sabbath in the
same manner. All the men mentioned above kept no Sabbaths, yet
they were just and pleasing in the sight of God. In *Dial.* 23 Justin
extends his argument from circumcision and Sabbaths to include festivals and sacrifices. He states that if circumcision was not required
before Abraham, and if there was no need of Sabbaths, festivals,
and sacrifices before Moses then they are not needed now.

---

[25] *Dial.* 19.6.
[26] *Dial.* 20.1.
[27] *Dial.* 46.5.
[28] *Dial.* 19.6.
[29] *Dial.* 18.2; 21.1; 22.1; 23.2; 27.2; 44.2; 46.5, 7; 47.2; 67.8; 114.4.
[30] This argument concerning uncircumcision at birth is extended to all men in
Dial. 29.2.

Yet the fact that the first Law was instituted only for the Jews and that the patriarchs were justified apart from carrying out the works of the Law does not fully explain Justin's belief in its obsolescence. It did serve its purpose for the Jews. But, in Justin's thinking, God's purpose in instituting the old Law was not merely to carry out the physical acts described therein. While it is true that the old Law was instituted to mark off the Jewish people, aid in keeping them from idolatry, and cause them to remember God, it is equally true that the old Law could not completely succeed in this.[31] In this light, Justin explains the further, and perhaps most important, significance of the old Law.

4. *Spiritual Obedience*

The crux of Justin's argument concerning the new Covenant lies here, in its "true" purpose. Since a new Covenant has been foretold, since the old Law was for Jews only, and since the patriarchs were justified apart from the old Law, it is necessary for Justin to offer explanation concerning the purpose of the Law. Here Justin's foundation is built upon the incarnation of the Logos.

The fact that the content of the old Law was for Jews only severely restricted its adequacy for a universal salvation.[32] But the effect of the Law was also inadequate. Its temporary purpose was fulfilled, but it also prefigured future realities of the new Law by preparing human minds for those future realities.[33] By insisting on the prediction of a new Law, Justin was thus insisting on a Law that could truly give a person salvation and righteousness before God.[34] This new Law is eternal and has the power to save all humankind, not just Jews.[35]

---

[31] Proof of this is seen where Justin gives the reasons for the institution of the old Law, but also claims that in spite of these reasons, the Jews still failed to remember God, fell into idolatry and continued to sin. See e.g., *Dial.* 19.6; 20.1; 21.1; 22.1; 23.2; 27.2; 44.2; 46.5, 7; 47.2; 67.8; 114.4.

[32] *Dial.* 11.2; 19.6.

[33] B. de Margerie, *An Introduction to the History of Exegesis Vol. I: The Greek Fathers* (ET L. Maluf; Petersham: St. Bede's, 1993) 31.

[34] *Dial.* 11; 24; 34; 67.

[35] *Dial.* 122.5. The concept of a new law is not new to Justin Martyr. Its foundation is in Jer 31:27–40. It is continued in the writings of the New Testament (e.g., Luke 22:20; 2 Cor 3:6; Heb 7:11ff.). The *Epistle of Barnabas* (2; 4; 13; 14), also an *Adversus Judaeos* writing, makes many appeals to this new law (Greek text and ET can be found in K. Lake (ed.), *The Apostolic Fathers* [LCL; 2 vols.; London: William Heinemann/New York: The Macmillan Co., 1914] 1.335–409). Christian

Fulfilling the precepts of the old Law, therefore, is not the foundation upon which the new Law is based. This is shown in Justin's discussions about the justification of Abraham. In explaining that Abraham received circumcision as a sign, Justin's main point is that he was justified because of his faith. Indeed, Abraham was justified *before* he was circumcised.[36] Thus, Abraham's justification was based not on doing the Law, but on faith in God. Further, the new Law is also not tied to fleshly descent from Abraham. Justin thus makes it clear that no Jew will participate in the legacy of benefits promised by Christ simply because they are descendants of Abraham. The only participants will be those who have the same ardent faith as Abraham.[37] The new Law, therefore, is not for Jews only, but for those who display this same faith.[38]

The necessity of faith and the expectation of an eternal Law is fulfilled ultimately in Jesus. He is the new and eternal Law whom the Prophets predicted.[39] Exemplary of Justin's claims for Jesus as the new and eternal Law is *Dial.* 43. There he asserts that, according to the will of the Father, circumcision, Sabbaths, sacrifices, oblations and festivals originating with Abraham and Moses have their end in Him who was born of the virgin, of the race of Abraham, of the tribe of Judah, and of the family of David. Justin continues, "... in Christ, the Son of God, who was proclaimed as coming to the whole world to be an eternal law and a new covenant, just as the prophecies which were mentioned before show."[40]

Justin thus argues that the new Law surpasses and fulfils the old. Because of this, he recognizes his responsibility to explain how he can use the Jewish scriptures, which clearly argue for strict adherence to the old Law, to prove that adherence to this old Law is no longer necessary. In other words, Justin must offer his reasons for denying the continuing validity of something that is clearly com-

---

art also illustrates this concept. On sarcophagus sculptures and on wall paintings and mosaics, Peter is frequently pictured as the new Moses. He is shown as receiving from Christ the lawgiver the scroll of the new covenant. This signifies the early Christian belief that the new law (the law of Christ) does not merely oppose the law of Moses, rather, it replaces it. See Simon, *Verus Israel*, 76.

[36] *Dial.* 23.4.
[37] *Dial.* 44.2.
[38] *Dial.* 119.5–6.
[39] *Dial.* 24; 34; 43; 51; 67; 110; 118; 121; 122.
[40] *Dial.* 43.1 υἱὸν τοῦ θεοῦ Χριστόν, ὅστις καὶ αἰώνιος νόμος καὶ καινὴ διαθήκη τῷ παντὶ κόσμῳ ἐκηρύσσετο προελευσόμενος, ὡς αἱ προλελεγμέναι προφητεῖαι σημαίνουσι.

manded in scripture. The issue really gets down to the basic question of the purpose of the old Law.

In this light Justin presents the old Law as a collection of symbols to prepare humankind's minds for Christ. He states in this connection, " 'And sincerely gentlemen,' I said, 'by enumerating all the other precepts of Moses, I would be able to demonstrate that they were types, and symbols, and proclamations of what was about to happen to Christ . . .' "[41] Without the fulfillment, the symbol is useless, there is no symbol without the reality. So, for Justin, the symbol is essential and the key to understanding the fulfillment since the fulfillment stands in direct continuity to the symbol.[42] The Law, therefore has a "true" or "real" meaning which surpasses its original intent and points to Christ. This concept is seen especially in the section devoted to a discussion on the Law (11–30).

a. *Perpetual Sabbath*

Thus in *Dial.* 12, after Justin quotes Isa 55:3–5 in support of a new Covenant, he explains the new Law demands observance of a perpetual Sabbath in contrast to the Sabbath which requires abstinence from work. Justin states that if one believes this abstinence on the Sabbath leads to piety, then the real meaning[43] of that precept is not understood. So Justin asserts that the way to keep the true Sabbath is repentance of evil ways.

b. *Unleavened Bread*

The same way of thinking is applied to the unleavened bread.[44] Justin states that the unleavened bread is a symbol (σύμβολον) to teach people not to commit the old deeds of the bad leaven. Justin takes issue with the fact that the Jews interpret this in a carnal (σαρκικῶς) way. That is, the Jews believe that practice of the precept of the unleavened bread leads to piety, even when souls are filled with deceit and other kinds of sin. Then, in explaining the true significance of the unleavened bread, Justin claims that its purpose was to implore the people not to repeat old sinful deeds.

---

[41] *Dial.* 42.4. καὶ τὰ ἄλλα δὲ πάντα ἁπλῶς, ὦ ἄνδρες, ἔφην, τὰ ὑπὸ Μωυσέως διαταχθέντα δύναμαι καταριθμῶν ἀποδεικνύμαι τύπους καὶ σύμβολα καὶ καταγγελίας τῶν τῷ Χριστῷ γίνεσθαι μελλόντων.

[42] See A. Schmemann, *For the Life of the World: Sacraments and Orthodoxy* (Crestwood, NY: St. Vladimir's Seminary Press, 1995) 135–151.

[43] *Dial.* 12.3. μὴ νοοῦντες διὰ τί ὑμῖν προσετάγη.

[44] *Dial.* 14.2–3.

c. *Fasting and Circumcision*

Fasting is also explained by Justin as having a "true" meaning.[45] In support of this he quotes Isa 58:1–2. The impact of the quotation is easily observed. Isaiah states that it is not the action of fasting that God desires, but the practical outworking of a person whose heart is truly repentant. In this context, true fasting is linked with true circumcision, that is, circumcision of the heart.[46] This is the true circumcision.[47]

d. *Lasting Precepts*

In the *Dialogue* Justin uses circumcision as representative of the old Law and its stress on outward action as a sign of piety. This being the case, Justin summarizes his position on the old Law versus the new Law, "But even if someone is a Scythian or a Persian, but has knowledge of God and his Christ, and keeps the eternal righteous [decrees], [this one] has been circumcised with the good and profitable circumcision, and is a friend of God, and his gifts and offerings cause God to be full of joy."[48] The point here is that there are lasting precepts which render the temporary precepts obsolete. It is these lasting and true precepts that Justin points to when he desires to show the purpose of the old Law.

In the *Dialogue* Justin has employed the new Covenant as a way to rescue the Jewish scriptures from an interpretation based on the old Covenant. Justin realizes that the old Law was imposed on the Jewish people for reasons that are now unnecessary since the coming of Jesus the Christ. Before Christ, the Jewish scriptures required interpretation based on the Law. But after the advent of Christ, because he was the new and eternal Covenant, interpretation needed to be based on him. Thus the old Law was seen as foreshadowing Christ or containing an underlying "true" or "real" meaning. It is this christocentric interpretation of the Jewish scriptures that Justin applies in the *Dialogue*. It is the key by which Justin unlocks the true and lasting precepts. But the Jews, because they do not accept Jesus

---

[45] *Dial.* 15.

[46] See also *Dial.* 16 where Justin quotes Deut 10:16–17 and Lev 26:40–41 in support of a circumcision of the heart.

[47] *Dial.* 18.2; 41.4.

[48] *Dial.* 28.4. ἀλλὰ κἂν Σκύθης ᾖ τις ἢ Πέρσης, ἔχει δὲ τὴν τοῦ θεοῦ γνῶσιν καὶ τοῦ Χριστοῦ αὐτοῦ καὶ φυλάσσει τὰ αἰώνια δίκαια, περιτέτμηται τὴν καλὴν καὶ ὠφέλιμον περιτομήν, καὶ φίλος ἐστὶ τῷ θεῷ, καὶ ἐπὶ τοῖς δώροις αὐτοῦ καὶ ταῖς προσφοραῖς χαίρει.

as Messiah, understand everything in a carnal (σαρκικῶς) way.[49] And although they read scriptures, they do not understand its sense or meaning (νοῦς).[50]

B. *Two Advents*

Because the new and eternal Law is Jesus himself, Justin is obligated to interpret scripture christocentrically. By so doing he has already ruled Trypho's method of interpretation, based as it is on the old Law, obsolete. Thus, Justin's overarching understanding of scripture is that some passages in the Prophets refer to the first advent of Christ, in which he is described as coming in disgrace and obscurity, and mortality, while other passages in the Prophets speak of his second advent, when he will appear in glory.[51]

Just as the Law had a true meaning that was represented by the rituals, so the two advents of Jesus have been foretold symbolically by the Prophets. For example, the scapegoat and the sacrificial goat which had to be offered up during the fast were an announcement (καταγγέλλω) of the two advents Jesus, ". . . the first in which the elders of your people, and the priests, sent him away as a scapegoat, laying hands upon him and putting him to death; and his second advent, because in that place in Jerusalem you will recognize him, the one who you dishonored, and was a sacrificial offering on behalf of all sinners willing to repent."[52]

Justin's discussion of the two advents in relation to the Law betrays an important aspect of his presentation. It was shown above that the core issue with respect to the Law was salvation. The old Law could not save people. A new and eternal Law was required that could provide that salvation. In placing the discussion of the two advents above in sacrificial language, Justin points to the issue of salvation as it relates to the advents as well.

---

[49] *Dial.* 14.2.
[50] *Dial.* 29.2.
[51] *Dial.* 14.8.
[52] *Dial.* 40.4 μιᾶς μέν, ἐν ᾗ ὡς ἀποπομπαῖον αὐτὸν παρεπέμψαντο οἱ πρεσβύτεροι τοῦ λαοῦ ὑμῶν καὶ οἱ ἱερεῖς, ἐπιβαλόντες αὐτῷ τὰς χεῖρας καὶ θανατώσαντες αὐτόν, καὶ τῆς δευτέρας δὲ αὐτοῦ παρουσίας, ὅτι ἐν τῷ αὐτῷ τόπῳ τῶν Ἱεροσολύμων ἐπιγνωσθήσεσθε αὐτόν, τὸν ἀτιμωθέντα ὑφ' ὑμῶν, καὶ προσφορὰ ἦν ὑπὲρ πάντων τῶν μετανοιεῖν βουλομένων ἁμαρτωλῶν . . .

1. *The Problem of a Suffering Messiah*

The implicit belief in the two advents of Jesus is dependent upon the belief that Jesus is Messiah. Justin adhered to this belief while Trypho did not. Trypho believes the Messiah is yet to come. In this light we may understand why much of the *Dialogue* records Trypho's objection to Justin's claim that Jesus is the Messiah. Trypho simply cannot accept a suffering Christ.[53] But Justin is clear in his understanding that Jesus is the long awaited Messiah and that he suffered in accordance with the plan of God.[54] By denying the Messiahship of Jesus, Trypho is thus denying the coming of a new and eternal Law.

Trypho has one overarching reason for denying messianic claims for Jesus—the fact that Jesus was crucified. Trypho believes that Justin's quotations from scripture prove that the Messiah will be glorious, but that the one whom the Christians call Christ was without glory and honor to the extent that he was crucified, thus incurring the last curse of God's law (Deut 21:23).[55] Later in the *Dialogue*, the seriousness of this for Trypho is clarified when he states,

> You are right . . . that the whole of our nation waits for the Christ, and that all the scriptures which you have quoted profess him . . . But we doubt if the Christ was to be crucified in this ignoble way. For the one crucified is declared to be accursed in the law. Consequently, I am still not convinced on this point. It is clear that the scriptures proclaim that the Christ is destined to suffer. But we wish to learn if you can demonstrate if it was by a suffering accursed in the law.[56]

Once again, the issue of the Law rears it head. This makes perfect sense, in the light of Trypho's attitude toward the Law as essential for salvation. If the Law places a curse upon the crucified one, it would be impossible for Trypho to accept an accursed one as Messiah. But in Justin's mind, accepting the obsolescence of the old Law is part and parcel of accepting Jesus as Messiah. Indeed, the old Law is obsolete *because* Jesus is Messiah. But Trypho is still hung up on the Law.

---

[53] *Dial.* 89.1.
[54] *Dial.* 89.3.
[55] *Dial.* 32.1.
[56] *Dial.* 89.1–2. Εὖ ἴσθι . . . ὅτι καὶ πᾶν τὸ γένος ἡμῶν τὸν Χριστὸν ἐκδέχεται, καὶ ὅτι πᾶσαι αἱ γραφαί, ἃς ἔφης, εἰς αὐτὸν εἴρηνται, ὁμολογοῦμεν . . . εἰ δὲ καὶ ἀτίμως οὕτως σταυρωθῆναι τὸν Χριστόν, ἀποροῦμεν· ἐπικατάρατος γὰρ ὁ σταυρούμενος ἐν τῷ νόμῳ λέγεται εἶναι· ὥστε πρὸς τοῦτο ἀκμὴν δυσπείστως ἔχω. παθητὸν μὲν τὸν Χριστὸν ὅτι αἱ γραφαὶ κηρύσσουσι, φανερόν ἐστιν· εἰ δὲ διὰ τοῦ ἐν τῷ νόμῳ κεκατηραμένου πάθους, βουλόμεθα μαθεῖν, εἰ ἔχεις καὶ περὶ τούτου ἀποδεῖξαι.

3. *The Prediction of a Suffering Messiah*

This necessitates a certain plan of action on Justin's part. He thus argues, in much the same way as in the above section on the Law, that the Prophets actually predicted the crucifixion and death of Christ. If the Prophets had not predicted these things, Trypho and the Jews would be justified in their feelings of surprise about the crucifixion. But Justin states that the event of the crucifixion is a distinguishing mark (τὸ χαρακτηρίζον) which declares or announces (μηνύω) the Christ to all. And if this is the distinguishing mark of the Messiah, the only choice is belief in Jesus as the Messiah.[57] The crucifixion as a τὸ χαρακτηρίζον is related to the σφραγίς.[58] In its technical sense the σφραγίς refers to the imposition of the sign of the cross on the forehead of the candidate at the rite of baptism. The word was used by both secular and Christian writers, but our interest in the term centers on its use by Christian writers.[59] In Christian writers the term may denote two general things.[60] First, a stone in a signet ring, the design or inscription which it bears, the stamp which it makes upon wax, and hence a seal which is an authentication, guarantee or proof. Second, it may denote a token of agreement or affirmation, a mark of ownership, a seal set upon a letter, parcel, book, or other object as a mark of ownership, and also a safeguard or protection against interference.[61] Thus, we see that it may mean that which closes or seals up and is equivalent to "completion" or "perfection," in the sense of that which completes and sums up a process or a series.[62] It could be that Justin has this idea of completion or perfection in mind when he describes the event of the crucifixion as a distinguishing mark (τό χαρακτηρίζον) which declares or announces the Christ to all. Justin's position is that the

---

[57] *Dial.* 89.3.

[58] This connection is also made by G. W. H. Lampe, *The Seal of the Spirit: A Study in the Doctrine of Baptism and Confirmation in the New Testament and the Fathers* (London: Longmans, Green and Co., 1956) 7. The classic work on the subject is F. J. Dölger, *Sphragis. Eine altchristliche Taufbezeichnung in ihren Beziehungen zur profanen und religiösen Kultur des Altertums* (Studien zur Geschichte und Kultur des Altertums; Paderborn: Druck und Verlag von Ferdinand Schöningh, 1911). See also, J. Daniélou, *The Bible and the Liturgy* (Liturgical Studies; Notre Dame, IN: University of Notre Dame Press, 1956) 54–69.

[59] For its use by non-Christian writers see, Dölger, *Sphragis*; Daniélou, *The Bible and the Liturgy*.

[60] Lampe, *The Seal of the Spirit*, 8.

[61] These various uses are detailed in Daniélou, *The Bible and the Liturgy*, 54–60.

[62] Lampe, *The Seal of the Spirit*, 8.

Messiah could be none other than Jesus because the events of his death prove that he is Messiah. The one who understands this understands the Prophets. "Whoever understands the Prophets, upon merely hearing that he was crucified, will say that this is he [the Christ] and no other."[63]

Trypho is intrigued by Justin's assertion that the Prophets predict a crucified Messiah. He thus states,

> Show us this [the prediction of a crucified messiah] therefore . . . from the scriptures, that you might seek to persuade us. For we know [that he was] to suffer and be led as a sheep. But prove to us that he had to be crucified and die such a dishonorable and ignoble death which is accursed in the law. For we cannot even bring ourselves to think of this.[64]

Justin's reply to Trypho's challenge continues in the vein of understanding what the Prophets really wrote—the "true" meaning. Justin thus states, "You know . . . that whatever the Prophets said and did they revealed in parables and types, as you confessed to us; so it was not easy for most to comprehend all [of what they were saying], since they concealed the truth by these means, that the ones who are searching to find and to learn will do so with much labor."[65] In saying this, Justin is claiming that there is something that unlocks the hidden truth—the crucifixion. The hidden truth would have remained so were it not for the event. Thus, the event of the crucifixion of the incarnate *Logos* was revelation. Truth has been made manifest and revealed by this event. Again, without the event, the symbol is useless. He then proceeds to show Trypho a number of symbolic acts which portray the cross and crucifixion in the scriptures.

---

[63] *Dial.* 89.3. καὶ ὅσοι νενοήκασι τὰ τῶν προφητῶν, τοῦτον φήσουσιν, οὐκ ἄλλον, εἰ μόνον ἀκούσειαν ὅτι οὗτος ἐσταυρωμένος.

[64] *Dial.* 90.1. Καὶ ἡμᾶς οὖν . . . προβίβασον ἐκ τῶν γραφῶν, ἵνα σοι πεισθῶμεν καὶ ἡμεῖς. παθεῖν μὲν γὰρ καὶ ὡς πρόβατον ἀχθήσεσθαι οἴδαμεν· εἰ δὲ καὶ σταυρωθῆναι καὶ οὕτως αἰσχρῶς καὶ ἀτίμως ἀποθανεῖν διὰ τοῦ κεκατηραμένου ἐν τῷ νόμῳ θανάτου, ἀπόδειξον ἡμῖν· ἡμεῖς γὰρ οὐδ᾽ εἰς ἔννοιαν τούτου ἐλθεῖν δυνάμεθα.

[65] *Dial.* 90.2. Οἶσθα . . . ὅτι ὅσα εἶπον καὶ ἐποίησαν οἱ προφῆται, ὡς καὶ ὡμολογήθη ὑμῖν, παραβολαῖς καὶ τύποις ἀπεκάλυψαν, ὡς μὴ ῥαδίως τὰ πλεῖστα ὑπὸ πάντων νοηθῆναι, κρύπτοντες τὴν ἐν αὐτοῖς ἀλήθειαν, ὡς καὶ πονέσαι τοὺς ζητοῦντας εὑρεῖν καὶ μαθεῖν.

3. *Examples of a Suffering Messiah*

Justin asserts that the actions of Moses and Joshua symbolically announced (προσκηρυσσόμενον συμβολικῶς) the crucifixion of the Messiah.[66] According to Justin, Moses is a type (τύπος) of the cross in Exod 17:8–15. This is the narrative of the war with Amalek. When Moses held his arms up, Israel prevailed. But when Moses let his arms down, Amalek prevailed. This is clearly a type for Justin because ". . . if he [Moses] gave up this figure, which was imitating the cross, the people were vanquished, as it is written in the writings of Moses. But if he was remaining in this disposition, Amalek was defeated, and the one prevailing was prevailing through the cross."[67]

Joshua, on the other hand, is a type of the name of Jesus. Justin places great importance in the fact that the Hebrew name Joshua in Greek is Ἰησοῦς. He thus asks Trypho to consider that it was Jesus (Joshua) who led the patriarchs into the promised land.[68] So the passage concerning the war with Amalek,[69] which records Joshua as victorious in this battle, was really a type of Christ who was also victorious over death.[70]

The cross was further announced through Jacob in the blessing pronounced over Joseph.[71] Contained in that blessing is a phrase which refers to the Lord having the horns of a rhinoceros,[72] with which he will push the nations from one end of the earth to another.[73] These horns represent (μιμέομαι) the type (τύπος) of the cross, while the reference to the pushing of the nations describes what is taking place among the nations.[74] Justin clarifies this by stating that people of all nations have been convicted and goaded into compunction by the mystery of the cross. They have thus turned from idols and

---

[66] *Dial.* 111.

[67] *Dial.* 90.4. εἰ γὰρ ἐνεδεδώκει τι τοῦ σχήματος τούτου τοῦ τὸν σταυρὸν μιμουμένου, ὡς γέγραπται ἐν ταῖς Μωυσέως γραφαῖς· ὁ λαὸς ἡττᾶτο· εἰ δὲ ἐν τῇ τάξει ἔμενε ταύτῃ, Ἀμαλὴκ ἐνικᾶτο τοσοῦτον, καὶ ἰσχύων διὰ τοῦ σταυροῦ ἴσχμεν.

[68] *Dial.* 75.2.

[69] Exod 17:8–15.

[70] *Dial.* 111.1.

[71] Deut 33:13–17.

[72] See, G. Q. Reijners, *The Terminology of the Holy Cross in Early Christian Literature As Based Upon Old Testament Typology* (Nijmegen: Dekker & Van de Vegt N. V., 1965) 97–107.

[73] *Dial.* 91.2. κέρατα μονοκέρωτος τὰ κέρατα αὐτοῦ, ἐν αὐτοῖς ἔθνη κερατιεῖ ἅμα ἕως ἀπὸ ἄκρου τῆς γῆς.

[74] *Dial.* 91.2.

demons to worship the true God. But the ones who do not believe are condemned and destroyed by the same figure of the cross. Just as when the people had come out of Egypt when Israel was victorious over Amalek by the sign of Moses' outstretched hands and by the imposition of the name Jesus upon the son of Nun.[75]

Just as Moses' outstretched hands, Joshua's victory over Amalek, and the horns of the rhinoceros were types of the cross, so was the type (τύπος) and sign (σημεῖον) erected to counteract the effects of the serpents that bit Israel.[76] It is here that Justin makes the link of the cross with salvation. He says that

> the type and the sign, which was erected to counteract the serpents, came into existence to bring to light the salvation of the ones believing that death was previously declared to come upon the serpent through the one who was about to be crucified, but salvation to the ones who had been bitten by it and those who fled for refuge to the one who was being crucified, the son of him who sent him into the world.[77]

Justin appeals to these four "types" of the cross because they show that the cross, in the writings of Moses, has an intimate relationship to salvation and victory. The above four types clearly show this, and it is in these types that Justin believes the Jews have a means of understanding that the man crucified on the cross is the Christ. But Justin is disgusted by the fact that, in spite of these signs described by Moses, the Jews still refuse to believe.[78]

4. Recapitulation of the Curse

Justin now furthers the discussion of the raising of the brazen serpent in the context of the Law in order to counteract Trypho's contention that Jesus is accursed by the Law because he was crucified.[79]

---

[75] *Dial.* 91.3. Κερατισθέντες γάρ, τοῦτ' ἔστι κατανυγέντες, οἱ ἐκ πάντων τῶν ἐθνῶν διὰ τούτου τοῦ μυστηρίου εἰς τὴν θεοσέβειαν ἐτράπησαν ἀπὸ τῶν ματαίων εἰδώλων καὶ δαιμόνων, τοῖς δὲ ἀπίστοις τὸ αὐτὸ σχῆμα εἰς κατάλυσιν καὶ καταδίκην δηλοῦται· ὃν τρόπον ἐν τῷ ἀπ' Αἰγύπτου ἐξελθόντι λαῷ διά τε τοῦ τύπου τῆς ἐκτάσεως τῶν χειρῶν τοῦ Μωυσέως καὶ τῆς τοῦ Ναυῆ υἱοῦ ἐπικλήσεως τοῦ ὀνόματος Ἰησοῦ ὁ Ἀμαλὴκ μὲν ἡττᾶτο, Ἰσραὴλ δὲ ἐνίκα.

[76] *Dial.* 91.4.

[77] *Dial.* 91.4. καὶ διὰ τοῦ τύπου δὲ καὶ σημείου τοῦ κατὰ τῶν δακόντων τὸν Ἰσραὴλ ὄφεων ἡ ἀνάθεσις φαίνεται γεγενημένη ἐπὶ σωτηρίᾳ τῶν πιστευόντων ὅτι διὰ τοῦ σταυροῦσθαι μέλλοντος θάνατος γενήσεσθαι ἔκτοτε προεκηρύσσετο τῷ ὄφει, σωτηρία δὲ τοῖς καταδακνομένοις ὑπ' αὐτοῦ καὶ προσφεύγουσι τῷ τὸν ἐσταυρωμένον υἱὸν αὐτοῦ πέμψαντι εἰς τὸν κόσμον·

[78] *Dial.* 93.5.

[79] *Dial.* 94.

He asks Trypho why God would command Moses to construct the serpent and set it up as a sign even though he had forbade the making of any image or likeness in the heavens or on the earth. Justin then repeats his belief that this is because it was the announcement of the mystery of the cross. Trypho and his companions are then challenged to refute Justin's interpretation, but no refutation is recorded. So, with respect to the brazen serpent, Justin concludes, "Therefore, when God commanded that a sign come into existence in the manner of the brazen serpent, he is innocent [of the charge of making graven images]; even so, a curse is established in the law upon men who are crucified. But no curse is established upon the Christ of God through whom all who have committed acts worthy of the curse are saved."[80]

The discussion on the curse continues in *Dial.* 95 where Justin claims that all men are under the curse. Both Jews and Gentiles fail to keep the whole Law. But God willed that the Christ would shoulder the curse of the whole human race on the cross for the remission of sins. The shouldering of the curse should force the Jews to bewail their own sin, rather than accusing Jesus of being accursed. The fact that Jesus was crucified actually strengthens hope because that which was predicted to happen to Christ has actually taken place.[81] This is what Justin then proceeds to show in the section with the concentrated references to the Memoirs of the Apostles.[82] Referring especially to Psalm 22, Justin proves, by an appeal to the writings of the Apostles as witnesses to the events, that the prophecies contained in Ps 22 actually took place.

Justin then comes full circle in his discussion on the curse by repeating his interpretations of the two goats, Moses' outstretched hands, and the victory of Joshua over Amalek.[83] Each show the importance of the cross as the means of salvation. Even though these types are expressed through various persons and events, the actual event which they prefigure is attributed to the suffering and crucified Christ who was not cursed by the law, but rather, showed that he

---

[80] *Dial.* 94.5. Ὅνπερ οὖν τρόπον τὸ σημεῖον διὰ τοῦ χαλκοῦ ὄφεως γενέσθαι ὁ θεὸς ἐκέλευσε καὶ ἀναίτιός ἐστιν, οὕτω δὴ καὶ ἐν τῷ νόμῳ κατάρα κεῖται κατὰ τῶν σταυρουμένων ἀνθρώπων· οὐκ ἔτι δὲ καὶ κατὰ τοῦ Χριστοῦ τοῦ θεοῦ κατάρα κεῖται, δι' οὗ σώζει πάντας τοὺς κατάρας ἄξια πράξαντας.

[81] *Dial.* 96.1.

[82] *Dial.* 99–107. See also above, Chapter 2.IV.B; Chapter 4.I.

[83] *Dial.* 111.1.

alone could save those who hold firm to faith in him.[84] In this light
Justin further explains the necessity of the crucifixion by focusing on
the blood of the Messiah. Thus, the Passover was a sign that salvation was to come to humankind through the blood of Christ. For
just as the blood of the Passover saved those who were in Egypt, so
shall the blood of Christ save those who believe in him.[85]

With this description of the necessity of the crucifixion of Jesus,
Justin has shown how the apparent disgrace of the crucifixion is
turned into the glory of salvation for humankind. He has shown how
something which the Jews understand as a curse must be understood
as a blessing and hope. For just as the old Law brought a curse
because of humankind's inability to keep it, the new Law brought
hope because it fulfilled and completed the old Law. All that was
now required was faith.

5. *Subjugation of the First Advent*

But still Justin views the first advent of Jesus as somehow subjugated
in importance to the second advent,

> But if he [Jesus] so shone forth and was so strong at his first advent
> (which was without honor and ugly and contemptible) that in no nation
> he is unknown, and citizens of all nations have repented of their old
> evil way of living, so that even the demons are submissive to his name,
> and all authorities and kingdoms fear his name more than they fear
> the dead; shall he not at his glorious advent destroy all the ones hat-
> ing him and the ones who unrighteously left him, but give rest to his
> own, rewarding them with all they have looked for?[86]

Reference is here made to the second advent being even greater
than the first.[87] For at that advent, Jesus' enemies will be destroyed,

---

[84] *Dial.* 111.2. οὗ καὶ τὸ ὄνομα πᾶσα ἀρχὴ δέδιεν, ὠδίνουσα ὅτι δι᾽ αὐτοῦ καταλύεσθαι
μέλλουσιν. ὁ οὖν παθητὸς ἡμῶν καὶ σταυρωθεὶς Χριστὸς οὐ κατηράθη ὑπὸ τοῦ νόμου,
ἀλλὰ μόνος σώσειν τοὺς μὴ ἀφισταμένους τῆς πίστεως αὐτοῦ ἐδήλου.

[85] *Dial.* 111.3–4.

[86] *Dial.* 121.3. εἰ δὲ ἐν τῇ ἀτίμῳ καὶ ἀειδεῖ καὶ ἐξουθενημένῃ πρώτῃ παρουσίᾳ αὐτοῦ
τοσοῦτον ἔλαμψε καὶ ἴσχυσεν, ὡς ἐν μηδενὶ γένει ἀγνοεῖσθαι αὐτὸν καὶ ἀπὸ παντὸς
μετάνοιαν πεποιῆσθαι ἀπὸ τῆς παλαιᾶς κακῆς ἑκάστου γένους πολιτείας, ὥστε καὶ τὰ
δαιμόνια ὑποτάσσεσθαι αὐτοῦ τῷ ὀνόματι καὶ πάσας τὰς ἀρχὰς καὶ τὰς βασιλείας
τούτου τὸ ὄνομα παρὰ πάντας τοὺς ἀποθανόντας δεδοικέναι, οὐκ ἐκ παντὸς τρόπου ἐν
τῇ ἐνδόξῳ αὐτοῦ παρουσίᾳ καταλύσει πάντας τοὺς μισήσαντας αὐτὸν καὶ τοὺς αὐτοῦ
ἀδίκως ἀποστάντας, τοὺς δὲ ἰδίους ἀναπαύσει, ἀποδιδοὺς αὐτοῖς τὰ προσδοκώμενα
πάντα;

[87] Justin is still very conscious of the possibility that some Jews may still accept

and his followers rewarded. This appears to be the glory of the second advent, of which Justin states that the Jews will recognize that the one they have pierced is indeed the messiah.[88]

The contrast between the first and second advents is employed by Justin as a means of showing Trypho that passages of scripture which speak of a glorious Messiah are references to this second advent. This is seen in an exchange between Justin and Trypho that is recorded in *Dial*. 32. In the preceding chapter Justin had just quoted Dan 7:9–28 to Trypho, which stresses the glory of the Messiah. Trypho, quite naturally objects to this on the grounds that the one called Christ by Christians was without this glory and honor.[89] Justin's response is to claim that there should be two advents, one in disgrace and the other in glory. Justin admits that a failure to understand this basic point results in a lack of understanding with respect to the prophetic descriptions of the Messiah.[90]

Ultimately, however, the glory of the second advent is shown to outshine the glory of the first advent because the second advent is the culmination of the plan of God.[91] Justin speaks fairly often of the divine οἰκονομία or plan.[92] In each occurrence[93] of the terms Justin has in view the fact that all things that happened to Christ were in accordance with the will of the Father. Thus, for example, by his crucifixion, Christ fulfilled the Father's οἰκονομία of our redemption.[94] And Jesus' birth through the virgin was in accordance with the divine οἰκονομία of our redemption.[95] In fact, the events of the life, death and resurrection of the Logos fulfilled the Father's plan of humankind's redemption.[96]

The first advent, therefore, may be described as being dependent upon the divine οἰκονομία. But it would be difficult to maintain a plan for only part of Justin's argument on the advents. Thus, Justin

salvation before the second advent. He has a very strong commitment that a remnant of the Jews remains to be saved (*Dial*. 32.2; 55.3; 64.2–3). See Stylianopoulos, *Justin Martyr and the Mosaic Law*, 39–44 and Chapter 1 where these passages and the eschatological remnant are discussed in greater detail.

[88] *Dial*. 14.8; 32.2; 64.7.
[89] *Dial*. 32.1.
[90] *Dial*. 32.2.
[91] For more on the plan of God see above, Chapter 2.V–VI.
[92] *Dial*. 30.3; 31.1; 45.4; 67.6; 87.5; 103.3; 107.3; 120.1; 134.2; 141.4.
[93] With the exception of 107.3.
[94] *Dial*. 103.3.
[95] *Dial*. 120.1.
[96] *Dial*. 34; 43; 53; 60; 63; 74; 76; 92.6; 110; 128; 136.

also maintains that the second advent is vital in the Father's plan. The second advent is shown by Justin to be dependent on the first. He explains that even though Christ was pre-existent, he still became incarnate and was born of the virgin, in order that by this οἰκονομία he might conquer death and bring it to an end, so that at the second advent the serpent would no longer have any power over those who believe in Christ and live according to his principles.[97]

Thus, the second advent is not only presented as being dependent on the first, but as also fulfilling it, much in the same way that the new Law fulfils the old Law. At the second advent the glory of the first will be recognized because no one will be able to deny the completion of God's plan through his Christ.

Because the Jews did not understand this concept of the two advents, Justin believes they were hampered in their ability to understand what scripture truly says about the Christ, thus making it impossible for the Jews to recognize that Jesus is the Christ.[98] Justin's answer, therefore, to Trypho's denial that the Prophets predict a crucified Messiah is that the things which the Prophets said or did were often veiled (ἀπεκάλυψαν) in parables (παραβολαῖς) and types (τύποις). Consequently, it is not easy for most people to understand what they actually said.[99] The way to understand these parables and types, however, is through an understanding of the advents. If one understands that the advents are the reason why parables were spoken,[100] then one is able to differentiate between prophecies of the first advent and prophecies of the second advent. Thus, the meaning of the words of the prophecy is dependent upon prior understanding that these two advents were foretold, and that they all fit into the plan of God.

III. *Baptism, Illumination, and Interpretation*

Justin believes that the Jews simply do not understand the true meaning of the scriptures, and as a result, they are unable to discern what scripture portrays.[101] But Christians, on the other hand, are presented

---

[97] *Dial.* 45.4.
[98] *Dial.* 89.
[99] *Dial.* 90.2.
[100] *Dial.* 52.1.
[101] *Dial.* 29.2; 38.2; 55.3; 112; 114.5.

as being able to discern what the Jews cannot.[102] This is not an arbitrary understanding on Justin's part, nor is it Justin's belief that Christians have received some sort of spiritual illumination, akin to the Prophets, which enables them to correctly discern scripture. Rather, Justin's assertion is based upon his thoroughly christological understanding of scripture. The key to Justin's meaning here is contained in what may be called his doctrine of illumination.[103] This doctrine of illumination is, in turn, helpful in understanding Justin's interpretation of scripture.

It is necessary here to start, as background, with a passage from Justin's *1 Apology*, which links baptism and illumination.[104] In this passage Justin describes the Christian rite of baptism. Christian baptism has been described as the *sine qua non* of being a Christian in the second century.[105] This is to say that the time had not yet arrived when people could think of themselves as being saved yet unbaptized—the two went together quite naturally through a more or less set order. In the passage at hand we see Justin Martyr reflecting this order.

Justin explains the manner in which Christians dedicate themselves to God after they had been made new through Christ.[106] The order of baptism, as Justin relates it, can be set out in four sections.

1) The candidate for baptism is one who is convinced of the truth of Christianity. In the words of Justin he or she is "persuaded and believe[s] that what we teach and say is true."[107] Because of the conviction of the truth of Christianity the candidate resolves to live accordingly.
2) The candidate is then instructed to pray and entreat God with fasting for the remission of past sins. In this step, Justin points out that the local congregation prays and fasts along with the candidate.[108]
3) The candidate is then brought to a place where there is water and "in the name of God, the Father and Lord of the universe,

---

[102] *Dial.* 39.1; 110.2.
[103] My designation.
[104] *1 Apol.* 61 & 65.
[105] J. P. Lewis, "Baptismal Practices in the Second and Third Century Church," *RestQ* 26 (1983) 1.
[106] *1 Apol.* 61.1.
[107] *1 Apol.* 61.2 . . . πεισθῶσι καὶ πιστεύωσιν ἀληθῆ ταῦτα τὰ ὑφ᾽ ἡμῶν διδασκόμενα καὶ λεγόμενα εἶναι.
[108] *1 Apol.* 61.2.

and of our Saviour Jesus Christ, and of the Holy Spirit" is baptized (ἀναγεννάω) in water.[109]
4) Following the baptism Justin explains that the one who has been
   convinced and assented to Christian teaching is brought to a place
   where all the brethren are assembled in order that they may
   pray,[110] salute one another with a kiss,[111] and partake of the
   Eucharist.[112]

Historians of the early church have concluded that the catechetical
instruction was a very important part of the rite of baptism.[113] Indeed,
this can be traced in the *Didache*,[114] Hippolytus' *Apostolic Tradition*,[115]
and into the later catechetical lectures of Cyril of Jerusalem, John
Chrysostom, and Augustine of Hippo. This order of baptism in *1
Apology* lends support to this conclusion. This instruction was concerned with both moral behavior and doctrinal training.[116] In Justin

---

[109] *1 Apol.* 61.3 ἐπ᾽ ὀνόματος γὰρ τοῦ πατρὸς τῶν ὅλων καὶ δεσπότου θεοῦ καὶ τοῦ
σωτῆρος ἡμῶν Ἰησοῦ Χριστοῦ καὶ πνεύματος ἁγίου . . .

[110] *1 Apol.* 65.1.

[111] *1 Apol.* 65.2. "The kiss of charity, the kiss of peace, or "the peace" (ἡ εἰρήνη),
was enjoined by the Apostle Paul in his Epistles to the Corinthians, Thessalonians,
and Romans, and thence passed into a common usage. It was continued in the
Western Church, under regulations to prevent its abuse, until the thirteenth century" (A. Roberts & J. Donaldson, *Ante Nicene Fathers* [10 Vols.; Peabody: Hendrickson,
1994] 1.185, FN #3).

[112] *1 Apol.* 65.3–66.4.

[113] L. W. Barnard, *Justin Martyr. His Life and Thought* (Cambridge: Cambridge
University Press, 1967) 135; E. Ferguson, "Baptismal Motifs in the Ancient Church,"
RestQ 7 (1963) 202–216; Lewis, "Baptismal Practices in the Second and Third
Century Church"; E. F. Osborn, *Justin Martyr*, (BHT Gerhard Ebeling; Tübingen:
J. C. B. Mohr [Paul Seibeck], 1973) 179. J. N. D. Kelly, in his monumental *Early
Christian Creeds* (London: Longmans, Green and Co., 1950) explains that there are
several situations that arose in the life of the church that called for a statement of
doctrine thus leading to development of declatory creeds. Of these situations baptismal catechism is said to be the most important. According to Kelly there are
two moments that stand out in the ritual of baptism that call for this doctrinal
statement. The first is the actual act of baptism while the second is the time of
baptismal preparation or catechetical instruction which led up to the rendering of
the creed (See Kelly, Chap. 2). G. Hinson ("Confessions or Creeds in the Early
Christian Tradition," *RevExp* 76 [1979] 6) indicates that this procedure for baptism
included five steps: 1) a preliminary presentation of Christian doctrine for inquir-
ers; 2) a cetechumate of up to three years; 3) a concluding period of instruction
and preparation for baptism; 4) baptism on Easter Sunday (or, in some cases
Pentecost); and 5) instruction in the "mysteries" (Baptism and the Eucharist) following baptism.

[114] 1–6.

[115] 16–19.

[116] S. G. Hall, *Doctrine and Practice in the Early Church* (Grand Rapids: Eerdmans,
1991) 16–17.

we see that the candidate is "persuaded and believe[s] that what we teach and say is true," and that the candidate is "instructed."[117] Later, in *1 Apol.* 65, Justin indicates once again that the one who has been baptized has been convinced and has assented to Christian teaching.[118] All of this implies some sort of catechetical instruction that was at least as important in the rite of baptism as the actual washing.[119] Justin calls this rite of baptism a new birth (ἀναγεννάω)[120] which was learned from the Apostles.

While this passage has tremendous importance for information on the liturgy of the second century church, it is not in that capacity where its interest for us lies. In this passage Justin also alludes to another washing—a washing that is called illumination (φωτισμός). It is with Justin Martyr that we see for the first time the connection between baptism and illumination or enlightenment.[121]

Justin believes that salvation occurs before baptism.[122] This is seen in five ways. The first two refer to the general context of Justin's extant writings while the final three refer to the specific context at

---

[117] *1 Apol.* 61.2 διδάσκονται.

[118] *1 Apol.* 65.1.

[119] Barnard (*Justin Martyr*, 137) states that a period of pre-baptismal instruction is presupposed in Justin.

[120] *1 Apol.* 61.3.

[121] Barnard, *Justin Martyr*, 141; Ferguson, "Baptismal Motifs in the Ancient Church," 214; Lewis, "Baptismal Practices of the Second and Third Century Church," 6; Osborn, *Justin Martyr*, 179. J. Ysebaert (*Greek Baptismal Terminology: Its Origin and Early Development* [Græcitas Christianorum Primæva; Nijmegen: Dekker & Van de Vegt N. V., 1962]157–178) points out that both the verb (φωτίζειν) and the noun (φωτισμός) are used metaphorically in the NT of Christian belief as enlightenment (2 Cor 4:4; Eph 1:18; 2 Tim 1:10). In Heb 6:4 (cf. 10:32) the verb is used in the passive voice of the enlightenment received at baptism. However, φωτίζειν only became a technical term for baptism from the second century onwards (Ignatius of Antioch, *ad Rom. Inscript.*). Justin clearly uses φωτίζειν in this technical way (*1 Apol.* 61.13; 65.1; *Dial.* 39.2; 122.1, 3), but he is the first to use the noun φωτισμός specifically of baptism (*1 Apol.* 61.12). By the time of Clement Alexandria it is used of baptism without further explanation. Lewis ("Baptismal practices of the Second and Third Century Church," 6) states that the term is no doubt an echo of Heb 6:4 and 10:32 and which Clement explains as a description of baptism (Clement of Alexandria, *Paed* 1.6.26). But in Cyril of Jerusalem (*Procat.* 1; *Cat.* 18.32) enlightenment is applied to the process of instruction before baptism. Irenaeus is explicit that it is the preaching of the truth which enlightens (*Haer.* 1.10.2 cf. 4.14). From this time on φωτισμός becomes common, cf. Clement of Alexandria (*Paed.* 1.6.26), Cf. Cyril of Jerusalem (*Procat.* 1–2) where a clear distinction is made between dipping in water and the illumination of the heart. Simon Magus, says Cyril, enjoyed only the former.

[122] For Justin's understanding of salvation see above, Chapter 2.VI.

issue. First, Justin urges repentance in all his writings.[123] Second,[124] Justin indicates that the acceptance of the doctrine of Christianity must be accompanied by repentance.[125] Christ died for those who are willing to repent.[126] This repentance is a condition of mercy,[127] and a prerequisite for baptism.[128] Third, there are several statements in *1 Apol.* 61.2 that indicate a volitional repentance before the actual rite of baptism is performed. In 61.2 Justin states that those who have been taught and believe Christianity undertake to live accordingly. 61.6 indicates that there must be repentance from past sins. 61.10 has two statements concerning the fact that the ones baptized are children of choice who have repented of past sins. 65.1 indicates that the one baptized is seen as a good citizen because of his/her good works. This dovetails with the statement in 61.2 which claims that Christians undertake to live accordingly. Fourth, Justin's uses a quotation from a passage in Isaiah[129] to show how it is only those who repent who shall be saved. This passage has no mention of an external washing or baptism, but exhorts the readers to wash their souls. This washing cleanses from sin. Fifth, Justin indicates in 61.3 that candidates for baptism "wash themselves" (λουτρὸν ποιοῦνται). This use of the middle voice may be taken in one of two ways.[130] It could mean that the candidate goes under the water unassisted while the 3-fold formula is pronounced over him. But, more probable is the idea that the rite cannot be possible without the complete volition of the participant.

---

[123] Goodenough, *The Theology of Justin Martyr. An Investigation Into the Consequences of Early Christian Literature and Its Hellenic and Judaistic Influences* (Amsterdam: Philo Press, 1968) 263. Cf. *1 Apol.* 40.7; *Dial.* 95.3; 108.3; 118.1; 138.3.

[124] Goodenough, *The Theology of Justin Martyr*, 263.

[125] *Dial.* 26.1.

[126] *Dial.* 40.4.

[127] *1 Apol.* 28.2; *Dial.* 26.1; 141.2–3.

[128] *1 Apol.* 61; *Dial.* 47.5.

[129] *1 Apol.* 61.7 quotes Isa 1:16–20. "Wash you, make you clean; put away the evil of your doings from you souls; learn to do well; judge the fatherless, and plead for the widow: and come and let us reason together saith the Lord. And though your sins be as scarlet, I will make them white like wool; and though they be as crimson; I will make them white as snow. But if ye refuse and rebel, the sword of the Lord hath spoken it." Translation from A. Roberts & J. Donaldson, *Ante-Nicene Fathers* (10 Vols.; Peabody: Hendrickson, 1994) 1.183.

[130] E. R. Goodenough, *The Theology of Justin Martyr*, 266. For a good explanation on the uses of the Greek middle voice see S. E. Porter, *Idioms of the Greek New Testament* (Biblical Languages: Greek 2; Sheffield: JSOT Press, 1992. ". . . the Greek middle voice expresses more direct participation, specific involvement, or even some form of benefit of the subject doing the action" (p. 67).

These five ways in which Justin indicates that salvation precedes baptism, along with the implied period of catechetical instruction, fit well with Justin's use in this passage of illumination in connection with baptism. The washing that is involved in the choice of being born again, and the repentance of sins is called illumination. "And this washing is called illumination, because they who learn these things are illuminated in their understandings. And in the name of Jesus Christ, who was crucified under Pontius Pilate, and in the name of the Holy Spirit, who through the Prophets foretold all things about Jesus, he who is illuminated is washed."[131]

In *1 Apol.* 61 Justin claims that the external rite of baptism is the manner in which Christians show devotion (ἀνατίθημι) to God. Although Justin describes the importance of this external rite for Christians, he stresses the washing of which Isaiah speaks. This washing is focused on an internal cleansing for sin. It is the internal washing that is called illumination, because by it individuals are illuminated in their understanding.[132] This understanding of baptism as illumination is continued, and even expounded more clearly in the *Dialogue with Trypho.*

A. *Baptism*

Justin repeats his admonition to the readers of *1 Apol.* 61.7 to wash their souls clean in *Dial.* 18.2.[133] He relates this washing with the true (ἀληθινός) circumcision. This is clearly an admonition to a spiritual obedience, since true circumcision is the lasting precept by which Abraham was saved.[134] Justin repeats his assertion that fleshly circumcision was not essential for all men, but only for Jews.[135] Fleshly circumcision is then compared to the Jewish baptism of cisterns which, "has nothing to do with this baptism of life."[136] The comparison of the baptism of life with the baptism of cisterns is Justin's

---

[131] *1 Apol.* 61.12–13. καλεῖται δὲ τοῦτο τὸ λουτρὸν φωτισμός, ὡς φωτιζομένων τὴν διάνοιαν τῶν ταῦτα μανθανόντων. καὶ ἐπῷ ὀνόματος δὲ Ἰησοῦ Χριστοῦ, τοῦ σταυ-ρωθέντος ἐπὶ Ποντίου Πιλάτου, καὶ ἐπ' ὀνόματος πνεύματος ἁγίου, ὃ διὰ τῶν προφητῶν προεκήρυξε τὰ κατὰ τὸν Ἰησοῦν πάντα, ὁ φωτιζόμενος λούεται.

[132] This fits well with Justin's doctrine of redemption as imparting saving knowledge. See above, Chapter 2.V.

[133] Again Justin quotes here the same passage (Isa 1:16) that he quoted in *1 Apol.* 61.7.

[134] See above, section II.A.4.

[135] *Dial.* 19.1.

[136] *Dial.* 19.2. οὐδὲν γὰρ πρὸς τὸ βάπτισμα τοῦτο τὸ τῆς ζωῆς ἐστι.

way of criticizing the minute regulations of the ceremonial use of
the *Miqweh* in baptism.[137] The concern that thus comes to the fore
with this comparison and with the above comparison to true circumcision, is a better baptism.

Earlier in the *Dialogue*, this better baptism is clarified by an appeal,
once again, to the washing mentioned in Isa 1,

> For Isaiah was not sending you to a bath, there to forgive murder
> and other sins which even all the water in the sea would be sufficient,
> but, as might have been expected, this was that saving bath of old
> which followed those who changed their minds and who were no
> longer cleansed by the blood of goats and sheep or ashes of an heifer
> or offerings of fine flour, but through the blood of Christ, and through
> his death, who died for this very reason . . .[138]

The baptism spoken of here is salvation.[139] In *Dial.* 14.1 Justin calls
it a baptism of repentance instituted for the sins of the people, which
alone can purify those who repent. The value of baptism which
cleanses only the flesh and the body is said to be useless. Justin thus
exhorts Trypho to wash his soul free of anger, avarice, jealously and
hatred—this purifies the body. This is clearly a reference to a spiritual baptism that is possible only through salvation.

Later in the *Dialogue* Justin refers to baptism in relation to salvation once more. In explaining that the rites of the Law found their
end in Jesus, the new and eternal Law, Justin asserts that Christians
have come to God through Jesus Christ. In so doing they have

---

[137] A. L. Williams, *Justin Martyr. The Dialogue with Trypho: Translation, Introduction,
and Notes.* (London: SPCK, 1930). Williams states, "Justin has a side hit at the
importance attributed by the Jews to the ceremonial use of the *Miqweh* (bath), and
the minute regulations about its size, and the amount and nature of the water for
it" (p. 38). On the *Miqweh* see Y. Magen, "The Ritual Baths (*miqva'ot*) at Qedumim
and the Observance of Ritual Purity Among the Samaritans," in F. Manns and
E. Alliata (eds.), *Early Christianity in Context: Monuments and Documents* (Studium Biblicum
Franciscanum Collectio Maior 38; Jerusalem: Franciscan Printing Press, 1993)
181–193.

[138] *Dial.* 13.1. Οὐ γὰρ δή γε εἰς βαλανεῖον ὑμᾶς ἔπεμπεν Ἡσαίας ἀπολουσομένους
ἐκεῖ τὸν φόνον καὶ τὰς ἄλλας ἁμαρτίας, οὓς οὐδὲ τὸ τῆς θαλάσσης ἱκανὸν πᾶν ὕδωρ
καθαρίσαι, ἀλλά, ὡς εἰκός, πάλαι τοῦτο ἐκεῖνο τὸ σωτήριον λουτρὸν ἦν, ὃ εἶπε, τὸ τοῖς
μεταγινώσκουσι καὶ μηκέτι αἵμασι τράγων καὶ προβάτων ἢ σποδῷ δαμάλεως ἢ σεμιδάλεως προσφοραῖς καθαριζομένοις, ἀλλὰ πίστει διὰ τοῦ αἵματος τοῦ Χριστοῦ καὶ τοῦ
θανάτου αὐτοῦ, ὃς διὰ τοῦτο ἀπέθανεν . . .

[139] This is supported in the same chapter where Justin quotes Isa 52:10–15;
53:1–12; and 54:1–6 as christological prophecies of the death of Christ for salvation. This must be understood through Justin's apparent belief that salvation is primarily the impartation of saving knowledge, see above, Chapter 2.VI.

received not a carnal circumcision, but a spiritual circumcision. This spiritual circumcision is then said to have been received by means of baptism.[140] The validity of taking these references to baptism as synonymous with salvation is dependent upon their connection with the obsolescence of the old Law. The old Law could not cleanse from sin, but the new Law does—and this is through faith in the blood of Christ, not animals. That is why Justin encourages Trypho to be washed with the true baptism of life. It is only through faith in the blood of Jesus Christ that one may be purified with this washing. Thus it is entirely consistent that the baptism of life is synonymous with salvation. As Justin expresses to Trypho, "There is no other way than this, that you come to know this Christ and be cleansed by the cleansing proclaimed by Isaiah for the forgiveness of sins; and thus live a life free of sin."[141] According to Justin, true baptism is that cleansing from sin which every person may receive through faith in Jesus Christ.

B. *Illumination or Enlightenment*

Just as true baptism, with its emphasis on salvation, is intimately linked with Christ, so is illumination. Thus, Justin claims that some Jews are actually becoming disciples in the name of Christ, and are thus "being illuminated through the name of this Christ."[142] Again, Justin does not describe what this illumination is here. But two things merit special attention in connection with this illumination. First, the ones who are being saved are illuminated, and second, Christ is the one who illuminates. The importance of these two observations will become clear as we proceed.

Justin makes no more mention of this illumination until the last part of *Dialogue*. And it is in *Dial.* 122 that Justin's meaning of the term becomes apparent. The larger context of the chapter lies within the section dealing with Christians as true Israel.[143] Chapters 119–120 contain Justin's claim that the Jews are not true Israel, but that Christians, by virtue of their standing in Christ, actually are. In *Dial.*

---

[140] *Dial.* 43.1–2.
[141] *Dial.* 44.4. ἔστι δ᾽οὐκ ἄλλη ἢ αὕτη, ἵνα τοῦτον τὸν Χριστὸν ἐπιγνόντες καὶ λουσάμενοι τὸ ὑπὲρ ἀφέσεως ἁμαρτιῶν διὰ Ἠσαίου κηρυχθὲν λουτρὸν ἀναμαρτήτως λοιπὸν ζήσητε.
[142] *Dial.* 39.2. φωτιζόμενοι διὰ τοῦ ὀνόματος τοῦ Χριστοῦ τούτου·
[143] *Dial.* 119–142.

121, Justin claims that it was prophesied that all nations would be blessed "in him". If all nations are blessed in Christ, and Christians from all nations believe in him, then, Justin reasons, Jesus is the Christ, and Christians are the ones who are blessed by him. It has been granted to Christians to hear, understand, and be saved by this Christ, and to recognize all the truths revealed by the Father.[144] In support of this, Justin offers Isa 49:6 as the Father speaking to Christ.[145]

In *Dial.* 122 Justin anticipates Trypho's objection to Isa 49:6 as being a reference to Christians. Jews would understand it as referring to Jewish proselytes, but Justin answers that it refers to Christians "who have been illumined by Jesus."[146] This line of argument continues as Justin offers scripture that he says refer to Christ and concern the "illumined nations" (Christians).[147] Finally Trypho and his companions speak. They protest that the passages which are quoted by Justin refer to the Law and to those who are illumined by it.[148] Justin's answer is worth quoting at length.

> For if the law was able to enlighten the nations, and the ones possessing it, why is there a need for a new covenant? But since God foretold that he would send a new covenant, and an eternal law and commandment, we will not understand this as of the old law and its proselytes, but of Christ and his proselytes—us Gentiles, whom he has enlightened, as he says somewhere, 'Thus says the Lord, In an acceptable time I have heard you, and in a day of salvation I have helped you, and I have given you for a covenant of the people, to establish the earth, and to inherit the deserted. What then is the inheritance of Christ? Is it not the nations? What is the covenant of God? Is it not Christ?[149]

---

[144] *Dial.* 121.4. ἀκοῦσαι καὶ συνεῖναι καὶ σωθῆναι διὰ τούτου τοῦ Χριστοῦ καὶ τὰ τοῦ πατρὸς ἐπιγνῶναι πάντα.

[145] "It is a great thing for thee to be called my servant, to raise up the tribes of Jacob, and turn again the dispersed of Israel, I have appointed thee for a light to the Gentiles, that thou mayest be their salvation unto the end of the earth."

[146] *Dial.* 122.1 τοὺς διὰ Ἰησοῦ πεφωτισμένους.

[147] *Dial.* 122.3 τῶν ἐθνῶν τῶν πεφωτισμένων.

[148] *Dial.* 122.4.

[149] *Dial.* 122.5–6 ἐπεὶ εἰ νόμος εἶχε τὸ φωτίζειν τὰ ἔθνη καὶ τοὺς ἔχοντας αὐτόν, τίς χρεία καινῆς διαθήκης; ἐπεὶ δὲ καινὴν διαθήκην καὶ νόμον αἰώνιον καὶ πρόσταγμα ὁ θεὸς προεκήρυσσε πέμψειν, οὐχὶ τὸν παλαιὸν νόμον ἀκουσόμεθα καὶ τοὺς προσηλύτους αὐτοῦ, ἀλλὰ τὸν Χριστὸν καὶ τοὺς προσηλύτους αὐτοῦ, ἡμᾶς τὰ ἔθνη, οὓς ἐφώτισεν, ὥς πού φησιν· Οὕτω λέγει κύριος· Καιρῷ δεκτῷ ἐπήκουσά σου, καὶ ἐν ἡμέρᾳ σωτηρίας ἐβοήθησά σοι, καὶ ἔδωκά σε εἰς διαθήκην ἐθνῶν, τοῦ καταστῆσαι τὴν γῆν καὶ κληρονομίαν κληρονομῆσαι ἐρήμους. τίς οὖν ἡ κληρονομία τοῦ Χριστοῦ; οὐχὶ τὰ ἔθνη; τίς ἡ διαθήκη τοῦ θεοῦ; οὐκ ὁ Χριστός;

The fact that Christ is the new Covenant becomes very important here in connection with Justin's doctrine of illumination. Once again (as in *Dial.* 39.2 above) it is those who are saved through Christ who are illumined, and it is Christ who is the "illuminator". It is here where the rubber meets the road, so to speak, in Justin's doctrine of illumination. We can at once see the connection of salvation with illumination. The old Law could illumine neither the Gentiles nor the Jews who possessed it. There was need, therefore, of a new and eternal Law—Christ himself. He has illumined the Gentiles. In the context, this can mean nothing less than salvation. For salvation was the whole purpose of the Law, and by it Jews believed they were reconciled to God.[150] But now, through Christ, all may be reconciled to God because he illumines.

Justin's doctrine of illumination may thus indicate one of two things, although the two are not necessarily mutually exclusive. First, it may indicate the fact that because of the baptismal catechism (which was synonymous with the act of baptism) the candidates are illuminated in their understanding.[151] Christ truly becomes the key by which all is understood. He makes sense of salvation history, and it is through him that Hebrew scripture is interpreted.

Second, it may build upon the idea in Justin's *2 Apology* of the spermatic Logos wherein illumination indicates that the candidate for baptism receives the whole *Logos*.[152] "For whatever the philosophers or lawgivers continually uttered well, they achieved by finding and contemplating part of the Word. But since they did not know all of the Word, which is Christ, they often contradicted themselves in what they said."[153] By becoming human the Logos thus completed the knowledge of the Father.[154] Thus, since the whole *Logos* has now come into a candidate's life, he or she was now empowered with a divine force which will enable them to live a truly moral life.[155] "It

---

[150] *Dial.* 8–11. See also, Chapter 3.V.B.3–V.C.4.

[151] Lewis, "Baptismal Practices of the Second and Third Century Church," 6; Osborn *Justin Martyr*, 179.

[152] *1 Apol.* 32.10; 33.6; *2 Apol.* 10.8; *Dial.* 128.2. Barnard, *Justin Martyr*, 141; Goodenough, *The Theology of Justin Martyr*, 266–268.

[153] *2 Apol.* 10.2 ὅσα γὰρ καλῶς ἀεὶ ἐφέγξαντο καὶ εὗρον οἱ φιλοσοφήσαντες ἢ νομοθετήσαντες, κατὰ λόγου μέρος δι᾽ εὑρέσεως καὶ θεωρίας ἐστὶ πονηθέντα αὐτοῖς. ἐπειδὴ δὲ οὐ πάντα τὰ τοῦ λόγου ἐγνώρισαν, ὅς ἐστι Χριστός, καὶ ἐναντία ἑαυτοῖς πολλάκις εἶπον.

[154] *1 Apol.* 32.10; 33.6; *2 Apol.* 10.8; *Dial.* 128.2.

[155] Barnard, *Justin Martyr*, 141.

is here [in baptism] that man receives the great enlightening from
God which gives the power of the entire Logos in place of the
defeated fragment which man naturally possesses."[156]

As stated, the two are not mutually exclusive. There is no denying that Justin is referring to an illumination of understanding. Because
the will of humanity is involved in his concept of salvation this must
be included. But of the second possibility in attempting to define
Justin's doctrine of illumination Justin is less clear. Justin clearly
regards the rite as external. Yet by indicating an illumination he is
also asserting that something takes place spiritually, "in a sense which
Justin does not explain."[157] So, because there is a definite illumination of understanding and a claim by Justin that the external rite
(taken as a whole) confers a spiritual benefit, I must conclude that the
two may be held together in a way that Justin does not fully explain.[158]

C. *Interpretation*

The fact that Justin's use of illumination here is a reference to salvation has implications for interpretation. It is clear that Justin is
not speaking of a special inspiration that Christians receive in some
supernatural way. Rather, Justin is speaking of the necessity and centrality of Christ in salvation. But this idea must also be understood
in light of the interpretation of scripture. For if the old Covenant
governed the understanding and interpretation before the coming of
the new Covenant, then Christ must govern the interpretation of
scripture since he is the new Covenant which fulfills the old.

Justin's doctrine of illumination goes hand in hand with what has
already been presented concerning the centrality of Jesus as the new
Covenant. Christ is the one who brings illumination to those who
believe in him because he is the one of whom scripture speaks.

---

[156] Goodenough, *The Theology of Justin Martyr*, 266.
[157] Goodenough, *The Theology of Justin Martyr*, 266.
[158] K. McDonnell (*The Baptism of Jesus in the Jordan: The Trinitarian and Cosmic Order
of Salvation* [Collegeville, MN: The Liturgical Press, 1996] 42) states, "Justin Martyr
is in a bind. He feels constrained to talk about baptism, but he cannot make too
much of it, as he has attacked the Jews for their exterior rites. How can he, then,
comfortably talk about the exterior rites of Christians?" While McDonnell relates
this to Jesus' baptism in the Jordan, it may also apply to the way he speaks of
Baptism in general. As we have seen, the external rite encompasses more than simply the act of baptism, but includes a catechism. Further, Justin is more than likely
claiming that the external rite confers a spiritual blessing that empowers the candidate to live a moral life.

Failure to believe in Jesus as the Christ virtually eradicates any hope of understanding the scriptures. But belief in Jesus as Messiah illuminates the believer to understand scripture, which ultimately prophesy about Christ. Christ is thus the key to understanding scripture. Christians, by virtue of their salvation, possess this key. But Jews, by virtue of their unbelief in Jesus as messiah, possess a key that no longer fits the lock—the old Law.

This explains why the two major themes throughout the *Dialogue* are the Law and the Messiah. For if Jesus is the new Law and the Messiah, the Jews have the answers before their very eyes.

IV. *Evaluation of Justin's OT Interpretation*

In evaluating Justin's method of interpreting scripture one thing becomes very clear—the belief in and importance of the historical figure of Jesus as the Christ. Justin's interpretation is thoroughly christocentric. That is, it has Jesus as Messiah at the forefront of interpretation. The OT scriptures must be interpreted through an understanding of the events of his pre-existence, incarnation, death, resurrection and ascension to the right hand of the Father. A proper understanding of the Law and prophecy are built upon this foundation.

Justin has expressed the importance of the Jesus of history to his interpretation in many ways throughout the *Dialogue with Trypho*. His argument from prophecy was designed to show that Jesus was the one of whom the Prophets spoke. He is the fulfillment of their predictions. That fulfillment is proved in the Memoirs of the Apostles. As records of the historical event of Jesus, the Memoirs show the various events in his life as corresponding to the various OT prophecies concerning him. The prophecies were spoken and they were actually fulfilled in the person and work of Jesus. They are grounded in history because Jesus was a historical figure who existed at a particular era in human history. This is clear for all to see because the events are recorded also for all to see and read.

The christocentrism which Justin employs governs his scriptural interpretation. It gives him a foundation upon which to base his arguments as well as a focus upon which all things are directed. The Prophets spoke of a coming Messiah, Jesus came as Messiah and fulfilled all the prophecies. As Messiah, Jesus made the old Law obsolete and provided a new Law—a way of salvation for all, not just

Jews. Without the historical reality of Jesus as Messiah, Justin's OT
interpretation collapses. He stakes his whole method on this one
incontrovertible fact.

The stress on the historical reality of Jesus by Justin must not be
underestimated if one is to properly evaluate Justin's exegesis. It is,
in fact, the key in defining his exegesis as typological as opposed to
allegorical.[159] Foundational to the typological interpretation of scripture is historical correspondence. This is in stark contrast to allegorical
interpretation which treats the text as a mere symbol, or allegory of
spiritual truths.[160] Typology does not mean that there is a relation
between things invisible and visible, but there is a correspondence
between historical realities at different stages in history. This definition
has three important points that must be understood.[161] First, it is not
a question of the hidden sense in the text of scripture, but the realities
themselves which are the types. Second, it is a question of a relation
between realities both of which are historical, and not between historical realities and a timeless world. Third, the resemblance between
the type and the anti-type, or the figure and the reality, is contributed not by anything in the persons or events in question, but
by the fact that both form part of a single divine plan and both
manifest the way the same God deals with his people.

Justin's exegesis clearly fits each of these three important points.
First, it is clear that Justin does not focus on some hidden meaning
in the text. While it is true that, for Justin, Christ is the key that
unlocks the meaning, that meaning is clear for all to see in light of
Christ. He focuses on the reality of Christ as fulfillment of the OT
types. Thus, his explanation of the sign of the serpent was a type of
the cross shows that there is historical reference to the type.[162] Second,

[159] D. L. Baker, "Typology and the Christian Use of the Old Testament, " *SJT*
29 (1976) 137; J. Daniélou, "The Fathers and the Scriptures," *ECQ* 10 (1954)
265–268; J. N. D. Kelly, *Early Christian Doctrines* (rev. ed.; San Francisco: Harper,
1978) 70–72; Kugel and Greer, *Early Biblical Interpretation*, 153; G. W. H. Lampe,
"The Reasonableness of Typology," in G. W. H. Lampe and K. J. Woolcombe,
Essays on Typology (Studies in Biblical Theology; London: SCM, 1957) 31; R. A.
Markus, "Presuppositions of the Typological Approach to Scripture," *CQR* 158
(1957) 444–445; T. F. Torrance, "Early Patristic Interpretation of the Holy Scriptures,"
in idem., *Divine Meaning. Studies in Patristic Hermeneutics* (Edinburgh: T & T Clark,
1995) 100–104; K. J. Woolcombe, "The Biblical origins and Patristic Development
of Typology," in G. W. H. Lampe and K. J. Woolcombe, *Essays in Typology* (Studies
in Biblical Typology; London: SCM, 1957) 39–40.
[160] J. N. D. Kelly, *Early Christian Doctrines* (rev. ed.; San Francisco: Harper, 1978) 70.
[161] Daniélou, "The Fathers and Scripture," 267–268.
[162] *Dial.* 91.4.

it is also clear that the relationship that Justin points out is a relationship between two historical realities. In other words, the connection Justin makes between Christ and something in the OT always corresponds to a reality. For example, the actions of Moses and Joshua are types of Christ because they display the victory which Christ also won on the cross.[163] The connection is made between the historical reality of the Moses and Joshua and the historical reality of the crucifixion. Third, it is also clear that all things are considered to be under the divine οἰκονομία or plan.[164] All this occurs as a fulfillment of the plan of the Father. He is at its beginning and end.

It is thus clear that Justin's OT interpretation is typological in its outworking. It was stated at the beginning of this chapter that Justin's exegesis was not governed by any precise rules, but that it followed the needs that Justin was required to meet. In other words, it was a functional exegesis. This is what has been seen in this chapter. Justin's task in relating Christianity to the Jew Trypho required Justin to explain certain doctrines in Christianity which were scoffed at by the Jews. Justin attempted to use the same foundational documents as the Jews to show them that Jesus was, in fact, their Messiah. He appealed to historical realities which shows that he remains in the typological tradition.

---

[163] *Dial.* 111.
[164] *Dial.* 30.3; 45.4; 67.6; 87.5; 103.3; 120.1; 134.2.

GOSPEL QUOTATIONS AND ALLUSIONS FOUND IN THE *DIALOGUE WITH TRYPHO*

I. *Passages in* Dialogue with Trypho *which are indicated by Justin to be contained in the Gospel or memoirs*[1]

A. *Dial.* 88.3, καὶ τότε ἐλθόντος τοῦ Ἰησοῦ ἐπὶ τὸν Ἰορδάνην ποταμόν, ἔνθα ὁ Ἰωάννης ἐβάπτιζε, κατελθόντος τοῦ Ἰησοῦ ἐπὶ τὸ ὕδωρ καὶ πῦρ ἀνήφθη ἐν τῷ Ἰορδάνῃ, καὶ ἀναδύντος αὐτοῦ ἀπὸ τοῦ ὕδατος ὡς περιστερὰν τὸ ἅγιον πνεῦμα ἐπιπτῆναι ἐπ᾽ αὐτὸν ἔγραψαν οἱ ἀπόστολοι αὐτοῦ τούτου τοῦ Χριστοῦ ἡμῶν.

"And then, when Jesus had gone to the river Jordan, where John was baptizing, and when he had stepped into the water, a fire was kindled in the Jordan; and when He came out of the water, the Holy Ghost lighted on Him like a dove, [as] the apostles of this very Christ of ours wrote."

* Mat 3:13–17; Mark 1:9–11; Luke 3:21–22. No canonical document mentions the fire igniting the waters.
* Mention of the fire igniting the waters may have been learned from oral tradition or from some apocryphal work. The Ebionite Gospel and the *Praedicatio Pauli* both mention this phenomenon.

B. *Dial.* 100.1, καὶ ἐν τῷ εὐαγγελίῳ δὲ γέγραπται εἰπών· Πάντα μοι παραδέδοται ὑπὸ τοῦ πατρός, καὶ οὐδεὶς γινώσκει τὸν πατέρα εἰ μὴ ὁ υἱός, οὐδὲ τὸν υἱὸν εἰ μὴ ὁ πατὴρ καὶ οἷς ἂν ὁ υἱὸς ἀποκαλύψῃ.

"... but also in the Gospel it is written that he said, 'All things have been delivered to me by my Father; and no one knows the Father except the Son; nor does anyone know the Son except the Father, and those to whom the Son will reveal him.'"

* Mat 11:27; Luke 10:22.

C. *Dial.* 100.3, ὅθεν καὶ ἐν τοῖς λόγοις αὐτοῦ ἔφη, ὅτε περὶ τοῦ πάσχειν αὐτὸν μέλλειν διελέγετο, ὅτι Δεῖ τὸν υἱὸν τοῦ ἀνθρώπου πολλὰ παθεῖν καὶ ἀποδοκιμασθῆναι ὑπὸ τῶν Φαρισαίων καὶ γραμματέων, καὶ σταυρωθῆναι καὶ τῇ τρίτῃ ἡμέρᾳ ἀναστῆναι.

---

[1] Translations from A. Roberts & J. Donaldson (eds.), *Ante-Nicene Fathers* (10 Vols.; Peabody, MA: Hendrickson, 1994). 1.194–270.

"Hence also, among His words he said, when he was discoursing about His future sufferings: 'The Son of man must suffer many things, and be rejected by the Pharisees and Scribes, and be crucified, and on the third day rise again.'"

* Mat 16:21; Mark 8:31; Luke 9:22.

D. *Dial.* 100.4, καὶ γὰρ υἱὸν θεοῦ, Χριστόν, κατὰ τὴν τοῦ πατρὸς αὐτοῦ ἀποκάλυψιν ἐπιγνόντα αὐτὸν ἕνα τῶν μαθητῶν αὐτοῦ, Σίμωνα πρότερον καλούμενον, ἐπωνόμασε Πέτρον.

"For [Christ] called one of his disciples—previously known by the name Simon—Peter; since he recognized Him to be Christ the Son of God, by the revelation of His Father."

* Mat 10:2; Mat 16:16–17; Mark 3:16; Luke 6:13–14

E. *Dial.* 100.5, πίστιν δὲ καὶ χαρὰν λαβοῦσα Μαρία ἡ παρθένος, εὐαγγελιζομένου αὐτῇ Γαβριὴλ ἀγγέλου ὅτι πνεῦμα κυρίου ἐπ᾽ αὐτὴν ἐπελεύσεται καὶ δύναμις ὑψίστου ἐπισκιάσει αὐτήν, διὸ καὶ τὸ γεννώμενον ἐξ αὐτῆς ἅγιόν ἐστιν υἱὸς θεοῦ, ἀπεκρίνατο· Γένοιτό μοι κατὰ τὸ ῥῆμά σου.

Jesus is called "Son of God."

* Mat 4:3; Mat 8:29; Mat 16:16–17; Mark 3:11; Mark 14:61; Luke 1:35; John 3:18; John 11:27.

F. *Dial.* 100 Jesus is said to be "born of a Virgin."

* Mat 1:23, 25; Luke 1:26–38; Luke 2:7.

G. *Dial.* 100.5, πίστιν δὲ καὶ χαρὰν λαβοῦσα Μαρία ἡ παρθένος, εὐαγγελιζομένου αὐτῇ Γαβριὴλ ἀγγέλου ὅτι πνεῦμα κυρίου ἐπ᾽ αὐτὴν ἐπελεύσεται καὶ δύναμις ὑψίστου ἐπισκιάσει αὐτήν, διὸ καὶ τὸ γεννώμενον ἐξ αὐτῆς ἅγιόν ἐστιν υἱὸς θεοῦ, ἀπεκρίνατο· Γένοιτό μοι κατὰ τὸ ῥῆμά σου.

"But the virgin Mary, filled with faith and joy, when the angel Gabriel announced to her the good tidings that the Spirit of the lord would come upon her, and the power of the highest would overshadow her, and therefore the Holy one born of her would be the Son of God, answered, 'Be it done according to they word.'"

* Luke 1:26–38.

H. *Dial.* 101.3, οἱ γὰρ θεωροῦντες αὐτὸν ἐσταυρωμένον τὰς κεφαλὰς ἕκαστος ἐκίνουν καὶ τὰ χείλη διέστρεφον, καὶ τοῖς μυξωτῆρσιν ἐν ἀλλήλοις διαρρινοῦντες ἔλεγον εἰρωνευόμενοι ταῦτα ἃ καὶ ἐν τοῖς ἀπομνημονεύμασι τῶν ἀποστόλων αὐτοῦ γέγραπται· Υἱὸν θεοῦ ἑαυτὸν ἔλεγε, καταβὰς περιπατείτω· σωσάτω αὐτὸν ὁ θεός.

"Those that beheld him on the cross wagged their heads, curled their lips in scorn, turned up their noses and said, "He called himself the

Son of God, let him come down from the cross and walk! Let God save him!"

* Mat 27:38–43; Mark 15:27–32; Luke 23:35–38.

I. *Dial.* 102.5, σιγήσαντος αὐτοῦ καὶ μηκέτι ἐπὶ Πιλάτου ἀποκρίνασθαι μηδὲν μηδενὶ βουλομένου, ὡς ἐν τοῖς ἀπομνημονεύμασι τῶν ἀποστόλων αὐτοῦ

"He kept silence, and chose to return no answer to any one in the presence of Pilate; as has been declared in the Memoirs of His apostles . . ."

* Mat 27:14; Mark 15:5; Luke 23:9; John—No mention of Jesus' silence but records a conversation between Jesus and Pilate.

J. *Dial.* 103.1, ἐκείνης γὰρ τῆς νυκτός, ὅτε ἀπὸ τοῦ Ὄρους τῶν Ἐλαιῶν ἐπῆλθον αὐτῷ οἱ ἀπὸ τοῦ λαοῦ ὑμῶν ὑπὸ τῶν Φαρισαίων καὶ γραμματέων κατὰ τὴν διδασκαλίαν ἐπιπεμφθέντες, ἐκύκλωσαν αὐτὸν οὓς μόσχους κερατιστὰς καὶ προώλεις ὁ λόγος ἔλεγε.

"For on that night when some of your nation, who had been sent by the Pharisees and Scribes, and teachers, came upon Him from the Mount of Olives, those whom scripture called butting and prematurely destructive calves surrounded Him."

* Mat 26:47–56; Mark 14:43–50; Luke 22:47–53; John 18:2–12.

K. *Dial.* 103.6, καὶ γὰρ οὗτος ὁ διάβολος ἅμα τῷ ἀναβῆναι αὐτὸν ἀπὸ τοῦ ποταμοῦ τοῦ Ἰορδάνου, τῆς φωνῆς αὐτῷ λεχθείσης· Υἱός μου εἶ σύ, ἐγὼ σήμερον γεγέννηκά σε· ἐν τοῖς ἀπομνημονεύμασι τῶν ἀποστόλων γέγραπται προσελθὼν αὐτῷ καὶ πειράζων μέχρι τοῦ εἰπεῖν αὐτῷ· Προσκύνησόν μοι· καὶ ἀποκρίνασθαι αὐτῷ τὸν Χριστόν· Ὕπαγε ὀπίσω μου, σατανᾶ· κύριον τὸν θεόν σου προσκυνήσεις καὶ αὐτῷ μόνῳ λατρεύσεις·

"For this devil, when [Jesus] went up from the river Jordan, at the time when the voice spake to Him, 'Thou art my Son: this day have I begotten Thee,' is recorded in the memoirs of the apostles to have come to Him and tempted him, even so far as to say to him, 'Worship me;' and Christ answered him, 'Get thee behind me Satan: thou shalt worship the Lord thy God and Him only shalt thou serve.'"

* Mat 3:16–17; Mark 1:10–11; Luke 3:21–22.

L. *Dial.* 103.6, καὶ γὰρ οὗτος ὁ διάβολος ἅμα τῷ ἀναβῆναι αὐτὸν ἀπὸ τοῦ ποταμοῦ τοῦ Ἰορδάνου, τῆς φωνῆς αὐτῷ λεχθείσης· Υἱός μου εἶ σύ, ἐγὼ σήμερον γεγέννηκά σε· ἐν τοῖς ἀπομνημονεύμασι τῶν ἀποστόλων γέγραπται προσελθὼν αὐτῷ καὶ πειράζων μέχρι τοῦ εἰπεῖν αὐτῷ· Προσκύνησόν μοι· καὶ ἀποκρίνασθαι αὐτῷ τὸν Χριστόν· Ὕπαγε ὀπίσω μου, σατανᾶ· κύριον τὸν θεὸν σου προσκυνήσεις καὶ αὐτῷ μόνῳ λατρεύσεις·

"For this devil, when [Jesus] went up from the river Jordan, at the time when the voice spake to Him, 'Thou art my Son: this day have

I begotten Thee,' is recorded in the memoirs of the apostles to have come to Him and tempted him, even so far as to say to him, 'Worship me;' and Christ answered him, 'Get thee behind me Satan: thou shalt worship the Lord thy God and Him only shalt thou serve.'"

    * Mat 4:9–10; Mark 1:13; Luke 4:7–8.

M. *Dial.* 103.8, ἐν γὰρ τοῖς ἀπομνημονεύμασιν, ἅ φημι ὑπὸ τῶν ἀποστόλων αὐτοῦ καὶ τῶν ἐκείνοις παρακολουθησάντων συντετάχθαι, γέγραπται ὅτι ἱδρὼς ὡσεὶ θρόμβοι κατεχεῖτο, αὐτοῦ εὐχομένου καὶ λέγοντος· Παρελθέτω, εἰ δυνατόν, τὸ ποτήριον τοῦτο·

"For in the memoirs which I say were drawn up by His apostles and those who followed them, [it is recorded] that His sweat fell down like drops of blood while he was praying, and saying, 'If it be possible, let this cup pass.'"

    * Mat 26:37–39; Mark 14:33–35; Luke 22:41–44; John 12:27.

N. *Dial.* 104.1–2, ὅπερ καὶ ἐν τοῖς ἀπομνημονεύμασι τῶν ἀποστόλων αὐτοῦ γέγραπ-ται γενόμενον. 2 καὶ ὅτι μετὰ τὸ σταυρωθῆναι αὐτὸν ἐμέρισαν ἑαυτοῖς οἱ σταυρώσαντες αὐτὸν τὰ ἱμάτια αὐτοῦ, ἐδήλωσα.

"And this is recorded to have happened in the memoirs of His apos-tles. And I have shown that, after His crucifixion, they who crucified Him parted His garments among them."

    * Mat 27:35; Mark 15:24; Luke 23:34; John 19:24.

O. *Dial.* 105.1, μονογενὴς γὰρ ὅτι ἦν τῷ πατρὶ τῶν ὅλων οὗτος, ἰδίως ἐξ αὐτοῦ λόγος καὶ δύναμις γεγεννημένος, καὶ ὕστερον ἄνθρωπος διὰ τῆς παρθένου γενόμενος, ὡς ἀπὸ τῶν ἀπομνημονευμάτων ἐμάθομεν, προεδήλωσα.

"For I have already proved that he was the only-begotten of the Father of all things, being begotten in peculiar manner Word and power by Him, and having afterwards become man through the Virgin, as we have learned from the memoirs."

    * John 1 (?)

P. *Dial.* 105.1, μονογενὴς γὰρ ὅτι ἦν τῷ πατρὶ τῶν ὅλων οὗτος, ἰδίως ἐξ αὐτοῦ λόγος καὶ δύναμις γεγεννημένος, καὶ ὕστερον ἄνθρωπος διὰ τῆς παρθένου γενόμενος, ὡς ἀπὸ τῶν ἀπομνημονευμάτων ἐμάθομεν, προεδήλωσα.

"For I have already proved that he was the only-begotten of the Father of all things, being begotten in peculiar manner Word and power by Him, and having afterwards *become man through the Virgin*, as we have learned from the memoirs."

    * Mat 1:24–25; Luke 1:26–38; Luke 2:7.

Q. *Dial.* 105.5, καὶ γὰρ ἀποδιδοὺς τὸ πνεῦμα ἐπὶ τῷ σταυρῷ εἶπε· Πάτερ, εἰς χεῖράς σου παρατίθεμαι τὸ πνεῦμά μου, ὡς καὶ ἐκ τῶν ἀπομνημονευμάτων καὶ τοῦτο ἔμαθον.

"For when Christ was giving up His spirit on the cross, He said, 'Father, into Thy hands I commend My spirit,' as I have learned also from the memoirs."

* Mat 27:50; Mark 15:37; Luke 23:46 (In the Greek, Jesus' words in Luke are identical with those recorded by Justin.); John 19:30.

R. *Dial.* 105.6, καὶ γὰρ πρὸς τὸ ὑπερβάλλειν τὴν Φαρισαίων πολιτείαν τοὺς μαθ-ητὰς αὐτοῦ συνωθῶν, εἰ δὲ μή γε, ἐπίστασθαι ὅτι οὐ σωθήσονται, ταῦτα εἰρηκέναι ἐν τοῖς ἀπομνημονεύμασι γέγραπται· Ἐὰν μὴ περισσεύσῃ ὑμῶν ἡ δικαιοσύνη πλεῖον τῶν γραμματέων καὶ Φαρισαίων, οὐ μὴ εἰσέλθητε εἰς τὴν βασιλείαν τῶν οὐρανῶν.

"For He exhorted His disciples to surpass the pharisaic way of living, with the warning, that if they did not, they might be sure they could not be saved: and these words are recorded in the memoirs: 'Unless your righteousness exceed that of the Scribes and Pharisees, ye shall not enter the kingdom of heaven.'"

* Mat 5:20 (Justin's quote matches exactly the Greek of Matthew.)

S. *Dial.* 106.1, καὶ μετ᾽ αὐτῶν διάγων ὕμνησε τὸν θεόν, ὡς καὶ ἐν τοῖς ἀπομν-ημονεύμασι τῶν ἀποστόλων δηλοῦται γεγενημένον, τὰ λείποντα τοῦ ψαλμοῦ ἐδήλωσεν.

". . . and when living with them [the apostles] sang praises to God, as is evident in the memoirs of the apostles."

* Mat 26:30; Mk 14:26.

T. *Dial.* 106.3, καὶ τὸ εἰπεῖν μετωνομακέναι αὐτὸν Πέρον ἕνα τῶν ἀποστόλων, καὶ γεγράφθαι ἐν τοῖς ἀπομνημονεύμασιν αὐτοῦ γεγενημένον καὶ τοῦτο,

"And when it is said that He changed the name of one of the apostles to Peter; and it is written in the memoirs of Him that this so happened . . ."

* Mat 10:2; Mat 16:16–17; Mark 3:16; Luke 6:13–14.

U. *Dial.* 106.3, καὶ γεγράφθαι ἐν τοῖς ἀπομνημονεύμασιν αὐτοῦ γεγενημένον καὶ τοῦτο, μετὰ τοῦ καὶ ἄλλους δύο ἀδελφούς, υἱοὺς Ζεβεδαίου ὄντας, ἐπωνο-μακέναι ὀνόματι τοῦ Βοανεργές, ὅ ἐστιν υἱοὶ βροντῆς,

". . . and it is written in the memoirs of Him that this so happened, as well as that he changed the names of other two brothers, the sons of Zebedee, to Boanerges, which means sons of thunder;"

* Mat 3:17.

V. *Dial.* 106.4, ἀνατείλαντος οὖν καὶ ἐν οὐρανῷ ἅμα τῷ γεννηθῆναι αὐτὸν ἀστέρος, ὡς γέγραπται ἐν τοῖς ἀπομνημονεύμασι τῶν ἀποστόλων αὐτοῦ. οἱ ἀπὸ Ἀρραβίας μάγοι, ἐκ τούτου ἐπιγνόντες, παρεγένοντο καὶ προσεκύνησαν αὐτῷ.

"Accordingly, a star arose in heaven at the time of His birth, as is recorded in the memoirs of His apostles, the magi from Arabia, recognizing the sign by this, came and worshipped Him."

    * Mat 2:10–11.

W. *Dial.* 107.1, Καὶ ὅτι τῇ τρίτῃ ἡμέρᾳ ἔμελλεν ἀναστήσεσθαι μετὰ τὸ σταυρωθῆναι, γέγραπται ἐν τοῖς ἀπομνημονεύμασιν ὅτι οἱ ἀπὸ τοῦ γένους ὑμῶν συζητοῦντες αὐτῷ ἔλεγον ὅτι Δεῖξον ἡμῖν σημεῖον. καὶ ἀπεκρίνατο αὐτοῖς· Γενεὰ πονηρὰ καὶ μοιχαλὶς σημεῖον ἐπιζητεῖ, καὶ σημεῖον οὐ δοθήσεται αὐτοῖς εἰ μὴ τὸ σημεῖον Ἰωνᾶ.

"And that he would rise again on the third day after the crucifixion, it is written in the memoirs that some of your nation, questioning Him, said, 'Show us a sign;' and he replied to them, 'An evil and adulterous generation seeketh after a sign; and no sign shall be given them, save the sign of Jonah.'"

    * Mat 12:38–39; Mat 16:1, 4; Mark 8:11–12; Luke 11:29.

II. *Passages in* Dialogue with Trypho *which are indicated by*
Justin to be the words or commands of Jesus

A. *Dial.* 17.3, δύσχρηστος γὰρ ὑμῖν ἔδοξεν εἶναι, βοῶν παρ' ὑμῖν· Γέγραπται· Ὁ οἶκός μου οἶκος προσευχῆς ἐστιν, ὑμεῖς δὲ πεποιήκατε αὐτὸν σπήλαιον λῃστῶν.

"For He appeared distasteful to you when he cried among you, 'It is written, My house is the house of prayer; but ye have made it a den of thieves!'"

    * Mat 21:13; Mark 11:17; Luke 19:46.
    * Cf. *Dial.* 112.4.

B. *Dial.* 17.4, Οὐαὶ ὑμιν, γραμματεῖς καὶ Φαρισαῖοι, ὑποκριταί, ὅτι ἀποδεκατοῦτε τὸ ἡδύοσμον καὶ τὸ πήγανον, τὴν δὲ ἀγάπην τοῦ θεοῦ καὶ τὴν χρίσιν οὐ κατανοεῖτε· τάφοι κεκονιαμένοι, ἔξωθεν φαινόμενοι ὡραῖοι, ἔσωθεν δὲ γέμοντες ὀστέων νεκρῶν.

"He overthrew also the tables of the money-changers in the temple, and exclaimed, 'Woe unto you, Scribes and Pharisees, hypocrites! Because ye pay tithe of mint and rue, but do not observe the love of God and justice. Ye whited sepulchers! Appearing beautiful outward, but are within full of dead men's bones.'"

    * Mat 23:23–27; Luke 11:42–44.
    * Cf. *Dial.* 112.4.

C. *Dial.* 17.4, καὶ τοῖς γραμματεῦσιν· Οὐαὶ ὑμῖν, γραμματεῖς, ὅτι τὰς κλεῖς ἔχετε, καὶ αὐτοὶ οὐκ εἰσέρχεσθε καὶ τοὺς εἰσερχομένους κωλύετε· ὁδηγοὶ τυφλοί.

"And to the Scribes, 'Woe unto you Scribes! For ye have the keys, and ye do not enter in yourselves, and them that are entering in ye hinder; ye blind guides!'"

* Mat 23:13; Luke 11:52.
* Cf. *Dial.* 112.4.

D. *Dial.* 35.3, εἶπε γάρ· Πολλοὶ ἐλεύσονται ἐπὶ τῷ ὀνόματί μου, ἔξωθεν ἐνδε-δυμένοι δέρματα προβάτων, ἔσωθεν δέ εἰσι λύκοι ἅρπαγες.

"For he said, 'many will come in my name, clothed outwardly in sheep's clothing, but inwardly they are ravening wolves.'"

* Mat 7:15.

E. *Dial.* 35.3, καί· Ἔσονται σχίσματα καὶ αἱρέσεις.

"And, 'There shall be schisms and heresies.'"

* Quoted in no canonical document.
* Also quoted in *Didascalia*, Didymus the Blind *De trinitate* 3.22, and Lactantius *De Inst.* 4.30.

F. *Dial.* 35.3, καί· Προσέχετε ἀπὸ τῶν ψευδοπροφητῶν, οἵτινες ἐλεύσονται πρὸς ὑμᾶς, ἔξωθεν ἐνδεδυμένοι δέρματα προβάτων, ἔσωθεν δέ εἰσι λύκοι ἅρπαγες.

"And, 'Beware of the false prophets, who shall come to you clothed outwardly in sheep's clothing, but inwardly they are ravening wolves.'"

* Mat 7:15.

G. *Dial.* 35.3, καί· Ἀναστήσονται πολλοὶ ψευδόχριστοι καὶ ψευδοαπόστολοι, καὶ πολλοὺς τῶν πιστῶν πλανήσουσιν.

"And, 'Many false Christs and false apostles shall arise, and shall deceive many of the faithful.'"

* Mat 24:5; Mat 24:11; Mat 24:24; Mark 13:5–6; Luke 21:8.

H. *Dial.* 47.5, διὸ καὶ ὁ ἡμέτερος κύριος Ἰησοῦς Χριστὸς εἶπεν· Ἐν οἷς ἂν ὑμᾶς καταλάβω, ἐν τούτοις καὶ κρινῶ.

"Wherefore also our Lord Jesus Christ said, 'In whatsoever things I shall take you, in these I shall judge you.'"

* In no canonical document. Perhaps in *Gospel of Hebrews*.
* Cf. John 12:47–48.

I. *Dial.* 48.4, ἐπειδὴ οὐκ ἀνθρωπείοις διδάγμασι κεκελεύσμεθα ὑπ᾽ αὐτοῦ τοῦ Χριστοῦ πείθεσθαι, ἀλλὰ τοῖς διὰ τῶν μακαρίων προφητῶν κηρυχθεῖσι καὶ δι᾽ αὐτοῦ διδαχθεῖσι.

". . . since we were enjoined by Christ Himself to put no faith in human doctrines, but in those proclaimed by the blessed prophets and taught by Himself."

   * Mat 23:1–36; Luke 11:42–54.

J. *Dial.* 49.3, Καὶ ὁ ἡμέτερος οὖν κύριος, ἔφην, τοῦτο αὐτὸ ἐν τοῖς διδάγμασιν αὐτοῦ παρέδωκε γενησόμενον, εἰπὼν καὶ Ἠλίαν ἐλεύσεσθαι·

"And, accordingly, our Lord in His teaching proclaimed that this very thing would take place, saying that Elijah would also come."

   * Mat 11:13–14; Mat 17:10–13; Mark 9:11–13; John 1:19–28.

K. *Dial.* 49.5, διὸ καὶ ὁ ἡμέτερος Χριστὸς εἰρήκει ἐπὶ γῆς τότε τοῖς λέγουσι πρὸ τοῦ Χριστοῦ Ἠλίαν δεῖν ἐλθεῖν· Ἠλίας μὲν ἐλεύσεται καὶ ἀποκαταστήσει πάντα· λέγω δὲ ὑμῖν ὅτι Ἠλίας ἤδη ἦλθε, καὶ οὐκ ἐπέγνωσαν αὐτόν, ἀλλ᾽ ἐποίησαν αὐτῷ ὅσα ἠθέλησαν. καὶ γέγραπται ὅτι Τότε συνῆκαν οἱ μαθηταὶ ὅτι περὶ Ἰωάννου τοῦ βαπτιστοῦ εἶπεν αὐτοῖς.

"Wherefore also our Christ said, [when He was] on earth, to those who were affirming that Elijah must come before Christ: 'Elijah shall come, and restore all things; but I say unto you, that Elijah has already come, and they knew him not, but have done to him whatsoever they chose.' And it is written, 'Then the disciples understood that he spake to them about John the Baptist.'"

   * Mat 17:10–13; Mark 9:11–13.

L. *Dial.* 51.3, εἰρήκει δὲ περὶ τοῦ μηκέτι γενήσεσθαι ἐν τῷ γένει ὑμῶν προφήτην καὶ περὶ τοῦ ἐπιγνῶναι ὅτι ἡ πάλαι κηρυσσομένη ὑπὸ τοῦ θεοῦ καινὴ διαθήκη διαταχθήσεσθαι ἤδη τότε παρῆν, τοῦτ᾽ ἔστιν αὐτὸς ὢν ὁ Χριστός, οὕτως· Ὁ νόμος καὶ οἱ προφῆται μέχρι Ἰωάννου τοῦ Βαπτιστοῦ· ἐξ ὅτου ἡ βασιλεία τῶν οὐρανῶν βιάζεται, καὶ βιασταὶ ἁρπάζουσιν αὐτήν. καὶ εἰ θέλετε δέξασθαι, αὐτός ἐστιν Ἠλίας ὁ μέλλων ἔρχεσθαι. ὁ ἔχων ὦτα ἀκούειν ἀκουέτω.

"Moreover, He [Jesus] referred to the fact that there would be no longer in your nation any prophet, and to the fact that men recognized how that the New Covenant, which God formerly announced [His intention of] promulgating, was then present, i.e., Christ Himself; and in the following terms: 'The law of the prophets were until John the Baptist; from that time the kingdom of heaven suffereth violence, and violent take it by force. And if you can receive it, he is Elijah, who was to come. He that hath ears to hear, let him hear.'"

   * Mat 11:12–15; Luke 16:16.

M. *Dial.* 76.3–4, ἃ γὰρ μεγάλα ἐβεβούλευτο ὁ πατὴρ εἴς τε πάντας τοὺς εὐαρέστους γενομένους αὐτῷ καὶ γενησομένους ἀνθρώπους, καὶ τοὺς ἀποστάντας τῆς βουλῆς αὐτοῦ ὁμοίως ἀνθρώπους ἢ ἀγγέλους, οὗτος μόνος ἀπαρακαλύπτως ἐδίδαξεν, εἰπών· 4 Ἥξουσιν ἀπὸ ἀνατολῶν καὶ δυσμῶν, καὶ ἀνακλιθήσονται μετὰ Ἀβραὰμ καὶ Ἰσαὰκ καὶ Ἰακὼβ ἐν τῇ βασιλείᾳ τῶν οὐρανῶν· οἱ δὲ υἱοὶ τῆς βασιλείας ἐκβληθήσονται εἰς τὸ σκότος τὸ ἐξώτερον.

"For He alone taught openly those mighty counsels which the FATHER designed both for all those who have been and shall be well-pleasing to Him, and also for those who have rebelled against His will, whether men or angels, when he said, 'They shall come from the east [and from the west], and shall sit down with Abraham, and Isaac, and Jacob, in the kingdom of heaven: but the children of the kingdom shall be cast out into outer darkness.' "

* Mat 8:11–12; Luke 7:28–29.
* Cf. *Dial.* 120.6; 140.4.

N. *Dial.* 76.5, καί· Πολλοὶ ἐροῦσί μοι τῇ ἡμέρᾳ ἐκείνῃ· Κύριε, κύριε, οὐ τῷ σῷ ὀνόματι ἐφάγομεν καὶ ἐπίομεν καὶ προεφητεύσαμεν καὶ δαιμόνια ἐξεβάλομεν; καὶ ἐρῶ αὐτοῖς· Ἀναχωρεῖτε ἀπ᾽ ἐμοῦ.

"And, 'Many shall say to me in that day, LORD, LORD, have we not eaten, and drunk, and prophesied, and cast out demons in Thy name? And I will say to them, Depart from Me.' "

* Mat 7:21–23; Luke: 25–27.

O. *Dial.* 76.5, καὶ ἐν ἄλλοις λόγοις, οἷς καταδικάζειν τοὺς ἀναξίους μὴ σώζεσθαι μέλλει, ἔφη ἐρεῖν· Ὑπάγετε εἰς τὸ σκότος τὸ ἐξώτερον, ὃ ἡτοίμασεν ὁ πατὴρ τῷ σατανᾷ καὶ τοῖς ἀγγέλοις αὐτοῦ.

"Again, in other words, by which He shall condemn those who are unworthy of salvation, he said, 'Depart into outer darkness which the Father has prepared for Satan and his angels.' "

* Mat 25:41.

P. *Dial.* 76.6, καὶ πάλιν ἐν ἑτέροις λόγοις ἔφη· Δίδωμι ὑμῖν ἐξουσίαν καταπατεῖν ἐπάνω ὄφεων καὶ σκορπίων καὶ σκολοπενδρῶν καὶ ἐπάνω πάσης δυνάμεως τοῦ ἐχθροῦ.

"And again, in other words, He said, 'I give unto you power to tread on serpents, and on scorpions, and on centipedes, and on all the might of the enemy.' "

* Mat 16:17–18; Luke 10:19.
* No mention of "centipedes" in the canonical documents.

Q. *Dial.* 76.7, ἐβόα γὰρ πρὸ τοῦ σταυρωθῆναι· Δεῖ τὸν υἱὸν τοῦ ἀνθρώπου πολλὰ παθεῖν καὶ ἀποδοκιμασθῆναι ὑπὸ τῶν γραμματέων καὶ Φαρισαίων, καὶ σταυρωθῆναι καὶ τῇ τρίτῃ ἡμέρα ἀναστῆναι.

"For He exclaimed before His crucifixion: 'The Son of man must suffer many things and be rejected by the Scribes and Pharisees, and be crucified, and on the third day rise again.'"

* Mat 16:21; Mark 8:31; Luke 9:22.

R. *Dial.* 81.4, ὅπερ καὶ ὁ κύριος ἡμῶν εἶπεν, ὅτι Οὔτε γαμήσουσιν οὔτε γαμηθήσονται, ἀλλὰ ἰσάγγελοι ἔσονται, τέκνα τοῦ θεοῦ τῆς ἀναστάσεως ὄντες.

"Just as our Lord also said, 'They shall neither marry nor be given in marriage, but shall be equal to the angels, the children of the God of the resurrection.'"

* Mat 22:30; Mark 12:25; Luke 20:34–36.

S. *Dial.* 82.1–2, ὅνπερ δὲ τρόπον καὶ ψευδοπροφῆται ἐπὶ τῶν παρ᾽ ὑμῖν γενομένων ἁγίων προφητῶν ἦσαν, καὶ παρ᾽ ἡμῖν νῦν πολλοί εἰσι καὶ ψευδοδιδάσκαλοι, οὓς φυλάσσεσθαι προεῖπεν ἡμῖν ὁ ἡμέτερος κύριος, ὡς ἐν μηδενὶ ὑστερεῖσθαι ἡμᾶς, ἐπισταμένους ὅτι προγνώστης ἦν τῶν μετὰ τὴν ἀνάστασιν αὐτοῦ τὴν ἀπὸ τῶν νεκρῶν καὶ ἄνοδον τὴν εἰς οὐρανὸν μελλόντων γίνεσθαι ἡμῖν. 2 εἶπε γὰρ ὅτι φονεύεσθαι καὶ μισεῖσθαι διὰ τὸ ὄνομα αὐτοῦ μέλλομεν, καὶ ὅτι ψευδοπροφῆται καὶ ψευδόχριστοι πολλοὶ ἐπὶ τῷ ὀνόματι αὐτοῦ παρελεύσονται καὶ πολλοὺς πλανήσουσιν· ὅπερ καὶ ἔστι.

"And just as there were false prophets contemporaneous with your holy prophets, so are there now many false teachers amongst us, of whom our Lord forewarned us to beware; so that in no respect are we deficient, since we know that He foreknew all that would happen to us after His resurrection from the dead and ascension to heaven. For He said we would be put to death, and hated for His name's sake; and that many false prophets and false Christs would appear in His name, and deceive many: and so it has come about."

* Mat 7:15; Mat 24:5, 9, 11, 24; Mark 13:5–6, 9; Luke 21:12, 18.

T. *Dial.* 88.8, τὸ πνεῦμα οὖν τὸ ἅγιον καὶ διὰ τοὺς ἀνθρώπους, ὡς προέφην, ἐν εἴδει περιστερᾶς ἐπέπτη αὐτῷ, καὶ φωνὴ ἐκ τῶν οὐρανῶν ἅμα ἐληλύθει, ἥτις καὶ διὰ Δαυεὶδ λεγομένη, ὡς ἀπὸ προσώπου αὐτοῦ λέγοντος ὅπερ αὐτῷ ἀπὸ τοῦ πατρὸς ἔμελλε λέγεσθαι· Υἱός μου εἶ σύ, ἐγὼ σήμερον γεγέννηκά σε·

". . . but then the Holy Ghost, and for man's sake, as I formerly stated, lighted on Him in the form of a dove, and there came at the same instant from the heavens a voice, which was uttered also by David when he spoke, personating Christ, what the father would say to Him: 'Thou art My Son: this day have I begotten Thee;' [the Father] saying that His generation would take place for men, at the time when they would become acquainted with Him: 'Thou art My Son: this day I have begotten thee.'"

    * Mat 3:16–17; Mark 1:10–11; Luke 3:21–22.

U. *Dial.* 93.2, ὅθεν μοι δοκεῖ καλῶς εἰρῆσθαι ὑπὸ τοῦ ἡμετέρου κυρίου καὶ σωτῆρος Ἰησοῦ Χριστοῦ, ἐν δυσὶν ἐντολαῖς πᾶσαν δικαιοσύνην καὶ εὐσέβειαν πληροῦσθαι· εἰσὶ δὲ αὗται· Ἀγαπήσεις κύριον τὸν θεόν σου ἐξ ὅλης τῆς καρδίας σου καὶ ἐξ ὅλης τῆς ἰσχύος σου, καὶ τὸν πλησίον σου ὡς σεαυτόν.

"And hence I think that our Lord and Savior Jesus Christ spoke well when He summed up all righteousness and piety in two commandments. They are these: 'Thou shalt love the Lord thy God with all thy heart, and with all thy strength, and thy neighbor as thyself.'"

    * Mat 22:37–40; Mark 12:29–31; Luke 10:27.

V. *Dial.* 96.3, καὶ πρὸς τούτοις πᾶσιν εὐχόμεθα ὑπὲρ ὑμῶν, ἵνα ἐλεηθῆτε ὑπὸ τοῦ Χριστοῦ. οὗτος γὰρ ἐδίδαξεν ἡμᾶς καὶ ὑπὲρ τῶν ἐχθρῶν εὔχεσθαι, εἰπών· Γίνεσθε χρηστοὶ καὶ οἰκτίρμονες, ὡς καὶ ὁ πατὴρ ὑμῶν ὁ οὐράνιος.

"And in addition to all this we pray for you, that Christ may have mercy upon you. For He taught us to pray for our enemies also, saying, 'Love your enemies; be kind and merciful, as your heavenly Father is.'"

    * Mat 5:38; Luke 6:36.

W. *Dial.* 99.1, ὃ οὖν εὐθὺς λέγει· ὁ θεός, ὁ θεός μου, πρόσχες μοι· ἵνα τί ἐγκατέλιπές με;

"For when crucified, He spake, 'O God, my God, why hast Thou forsaken me?'"

    * Mat 27:46; Mark 15:34.

X. *Dial.* 99.2, τῇ γὰρ ἡμέρᾳ, ἥπερ ἔμελλε σταυροῦσθαι, τρεῖς τῶν μαθητῶν αὐτοῦ παραλαβὼν εἰς τὸ ὄρος τὸ λεγόμενον Ἐλαιών, παρακείμενον εὐθὺς τῷ ναῷ τῷ ἐν Ἰερουραλήμ, ηὔχετο λέγων· Πάτερ, εἰ δυνατόν ἐστι, παρελθέτω τὸ ποτήριον τοῦτο ἀπ᾽ ἐμοῦ. καὶ μετὰ τοῦτο εὐχόμενος λέγει· Μὴ ὡς ἐγὼ βούλομαι, ἀλλ᾽ ὡς σὺ θέλεις·

"For on the day on which he was to be crucified, having taken three of His disciples to the hill called Olivet, situated opposite to the temple in Jerusalem, He prayed in these words: 'Father, if it be possible, let this cup pass from me.' And again He prayed: 'Not as I will, but as Thou wilt;' showing by this that he had become truly a suffering man."

    * Mat 26:37–39; Mark 14:33–36; Luke 22:41–42; John 12:27.

Y. *Dial.* 101.2, καὶ γὰρ ἐπὶ γῆς τὸ αὐτὸ ἔπραξε· λέγοντος αὐτῷ τινος· Διδάσκαλε
ἀγαθέ, ἀπεκρίνατο· Τί με λέγεις ἀγαθόν; εἷς ἐστιν ἀγαθός, ὁ πατήρ μου ὁ ἐν
τοῖς οὐρανοῖς.

"For when on earth He acted in the very same manner, and answered
to the one who addressed Him as 'Good Master:' 'Why callest thou me
good? One is good, my Father who is in heaven.' "

   * Mat 19:16–17; Mark 10:17–18; Luke 18:18–19.

Z. *Dial.* 112.4, οὐχὶ δικαίως ἀκούσονται ἅπερ πρὸς αὐτοὺς ἔφη ὁ ἡμέτερος κύριος
Ἰησοῦς Χριστός· Τάφοι κεκονιαμένοι, ἔξωθεν φαινόμενοι ὡραῖοι καὶ ἔσωθεν
γέμοντες ὀστέων νεκρῶν, τὸ ἡδύοσμον ἀποδεκατοῦντες, τὴν δὲ κάμηλον
καταπίνοντες, τυφλοὶ ὁδηγοί;

". . . will they not deserve to hear what our Lord Jesus Christ said to
them [Trypho's teachers]: 'Whited sepulchers, which appear beautiful
outward, and within are full of dead men's bones; which pay tithe of
mint, and swallow a camel: ye blind guides!' "

   * Mat 23:1–36; Luke 11:42–54.
   * Cf. *Dial.* 17.3–4.

AA. *Dial.* 120.6, Ἥξουσι γάρ, εἶπεν, ἀπὸ δυσμῶν καὶ ἀνατολῶν, καὶ ἀνακλιθήσονται μετὰ Ἀβραὰμ καὶ Ἰσαὰκ καὶ Ἰακὼβ ἐν τῇ βασιλείᾳ τῶν οὐρανῶν·
οἱ δὲ υἱοὶ τῆς βασιλείας ἐκβληθήσονται εἰς τὸ σκότος τὸ ἐξώτερον

" 'For they shall come,' He said, 'from the west and from the east,
and shall sit down with Abraham, and Isaac, and Jacob in the kingdom of heaven; but the children of the kingdom shall be cast out
into outer darkness.' "

   * Mat 8:11–12; Luke 7:28–29.
   * Cf. *Dial.* 76.4; 140.4.

BB. *Dial.* 122.1, ἢ γὰρ ἂν κἀκείνοις ἐμαρτύρει ὁ Χριστός· νῦν δὲ διπλότερον
υἱοὶ γεέννης, ὡς αὐτὸς εἶπε, γίνεσθε.

"For Christ would have borne witness even to them; but now you
are become twofold more the children of hell, as he said Himself."

   * Mat 23:15.

CC. *Dial.* 125.1, ἀλλὰ πάντα ἁπλῶς καὶ ἀδόλως λέγειν, ὡς ὁ ἐμὸς κύριος εἶπεν·
Ἐξῆλθεν ὁ σπείρων τοῦ σπεῖραι τὸν σπόρον· καὶ ὃ μὲν ἔπεσεν εἰς τὴν ὁδόν,
ὃ δὲ εἰς τὰς ἀκάνθας, ὃ δὲ ἐπὶ τὰ πετρώδη, ὃ δὲ ἐπὶ τὴν γῆν τὴν καλήν.

". . . but I speak all things simply and candidly, as my Lord said: 'A
sower went forth to sow the seed; and some fell by the wayside, and
some among thorns, and some on stony ground, and some on good
ground.' "

   * Mat 13:3–9; Mark 4:3–9; Luke 8:5–8.

DD. *Dial.* 125.4, ὁ δὲ αὐτὸν κατέλυσε καὶ κατέβαλεν, ἐλέγξας ὅτι πονηρός ἐστι, παρὰ τὴν γραφὴν ἀξιῶν προσκυνεῖσθαι ὡς θεός, ἀποστάτης τῆς τοῦ θεοῦ γνώμης γεγενημένος. ἀποκρίνεται γὰρ αὐτῷ· Γέγραπται· Κύριον τὸν θεόν σου προσκυνήσεις καὶ αὐτῷ μόνῳ λατρεύσεις.

"But He destroyed and overthrew the devil, having proved him to be wicked, in that he asked to be worshipped as God, contrary to the Scripture; who is an apostate from the will of God. For He answers him, 'It is written, Thou shalt worship the Lord thy God, and Him only shalt thou serve.'"

* Mat 4:10; Luke 4:8.

EE. *Dial.* 140.4, καὶ ὁ κύριος ἡμῶν κατὰ τὸ θέλημα τοῦ πέμψαντος αὐτὸν πατρὸς καὶ δεσπότου τῶν ὅλων οὐκ ἂν εἶπεν· Ἥξουσιν ἀπὸ δυσμῶν καὶ ἀνατολῶν, καὶ ἀνακλιθήσονται μετὰ Ἀβραὰμ καὶ Ἰσαὰκ καὶ Ἰακὼβ ἐν τῇ βασιλείᾳ τῶν οὐρανῶν· οἱ δὲ υἱοὶ τῆς βασιλείας ἐκβληθήσονται εἰς τὸ σκότος τὸ ἐξώτερον

"And our Lord, according to the will of Him that sent Him, who is the father and lord of all, would not have said, 'The shall come from the east, and from the west, and shall sit down with Abraham, and Isaac, and Jacob in the kingdom of heaven. But the children of the kingdom shall be cast out into outer darkness.'"

* Mat 8:11–12; Luke 7:28–29.
* Cf. *Dial.* 76.4; 120.6.

III. *Passages in* Dialogue with Trypho *which contain no indication of source*

A. *Dial.* 12.2, πάρεστιν ὁ νομοθέτης, καὶ οὐχ ὁρᾶτε· πτωχοὶ εὐαγγελίζονται, τυφλοὶ βλέπουσι, καὶ οὐ συνίετε.

"The Lawgiver is present, yet you do not see Him; to the poor the Gospel is preached, the blind see, yet you do not understand."

* Mat 11:4–5; Luke 7:22.

B. *Dial.* 23.3, εἰ γὰρ πρὸ τοῦ Ἀβραὰμ οὐκ ἦν χρεία περιτομῆς οὐδὲ πρὸ Μωυσέως σαββατισμοῦ καὶ ἑορτῶν καὶ προσφορῶν, οὐδὲ νῦν, μετὰ τὸν κατὰ τὴν βουλὴν τοῦ θεοῦ διὰ Μαρίας τῆς ἀπὸ γένους τοῦ Ἀβραὰμ παρθένου γεννηθέντα υἱὸν θεοῦ Ἰησοῦν Χριστόν, ὁμοίως ἐστὶ χρεία.

"For if there was no need of circumcision before Abraham, or of the observances of Sabbaths, of feasts and sacrifices, before Moses; no more need of them is there now, after that, according to the will of God, Jesus Christ the Son of God has been born without sin, of a virgin sprung from the stock of Abraham."

* Born of a virgin—Mat 1:23, 25; Luke 1:26–38; 2:7.
* Descendant of Abraham—Mat 1:1–17.

C. *Dial.* 27.3, καὶ πάντες γὰρ ἐξέκλιναν, βοᾷ, πάντες ἄρα ἠχρειώθησαν· οὐκ ἔστιν ὁ συνίων, οὐκ ἔστιν ἕως ἑνός. ταῖς γλώσσαις αὐτῶν ἐδολιοῦσαν, τάφος ἀνεῳγμένος ὁ λάρυγξ αὐτῶν, ἰὸς ἀσπίδων ὑπὸ τὰ χείλη αὐτῶν, σύντριμμα καὶ ταλαιπωρία ἐν ταῖς ὁδοῖς αὐτῶν, καὶ ὁδὸν εἰρήνης οὐκ ἔγνωσαν.

" 'For they are all gone aside,' He [God] exclaims, 'they are all become useless. There is none that understands, there is not so much as one. With their tongues they have practiced deceit, their throat is an open sepulcher, the poison of asps is under their lips, destruction and misery are in their paths, and the way of peace they have not known.' "

* Rom 3:10–17.
* The Romans passage contains various OT quotations: Ps 14:1–3; 53:1–3; 5:9; 140:3; 10:7; Isa 59:7.

D. *Dial.* 30.3, Ἰησοῦ Χριστοῦ, τοῦ σταυρωθέντος ἐπὶ Ποντίου Πιλάτου, τοῦ γενομένου ἐπιτρόπου τῆς Ἰουδαίας,

". . . Jesus Christ, crucified under Pontius Pilate, governor of Judea . . ."

* Mat 27; Mark 15; Luke 8:1; John 19.

E. *Dial.* 32.3, ἵνα οὖν καὶ σαφέστερον ὑμῖν τὸ ζητούμενον νῦν γένηται, ἐρῶ ὑμῖν καὶ ἄλλους λόγους τοὺς εἰρημένους διὰ Δαυεὶδ τοῦ μακαρίου, ἐξ ὧν καὶ κύριον τὸν Χριστὸν ὑπὸ τοῦ ἁγίου προφητικοῦ πνεύματος λεγόμενον νοήσετε, καὶ τὸν κύριον πάντων πατέρα ἀνάγοντα αὐτὸν ἀπὸ τῆς γῆς καὶ καθίζοντα αὐτὸν ἐν δεξιᾷ αὐτοῦ, ἕως ἂν θῇ τοὺς ἐχθροὺς ὑποπόδιον τῶν ποδῶν αὐτοῦ· ὅπερ γίνεται ἐξ ὅτου εἰς τὸν οὐρανὸν ἀνελήφθη μετὰ τὸ ἐκ νεκρῶν ἀναστῆναι ὁ ἡμέτερος κύριος Ἰησοῦς Χριστός,

"In order, therefore, that the matter inquired into may be plainer to you, I will mention to you other words also spoken by the blessed David, from which you will perceive that the Lord is called the Christ by the Holy Spirit of prophecy; and that the Lord, the FATHER of all, has brought Him again from the earth, setting Him at His own right hand, until He makes His enemies His footstool; which indeed happens from the time that our Lord Jesus Christ ascended to heaven, after he rose again from the dead . . ."

* Ascension—Mark 16:19; Luke 24:51; Acts 1:2, 9–11.
  Placed at Father's right hand—Mark 16:19; Acts 2:33–36; 5:31; 7:55–56; Rom 8:33–34; Col 3:1; Heb 1:3, 13; 8:1; 10:12; 12:2; 1 Pet 3:21–22.
* Enemies His footstool—Acts 2:33–36; 7:49; 1 Cor 15:25–27; Eph 1:22; Heb 1:13; 2:8; 10:13.
* Resurrection from dead—Mat 16:21; 28; Mark 8:31; 16; Luke 9:22; 24; John 20.

F. *Dial.* 41.1, Καὶ ἡ τῆς σεμιδάλεως δὲ προσφορά, ὦ ἄνδρες, ἔλεγον, ἡ ὑπὲρ τῶν καθαριζομένων ἀπὸ τῆς λέπρας προσφέρεσθαι παραδοθεῖσα, τύπος ἦν τοῦ ἄρτου τῆς εὐχαριστίας, ὃν εἰς ἀνάμνησιν τοῦ πάθους, οὗ ἔπαθεν ὑπὲρ τῶν καθαιρομένων τὰς ψυχὰς ἀπὸ πάσης πονηρίας ἀνθρώπων, Ἰησοῦς Χριστὸς ὁ κύριος ἡμῶν παρέδωκε ποιεῖν, ἵνα ἅμα τε εὐχαριστῶμεν τῷ θεῷ ὑπέρ τε τοῦ τὸν κόσμον ἐκτικέναι σὺν πᾶσι τοῖς ἐν αὐτῷ διὰ τὸν ἄνθρωπον, καὶ ὑπὲρ τοῦ ἀπὸ τῆς κακίας, ἐν ᾗ γεγόναμεν, ἠλευθερωκέναι ἡμᾶς, καὶ τὰς ἀρχὰς καὶ τὰς ἐξουσίας καταλελυκέναι τελείαν κατάλυσιν διὰ τοῦ παθητοῦ γενομένου κατὰ τὴν βουλὴν αὐτοῦ.

"And the offering of the fine flour, sirs, which was prescribed to be presented on behalf of those purified from leprosy, was a type of the bread of the Eucharist, the celebration of which our Lord Jesus Christ prescribed, in remembrance of the suffering which he endured on behalf of those who are purified in soul from all iniquity, in order that we may at the same time thank God for having created the world, with all things therein, for the sake of Man, and for delivering us from the evil in which we were, and for utterly overthrowing principalities and powers by Him who suffered according to His will."

 * Mat 16:26–29; Mark 14:22–25; Luke 22:15–20; 1 Cor 11:23–25.

G. *Dial.* 49.3, ὅστις ἐπὶ τὸν Ἰορδάνην ποταμὸν καθεζόμενος ἐβόα· Ἐγὼ μὲν ὑμᾶς βαπτίζω ἐν ὕδατι εἰς μετάνοιαν· ἥξει δὲ ὁ ἰσχυρότερός μου, οὗ οὐκ εἰμὶ ἱκανὸς τὰ ὑποδήματα βαστάσαι· αὐτὸς ὑμᾶς βαπτίσει ἐν πνεύματι ἁγίῳ καὶ πυρί. οὗ τὸ πτύον αὐτοῦ ἐν τῇ χειρὶ αὐτοῦ, καὶ διακαθαριεῖ τὴν ἅλωνα αὐτοῦ καὶ τὸν σῖτον συνάξει εἰς τὴν ἀποθήκην, τὸ δὲ ἄχυρον κατακαύσει πυρὶ ἀσβέστῳ.

"He [John the Baptist] cried, as he sat by the river Jordan, 'I baptize you with water to repentance; but He that is stronger than I shall come, whose shoes I am not worthy to bear: He shall baptize you with the Holy Ghost and with fire: whose fan is in His hand, and He will thoroughly purge His floor, and will gather the wheat into the barn; but the chaff He will burn up with unquenchable fire.' "

 * Mat 3:11–12; Mark 1:7–8; Luke 3:16–17; John 1:26–27.

H. *Dial.* 49.4, καὶ τοῦτον αὐτὸν τὸν προφήτην συνεκεκλείκει ὁ βασιλεὺς ὑμῶν Ἡρώδης εἰς φυλακήν, καὶ γενεσίων ἡμέρας τελουμένης, ὀρχουμένης τῆς ἐξαδέλφης αὐτοῦ τοῦ Ἡρώδου εὐαρέστως αὐτῷ, εἶπεν αὐτῇ αἰτήσασθαι ὃ ἐὰν βούληται. καὶ ἡ μήτηρ τῆς παιδὸς ὑπέβαλεν αὐτῇ αἰτήσασθαι τὴν κεφαλὴν Ἰωάννου τοῦ ἐν τῇ φυλακῇ· καὶ αἰτησάσης ἔπεμψε καὶ ἐπὶ πίνακι ἐνεχθῆναι τὴν κεφαλὴν Ἰωάννου ἐκέλευσε.

"And this very prophet your King Herod had shut up in prison; and when his birth-day was celebrated, and the niece of the same Herod by her dancing had pleased him, he told her to ask whatever she pleased. Then the mother of the maiden instigated her to ask the head of John, who was in prison; and having asked it, [Herod] sent and ordered the head of John to be brought in on a charger."

  * Mat 14:6–11; Mark 6:21–28.

I. *Dial.* 51.1–2, Εἰ μὲν μὴ ἐπαύσαντο καὶ εἰσέτι ἐγένοντο οἱ προφῆται ἐν τῷ γένει ὑμῶν, ὦ Τρύφων, μετὰ τοῦτον τὸν Ἰωάννην, ἴσως ἀμφίβολα ἐνοεῖτε εἶναι τὰ λεγόμενα. 2 εἰ δὲ Ἰωάννης μὲν προελήλυθε βοῶν τοῖς ἀνθρώποις μετανοεῖν, καὶ Χριστὸς ἔτι αὐτοῦ καθεζομένου ἐπὶ τοῦ Ἰορδάνου ποταμοῦ ἐπελθὼν ἔπαυσέ τε αὐτὸν τοῦ προφητεύειν καὶ βαπτίζειν, καὶ εὐηγγελίζετο, καὶ αὐτὸς λέγων ὅτι ἐγγύς ἐστιν ἡ βασιλεία τῶν οὐρανῶν, καὶ ὅτι δεῖ αὐτὸν πολλὰ παθεῖν ἀπὸ τῶν γραμματέων καὶ Φαρισαίων, καὶ σταυρωθῆναι καὶ τῇ τρίτῃ ἡμέρᾳ ἀναστῆναι, καὶ πάλιν παραγενήσεσθαι ἐν Ἰερουσαλὴμ καὶ τότε τοῖς μαθηταῖς αὐτοῦ συμπιεῖν πάλιν καὶ συμφαγεῖν, καὶ ἐν τῷ μεταξὺ τῆς παρουσίας αὐτοῦ χρόνῳ, ὡς προέφην, γενήσεσθαι ἱερεῖς καὶ ψευδοπροφήτας ἐπὶ τῷ ὀνόματι αὐτοῦ προεμήνυσε, καὶ οὕτω φαίνεται ὄντα· πῶς ἔτι ἀμφιβάλλειν ἔστιν, ἔργῳ πεισθῆναι ὑμῶν ἐχόντων;

"If the prophets had not ceased, so that there were no more in your nation, Trypho, after this John, it is evident that what I say in reference to Jesus Christ might be regarded perhaps as ambiguous. But if John came first calling on men to repent, and Christ, while [John] still sat by the river Jordan, having come, put an end to this prophesying and baptizing and preached also Himself, saying that the kingdom of heaven is at hand, and that He must suffer many things from the Scribes and Pharisees, and be crucified, and on the third day rise again, and would appear again in Jerusalem, and would again eat and drink with His disciples; and foretold that in the interval between His [first and second] advent, as I previously said, priests and false prophets would arise in His name, which things do actually appear; then how can they be ambiguous, when you may be persuaded by the facts?"

  * Prophets ceasing in Israel—Mat 11:13; Luke 7:16.
  * John as forerunner—Mat 3:1–12; 11:7–19; Mark 1:2–8; Luke 3:1–18; 7:24–35; John 1:19–28.
  * John exhorting men to repent—Mat 3:2; Mark 1:4; Luke 3:3.
  * Jesus predicting his suffering at the hands of the scribes and Pharisees, to be crucified, and rise again on third day—Mat 16:21; Mark 8:31; Luke 9:22.
  * Jesus appears at Jerusalem to eat and drink with his disciples— Mark 16:14; Luke 24:36–43.
  * Prediction of Jesus that there would arise heresies and false prophets in his name—Mat 7:15; 24:5, 11, 25; Mark 13:5–6; Luke 21:8. These passages contain no mention of heresies, but only false prophets.

J. *Dial.* 53.2, καὶ ὄνον δέ τινα ἀληθῶς σὺν πώλῳ αὐτῆς προσδεδεμένην ἔν τινι εἰσόδῳ κώμης Βεθσφαγῆς λεγομένης, ὅτε ἔμελλεν εἰσέρχεσθαι εἰς τὰ Ἰεροσόλυμα ὁ κύριος ἡμῶν Ἰησοῦς Χριστός, ἐκέλευσε τοὺς μαθητὰς αὐτοῦ ἀγαγεῖν αὐτῷ, καὶ ἐπικαθίσας ἐπεισελήλυθεν εἰς τὰ Ἰεροσόλυμα·

"And truly our Lord Jesus Christ, when He intended to go into Jerusalem, requested His disciples to bring to Him a certain ass, along with its foal, which was bound in an entrance of a village called Bethpage; and having seated Himself on it, He entered Jerusalem."

* Mat 21:1–9; Mark 11:1–10; Luke 19:28–40.

K. *Dial.* 53.5, ἀλλὰ καὶ διὰ τοῦ προφήτου Ζαχαρίου, ὅτι παταχθήσεται αὐτὸς οὗτος ὁ Χριστὸς καὶ διασκορπισθήσονται οἱ μαθηταὶ αὐτοῦ, προεφητεύθη· ὅπερ καὶ γέγονε. μετὰ γὰρ τὸ σταυρωθῆναι αὐτὸν οἱ σὺν αὐτῷ ὄντες μαθηταὶ αὐτοῦ διεσκεδάσθησαν, μέχρις ὅτου ἀνέστη ἐκ νεκρῶν καὶ πέπεικεν αὐτοὺς ὅτι οὕτως προεπεφήτευτο περὶ αὐτοῦ παθεῖν αὐτόν· καὶ οὕτω πεισθέντες καὶ εἰς τὴν πᾶσαν οἰκουμένην ἐξελθόντες ταῦτα ἐδίδαξαν.

"Moreover, the prophet Zechariah foretold that this same Christ would be smitten, and His disciples scattered: which also took place. For after His crucifixion, the disciples that accompanied Him were dispersed, until He rose from the dead, and persuaded them that so it had been prophesied concerning Him, and that He would suffer; and being thus persuaded, they went into all the world, and taught these truths."

* Mat 18:16–20; Mark 16:9–20; Luke 24:44–53.

L. *Dial.* 77.4, ἅμα γὰρ τῷ γεννηθῆναι αὐτὸν μάγοι ἀπὸ Ἀρραβίας παραγενόμενοι προσεκύνησαν αὐτῷ, πρότερον ἐλθόντες πρὸς Ἡρώδην τὸν ἐν τῇ γῇ ὑμῶν τότε βασιλεύοντα, ὃν ὁ λόγος καλεῖ βασιλέα Ἀσσυρίων διὰ τὴν ἄθεον καὶ ἄνομον αὐτοῦ γνώμην.

"For at the time of His birth, Magi who came from Arabia worshipped Him, coming first to Herod, who then was sovereign in your land, and whom the Scripture calls king of Assyria on account of his ungodly character."

* Mat 2:1–12. Does not state that the Magi came form Arabia, but from the east.

M. *Dial.* 78.1, Καὶ γὰρ οὗτος ὁ βασιλεὺς Ἡρώδης, μαθὼν παρὰ τῶν πρεσβυτέρων τοῦ λαοῦ ὑμῶν, τότε ἐλθόντων πρὸς αὐτὸν τῶν ἀπὸ Ἀρραβίας μάγων, καὶ εἰπόντων ἐξ ἀστέρος τοῦ ἐν τῷ οὐρανῷ φανέντος ἐγνωκέναι ὅτι βασιλεὺς γεγένηται ἐν τῇ χώρᾳ ὑμῶν, καὶ ἤλθομεν προσκυνῆσαι αὐτόν, καὶ ἐν Βηθλεὲμ τῶν πρεσβυτέρων εἰπόντων, ὅτι γέγραπται ἐν τῷ προφήτῃ οὕτως· Καὶ σὺ Βηθλεέμ, γῆ Ἰούδα, οὐδαμῶς ἐλαχίστη εἶ ἐν τοῖς ἡγεμόσιν Ἰούδα· ἐκ σοῦ γὰρ ἐξελεύσεται ἡγούμενος, ὅστις ποιμανεῖ τὸν λαόν μου.

"Now this King Herod, at the time when the Magi came to him from Arabia, and said they knew from a star which appeared in the heavens that a King had been born in your country, and that they had come to worship Him learned from the elders of your people that it was thus written regarding Bethlehem in the prophets: 'And thou, Bethlehem, in the land of Judah, art by no means least among the princes of Judah; for out of thee shall go forth the leader who shall feed my people.'"

   * Mat 2:2–6.

N. *Dial.* 78.2, τῶν ἀπὸ Ἀρραβίας οὖν μάγων ἐλθόντων εἰς Βηθλεὲμ καὶ προσκυνησάντων τὸ παιδίον καὶ προσενεγκάντων αὐτῷ δῶρα, χρυσον καὶ λίβανον καὶ σμύρναν, ἔπειτα κατὰ ἀποκάλυψιν, μετὰ τὸ προσκυνῆσαι τὸν παῖδα ἐν Βηθλεέμ, ἐκελεύσθησαν μὴ ἐπανελθεῖν πρὸς τὸν Ἡρώδην.

"Accordingly, the Magi from Arabia came to Bethlehem and worshipped the Child, and presented Him with gifts, gold and frankincense, and myrrh; but returned not to Herod, being warned in a revelation after worshipping the Child in Bethlehem."

   * Mat 2:9–12.

O. *Dial.* 78.3, καὶ Ἰωσὴφ δέ, ὁ τὴν Μαρίαν μεμνηστευμένος, βουληθεὶς πρότερον ἐκβαλεῖν τὴν μνηστὴν αὐτῷ Μαριάμ, νομίζων ἐγκυμονεῖν αὐτὴν ἀπὸ συνουσίας ἀνδρός, τοῦτ, ἔστιν ἀπὸ πορνείας, δι᾽ ὁράματος κεκέλευστο μὴ ἐκβαλεῖν τὴν γυναῖκα αὐτοῦ, εἰπόντος αὐτῷ τοῦ φανέντος ἀγγέλου ὅτι ἐκ πνεύματος ἁγίου ὃ ἔχει κατὰ γαστρός ἐστι.

"And Joseph, the spouse of Mary, supposing her to be pregnant by intercourse with a man, i.e., from fornication, was commanded in a vision not to put away his wife; and the angel who appeared to him told him that what is in her womb is of the Holy Ghost."

   * Mat 1:18–21.

P. *Dial.* 78.4, φοβηθεὶς οὖν οὐκ ἐκβέβληκεν αὐτήν, ἀλλά, ἀπογραφῆς οὔσης ἐν τῇ Ἰουδαίᾳ τότε πρώτης ἐπὶ Κυρηνίου, ἀνεληλύθει ἀπὸ Ναζαρέτ, ἔνθα ᾤκει, εἰς Βηθλεέμ, ὅθεν ἦν, ἀπογράψασθαι· ἀπὸ γὰρ τῆς κατοικούσης τὴν γῆν ἐκείνην φυλῆς Ἰούδα τὸ γένος ἦν. καὶ αὐτὸς ἅμα τῇ Μαρίᾳ κελεύεται ἐξελθεῖν εἰς Αἴγυπτον καὶ εἶναι ἐκεῖ ἅμα τῷ παιδίῳ, ἄχρις ἂν αὐτοῖς πάλιν ἀποκαλυφθῇ ἐπανελθεῖν εἰς τὴν Ἰουδαίαν.

"Then he was afraid, and did not put her away; but on the occasion of the first census which was taken in Judea, under Cyrenius, he went up from Nazareth, where he lived, to Bethlehem, to which he belonged, to be enrolled; for his family was of the tribe of Judah, which then inhabited that region. Then along with Mary he is ordered to proceed into Egypt, and remain there with the Child until another revelation warn them to return into Judea."

   * Mat 2:13; Luke 2:1–5.

Q. *Dial.* 78.5, γεννηθέντος δὲ τότε τοῦ παιδίου ἐν Βεθλεέμ, ἐπειδὴ Ἰωσὴφ οὐκ εἶχεν ἐν τῇ κώμῃ ἐκείνῃ που καταλῦσαι, ἐν σπηλαίῳ τινὶ σύνεγγυς τῆς κώμης κατέλυσε· καὶ τότε, αὐτῶν ὄντων ἐκεῖ, ἐτετόκει ἡ Μαρία τὸν Χριστὸν καὶ ἐν φάτνῃ αὐτὸν ἐτεθείκει, ὅπου ἐλθόντες οἱ ἀπὸ Ἀρραβίας μάγοι εὗρον αὐτόν.

"But when the Child was born in Bethlehem, since Joseph could not find a lodging in that village, he took up his quarters in a certain cave near the village; and while they were there Mary brought forth the Christ and placed Him in a manger, and here the Magi who came from Arabia found Him."

> * Mat 2:1–25; Luke 2:7. The cave as the birthplace is mentioned in no canonical document. Matthew states that the birth was in a "house" (οἰκίαν).

R. *Dial.* 78.7, Καὶ ὁ Ἡρώδης, μὴ ἐπανελθόντων πρὸς αὐτὸν τῶν ἀπὸ Ἀρραβίας μάγων, ὡς ἠξίωσεν αὐτοὺς ποιῆσαι, ἀλλὰ κατὰ τὰ κελευσθέντα αὐτοῖς δι᾽ ἄλλης ὁδοῦ εἰς τὴν χώραν αὐτῶν ἀπαλλαγέντων, καὶ τοῦ Ἰωσὴφ ἅμα τῇ Μαρίᾳ καὶ τῷ παιδίῳ, ὡς καὶ αὐτοῖς ἀποκεκάλυπτο, ἤδη ἐξελθόντων εἰς Αἴγυπτον, οὐ γινώσκων τὸν παῖδα, ὃν ἐληλύθεισαν προσκυνῆσαι οἱ μάγοι, πάντας ἁπλῶς τοὺς παῖδας τοὺς ἐν Βηθλεὲμ ἐκέλευσεν ἀναιρεθῆναι.

"So Herod, when the Magi from Arabia did not return to him, as he had asked them to do, but had departed by another way to their own country, according to the commands laid on them; and when Joseph, with Mary and the Child, had now gone into Egypt, as it was revealed to them to do; as he did not know the Child whom the Magi had gone to worship, ordered simply the whole of the children then in Bethlehem to be massacred."

> * Mat 2:12–16.

S. *Dial.* 81.4, καὶ ἔπειτα καὶ παρ᾽ ἡμῖν ἀνήρ τις, ᾧ ὄνομα Ἰωάννης, εἷς τῶν ἀποστόλων τοῦ Χριστοῦ, ἐν ἀποκαλύψει γενομένῃ αὐτῷ χίλια ἔτη ποιήσειν ἐν Ἰερουσαλὴμ τοὺς τῷ ἡμετέρῳ Χριστῷ πιστεύσαντας προεφήτευσε, καὶ μετὰ ταῦτα τὴν καθολικὴν καί, συνελόντι φάναι, αἰωνίαν ὁμοθυμαδὸν ἅμα πάντων ἀνάστασιν γενήσεσθαι καὶ κρίσιν.

"And further, there was a certain man with us, whose name was John, one of the apostles of Christ, who prophesied, by a revelation that was made to him, that those who believed in our Christ would dwell a thousand years in Jerusalem; and that thereafter the general, and, in short, the eternal resurrection and judgment of all men would take place."

> * Rev 20:4–5.

T. *Dial.* 88.1, μαρτύριον δὲ καὶ τοῦτο ἔστω ὑμῖν, ὃ ἔφην πρὸς ὑμᾶς γεγονέναι ὑπὸ τῶν Ἀρραβίας μάγων, οἵτινες ἅμα τῷ γεννηθῆναι τὸ παιδίον ἐλθόντες προσεκύνησαν αὐτῷ.

"And let this be proof to you, namely, what I told you was done by the Magi from Arabia, who as soon as the Child was born came to worship Him . . ."

* Mat 2:9–12.

U. *Dial.* 88.2, καὶ γὰρ γεννηθεὶς δύναμιν τὴν αὐτοῦ ἔσχε· καὶ αὐξάνων κατὰ τὸ κοινὸν τῶν ἄλλων ἁπάντων ἀνθρώπων, χρώμενος τοῖς ἁρμόζουσιν, ἑκάστῃ αὐξήσει τὸ οἰκεῖον ἀπένειμε, τρεφόμενος τὰς πάσας τροφάς, καὶ τριάκοντα ἔτη ἢ πλείονα ἢ καὶ ἐλάσσονα μείνας, μέχρις οὗ προελήλυθεν Ἰωάννης κῆρυξ αὐτοῦ τῆς παρουσίας καὶ τὴν τοῦ βαπτίσματος ὁδὸν προϊών, ὡς καὶ προαπέδειξα.

". . . for even at His birth he was in possession of His power; and as He grew up as all other men, by using the fitting means, He assigned its own [requirements] to each development, and was sustained by all kinds of nourishment, and waited for thirty years, more or less, until John appeared before Him as the herald of His approach, and preceded Him in the way of baptism, as I have already shown."

* Possessed his powers at birth—No canonical document.
* Grew up like any other man—Circumcised (Luke 2:21); Grew and became strong (Luke 2:40); Continued in subjection to his parents (Luke 2:51).
* Exercised appropriate powers at each stage of growth—Luke 2:40 (?)
* Waited thirty years—No canonical document.
* John as herald—Mat 3:11–12; 11:13–14; 17:10–13; Mark 1:7–8; 9:11–13; Luke 3:16–17; John 1:19–20, 26–27.

V. *Dial.* 88.7, Ἰωάννου γὰρ καθεζομένου ἐπὶ τοῦ Ἰορδάνου καὶ κηρύσσοντος Βάπτισμα μετανοίας, καὶ ζώνην δερματίνην καὶ ἔνδυμα ἀπὸ τριχῶν καμήλου μόνον φοροῦντος καὶ μηδὲν ἐσθίοντος πλὴν ἀκρίδας καὶ μέλι ἄγριον, οἱ ἄνθρωποι ὑπελάμβανον αὐτὸν εἶναι τὸν Χριστόν· πρὸς οὓς καὶ αὐτὸς ἐβόα· Οὐκ εἰμὶ ὁ Χριστός, ἀλλὰ φωνὴ βοῶντος· ἥξει γὰρ ὁ ἰσχυρότερός μου, οὗ οὐκ εἰμὶ ἱκανὸς τὰ ὑποδήματα βαστάσαι.

"For when John remained by the Jordan, and preached the baptism of repentance, wearing only a leather girdle and a vesture made of camels' hair, eating nothing but locusts and wild honey, men supposed him to be Christ; but he cried to them, 'I am not the Christ, but the voice of one crying; for He that is stronger than I shall come, whose shoes I am not worthy to bear.'"

* Mat 3:1–6, 11; Mark 1:4–7; Luke 3:3, 15–16; John 1:19–23, 25–27.

W. *Dial.* 88.8, καὶ ἐλθόντος τοῦ Ἰησοῦ ἐπὶ τὸν Ἰορδάνην, καὶ νομιζομένου Ἰωσὴφ τοῦ τέκτονος υἱοῦ ὑπάρχειν, καὶ ἀειδοῦς, ὡς αἱ γραφαὶ ἐκήρυσσον, φαινομένου, καὶ τέκτονος νομιζομένου (ταῦτα γὰρ τὰ τεκτονικὰ ἔργα εἰργάζετο, ἐν ἀνθρώποις ὤν, ἄροτρα καὶ ζυγά, διὰ τούτων καὶ τὰ τῆς δικαιοσύνης σύμβολα διδάσκων καὶ ἐνεργῆ βίον)

"And when Jesus came to the Jordan, He was considered to be the son of Joseph the carpenter; and he appeared without comeliness, as the Scriptures declared; and He was deemed a carpenter (for He was in the habit of working as a carpenter among men, making ploughs and yokes; by which He taught the symbols of righteousness and an active life) . . ."

* Mat 13:55; Mark 6:3; Luke 4:22; John 6:42.
* None of the above mention that Jesus used to work as a carpenter making ploughs and yokes.

X. *Dial.* 94.5, Ὅνπερ οὖν τρόπον τὸ σημεῖον διὰ τοῦ χαλκοῦ ὄφεως γενέσθαι ὁ θεὸς ἐκέλευσε καὶ ἀναίτιός ἐστιν, οὕτω δὴ καὶ ἐν τῷ νόμῳ κατάρα κεῖται κατὰ τῶν σταυρουμένων ἀνθρώπων· οὐκ ἔτι δὲ καὶ κατὰ τοῦ Χριστοῦ τοῦ θεοῦ κατάρα κεῖται, δι᾽ οὗ σῴζει πάντας τοὺς κατάρας ἄξια πράξαντας.

"Just as God commanded the sign to be made by the brazen serpent, and yet He is blameless; even so, though a curse lies in the law against persons who are crucified, yet no curse lies on the Christ of God, by whom all that have committed things worthy of a curse are saved."

* Gal 3:13.

Y. *Dial.* 97.1, καὶ γὰρ ὁ κύριος σχεδόν μέχρις ἑσπέρας ἔμεινεν ἐπὶ τοῦ ξύλου, καὶ πρὸς ἑσπέραν ἔθαψαν αὐτόν· εἶτα ἀνέστη τῇ τρίτῃ ἡμέρᾳ.

"For indeed the Lord remained upon the tree almost until evening, and they buried Him at eventide; then on the third day He rose again."

* Remained on cross until evening—Mat 27:57; Mark 15:42.
* Rose from the dead on third day—Mat 28; Mark 16; Luke 24; John 20.

Z. *Dial.* 97.3, ὅτε γὰρ ἐσταύρωσαν αὐτόν, ἐμπήσσοντες τοὺς ἥλους τὰς χεῖρας καὶ τοὺς πόδας αὐτοῦ ὤρυξαν, καὶ οἱ σταυρώσαντες αὐτὸν ἐμέρισαν τὰ ἱμάτια αὐτοῦ ἑαυτοῖς, λαχμὸν βάλλοντες ἕκαστος κατὰ τὴν τοῦ κλήρου ἐπιβολὴν ὃ ἐκλέξασθαι ἐβεβούλητο.

"For when they crucified Him, driving in the nails, they pierced His hands and feet; and those who crucified Him parted His garments among themselves, each casting lots for what he chose to have, and receiving according to the decision of the lot."

* Mat 27:35; Mark 15:24; Luke 23:33–34; John 19:18, 24.

AA. *Dial.* 115.6, ἵνα τῇ αὐτῇ ὁμοίᾳ κρίσει ὑπὸ τοῦ θεοῦ κρινόμενοι πολὺ μᾶλλον ὑπὲρ τῶν μεγάλων τολμημάτων, εἴτε κακῶν πράξεων εἴτε φαύλων ἐξηγήσεων, ἃς παραποιοῦντες ἐξηγεῖσθε, λόγον δώσετε. Ὁ γὰρ κρίμα κρίνετε, δίκαιόν ἐστιν ὑμᾶς κριθῆναι.

". . . in order that, when you are judged with the very same judgment by God, you may have a much heavier account to render for your great audacities, whether evil actions, or bad interpretations which you obtain by falsifying the truth. For with what judgment you judge, it is righteous that you be judged withal."

* Mat 7:1–2; Luke 6:37–38.

BIBLIOGRAPHY

I. *Greek Text*

Goodspeed, E. J. (ed.), *Die ältesten Apologeten. Texte mit kurzen Einleitungen.* Göttingen: Vandenhoeck & Ruprecht, 1915.

II. *English Translations*

Falls, T. B., *Writings of Justin Martyr.* The Fathers of the Catholic Church Vol. 6; Washington, D. C.: The Catholic University of America Press, 1948.
Roberts, A. and J. Donaldson (eds.), *Ante-Nicene Fathers Vol. 1.* Peabody, MA: Hendrickson, 1994. Reprint from original, Buffalo: The Christian Literature Publishing Company, 1885.
Williams, A. L. *Justin Martyr. The Dialogue with Trypho: Translation, Introduction, and Notes.* London: SPCK, 1930.

III. *Secondary Sources*

Aland, K., *A History of Christianity Vol. 1: From the Beginnings to the Threshold of the Reformation.* ET J. L. Schaaf; Philadelphia: Fortress, 1985.
Albinus, *Enseignement des doctrines de Platon/Alcinoos; introduction, texte établi et commenté par John Whittaker ettraduit par Pierre Louis.* Paris: Belles Lettres, 1990.
——, *Didaskalikos* in J. P. Hershbell (ed.), *The Platonic Doctrines of Albinus.* ET J. Reedy; Grand Rapids: Phanes Press, 1991.
Albl, M. C., *"And Scripture Cannot Be Broken": The Form and Function of the Early Christian Testimonia Collections.* NovTSup 96; Leiden: E. J. Brill, 1999.
Alexander, J. N. S., "The Interpretation of Scripture in the Ante-Nicene Period," *Int* 12 (1958) 272–280.
Alexander, L., "Ancient Book Production and the Circulation of the Gospels," in R. Bauckham (ed.), *The Gospels for All Christians. Rethinking the Gospel Audiences.* Grand Rapids/Cambridge: Eerdmans, 1998, 71–105.
Altaner, B., *Patrology.* Frieburg: Herder, 1960.
Andresen, C., "Justin und der mittlere Platonismus," *ZNW* 44 (1952/53) 157–195.
Armstrong, A. H., (ed.), *The Cambridge History of Later Greek and Early Medieval Philosophy.* Cambridge: Cambridge University Press, 1970.
——, "On Not Knowing Too Much About God," in G. Vesey (ed.), *The Philosophy in Christianity.* Cambridge: Cambridge University Press, 1989, 129–145.
Armstrong, A. H., and R. A. Markus, *Christian Faith and Greek Philosophy.* London: Darton, Longman & Todd, 1960.
Aulén, G., *Christus Victor: An Historical Study of the Three Main Types of the Idea of the Atonement.* ET A. G. Hebert; London: SPCK, 1950.
Aune, D. E., "Justin Martyr's Use of the Old Testament," *BETS* 9 (1966) 179–197.
Baarda, Tj., "Διαφωνία-Συμφωνία. Factors in the Harmonization of the Gospels, Especially in the Diatessaron of Tatian," in *Essays on the Diatessaron.* Contributions to Biblical Exegesis and Theology 11; Kampen: Pharos, 1994, 29–47.
Baker, A., "Justin's Agraphon in the Dialogue with Trypho," *JBL* 87 (1968) 277–287.

Baker, D. L., "Typology and the Christian Use of the Old Testament," *SJT* 29 (1976) 137–157.

Balás, D. L., "Marcion Revisited: A 'Post-Harnack' Perspective," in W. E. March (ed.), *Texts and Testaments: Critical Essays on the Bible and Early Church Fathers.* FS S. D. Currie; San Antonio: Trinity University Press, 1980, 95–108.

Baldus, A., *Das Verhältnis Justins des Märtyrers zu unsern synoptischen Evangelien.* Münster, 1895.

Banner, W. A., "Origen and the Tradition of Natural Law," *Dumbarton Oaks Papers* 8 (1954) 49–82. Reprinted in E. Ferguson, D. M. Scholer & P. C. Finney (eds.), *Studies in Early Christianity Vol. 8: The Early Church and Greco-Roman Thought.* New York/London: Garland, 1993, 181–214.

Barker, M., *The Great Angel. A Study of Israel's Second God.* London: SPCK, 1992.

Barnard, L. W., *Justin Martyr. His Life and Thought.* Cambridge: Cambridge University Press, 1967.

———, "Justin Martyr in Recent Study," *SJT* 22 (1969) 152–164.

———, "The Logos Theology of St. Justin Martyr," *Downside Review* 89 (1971) 132–141.

———, "The Old Testament and Judaism in the Writings of Justin Martyr," *VT* 14 (1964) 395–406. Reprinted as "Justin Martyr's Knowledge of Judaism," in idem, *Studies in Church History and Patristics.* Thessaloniki: Patriarchal Institute for Patristic Studies, 1978, 107–118.

Barnes, T. D., *Tertullian: A Historical and Literary Study.* Oxford: Oxford University Press, 1971.

Barton. J., *Holy Writings, Sacred Text. The Canon in Early Christianity.* Louisville, KY: Westminster John Knox Press, 1997.

Bate, H. N., "Some Technical Terms of Greek Exegesis," *JTS* 24 (1922–23) 59–66.

Bauckham, R., "For Whom Were the Gospels Written?" in idem, *The Gospels for All People. Rethinking the Gospel Audiences.* Grand Rapids/Cambridge: Eerdmans, 1998, 9–48.

Bauer, W., W. F. Arndt, F. W. Gingrich, and F. W. Danker, *A Greek-English Lexicon of the New Testament and Other Early Christian Literature.* 2d ed. rev; Chicago and London: University of Chicago Press, 1979.

Becker, U., "εὐαγγέλιον," in C. Brown (ed.), *The New International Dictionary of New Testament Theology.* 3 vols.; Grand Rapids: Zondervan, 1976, 2.107–115.

Behm, J., "αἷμα" in G. Kittel (ed.), *Theological Dictionary of the New Testament.* 10 vols.; Grand Rapids: Eerdmans, 1964, 1.172–177.

Bellinzoni, A. J., *The Sayings of Jesus in the Writings of Justin Martyr.* NovTSup 17; Leiden: E. J. Brill, 1967.

———, "The Source of the Agraphon in Justin Martyr's Dialogue with Trypho 47:5," *VC* 17 (1963) 65–70.

Benoit, A., *Saint Irénée: Introduction à l'Étude de sa théologie* (Paris: Presses Universities de France, 1960) 82–87; 96–101.

Bethune-Baker, J. F., *An Introduction to the Early History of Christian Doctrine to the Time of the Council of Chalcedon.* London: Methuen & Co., 1962.

Betz, H. D., "The Literary Composition and Function of Paul's Letter to the Galatians," *NTS* 21 (1975) 353–379.

Bishop, E. F. F., "Some Reflections on Justin Martyr and the Nativity Narratives," *EvQ* 39 (1967) 30–39.

Blackman, E. C., *Marcion and His Influence.* London: SPCK, 1948.

Bloesch, D. G., *Essentials of Evangelical Theology Volume I: God, Authority, & Salvation.* San Francisco: Harper & Row, 1978.

Bokser, B. Z., "Justin Martyr and the Jews," *JQR* 64 (1973–74) 97–122; 204–211.

Bousset, W., *Die Evangeliencitate Justins des Märtyrers in ihrem Wert für die Evangelienkritik.* Göttingen: Vandenhoeck & Ruprecht, 1891.

Bouyer, L., *The Christian Mystery. From Pagan Myth to Christian Mysticism.* ET I. Trethowan; Edinburgh: T. & T. Clark, 1990.

Brandt, R. B., "Happiness," in P. Edwards (ed.), *The Encyclopedia of Philosophy*. 8 vols.; New York: Macmillan/The Free Press, 1967, 3.413–414.

Bray, G., *Creeds, Councils and Christ*. Leicester/Downers Grove: Inter-Varsity Press, 1984.

Breck, J., "Divine Initiative: Salvation in Orthodox Theology," in J. Meyendorff & R. Tobias (eds.), *Salvation in Christ: A Lutheran-Orthodox Dialogue*. Minneapolis: Augsburg, 1992, 105–120.

Bréhier, E., *The Hellenic Age*. ET J. Thomas; Chicago: University of Chicago Press, 1963.

Bruce, F. F., *The Canon of Scripture*. Downers Grove: Inter-Varsity Press, 1988.

Buchanan, G. W., *The Consequences of the Covenant*. NovTSup; Leiden: E. J. Brill, 1970.

Buckley, E. R., "Justin Martyr's Quotations from the Synoptic Tradition," *JTS* 36 (1935) 173–176.

Burghardt, W. J., "On Early Christian Exegesis," *TS* 11 (1950) 78–116.

Burke, G. T., "Celsus and Justin: Carl Andresen Revisited," *ZNW* 76 (1985) 107–116.

Burns, J. P., "The Economy of Salvation: Two Patristic Traditions," *TS* 37 (1976) 598–619. Reprinted in E. Ferguson, D. M. Scholer, & P. C. Finney (eds.), *Studies in Early Christianity Vol. X: Doctrines of Human Nature, Sin, and Salvation in the Early Church*. New York/London: Garland, 1993, 224–245.

Burridge, R. A., "About People, by People, for People: Gospel Genre and Audiences," in R. Bauckham (ed.), *The Gospels for All Christians. Rethinking the Gospel Audiences*. Grand Rapids/Cambridge: Eerdmans, 1998, 113–145.

Cairns, H., "Introduction," in E. Hamilton & H. Cairns (eds.), *The Collected Dialogues of Plato*. Bollingen Series 71; New Jersey: Princeton University Press, 1993.

Campenhausen, H. F. von, "The Authority of Jesus' Relatives in the Early Church," in H. F. von Campenhausen and H. Chadwick, *Jerusalem and Rome: The Problem of Authority in the Early Church*. Historical Series 4; Philadelphia: Fortress Press, 1966, 1–19.

——, *The Formation of the Christian Bible*. ET J. A. Baker; London: Adam & Charles Black, 1972.

Carabine, D., *The Unknown God. Negative Theology in the Platonic Tradition: Plato to Eriugena*. Louvain Theological & Pastoral Monographs 19; Louvain: Peeters Press/Grand Rapids: Eerdmans, 1995.

Chadwick, H., "The Bible and the Greek Fathers," in D. E. Nineham (ed.), *The Church's Use Of the Bible*. London: SPCK, 1963.

——, "The Circle and the Ellipse: Rival Concepts of Authority in the Early Church," in H. F. von Campenhausen and H. Chadwick, *Jerusalem and Rome: The Problem of Authority in the Early Church*. Historical Series 4; Philadelphia: Fortress Press, 1966, 21–36.

——, *Early Christian Thought and the Classical Tradition. Studies in Justin, Clement, and Origen*. Oxford/New York: Oxford University Press, 1984.

——, "Justin Martyr's Defense of Christianity," *BJRL* 47 (1965) 275–297.

——, *The Early Church*. The Pelican History of the Church Vol. 1; Middlesex: Penguin, 1974.

Chauvet, L. M., *Symbol and Sacrament. A Sacramental Reinterpretation of Christian Existence*. ET P. Madigan and M. Beaumont; Collegeville, Min.: The Liturgical Press, 1995.

Copleston, F., *A History of Philosophy Vol. I, Parts I & II: Greece & Rome*. Rev. ed.; Garden City, NY: Image Books, 1962.

Cosgrove, C. H., "Justin Martyr and the Emerging Christian Canon. Observations on the Purpose and Destination of the Dialogue with Trypho," *VC* 36 (1982) 209–232.

Credner, C. A., *Beiträge zur Einleitung in die biblischen Schriften*. Halle, 1832.

Cullmann, O., "The Plurality of the Gospels as a Theological Problem in Antiquity," in idem, *The Early Church*. London: SCM, 1956, 37–54.

——, *The Earliest Christian Confessions*. ET J. K. S. Reid; London: Lutterworth, 1949.

Cunliffe-Jones, H. (ed), *A History of Christian Doctrine*. Edinburgh: T. & T. Clark, 1980.

Dahl, N. A., "Anamnesis. Memory and Commemoration in Early Christianity," in idem, *Jesus in the Memory of the Early Church. Essays by Nils Alstrup Dahl*. Minneapolis: Augsburg, 1976, 11–29.

Daly, R. J., *Christian Sacrifice. The Judeo-Christian Background Before Origen*. Washington, D.C.: The Catholic University of America Press, 1978.

Daniélou, J., *The Theology of Jewish Christianity*. The Development of Christian Doctrine Before the Council of Nicaea Vol. 1; ET J. A. Baker; London: Darton, Longman & Todd, 1964.

——, *Gospel Message and Hellenistic Culture*. The Development of Christian Doctrine Before the Council of Nicaea Vol. 2; ET J. A. Baker; London: Darton, Longman & Todd, 1973.

——, *From Shadows to Reality. Studies in the Biblical Typology of the Fathers*. ET W. Hibberd; Westminster, Maryland: The Newman Press, 1960.

——, "The Fathers and the Scriptures," *ECQ* 10 (1954) 265–273.

——, *Primitive Christian Symbols*. ET D. Attwater; Baltimore: Helicon Press, 1964.

——, *The Bible and the Liturgy*. Liturgical Studies; Notre Dame, IN: University of Notre Dame Press, 1956.

Denning-Bolle, S., "Christian Dialogue as Apologetic: The Case of Justin Martyr in Historical Context," *BJRL* 69 (1987) 492–510.

De Vogel, C. J., "Platonism and Christianity: A Mere Antagonism or a Profound Common Ground?" *VC* 39 (1985) 1–62.

Dillon, J., "Logos and Trinity: Patterns of Platonist Influence on Early Christianity," in G. Vesey (ed.), *The Philosophy in Christianity*. Cambridge: Cambridge University Press, 1989, 1–13.

——, *The Middle Platonists: A Study of Platonism 80 B.C. to A.D. 220*. London: Duckworth, 1977.

Dölger, F. J., *Sphragis. Eine altchristliche Taufbezeichnung in ihren Beziehungen zur profanen und religiösen Kultur des Altertums*. Studien zur Geschichte und Kultur des Altertums; Paderborn: Druck und Verlag von Ferdinand Schöningh, 1911.

Donahue, P. J., *Jewish-Christian Controversy in the Second Century: A Study in the Dialogue of Justin Martyr*. Yale University Ph.D. Dissertation, 1973.

Droge, A. J., "Justin Martyr and the Restoration of Philosophy," *CH* 56 (1987) 303–319.

Duschesne, L., *Early History of the Christian Church Vol. 1: To the End of the Third Century*. 4th ed.; London: John Murray, 1950.

Edwards, M. J., "Justin's Logos and the Word of God," *J Early Chr St* 3 (1995) 261–280.

——, "On the Platonic Schooling of Justin Martyr," *JTS* ns 42 (1991) 17–34.

Engelhardt, M. von, *Das Christentum Justins des Märtyrers, Eine Untersuchung über die Anfänge der katholischen Glaubenslehre*. Erlangen: A. Deichert, 1878.

Eusebius of Caesarea, *Ecclesiastical History* in P. Schaff and H. Wace (eds.), *Nicene and Post-Nicene Fathers*. 14 vols.; Buffalo: The Christian Literature Publishing Company, 1890. Reprinted: Peabody, MA: Hendrickson, 1994, 1.73–403.

Fee, G. D., "Modern Text Criticism and the Synoptic Problem," in B. Orchard and T. R. W. Longstaff (eds.), *J. J. Griesbach: Synoptic and Text-Critical Studies 1776–1976*. SNTSMS 34; Cambridge: Cambridge University Press, 1978, 154–169.

Ferguson, E., *Backgrounds of Early Christianity*. 2nd ed.; Grand Rapids: Eerdmans, 1993.

——, "Baptismal Motifs in the Ancient Church," *RestQ* (1963) 202–216.

——, "The Covenant Idea in the Second Century," in W. E. March (ed.), *Texts and Testaments: Critical Essays on the Bible and the Early Church Fathers*. FS S. D. Currie; San Antonio: Trinity University Press, 1980, 135–162.

——, "The Disgrace and the Glory: A Jewish Motif in Early Christianity," *StudPat* 21 (1989) 86–94.

——, "Justin Martyr on Jews, Christians and the Covenant," in F. Manns and

E. Alliata (eds.), *Early Christianity in Context: Monuments and Documents*. Studium Biblicum Franciscanum Collectio Maior 38; Jerusalem: Franciscan Printing press, 1993, 395–405.
——, "Justin Martyr and the Liturgy," *RestQ* 36 (1994) 267–278.
Filson, F. V., *Which Books Belong in the Bible?* Philadelphia: Westminster, 1957.
Flesseman-Van Leer, E., *Tradition and Scripture in the Early Church*. Van Gorcum's Theologische Bibliotheek 26; Assen: Van Gorcum, 1954.
Ford, J. M., "Was Montanism a Jewish-Christian Heresy?" *JEH* 17 (1966) 145–158.
Freimann, M., "Die Wortführer des Judentums in den ältesten Kontroversen zwischen Juden und Christen," *MGWJ* 55 (1893) 555–585.
Frend, W. H. C., *The Early Church*. Knowing Christianity; London: Hodder and Stoughton, 1965.
——, *The Rise of Christianity*. Philadelphia: Fortress, 1984.
——, "The Old Testament in the Age of the Greek Apologists A.D. 130–180," *SJT* 26 (1973) 129–150.
Friedländer, P., *Plato Vol. 1: An Anthology*. ET H. Meyerhoff; Bollingen Series 59; New York, Pantheon, 1958.
Friedrich, G., "εὐαγγέλιον," in G. Kittel (ed.), *Theological Dictionary of the New Testament*. 10 vols.; Grand Rapids: Eerdmans, 1964, 2.721–737.
Gadamer, H.-G., *Plato's Dialectical Ethics*. ET R. M. Wallace; New Haven and London: Yale University Press, 1991.
Gamble, H. Y., *Books and Readers in the Early Church: A History of Early Christian Texts*. New Haven and London: Yale University Press, 1995.
——, "Canon—New Testament," in N. D. Freedman (ed.), *ABD*. 6 vols.; New York: Doubleday, 1992, 1.852–861.
——, "The Canon of the New Testament," in E. J. Epp and G. W. MacRae (eds.), *The New Testament and Its Modern Interpreters*. Atlanta: Scholars Press, 1989, 201–243.
——, *The New Testament Canon. Its Making and Meaning*. Guides to Biblical Scholarship; Philadelphia: Fortress, 1985.
Garrison, R. *The Graeco-Roman Context of Early Christianity*. JSNTSup 137; Sheffield: Sheffield Academic Press, 1997.
Gaster, T. H., *Customs and Folkways of Jewish Life*. New York: William Sloane, 1955.
Gilkey, L., "God," in Hodgson & King (eds.), *Christian Theology. An Introduction to Its Traditions and Tasks*. London: SPCK, 1983, 62–87.
Gill, D., "A Liturgical Fragment in Justin, Dialogue 29.1," *HTR* 59 (1966) 98–100.
Gilson, E., *God and Philosophy*. New Haven: Yale University Press, 1941.
Ginzberg, L., *On Jewish Law and Lore*. New York: Atheneum, 1970.
Glover, R., "Patristic Quotations and Gospel Sources," *NTS* 31 (1985) 234–251.
Goldfahn, A. H., "Justinus Martyr und die Agada," *MGWJ* 22 (1873) 49–60, 104–115, 145–153, 193–202, 257–269.
Goodenough, E. R., *Jewish Symbols in the Graeco-Roman Period Vol. 1: The Archeological Evidence from Palestine*. New York: Pantheon, 1953.
——, *The Theology of Justin Martyr. An Investigation Into the Conceptions of Early Christian Literature and Its Hellenistic and Judaistic Influences*. Jena: Verlag Frommannsche Buchhandlung, 1923. Reprinted: Amsterdam: Philo Press, 1968.
Goodspeed, E. J., *The Formation of the New Testament*. Chicago: University of Chicago Press, 1962.
——, *A History of Early Christian Literature*. rev by R. M. Grant; Chicago: University of Chicago Press, 1966.
——, (ed.), *Index Apologeticus sive clavis Iustini Martyris Operum*. Leipzig: J. C. Hinrichs'sche Buchhandlung, 1912.
Goppelt, L., *Typos: The Typological Interpretation of the Old Testament in the New*. ET D. H. Madvig; Grand Rapids: Eerdmans, 1982.
Grant, R. M., *Augustus to Constantine. The Thrust of the Christian Movement into the Roman World*. London: Collins, 1971.

——, *The Earliest Lives of Jesus*. New York: Harper & Brothers, 1961.

——, *The Formation of the New Testament*. London: Hutchinson University Library, 1965.

——, *Gods and the One God*. Library of Early Christianity 1; Philadelphia: Westminster, 1986.

——, *Greek Apologists of the Second Century*. Philadelphia: Westminster, 1988.

——, *Jesus After the Gospels. The Christ of the Second Century*. London: SCM, 1990.

——, *The Letter and the Spirit*. London: SPCK, 1957.

——, "Aristotle and the Conversion of Justin," *JTS* ns 7 (1956) 246–248.

——, "The Fragments of the Greek Apologists and Irenaeus," in J. N. Birdsall and R. N. Thompson (eds.), *Biblical and Patristic Studies in Memory of Robert Pierce Casey*. Freiberg: Herder, 1963.

——, "The Social Setting of Second-Century Christianity," in E. P. Sanders (ed.), *Jewish and Christian Self-Definition Vol. 1: The Shaping of Christianity in the Second and Third Centuries*. London: SCM, 1980.

Grensted, L. W., *A Short History of the Doctrine of the Atonement*. Manchester: Manchester University Press, 1962 (1920).

Grenz, S. J., *Theology for the Community of God*. Nashville: Broadman & Holman, 1994.

Grillmeier, A., *Christ in Christian Tradition Vol. 1: From the Apostolic Age to Chalcedon (451)*. 2d ed. rev.: ET J. Bowden; Atlanta: John Know Press, 1975.

Guerra, A. J., "The Conversion of Marcus Aurelius and Justin Martyr: The Purpose, Genre, and Content of the First Apology," *TSC* 9 (1992) 171–187.

Gunton, C. E., *A Brief Theology of Revelation*. Edinburgh: T. & T. Clark, 1995.

Hagner, D. A., "The Sayings of Jesus in the Apostolic Fathers and Justin Martyr," in D. Wenham (ed.), *Gospel Perspectives Vol. 5: The Jesus Tradition Outside the Gospels*. Sheffield: JSOT Press, 1984, 233–268.

Hahneman, G. M., *The Muratorian Fragment and the Development of the Canon*. Oxford Theological Monographs; Oxford: Clarendon Press, 1992.

Hall, R., "Dialectic," in P. Edwards (ed.), *The Encyclopedia of Philosophy Vols. 1–2*. New York: Macmillan & The Free Press/London: Collier Macmillan, 1972.

Hall, S. G., *Doctrine and Practice in the Early Church*. London: SPCK, 1991/Grand Rapids: Eerdmans, 1992.

Hanson, R. P. C., *Tradition in the Early Church*. London: SCM, 1962.

——, "The Bible in the Early Church," in P. R. Ackroyd and C. F. Evans (eds.), *The Cambridge History of the Bible Vol. I: From the Beginnings to Jerome*. Cambridge: Cambridge University Press, 1970, 412–453.

Harnack, A., *The Mission and Expansion of Christianity in the First Three Centuries*. ET J. Moffat; New York: Harper & Brothers, 1962.

——, *The Origin of the New Testament and the Most Important Consequences of the New Creation*. Crown Theological Library 45; New Testament Studies 6; ET J. R. Wilkinson; London: Williams & Norgate, 1925.

——, *History of Dogma*. Vol. 2; 2nd ed.; ET N. Buchanan; London: Williams & Norgate, 1905.

——, *Marcion. The Gospel of the Alien God*. ET J. E. Steely & L. D. Bierma; Durham, NC: Labyrinth, 1990.

——, Judentum und Judenchristentum in Justins Dialog mit Trypho," TU 39; Leipzig, 1913, 47–92.

——, "Die Altercatio Simonis Judaei et Thophili Christiani nebst Untersuchungen über die antijüdische Polemik in der alten Kirche," TU 1; Leipzig, 1883.

Harris, J. R., *Testimonies*. 2 vols.; Cambridge: Cambridge University Press, 1916, 1920.

Harris, R. L., *Inspiration and Canonicity of the Bible. An Historical and Exegetical Study*. Contemporary Evangelical Perspectives; Grand Rapids: Zondervan, 1969.

Hart, J. N., "Creation and Providence," in Hodgson & King (eds.), *Christian Theology. An Introduction to Its Tasks and Traditions*. London: SPCK, 1983, 115–140.

Hatch, E., *Essays in Biblical Greek*. Oxford: Oxford University Press, 1889.

——, *The Influence of Greek Ideas and Usages Upon the Christian Church*. repr; Peabody, MA: Hendrickson, 1995 [London: Williams and Norgate, 1895].

Hazlett, I. (ed.), *Early Christianity: Origins and Evolution to AD 600*. London: SPCK, 1991.

Heard, R.G., "The ΑΠΟΜΝΗΜΟΝΕΥΜΑΤΑ in Papias, Justin, and Irenaeus," *NTS* 1 (1954–55) 122–129.

Henninger, J., "Sacrifice," in M. Eliade (ed.), *The Encyclopedia of Religion*. 16 vols.; New York: MacMillan, 1987, 12.544–557.

Henrichs, A., "Philosophy, the Handmaiden of Theology," *Greek, Roman and Byzantine Studies* 9 (1968) 437–450.

Heron, A., "'Logos, Image, Son': Some Models and Paradigms in Early Christology," in R. W. A McKinney (ed.), *Creation, Christ and Culture: Studies in Honor of T. F. Torrance*. Edinburgh: T. & T. Clark, 1976, 43–62.

Higgins, A. J. B., "Jewish Messianic Belief in Justin Martyr's *Dialogue with Trypho*," *NovT* 9 (1967) 298–305.

Hilgenfeld, A., *Kristische Untersuchungen über die Evangelien Justin's, der Clementinischen Homilien und Marcion's*. Halle, 1850.

Hill, C. E., "Justin and the New Testament Writings," *StudPat* 30 (1997) 42–48.

Hinson, G., "Confessions or Creeds in the Early Christian Tradition," *RevExp* 76 (1979) 6.

Hirsch, E. G., "Sacrifice," in I. Singer (ed.), *The Jewish Encyclopedia*. 12 vols.; New York: Ktav, 1901, 10.615–628.

Hirshman, M., "Polemic Literary Units in the Classical Midrashim and Justin Martyr's *Dialogue with Trypho*," *JQR* 83 (1993) 369–384.

Hirzel, R., *Der Dialog. Ein literarhistorischer Versuch*. 2 vols.; Leipzig: S. Hirzel, 1895.

Hodgson, R., "The Testimony Hypothesis," *JBL* 98 (1979) 361–378.

Holte, R., "Logos Spermatikos: Christianity and Ancient Philosophy According to St. Justin's Apologies," *ST* 12 (1958) 109–168.

Horbury, W., "Jewish-Christian Relations in Barnabas and Justin Martyr," in J. D. G. Dunn (ed.), *Jews and Christians. The Parting of the Ways AD 70 to 135*. Tübingen: J. C. B. Mohr (Paul Siebeck), 1992, 315–345.

——, "Old Testament Interpretation in the Writings of the Church Fathers," in J. M. Mulder (ed.), *Mikra. Text, Translation and Interpretation in the Hebrew Bible in Ancient Judaism and Early Christianity*. Assen, The Netherlands: Van Gorcum/ Philadelphia: Fortress, 1988.

Hughes, P. E., "Some Observations on the History of the Interpretation of Holy Scripture," in J. E. Bradley and R. A. Muller (eds.), *Church, Word, and Spirit: Historical and Theological Essays in Honor of Geoffrey W. Bromiley*. Grand Rapids: Eerdmans, 1987, 93–106.

Hulen, A. B., "The 'Dialogues with the Jews' as Sources for the Early Jewish Argument Against Christianity," *JBL* 51 (1932) 58–71.

Hyldahl, N., *Philosophie und Christentum. Eine Interpretation der Einleitung zum Dialog Justins*. Acta Theologica Danica 9; Copenhagen: Munksgaard, 1966.

Ignatius of Antioch, *Epistle to the Philadelphians* in K. Lake (ed.), *The Apostolic Fathers*. LCL; 2 vols.; London: William Heinemann/New York: The Macmillan Co., 1914.

Irenaeus of Lyons, *Against Heresies* in A. Roberts and J. Donaldson (eds.), *Ante-Nicene Fathers*. 10 vols.; Peabody: Hendrickson, 1994, 1.309–567.

Jaeger, W., *Early Christianity and Greek Paideia*. Cambridge, Mass./London: The Belknap Press, 1961.

Jannaris, A. N., "St. John's Gospel and the Logos," *ZNW* 2 (1901) 13–25.

Jewett, P. K., "Concerning the Allegorical Interpretation of Scripture," *WTJ* 17 (1954) 1–21.

Joad, C. E. M., *Great Philosophies of the World*. Benn's Sixpenny Library 23; London: Ernest Benn Limited, 1928.

Joly, R., *Christianisme et Philosophie. Études sur Justin et les Apologistes grecs du deuxième siècle*. Bruxelles: Editions de l'Universite de Bruxelles, 1973.

Katz, P., "Justin's Old Testament Quotations and the Greek Dodekapropheton Scroll," *StudPat* 1 (1957) 343–353.

Kaufman, G. D., *Systematic Theology: A Historicist Perspective*. New York: Charles Scribner's Sons, 1968.

Kee, H. C., E. Albu, C. Lindberg, W. J. Frost & D. L. Robert, *Christianity: A Social and Cultural History*. 2nd ed.; Upper Saddle River, NJ: Prentice-Hall, 1998.

Kelly, J. F., *Why is There a New Testament?* London: Geoffrey Chapman, 1986.

Kelly, J. N. D., *Early Christian Creeds*. London: Longmans, Green and Co., 1950.

——, *Early Christian Doctrines*. rev ed; San Francisco: Harper, 1978.

Kenyon, F., *Greek Papyri in the British Museum*. Oxford: Oxford University Press, 1898.

——, "The Date of the Apology of Justin Martyr," *The Academy* 49 (1896) 98.

Kerford, G. B., "Logos" in P. Edwards (ed.), *The Encyclopedia of Philosophy*. 8 vols.; Macmillan/The Free Press, 1967, 5.83–84.

Kline, L. K., "Harmonized Sayings of Jesus in the Pseudo-Clementine Homilies and Justin Martyr," *ZNW* 66 (1975) 223–241.

Koester, H., *Ancient Christian Gospels. Their History and Development*. London: SCM/Philadelphia: Trinity Press International, 1990.

——, and J. M. Robinson, *Trajectories in Early Christianity*. Philadelphia: Fortress, 1971.

——, "From the Kerygma-Gospel to Written Gospels," *NTS* 35 (1989) 361–381.

——, "The Text of the Synoptic Gospels in the Second Century," in W. L. Petersen (ed.), *Gospel Traditions in the Second Century. Origins, Rescensions, Text and Transmission*. Notre Dame: University of Notre Dame Press, 1989, 19–37.

Kugel, J. L., and R. A. Greer, *Early Biblical Interpretation*. Library of Early Christianity 3; Philadelphia: Westminster, 1986.

Lampe, G. W. H. (ed.), *A Patristic Greek Lexicon*. Oxford: Clarendon Press, 1995.

——, "Christian Theology in the Patristic Period," in H. Cunliffe-Jones with B. Drewery (eds.), *A History of Christian Doctrine*. Edinburgh: T. & T. Clark, 1978.

——, "The Reasonableness of Typology," in G. W. H. Lampe and K. L. Woollcombe, *Essays on Typology*. Studies in Biblical Theology; London: SCM, 1957, 9–38.

——, *The Seal of the Spirit. A Study in the Doctrine of Baptism and Confirmation in the New Testament and the Fathers*. London: Longmans, Green and Co., 1956.

Lewis, J. P., "Baptismal Practices of the Second and Third Century Church," *RestQ* 26 (1983) 1–17.

Lienhard, J. T., *The Bible, the Church, and Authority. The Canon of the Christian Bible in History and Theology*. Collegeville, MN: The Liturgical Press, 1995

Lietzmann, H., *A History of the Early Church Vol. 1: The Beginnings of the Christian Church; Vol. 2: The Founding of the Church Universal*. rev ed.; Woolf; Cleveland and New York: The World Publishing Company, 1953.

Lippelt, E., *Quae fuerint Justini Martyris APOMNHMONEUMATA quaque ratione cum forma Evangeliorum syro-latina cohaeserint*. Halle, 1901.

Lohse, B., *A Short History of Christian Doctrine*. ET F. E. Stoeffler; Philadelphia: Fortress, 1980.

Lyonnet, S. and L. Sabourin, *Sin, Redemption, and Sacrifice. A Biblical and Patristic Study*. AnBib 48; Rome: Biblical Institute Press, 1970.

MacLennan, R. S., *Early Christian Texts on Jews and Judaism*. Brown Judaic Studies 194; Atlanta: Scholars Press, 1990.

MacMullen, R., "Two Types of Conversion to Early Christianity," *VC* 37 (1983) 174–192. Reprinted in E. Ferguson (ed.), *Studies in Early Christianity Vol. II: Conversion, Catechumenate, and Baptism in the Early Church*. New York/London: Garland, 1993, 26–44.

Magen, Y., "The Ritual Baths (*miqva'ot*) at Qedumim and the Observance of Ritual Purity Among the Samaritans," in F. Manns and E. Alliata (eds.), *Early Christianity in Context: Monuments and Documents.* Studium Biblicum Franciscanum Collectio Maior 38; Jerusalem: Franciscan Printing Press, 1993, 181–193.

Manson, T. W., "The Argument from Prophecy," *JTS* 46 (1945) 129–136.

Margerie, B. de, *An Introduction to the History of Exegesis Vol. 1: The Greek Fathers.* ET L. Maluf; Petersham, MA: Saint Bede's Publications, 1993.

Markus, R. A., "Presuppositions of the Typological Approach to Scripture," *CQR* 158 (1957) 442–451.

Martens, E. A., *God's Design. A Focus on Old Testament Theology.* Grand Rapids: Baker, 1981.

Massaux, E., *The Influence of the Gospel of Saint Matthew on Christian Literature Before Saint Irenaeus. Book 3: The Apologists and the Didache.* ET N. J. Belval and S. Hecht; New Gospel Studies 5/2; Macon, GA: Mercer University Press, 1993.

——, "La Texte du Sermone sur la Montagne de Mattieu utilisé par Saint Justin," *EThL* 28 (1952) 411–448.

Massingberd Ford, J., "Was Montanism a Jewish-Christian Heresy?" *JEH* 17 (1966) 145–158.

May, G., *Creatio Ex Nihilo: The Doctrine of 'Creation out of Nothing' in Early Christian Thought.* ET A. S. Worall; Edinburgh: T. & T. Clark, 1994.

McComiskey, T. H., *The Covenants of Promise. A Theology of the Old Testament Covenants.* Grand Rapids: Baker, 1985.

McDaniel, M. C., "Salvation and Justification as *Theosis*," in J. Meyendorff & R. Tobias (eds.), *Salvation in Christ: A Lutheran-Orthodox Dialogue.* Minneapolis: Augsburg, 1992, 67–83.

McDonald, L. M., *The Formation of the Christian Biblical Canon.* rev. ed.; Peabody, MA, Hendrickson, 1995.

——, "The Integrity of the Biblical Canon in Light of Its Historical Development," *BBR* 6 (1996) 95–132.

McDonnell, K., *The Baptism of Jesus in the Jordan: The Trinitarian and Cosmic Order of Salvation.* Collegeville, MN: The Liturgical Press, 1996.

McGarthy, D. J., *Treaty and Covenant.* Rome: Pontifical Biblical Institute, 1963.

——, *Old Testament Covenant.* Richmond: John Knox, 1972.

McGuire, M. R. P., A. Closs, E. Des Places, J. S. Homlish, B. J. Cooke, & A. P. Hennessy, "Sacrifice," in W. J. McDonald (ed.), *The New Catholic Encyclopedia.* 15 vols.; New York: McGraw-Hill, 1967, 12.831–842.

McIntyre, J., *The Shape of Soteriology: Studies in the Doctrine of the Death of Christ.* Edinburgh: T. & T. Clark, 1992.

Metzger, B. M., *The Canon of the New Testament. Its Origin, Development, Significance.* Oxford: Clarendon Press, 1992.

Meyrick, F., "The Life and Times of Justin Martyr," in W. Lefroy (ed.), *Church Leaders in Primitive Times.* 2nd ed.; London: Thynne & Jarvis Ltd., 1896, 55–80.

Migne, J. P. (ed.), *Patrologia Graeca* 25–26 (Athanasius). Paris: Lutetiae, 1857–1866.

Morgan-Wynne, J. E., "The Holy Spirit and Christian Experience in Justin Martyr," *VC* 38 (1984) 172–177.

Nahm, C., "The Debate on the 'Platonism' of Justin Martyr," *SecCent* 9 (1992) 129–151.

Neusner, J, *Judaism in the Beginning of Christianity.* Philadelphia: Fortress, 1984.

Nilson, J., "To Whom is Justin's *Dialogue with Trypho* Addressed?" *TS* 38 (1977) 538–546.

Nispel, M. D., "Christian Deification and the Early *Testimonia*," *VC* 53 (1999) 289–304.

Norman, R. J., "Happiness," in T. Honderich (ed.), *The Oxford Companion to Philosophy.* Oxford/New York: Oxford University Press, 1995, 332–333.

Norris, F. W., "Wonder, Worship and Writ: Patristic Christology," *Ex Audita* 7 (1991) 59–72.

Norris, R. A., *God and World in Early Christian Theology. A Study in Justin Martyr, Irenaeus, Tertullian and Origen.* Studies in Patristic Thought; London: Adam & Charles Black, 1966.

Oberman, H. A., "*Quo Vadis, Petre?* Tradition from Irenaeus to *Humani Generis*," in idem, *The Dawn of the Reformation. Essays in Late Medieval and Early Reformation Thought.* Edinburgh: T. & T. Clark, 1986, 269–296.

Oden, T. C., *The Living God. Systematic Theology: Volume One.* San Francisco: Harper, 1992.

Olbricht, T. H., "Understanding the Church of the Second Century: American Research and Teaching 1890–1940," in W. E. March (ed.), *Text and Testaments: Critical Essays on the Bible and Early Church Fathers.* FS S. D. Currie; San Antonio: Trinity University Press, 1980, 237–261.

Opitz, H.-G., *Athanasius Werke* II.1. Berlin, 1935–40.

Origen of Alexandria, *Dialogue with Heraclides* in H. Chadwick and J. E. L. Oulton (eds.), *Alexandrian Christianity.* Library of Christian Classics; 26 vols.; London: SCM, 1954, 2.430–455.

Osborn, E. F., *Justin Martyr.* BHT Gerhard Ebeling; Tübingen: J. C. B. Mohr (Paul Siebeck), 1973.

——, "From Justin to Origen: The Pattern of Apologetic," *Prudentia* 4 (1972) 1–22. Reprinted in E. Ferguson, D. M. Scholer and P. C. Finney (eds.), *Studies in Early Christianity Vol. VIII: The Early Church and Greco-Roman Thought.* New York/London: Garland, 1993, 1–22.

——, "Justin Martyr and the Logos Spermatikos," *StudMiss* 42 (1993) 143–159.

——, *The Emergence of Christian Theology.* Cambridge: Cambridge University Press, 1993.

——, "Reason and the Rule of Faith in the Second Century," in R. R. Williams (ed.), *The Making of Orthodoxy.* Cambridge: Cambridge University Press, 1989, 40–61.

Outler, A. C., "The 'Logic' of Canon-Making and the Tasks of Canon Criticism," in W. E. March (ed.), *Text and Testaments: Critical Essays on the Bible and Early Church Fathers.* FS S. D. Currie; San Antonio: Trinity University Press, 1980, 263–276.

Palmer, D. W., "Atheism, Apologetic, and Negative Theology in the Greek Apologists of the Second Century," *VC* 37 (1983) 234–259.

Pannenberg, W., *Jesus—God and Man.* ET W. Wilkens & D. A. Priebe; Philadelphia: Westminster, 1968.

——, *Systematic Theology: Vol. I.* Edinburgh: T. & T. Clark, 1991.

——, "What is Truth?" in idem, *Basic Questions in Theology: Collected Essays.* 2 vols.; ET G. H. Kehm; Philadelphia: Fortress, 1971, 2.1–27.

Patzia, A. G., *The Making of the New Testament. Origin, Collection, Text & Canon.* Leicester: Apollos, 1995.

Pelikan, J., *The Emergence of Catholic Tradition (100–600). The Christian Tradition.* A History of the Development of Doctrine Vol. 1; Chicago and London: University of Chicago Press, 1971.

——, *The Light of the World. A Basic Image in Early Christian Thought.* New York: Harper & Brothers, 1962.

Petersen, S. E., "The Fall and Misogeny in Justin Martyr and Clement of Alexandria," in D. Foster and P. Mojzes (eds.), *Society and Original Sin: Ecumenical Essays on the Impact of the Fall.* New York, Paragon House, 1985, 37–51.

Petersen, W. L., "From Justin to Pepys: The History of the Harmonized Gospel Tradition," *StudPat* 30 (1997) 71–96.

——, *Gospel Traditions in the Second Century. Origins, Recensions, Text and Transmission.* Notre Dame: University of Notre Dame Press, 1989.

——, "Textual Evidence of Tatian's Dependence Upon Justin's ΑΠΟΜΝΗΜΟΝΕΥ-ΜΑΤΑ," *NTS* 36 (1990) 512–534.

Piper, O. A., "The Nature of the Gospel According to Justin Martyr," *JR* 41 (1961) 155–168.

Plato, *Republic.* ET B. Jowett; New York: Vintage Books, no date.

——, *Parmenides.* LCL 12 vols.; ET H. N. Fowler; Cambridge, MA: Harvard University Press/London: William Heinemann Ltd., 1977, 4.193–331.

——, *Phaedo*. LCL 12 vols.; ET H. N. Fowler; Cambridge, MA: Harvard University Press/London: William Heinemann Ltd., 1977, 1.193–403.

——, *Phaedrus*. LCL 12 vols.; ET H. N. Fowler; Cambridge, MA: Harvard University Press/London: William Heinemann Ltd., 1977, 1.405–579.

——, *Theaetetus*. LCL 12 vols.; ET H. N. Fowler; Cambridge, MA: Harvard University Press/London: William Heinemann Ltd., 1977, 7.1–257.

——, *Timaeus*. LCL 12 vols.; ET R. G. Bury; Cambridge, MA: Harvard University Press/London: William Heinemann Ltd., 1975, 9.1–253.

Pollack, A. J., *The Blood of Christ in Christian Greek Literature Till the Year 444 A.D.* Carthagena, OH: The Messenger Press, 1956.

Pollard, T. E., *Johannine Christology and the Early Church*. Cambridge: Cambridge University Press, 1970.

Porter, S. E., *Idioms of the Greek New Testament*. Biblical Languages: Greek 2; Sheffield: JSOT Press, 1992.

Posidonius, *The Fragments* in L. Edelstein & I. G. Kidd (eds.), *Posidonius Volume I: The Fragments*. Cambridge Classical Texts and Commentaries 13; Cambridge: Cambridge University Press, 1972.

——, *The Translation of the Fragments* in I. G. Kidd (ed.), *Posidonius Volume III: The Translation of the Fragments*. Cambridge Classical Texts and Commentaries 36; Cambridge: Cambridge University Press, 1999.

Prestige, G. L., *God in Patristic Thought*. London: SPCK, 1956.

Price, R. M., "'Hellenization' and Logos Doctrine in Justin Martyr," *VC* 42 (1988) 18–23.

——, "Are There 'Holy Pagans' in Justin Martyr?" *StudPat* 31 (1997) 167–171.

Prigent, P., *Justin l'Ancien Testament*. Paris: Gabalda, 1964.

Pryor, J. W. "Justin Martyr and the Fourth Gospel," *SecCent* 9 (1992) 153–169.

Pseudo-Dionysius, *The Mystical Theology* in C. Luinheid (ed.), *Pseudo-Dionysius: The Complete Works*. New York: Paulist, 1987, 133–141.

Quasten, J., *Patrology*. 3 Vols.; Maryland: The Newman Press, 1950.

Quell, G., G. Kittel, and R. Bultmann, "ἀλήθεια, ἀληθής, ἀληθινός, ἀληθεύω" in G. Kittel (ed.), *Theological Dictionary of the New Testament*. 10 Vols.; Grand Rapids: Eerdmans, 1964, 1.232–251.

Ratcliff, E. C., "The Eucharistic Institution Narrative of Justin Martyr's First *Apology*," *JEH* 22 (1971) 97–102.

Rees, D. A., "Platonism and the Platonic Tradition," in P. Edwards (ed.), *The Encyclopedia of Philosophy*. 8 vols.; New York: Macmillan/The Free Press, 1967, 6.333–341.

Reijners, G. Q., *The Terminology of the Holy Cross in Early Christian Literature*. Græcitas Christianorum Primæva; Nijmegen: Dekker & Van De Vegt N. V., 1965.

Remus, H., "Justin Martyr's Argument with Judaism," in S. G. Wilson (ed.), *Anti-Judaism in Early Christianity Vol. 2: Separation and Polemic*. Studies in Christianity and Judaism 2; Waterloo: Wilfred Laurier University Press, 1986.

Riegel, S. K., "Jewish Christianity: Definitions and Terminology," *NTS* 24 (1978) 410–415.

Riley, H. M., *Christian Initiation: A Comparative Study of the Interpretation Of the Baptismal Liturgy in the Mystagogical Writings of Cyril of Jerusalem, John Chrysostom, Theodore of Mopsuestia, and Ambrose of Milan*. The Catholic University of America Studies in Christian Antiquity 17; Washington, D.C.: The Catholic University of America Press, 1974.

Robbins, G. A., "Eusebius' Lexicon of 'Canonicity'," *StudPat* 15 (1993) 134–141.

Robinson, R., *Plato's Earlier Dialectic*. 2nd ed.; Oxford: Clarendon, 1962.

Runia, D. T., *Philo in Early Christian Literature: A Survey*. CRINT 3/3; Assen: Van Gorcum/Philadelphia: Fortress, 1993.

Russell, D. S., *From Early Judaism to Early Church*. Philadelphia: Fortress, 1986.

Ryle, G., "Aristotle," in P. Edwards (ed.), *The Encyclopedia of Philosophy*. 8 vols.; New York: Macmillan/The Free Press, 1967, 1.151–162.

——, "Plato," in P. Edwards (ed.), *The Encyclopedia of Philosophy*. 8 vols.; New York: Macmillan/The Free Press, 1967, 6.314–333.

Sanday, W., *The Gospels in the Second Century*. London: Macmillan and Co., 1876.

Sanders, E. P., *Jewish Law from Jesus to the Mishnah*. London: SCM Press/Philadelphia: Trinity Press International, 1990.

——, *Judaism: Practice & Belief 63 BCE–66 CE*. London: SCM Press/Philadelphia: Trinity Press International, 1992.

——, *Paul and Palestinian Judaism: A Comparison of Patterns of Religion*. London: SCM Press, 1977.

Schaff, P., *The Creeds of Christendom*. 3 vols.; Rev. Ed. by D. S. Schaff; Grand Rapids: Baker, 1996.

Schmemann, A., *For the Life of the World: Sacraments and Orthodoxy*. Crestwood, NY: St. Vladimir's Seminary Press, 1995.

Schneemelcher, W. (ed.), *New Testament Apocrypha Vol. I: Gospels and Related Writings*. ET R. McL. Wislon; rev. ed.; Cambridge: James Clarke & Co./Louisville: Westminster/John Knox Press, 1991.

Schneider, H. P., "Some Reflections on the Dialogue of Justin Martyr with Trypho," *SJT* 15 (1962) 164–175.

Segal, A. F., *Rebecca's Children. Judaism and Christianity in the Roman World*. Cambridge: Harvard University Press, 1986.

Semisch, K., *Die apostolischen Denkwürdigkeiten des Märtyrers Justinus*. Hamburg, 1848.

——, *Justin der Märtyrer*. 2 vols.; Breslau 1840–1842.

Sheppard, G. T., "Canon," in M. Eliade (ed.), *The Encyclopedia of Religion*. 10 vols.; New York: MacMillan, 1987, 3.62–69.

Shotwell, W. A., *The Biblical Exegesis of Justin Martyr*. London: SPCK, 1965.

Simon, M., *Verus Israel. A Study of the Relations Between Christians and Jews in the Roman Empire (135–425)*. ET H. McKeating; The Littman Library of Jewish Civilization; Oxford: Oxford University Press, 1986.

Simonetti, M., *Biblical Interpretation in the Early Church. An Historical Introduction to Patristic Exegesis*. ET J. A. Hughes; Edinburgh: T. & T. Clark, 1994.

Skarsaune, O., *The Proof from Prophecy. A Study in Justin Martyr's Proof-Text Tradition: Text-Type, Provenance, Theological Profile*. NovTSup 56; Leiden: E. J. Brill, 1987.

——, "The Conversion of Justin Martyr," *ST* 30 (1976) 53–73.

Sloyan, G.S., *Jesus: Redeemer and Divine Word*. Theology and Life 28; Wilmington: Michael Glazier, 1989.

Smart, N., "Soteriology," in M. Eliade (ed.), *The Encyclopedia of Religion*. 16 vols.; New York: MacMillan, 1987, 13.418–423.

Soccio, D. J., *Archetypes of Wisdom: An Introduction to Philosophy*. 2nd ed.; Belmot, CA: Wadsworth, 1995.

Stanton, G. N., "Aspects of Early Christian-Jewish Polemic and Apologetic," *NTS* 31 (1985) 377–392.

——, "The Fourfold Gospel," *NTS* 43 (1997) 317–346.

Story, C. I. K., *The Nature of Truth in "The Gospel of Truth" and in the Writings of Justin Martyr*. NovTSup 25; Leiden: E. J. Brill, 1970.

——, "Justin's Apology I.62–64: Its Importance for the Author's Treatment of Christian Baptism," *VC* 16 (1962) 172–178.

Stroup, G., "Revelation," in P. C. Hodgson & R. H. King (eds.), *Christian Theology. An Introduction to Its Traditions and Tasks*. London: SPCK, 1983, 88–114.

Stylianopulos, T., *Justin Martyr and the Mosaic Law*. SBLDS 20; Missoula, MON: Scholars Press, 1975.

——, *The New Testament: An Orthodox Perspective*. Brookline, MA: Holy Cross Orthodox Press, 1997.

Sundberg, A. C. Jr., "The Making of the New Testament Canon," in C. M. Laymon (ed.), *The Interpreter's One Volume Commentary on the Bible*. London: Collins, 1972, 1216–1224.

——, "Towards a Revised History of the New Testament Canon," *StudEv* 4 (1968) 452–461.

Swete, H. B., *The Holy Spirit in the Ancient Church. A Study of Christian Teaching in the Age of the Fathers*. London: MacMillan, 1912.

Tate, J., "On the History of Allegorism," *CQ* 28 (1934) 105–114.

——, "Plato and Allegorical Interpretation," *CQ* 23 (1929) 142–154; 24 (1930) 1–10.

Taylor, R., "Causation," in P. Edwards (ed.), *The Encyclopedia of Philosophy*. 8 vols.; New York: Macmillan/The Free Press, 1967, 2.56–66.

Tertullian of Carthage, *The Prescription Against Heretics* in A. Roberts and J. Donaldson (eds.), *Ante-Nicene Fathers*. 10 vols.; Peabody: Hendrickson, 1994, 3.243–267.

Thoma, A., "Justins literarisches Verhältnis zu Paulus und zum Johannesevangelium," *ZWT* 18 (1875) 383–412.

Thomson, R.W., *Athanasius, Contra Gentes and De Inarnatione*. Oxford: Oxford University Press, 1971.

Torrance, T. F., "Early Patristic Interpretation of the Holy Scriptures," in idem, *Divine Meaning. Studies in Patristic Hermeneutics*. Edinburgh: T. & T. Clark, 1995, 93–129. Originally in ΕΚΚΛΕΣΙΑ και ΘΗΕΟΛΟΓΙΑ, Athens, 1988, vol. ix, pp. 137–170.

Trakatellis, D., "Justin Martyr's Trypho," *HTR* 79 (1986) 289–297. Reprinted in G. W. H. Nickelsburg and G. W. Mackae (eds.), *Christians Among Jews and Gentiles*. FS K. Stendhal; Philadelphia: Fortress, 1986, 289–297.

Turner, H. E. W., *The Pattern of Christian Truth. A Study in the Relations Between Orthodoxy and Heresy in the Early Church*. London: A. R. Mowbray & Co., 1954.

——, *The Patristic Doctrine of Redemption. A Study of the Development of Doctrine During the First Five Centuries*. London: A. R. Mowbray & Co., 1952.

Vielhauer, P. and G. Strecker, "Jewish-Christian Gospels,"in W. Schneemelcher (ed.), *New Testament Apocrypha Vol. I: Gospels and Related Writings*. Et R.McL. Wilson; rev. ed.; Cambridge: James Clarke & Co./Westminster/John Knox Press, 1991, 134–178.

Volkmar, G., *Über Justin den Märtyrer und sein Verhältnis zu unsern Evangelien*. Zurich, 1853.

Wagner, W. H., *After the Apostles. Christianity in the Second Century*. Minneapolis: Fortress, 1994.

Watson, F., *Text and Truth: Redefining Biblical Theology*. Grand Rapids: Eerdmans, 1997.

Weiss, P. R., "Some Samaritanisms of Justin Martyr," *JTS* 45 (1944) 199–205.

Werline, "The Transformation of Pauline Arguments in Justin Martyr's *Dialogue with Trypho*," *HTR* 92 (1999) 79–93.

Westcott, B. F., *A General Survey of the History of the New Testament Canon*. 5th ed.; Cambridge and London: Macmillan and Co., 1881.

Wick, W., "Aristotelianism," in P. Edwards (ed.), *The Encyclopedia of Philosophy*. 8 vols.; New York: Macmillan/The Free Press, 1967, 1.148–151.

Widdicombe, P., "Justin Martyr, Allegorical Interpretation, and the Greek Myths," *StudPat* 31 (1997) 234–239.

Wiles, M., *The Christian Fathers*. Knowing Christianity; London: Hodder and Stoughton, 1966.

Wilken, R. L., "Pagan Criticism of Christianity: Greek Religion and Christian Faith," In W. R. Schoedel and R. L. Wilken (eds.), *Early Christian Literature and the Classical Intellectual Tradition. In Honorem Robert M. Grant*. Théologie Historique 54; Paris: Éditions Beauschesne, 1979, 117–134.

——, "The Old Testament in Controversy with the Jews," *SJT* 8 (1955) 113–126.

Williams, G. H., "Baptismal Theology and Practice in Rome as Reflected in Justin Martyr," in A. Blane and T. E. Bird (eds.), *The Ecumenical World of Orthodox Civilization. Russia and Orthodoxy: Vol. III. Essays in Honor of Georges Florovsky*. Slavistic Printings and Reprintings; The Hague/Paris: Mouton, 1974, 9–34.

———, "Justin Glimpsed as Martyr Among His Roman Contemporaries," in A. J. Mackelway & E. D. Willis (eds.), *The Context of Contemporary Theology: Essays in Honor of Paul Lehman.* Atlanta: John Knox Press, 1974, 99–126. Reprinted in E. Ferguson, D. M. Scholer and P. C. Finney (eds.), *Studies in Early Christianity Vol. I: Personalities of the Early Church.* New York/London: Garland, 1993, 81–108.

Williams, N. P., *The Ideas of the Fall and of Original Sin: A Historical and Critical Study.* London: Longmans, Green and Co. Ltd., 1927.

Williams, R. R., "Does it Make Sense to Speak of Pre-Nicene Orthodoxy?" in idem. (ed.), *The Making of Orthodoxy.* Cambridge: Cambridge University Press, 1989, 1–23.

Williamson, C. M., "The 'Adversus Judaeos' Tradition in Christian Theology," *Enc.* 39 (1978) 273–296.

Wilson, S. G., *Related Strangers. Jews and Christians 70–170 CE.* Minneapolis: Fortress, 1995.

Winden, J. C. M. van, *An Early Christian Philosopher. Justin Martyr's Dialogue with Trypho Chapters One to Nine.* Philosophia Patrum 1; Leiden: E. J. Brill, 1971.

Witt, R. E., *Albinus and the History of Middle Platonism.* Cambridge: Cambridge University Press, 1937.

Wolfson, H. A., *The Philosophy of the Church Fathers Vol. I: Faith, Trinity, Incarnation.* 2nd ed. rev.; Cambridge, Mass.: Harvard University Press, 1964.

Woollcombe, K. J., "The Biblical Origins and Patristic Development of Typology," in G. W. H. Lampe and K. J. Woollcombe, *Essays in Typology.* Studies in Biblical Theology; London: SCM, 1957, 39–75.

Woozley, A. D., "Universals," in P. Edwards (ed.), *The Encyclopedia of Philosophy.* 8 vols.; New York: Macmillan/The Free Press, 1967, 8.194–206.

Wright, D. F., Christian Faith in the Greek World: Justin Martyr's Testimony," *EvQ* 54 (1982) 77–87.

Young, M. O., "Justin, Socrates, and the Middle-Platonists," *StudPat* 18 (1989) 161–165.

Ysebaert, J., *Greek Baptismal Terminology. Its Origins and Early Development.* Græcitas Christianorum Primæva; Nijmegen: Dekker & Van de Vegt N. V., 1962.

Zeller, E., *Outlines of the History of Greek Philosophy.* ET L. R. Palmer; 13th ed. rev.; London: Kegan Paul, Trench, Trubner & Co./New York: Harcourt, Brace & Co., 1931.

Zahn, J. C., "Ist Ammon oder Tatian Verfasser der ins Lateinische, Altfrankische und Arabische übersetzten Evangelien-Harmonie? Und was hat Tatian bei seinem bekannten Diatessaron oder Diapente vor sicht gahabt und zum Grunde gelegt?" in C. A. G. Keil and H. G. Tzschirner, *Analekten für das Studium der exegetischen und systematischen theologie.* Leipzig, 1814.

Zahn, T., *Geschichte des neutestamentlichen Kanons.* Erlangen: Andreas Deichert, 1881.

———, "Studien zu Justin III," *ZKG* 8 (1885–1886) 56–61.

Zizioulas, J. D., *Being as Communion: Studies in Personhood and the Church.* Crestwood, NY: St. Vladimir's Seminary Press, 1993 (1985).

INDEX OF JUSTIN MARTYR'S WRITINGS

Dialogue with Trypho

40.1	194
40.4	231; 244
41	152; 166; 172; 180
41.1	115; 269
41.2	156; 189
41.3	28
41.4	230
42	101; 172; 180
42.1–2	99; 217
42.1	23
42.4	170; 172; 229
43	44; 96; 107; 152; 159; 166; 172; 174; 228; 239
43.1–2	172; 247
43.1	97; 117; 169; 171; 175; 228
43.2	48; 104; 106; 109
43.3	156
43.4	189
43.7	159
44	152; 166; 172
44.1	57; 60
44.2	156; 171; 172; 173; 189; 226; 227; 228
44.3	156; 189
44.4	247
45.2	170
45.3–4	107
45.3	170
45.4	108; 239; 240; 253
46	86; 152
46.1–2	170
46.2	170
46.5	156; 170; 171; 189; 226; 227
46.7	226; 227
47	58
47.1–3	58
47.1	58
47.2	58; 171; 226; 227
47.3	170
47.4	58; 170
47.5	244; 161
48–49	165
48	165; 186
48.4	262
48.8	195
49	86; 118
49.1	165
49.3	262; 269
49.3–5	195
49.4	269

49.5	262
49.8	106; 109
51–52	162
51	104; 109; 164; 166; 174; 228
51.1–2	194; 195; 270
51.2	21; 99
51.3	99; 104; 109; 117; 195; 262
52	172
52.1	240
52.3	170
52.4	104; 109
53	107; 152; 163; 164; 239
53.2	163; 194; 271
53.4	156; 189
53.5	164; 271
54	118; 172
54.2	97
55.3	59; 194; 239; 240
56–58	109; 110
56	86; 104; 108; 109; 175; 176; 177
56.1	84; 176; 179; 181
56.11	104; 109; 183
56.12	97
56.16	34; 38; 86; 155; 189
57	86
58	96; 177
58.3	57
59	175; 176; 177
59.1	97
60	107; 239
60.2–3	84
61–64	109; 110
61	104; 108; 177
61.1–2	109; 182; 183
61.1	105; 108; 109; 177; 179; 181; 183
61.3–7	181
61.3	179; 181
62	152
62.1	97
62.2–4	181
62.2	46; 114
62.4	181; 182
63	86; 107; 152; 239
63.3	181
63.5	104; 181
64	86; 162
64.2–3	59; 60; 239
64.2	45; 49; 57

INDEX OF SCRIPTURE

Old Testament

New Testament

INDEX OF ANCIENT AUTHORS

INDEX OF MODERN AUTHORS

INDEX OF GREEK TERMS AND PHRASES

INDEX OF SUBJECTS

epistemology 66–73; 74; 76; 77;
124
Forms (Ideas) 11; 68; 69; 70; 71;
72; 75; 76; 82; 84; 124; 127; 129;
130; 147; 148
Good, the 76; 84; 124; 127; 129;
147; 148; 168
similie of the sun 124; 127–129
truth 123
Plotinus 81
Plutarch
Polemo 142
Posidonius of Apamaea 141
Prologue of the *Dialogue* 40–42; 136;
178
prophecy 101
Prophets (Prophetic writings) 5; 8; 10;
16; 23; 25; 29; 41; 52; 64; 76; 77;
92–98; 99; 101; 102; 103; 104; 107;
109; 110; 111; 131; 141; 143; 144;
145; 146; 151; 152; 153; 154; 155;
156; 157; 167; 174; 188; 189; 216;
217; 224; 228; 231; 233; 234; 240;
241; 251
Pseudo-Dionysius 87

"Q" 197
Qumran 160

Revelation 4–9
Rule of Faith 13; 24; 166; 167; 168;
203–211
relation to canon 207–211
In Irenaeus 204–206; 209–210
In Tertullian 206–207; 210

Sabbath(s) 55; 78; 175; 225; 226; 228
sacrifice(s) 55; 175; 225; 226; 228
salvation (redemption) 55; 60; 65; 94;
95; 96; 104; 105; 107; 109;
110–119; 154; 155; 169; 170; 171;
183; 209; 210; 216; 217; 224; 225;
226; 227; 231; 232; 236; 237; 238;
239; 241; 243; 245; 246; 247; 248;
250; 251
scripture 18; 24; 26; 197; 198; 210
Apostolic writings 216–217
Hebrew & Jewish 25; 42–45; 59;
60; 64; 86; 155; 156; 157; 159;
163; 164; 171; 189; 190; 207–215;
224; 230; 231; 234; 239; 241;
248; 249; 251
true meaning 60; 240
sense perception 69; 70; 152; 163; 168

Serpent, the 116; 117; 236; 237
Septuagint 43–45; 156; 160
sign 236; 237; 238
Simon 142
sin 113; 116; 117; 237; 243; 246
Socrates 127; 128; 132; 133; 134;
135; 136; 145
socratic method 135
Solomon 156
Sophists 133
soul(s) 75; 76; 77; 92; 127; 150
spermatic *Logos* 145; 146; 183
Speusippus 142
Spirit (Holy Spirit) 94; 150; 152–155
filling of 94; 103; 151; 152
of prophecy 104; 152; 153; 156
resting of 103; 104
spiritual obedience 224; 227–231; 245
Stoicism 178
symbol (symbolic) 229; 231; 234; 235
synoptic Gospels 100; 195; 196; 199;
201; 218

Tabernacle 154
Tatian 20; 28; 30; 31; 197
Diatessaron 20; 197
Temple 154
Tertullian 203–211
testimonia 160–161
Theology Proper 77–91
theophanies 109; 110; 175; 177; 182
Theophilus of Antioch 197
Torah 168; 169
Tradition 22; 85; 157; 165–168; 190;
205; 206; 207; 208; 209; 210
transcendence of God
in Hellenistic Judaism
in Middle Platonism
Trinity 153
Truth 10–13; 94; 96; 97; 118; 147;
149; 151; 152; 153
Greek concept 12
Hebrew concept 123–124
Justin's concept of 91; 103
Middle Platonic concept 12
NT concept 11; 12; 129–131
philosophy as search for 138–155
Platonic concept 124–129
second century context 123–131
unchangeableness of 130
Trypho 42; 47–49; 51; 52; 54; 56;
58; 59; 60; 67; 78; 79; 83; 84–87;
88; 89; 90; 91; 95; 96; 98; 103;
104; 106; 107; 136; 138; 139; 155;